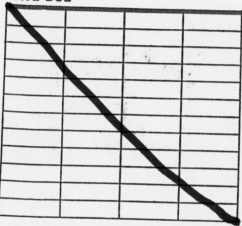

Francis Parkman's Works.

NEW LIBRARY EDITION.

VOL. IV.

FRANCIS PARKMAN'S WORKS.

New Library Edition.

Goupil & C° Paris.

THE

OLD RÉGIME IN CANADA.

FRANCE AND ENGLAND IN NORTH AMERICA.

PART FOURTH.

BY

FRANCIS PARKMAN.

BOSTON:
LITTLE, BROWN, AND COMPANY.
1908.

Printers
S. J. PARKHILL & CO., BOSTON, U. S. A.

TO

GEORGE EDWARD ELLIS, D.D.

My Dear Dr. Ellis :

When, in my youth, I proposed to write a series of books on the French in America, you encouraged the attempt, and your helpful kindness has followed it from that day to this. Pray accept the dedication of this volume in token of the grateful regard of

Very faithfully yours,

FRANCIS PARKMAN.

NOTE TO REVISED EDITION.

WHEN this book was written, I was unable to gain access to certain indispensable papers relating to the rival claimants to Acadia, — La Tour and D'Aunay, — and therefore deferred all attempts to treat that subject. The papers having at length come to hand, the missing chapters are supplied in the present edition, which also contains some additional matter of less prominence.

The title of " The Old Régime in Canada " is derived from the third and principal of the three sections into which the book is divided.

JUNE 16, 1893.

PREFACE.

---◆---

" THE physiognomy of a government," says
De Tocqueville, " can best be judged in its colonies, for there its characteristic traits usually
appear larger and more distinct. When I wish
to judge of the spirit and the faults of the administration of Louis XIV., I must go to Canada. Its deformity is there seen as through a
microscope."

The monarchical administration of France, at
the height of its power and at the moment of
its supreme triumph, stretched an arm across the
Atlantic and grasped the North American continent. This volume attempts to show by what
methods it strove to make good its hold, why it
achieved a certain kind of success, and why it
failed at last. The political system which has
fallen, and the antagonistic system which has
prevailed, seem, at first sight, to offer nothing
but contrasts ; yet out of the tomb of Canadian
absolutism come voices not without suggestion

even to us.   Extremes meet, and Autocracy and
Democracy often touch hands, at least in their
vices.

The means of knowing the Canada of the past
are ample.   The pen was always busy in this
outpost of the old monarchy.   The king and the
minister demanded to know everything; and
officials of high and low degree, soldiers and
civilians, friends and foes, poured letters, despatches, and memorials, on both sides of every
question, into the lap of government.   These
masses of paper have in the main survived the
perils of revolutions and the incendiary torch of
the Commune.   Add to them the voluminous
records of the Superior Council of Quebec, and
numerous other documents preserved in the civil
and ecclesiastical depositories of Canada.

The governments of New York and of Canada
have caused a large part of the papers in the
French archives relating to their early history to
be copied and brought to America, and valuable
contributions of material from the same quarter
have been made by the State of Massachusetts
and by private Canadian investigators.   Nevertheless, a great deal has still remained in France
uncopied and unexplored.   In the course of several visits to that country, I have availed myself

of these supplementary papers, as well as of those which had before been copied, sparing neither time nor pains to explore every part of the field. With the help of a system of classified notes, I have collated the evidence of the various writers, and set down without reserve all the results of the examination, whether favorable or unfavorable. Some of them are of a character which I regret, since they cannot be agreeable to persons for whom I have a very cordial regard. The conclusions drawn from the facts may be matter of opinion, but it will be remembered that the facts themselves can be overthrown only by overthrowing the evidence on which they rest, or bringing forward counter-evidence of equal or greater strength; and neither task will be found an easy one.[1]

I have received most valuable aid in my inquiries from the great knowledge and experience of M. Pierre Margry, Chief of the Archives of the Marine and Colonies at Paris. I beg also warmly to acknowledge the kind offices of Abbé Henri Raymond Casgrain and Grand

[1] Those who wish to see the subject from a point of view opposite to mine cannot do better than consult the work of the Jesuit Charlevoix, with the excellent annotation of Mr. Shea. (History and General Description of New France, by the Rev. P. F. X. de Charlevoix, S.J., translated with notes by John Gilmary Shea. 6 vols. New York: 1866–1872.)

Vicar Cazeau, of Quebec ; together with those of
James Le Moine, Esq., M. Eugène Taché, Hon.
P. J. O. Chauveau, and other eminent Canadians,
and Henry Harrisse, Esq.

The few extracts from original documents
which are printed in the Appendix may serve as
samples of the material out of which the work
has been constructed. In some instances their
testimony might be multiplied twenty-fold.
When the place of deposit of the documents
cited in the margin is not otherwise indicated,
they will, in nearly all cases, be found in the
Archives of the Marine and Colonies.

In the present book we examine the political
and social machine; in the next volume of the
series we shall see this machine in action.

BOSTON, July 1, 1874.

CONTENTS.

SECTION SECOND.

CANADA A MISSION.

CHAPTER IV.

1653–1658.

THE JESUITS AT ONONDAGA.

CHAPTER V.

1642–1661.

THE HOLY WARS OF MONTREAL.

CHAPTER VI.

1660, 1661.

THE HEROES OF THE LONG SAUT.

CONTENTS.

CHAPTER XII.

1662–1680.

LAVAL AND THE SEMINARY.

SECTION THIRD.

THE COLONY AND THE KING.

CHAPTER XIII.

1661–1665.

ROYAL INTERVENTION.

CHAPTER XIV.

1666, 1667.

THE MOHAWKS CHASTISED.

CHAPTER XV.

1665–1672.

PATERNAL GOVERNMENT.

CONTENTS.

CHAPTER XVI.

1661–1673.

MARRIAGE AND POPULATION.

CHAPTER XVII.

1665–1672.

THE NEW HOME.

CHAPTER XVIII.

1663–1763.

CANADIAN FEUDALISM.

CHAPTER XIX.

1663–1763.

THE RULERS OF CANADA.

CHAPTER XX.

1663–1763.

TRADE AND INDUSTRY.

CHAPTER XXI.

1663–1702.

THE MISSIONS. — THE BRANDY QUESTION.

CHAPTER XXII.

1663–1763.

PRIESTS AND PEOPLE.

CHAPTER XXIII.

1640–1763.

MORALS AND MANNERS.

CHAPTER XXIV.

1663–1763.

CANADIAN ABSOLUTISM.

APPENDIX.

THE OLD RÉGIME IN CANADA.

SECTION FIRST.

THE FEUDAL CHIEFS OF ACADIA.

CHAPTER I.

1497–1643.

LA TOUR AND D'AUNAY.

THE ACADIAN QUARREL. — BIENCOURT. — CLAUDE AND CHARLES
DE LA TOUR. — SIR WILLIAM ALEXANDER. — CLAUDE DE RA-
ZILLY. — CHARLES DE MENOU D'AUNAY CHARNISAY. — CAPE
SABLE. — PORT ROYAL. — THE HERETICS OF BOSTON AND PLY-
MOUTH. — MADAME DE LA TOUR. — WAR AND LITIGATION. — LA
TOUR WORSTED: HE ASKS HELP FROM THE BOSTON PURITANS.

WITH the opening of the seventeenth century
began that contest for the ownership of North
America which was to remain undecided for a century
and a half. England claimed the continent through
the discovery by the Cabots in 1497 and 1498, and
France claimed it through the voyage of Verrazzano
in 1524. Each resented the claim of the other; and
each snatched such fragments of the prize as she
could reach, and kept them if she could. In 1604,
Henry IV. of France gave to De Monts all America
from the 40th to the 46th degree of north latitude.

including the sites of Philadelphia on the one hand
and Montreal on the other;[1] while, eight years after,
Louis XIII. gave to Madame de Guercheville and
the Jesuits the whole continent from Florida to the
St. Lawrence, — that is, the whole of the future
British colonies. Again, in 1621, James I. of England made over a part of this generous domain to a
subject of his own, Sir William Alexander, — to
whom he gave, under the name of Nova Scotia, the
peninsula which is now so called, together with a
vast adjacent wilderness, to be held forever as a fief
of the Scottish Crown.[2] Sir William, not yet satisfied, soon got an additional grant of the "River and
Gulf of Canada," along with a belt of land three
hundred miles wide, reaching across the continent.[3]
Thus the King of France gave to Frenchmen the
sites of Boston, New York, and Washington, and
the King of England gave to a Scotchman the sites
of Quebec and Montreal. But while the seeds of
international war were thus sown broadcast over the
continent, an obscure corner of the vast regions in
dispute became the scene of an intestine strife like
the bloody conflicts of two feudal chiefs in the depths
of the Middle Ages.

After the lawless inroads of Argall, the French,
with young Biencourt at their head, still kept a

---

[1] See "Pioneers of France in the New World," 247.

[2] *Charter of New Scotland in favour of Sir William Alexander.*

[3] *Charter of the Country and Lordship of Canada in America,* 2 Feb.,
1628–29, in *Publications of the Prince Society,* 1873.

feeble hold on Acadia. After the death of his father, Poutrincourt, Biencourt took his name, by which thenceforth he is usually known. In his distress he lived much like an Indian, roaming the woods with a few followers, and subsisting on fish, game, roots, and lichens. He seems, however, to have found means to build a small fort among the rocks and fogs of Cape Sable. He named it Fort Loméron, and here he appears to have maintained himself for a time by fishing and the fur-trade.

Many years before, a French boy of fourteen years, Charles Saint-Étienne de la Tour, was brought to Acadia by his father, Claude de la Tour, where he became attached to the service of Biencourt (Poutrincourt), and, as he himself says, served as his ensign and lieutenant. He says, further, that Biencourt on his death left him all his property in Acadia. It was thus, it seems, that La Tour became owner of Fort Loméron and its dependencies at Cape Sable, whereupon he begged the King to give him help against his enemies, especially the English, who, as he thought, meant to seize the country; and he begged also for a commission to command in Acadia for his Majesty.[1]

In fact, Sir William Alexander soon tried to dispossess him and seize his fort. Charles de la Tour's father had been captured at sea by the privateer "Kirke," and carried to England. Here, being a widower, he married a lady of honor of the Queen,

[1] *La Tour au Roy,* 25 *July,* 1627.

and, being a Protestant, renounced his French allegiance.

Alexander made him a baronet of Nova Scotia, a new title which King James had authorized Sir William to confer on persons of consideration aiding him in his work of colonizing Acadia. Alexander now fitted out two ships, with which he sent the elder La Tour to Cape Sable. On arriving, the father, says the story, made the most brilliant offers to his son if he would give up Fort Loméron to the English, — to which young La Tour is reported to have answered in a burst of patriotism, that he would take no favors except from his sovereign, the King of France. On this, the English are said to have attacked the fort, and to have been beaten off. As the elder La Tour could not keep his promise to deliver the place to the English, they would have no more to do with him, on which his dutiful son offered him an asylum under condition that he should never enter the fort. A house was built for him outside the ramparts; and here the trader, Nicolas Denys, found him in 1635. It is Denys who tells the above story,[1] which he probably got from the younger La Tour, — and which, as he tells it, is inconsistent with the known character of its pretended hero, who was no model of loyalty to his king, being a chameleon whose principles took the color of his interests. Denys says, further, that the elder La Tour had been invested with the Order of the Garter, and that

---

[1] Denys, *Description géographique et historique.*

the same dignity was offered to his son; which is
absurd.   The truth is, that Sir William Alexander,
thinking that the two La Tours might be useful to
him, made them both baronets of Nova Scotia.[1]

Young La Tour, while begging Louis XIII. for a
commission to command in Acadia, got from Sir
William Alexander not only the title of baronet, but
also a large grant of land at and near Cape Sable, to
be held as a fief of the Scottish Crown.[2]   Again, he
got from the French King a grant of land on the river
St. John, and, to make assurance doubly sure, got
leave from Sir William Alexander to occupy it.[3]
This he soon did, and built a fort near the mouth of
the river, not far from the present city of St. John.

Meanwhile the French had made a lodgment on
the rock of Quebec, and not many years after, all
North America from Florida to the Arctic circle,
and from Newfoundland to the springs of the St.
Lawrence, was given by King Louis to the Company
of New France, with Richelieu at its head.[4]   Sir
William Alexander, jealous of this powerful rivalry,
caused a private expedition to be fitted out under the
brothers Kirke.   It succeeded, and the French settle-

---

[1] *Grant from Sir William Alexander to Sir Claude de St. Étienne
(de la Tour)*, 30 *Nov.*, 1629.   *Ibid. to Charles de St. Étienne, Esq.,
Seigneur de St. Denniscourt and Baigneux,* 12 *May,* 1630.   (Hazard,
State Papers, i. 294, 298.)   The names of both father and son appear
on the list of baronets of Nova Scotia.

[2] *Patent from Sir William Alexander to Claude and Charles de la
Tour,* 30 *April,* 1630.

[3] Williamson, *History of Maine,* i. 246.

[4] See "Pioneers of France," 440.

ments in Acadia and Canada were transferred by
conquest to England. England soon gave them
back by the treaty of St. Germain;[1] and Claude de
Razilly, a Knight of Malta, was charged to take possession of them in the name of King Louis.[2] Full
powers were given him over the restored domains,
together with grants of Acadian lands for himself.[3]

Razilly reached Port Royal in August, 1632, with
three hundred men, and the Scotch colony planted
there by Alexander gave up the place in obedience to
an order from the King of England. Unfortunately
for Charles de la Tour, Razilly brought with him an
officer destined to become La Tour's worst enemy.
This was Charles de Menou d'Aunay Charnisay, a
gentleman of birth and character, who acted as his
commander's man of trust, and who, in Razilly's
name, presently took possession of such other feeble
English and Scotch settlements as had been begun
by Alexander or the people of New England along
the coasts of Nova Scotia and Maine. This placed
the French Crown and the Company of New France
in sole possession for a time of the region then called
Acadia.

When Acadia was restored to France, La Tour's

[1] *Traité de St. Germain en Laye*, 29 *Mars*, 1632, *Article* 3. For
reasons of the restitution, see "Pioneers of France," 454.

[2] *Convention avec le Sieur de Razilly pour aller reçevoir la Restitution
du Port Royal*, etc., 27 *Mars*, 1632. *Commission du Sieur de Razilly*,
10 *May*, 1632.

[3] *Concession de la rivière et baye Saincte Croix à M. de Razilly*, 29
May, 1632.

English title to his lands at Cape Sable became worthless. He hastened to Paris to fortify his position; and, suppressing his dallyings with England and Sir William Alexander, he succeeded not only in getting an extensive grant of lands at Cape Sable, but also the title of lieutenant-general for the King in Fort Loméron and its dependencies,[1] and commander at Cape Sable for the Company of New France.

Razilly, who represented the King in Acadia, died in 1635, and left his authority to D'Aunay Charnisay, his relative and second in command. D'Aunay made his headquarters at Port Royal; and nobody disputed his authority except La Tour, who pretended to be independent of him in virtue of his commission from the Crown and his grant from the Company. Hence rose dissensions that grew at last into war.

The two rivals differed widely in position and qualities. Charles de Menou, Seigneur d'Aunay Charnisay, came of an old and distinguished family of Touraine,[2] and he prided himself above all things on his character of *gentilhomme français*. Charles

[1] *Revocation de la Commission du Sieur Charles de Saint-Étienne, Sieur de la Tour*, 23 *Fév.*, 1641.

[2] The modern representative of this family, Comte Jules de Menou, is the author of a remarkable manuscript book, written from family papers and official documents, and entitled *L'Acadie colonisée par Charles de Menou d'Aunay Charnisay*. I have followed Comte de Menou's spelling of the name. It is often written D'Aulnay, and by New England writers D'Aulney. The manuscript just mentioned is in my possession. Comte de Menou is also the author of a printed work called *Preuves de l'Histoire de la Maison de Menou*.

Saint-Étienne de la Tour was of less conspicuous
lineage.[1] In fact, his father, Claude de la Tour, is
said by his enemies to have been at one time so
reduced in circumstances that he carried on the trade
of a mason in Rue St. Germain at Paris.   The son,
however, is called *gentilhomme d'une naissance dis-
tinguée*, both in papers of the court and in a legal
document drawn up in the interest of his children.
As he came to Acadia when a boy he could have had
little education, and both he and D'Aunay carried
on trade, — which in France would have derogated
from their claims as gentlemen, though in America
the fur-trade was not held inconsistent with *noblesse*.

Of La Tour's little kingdom at Cape Sable, with
its rocks, fogs, and breakers, its seal-haunted islets
and iron-bound shores guarded by Fort Loméron,
we have but dim and uncertain glimpses.   After the
death of Biencourt, La Tour is said to have roamed
the woods with eighteen or twenty men, "living a
vagabond life with no exercise of religion."[2]   He
himself admits that he was forced to live like the
Indians, as did Biencourt before him.[3]   Better times
had come, and he was now commander of Fort

[1] The true surname of La Tour's family, which belonged to the
neighborhood of Evreux, in Normandy, was Turgis. The designa-
tion of La Tour was probably derived from the name of some
family estate, after a custom common in France under the old
régime. The Turgis's arms were "d'or au chevron de sable, accompagné de trois palmes de même."

[2] Menou, *L'Acadie colonisée par Charles de Menou d'Aunay
Charnisay.*

[3] *La Tour au Roy*, 25 *Juillet*, 1627.

Loméron, — or, as he called it, Fort La Tour, — with a few Frenchmen and abundance of Micmac Indians. His next neighbor was the adventurer Nicolas Denys, who with a view to the timber trade had settled himself with twelve men on a small river a few leagues distant. Here Razilly had once made him a visit, and was entertained under a tent of boughs with a sylvan feast of wild pigeons, brant, teal, woodcock, snipe, and larks, cheered by profuse white wine and claret, and followed by a dessert of wild raspberries.[1]

On the other side of the Acadian peninsula D'Aunay reigned at Port Royal like a feudal lord, which in fact he was. Denys, who did not like him, says that he wanted only to rule, and treated his settlers like slaves; but this, even if true at the time, did not always remain so. D'Aunay went to France in 1641, and brought out, at his own charge, twenty families to people his seigniory.[2] He had already brought out a wife, having espoused Jeanne Molin (or Motin), daughter of the Seigneur de Courcelles. What with old settlers and new, about forty families were gathered at Port Royal and on the river Annapolis, and over these D'Aunay ruled like a feudal Robinson Crusoe.[3] He gave each colonist a farm charged with a perpetual rent of one sou an arpent, or French acre. The houses of the settlers

[1] Denys, *Description géographique et historique.*
[2] Rameau, *Une Colonie féodale en Amérique,* i. 93 (ed. 1889).
[3] *Ibid.,* i. 96, 97.

were log cabins, and the manor-house of their lord
was a larger building of the same kind. The most
pressing need was of defence, and D'Aunay lost no
time in repairing and reconstructing the old fort on
the point between Allen's River and the Annapolis.
He helped his tenants at their work; and his confessor describes him as returning to his rough manor-
house on a wet day, drenched with rain and
bespattered with mud, but in perfect good humor,
after helping some of the inhabitants to mark out a
field. The confessor declares that during the eleven
months of his acquaintance with him he never heard
him speak ill of anybody whatever, a statement which
must probably be taken with allowance. Yet this
proud scion of a noble stock seems to have given
himself with good grace to the rough labors of the
frontiersman; while Father Ignace, the Capuchin
friar, praises him for the merit, transcendent in
clerical eyes, of constant attendance at mass and frequent confession.[1]

With his neighbors, the Micmac Indians, he was
on the best of terms. He supplied their needs, and
they brought him the furs that enabled him in some
measure to bear the heavy charges of an establishment that could not for many years be self-support-
ing. In a single year the Indians are said to have
brought three thousand moose-skins to Port Royal,
besides beaver and other valuable furs. Yet, from
a commercial point of view, D'Aunay did not

[1] *Lettre du Père Ignace de Paris, Capucin, 6 Aoust,* 1653.

prosper. He had sold or mortgaged his estates in France, borrowed large sums, built ships, bought cannon, levied soldiers, and brought over immigrants. He is reported to have had three hundred fighting men at his principal station, and sixty cannon mounted on his ships and forts; for besides Port Royal he had two or three smaller establishments.[1]

Port Royal was a scene for an artist, with its fort; its soldiers in breastplate and morion, armed with pike, halberd, or matchlock; its manor-house of logs, and its seminary of like construction; its twelve Capuchin friars, with cowled heads, sandalled feet, and the cord of Saint Francis; the birch canoes of Micmac and Abenaki Indians lying along the strand, and their feathered and painted owners lounging about the place or dozing around their wigwam fires. It was mediævalism married to primeval savagery. The friars were supported by a fund supplied by Richelieu, and their chief business was to convert the Indians into vassals of France, the Church, and the Chevalier d'Aunay. Hard by was a wooden chapel, where the seignior knelt in dutiful observance of every rite, and where, under a stone chiselled with his ancient scutcheon, one of his children lay buried. In the fort he had not forgotten to provide a dungeon for his enemies.

[1] *Certificat à l'égard de M. d'Aunay Charnisay, signé Michel Boudrot, Lieutenant Général en l'Acadie, et autres, anciens habitans au pays,* 5 Oct., 1687. *Lettre du Roy de gouverneur et lieutenant général es costes de l'Acadie pour Charles de Menou, Sieur d'Aulnay Charnisay, Février,* 1647.

The worst of these was Charles de la Tour. Before the time of Razilly and his successor D'Aunay, La Tour had felt himself the chief man in Acadia; but now he was confronted by a rival higher in rank, superior in resources and court influence, proud, ambitious, and masterful.[1] He was bitterly jealous of D'Aunay; and, to strengthen himself against so formidable a neighbor, he got from the Company of New France the grant of a tract of land at the mouth of the river St. John, where he built a fort and called it after his own name, though it was better known as Fort St. Jean.[2] Thither he removed from his old post at Cape Sable, and Fort St. Jean now became his chief station. It confronted its rival, Port Royal, across the intervening Bay of Fundy.

Now began a bitter feud between the two chiefs, each claiming lands occupied by the other. The Court interposed to settle the dispute, but in its ignorance of Acadian geography its definitions were so obscure that the question was more embroiled than ever.[3]

[1] Besides succeeding to the authority of Razilly, D'Aunay had bought of his heirs their land claims in Acadia. *Arrêts du Conseil,* 9 *Mars,* 1642.

[2] *Concession de la Compagnie de la Nouvelle France à Charles de Saint-Étienne, Sieur de la Tour, Lieutenant Général de l'Acadie, du Fort de la Tour, dans la Rivière de St. Jean, du* 15 *Jan.,* 1635, in *Mémoires des Commissaires,* v. 113 (ed. 1756, 12mo).

[3] *Louis XIII à d'Aunay,* 10 *Fév.,* 1638. This seems to be the occasion of Charlevoix's inexact assertion that Acadia was divided into three governments, under D'Aunay, La Tour, and Nicolas Denys, respectively. The title of Denys, such as it was, had no existence till 1654.

While the domestic feud of the rivals was gathering to a head, foreign heretics had fastened their clutches on various parts of the Atlantic coast which France and the Church claimed as their own. English heretics had made lodgment in Virginia, and Dutch heretics at the mouth of the Hudson; while other sectaries of the most malignant type had kennelled among the sands and pine-trees of Plymouth; and others still, slightly different, but equally venomous, had ensconced themselves on or near the small peninsula of Shawmut, at the head of La Grande Baye, or the Bay of Massachusetts. As it was not easy to dislodge them, the French dissembled for the present, yielded to the logic of events, and bided their time. But the interlopers soon began to swarm northward and invade the soil of Acadia, sacred to God and the King. Small parties from Plymouth built trading-houses at Machias and at what is now Castine, on the Penobscot. As they were competitors in trade, no less than foes of God and King Louis, and as they were too few to resist, both La Tour and D'Aunay resolved to expel them; and in 1633 La Tour attacked the Plymouth trading-house at Machias, killed two of the five men he found there, carried off the other three, and seized all the goods.[1] Two years later D'Aunay attacked the Plymouth trading-station at Penobscot, the Pentegoet of the French, and took it in the name of King Louis. That he might not appear in the part of a pirate, he set a

[1] Hubbard, *History of New England*, 163.

price on the goods of the traders, and then, having seized them, gave in return his promise to pay at some convenient time if the owners would come to him for the money.

He had called on La Tour to help him in this raid against Penobscot; but La Tour, unwilling to recognize his right to command, had refused, and had hoped that D'Aunay, becoming disgusted with his Acadian venture, which promised neither honor nor profit, would give it up, go back to France, and stay there. About the year 1638 D'Aunay did in fact go to France, but not to stay; for in due time he reappeared, bringing with him his bride, Jeanne Motin, who had had the courage to share his fortunes, and whom he now installed at Port Royal, — a sure sign, as his rival thought, that he meant to make his home there. Disappointed and angry, La Tour now lost patience, went to Port Royal, and tried to stir D'Aunay's soldiers to mutiny; then set on his Indian friends to attack a boat in which was one of D'Aunay's soldiers and a Capuchin friar, — the soldier being killed, though the friar escaped.[1] This was the beginning of a quarrel waged partly at Port Royal and St. Jean, and partly before the admiralty court of Guienne and the royal council, partly with bullets and cannon-shot, and partly with edicts, decrees, and *procès verbaux*. As D'Aunay had taken a wife, so too would La Tour; and he charged his agent Desjardins to bring him one from France.

[1] Menou, *L'Acadie colonisée par Charles de Menou d'Aunay.*

The agent acquitted himself of his delicate mission, and shipped to Acadia one Marie Jacquelin, — daughter of a barber of Mans, if we may believe the questionable evidence of his rival. Be this as it may, Marie Jacquelin proved a prodigy of mettle and energy, espoused her husband's cause with passionate vehemence, and backed his quarrel like the intrepid Amazon she was. She joined La Tour at Fort St. Jean, and proved the most strenuous of allies.

About this time, D'Aunay heard that the English of Plymouth meant to try to recover Penobscot from his hands. On this he sent nine soldiers thither, with provisions and munitions. La Tour seized them on the way, carried them to Fort St. Jean, and, according to his enemies, treated them like slaves.

D'Aunay heard nothing of this till four months after, when, being told of it by Indians, he sailed in person to Penobscot with two small vessels, reinforced the place, and was on his way back to Port Royal when La Tour met him with two armed pinnaces. A fight took place, and one of D'Aunay's vessels was dismasted. He fought so well, however, that Captain Jamin, his enemy's chief officer, was killed; and the rest, including La Tour, his new wife, and his agent Desjardins, were forced to surrender, and were carried prisoners to Port Royal.

At the request of the Capuchin friars D'Aunay set them all at liberty, after compelling La Tour to sign a promise to keep the peace in future.[1]   Both parties

[1] Menou, *L'Acadie colonisée par Charles de Menou d'Aunay.*

2

now laid their cases before the French courts, and, whether from the justice of his cause or from superior influence, D'Aunay prevailed. La Tour's commission was revoked, and he was ordered to report himself in France to receive the King's commands. Trusting to his remoteness from the seat of power, and knowing that the King was often ill served and worse informed, he did not obey, but remained in Acadia exercising his authority as before. D'Aunay's father, from his house in Rue St. Germain, watched over his son's interests, and took care that La Tour's conduct should not be unknown at court. A decree was thereupon issued directing D'Aunay to seize his rival's forts in the name of the King, and place them in charge of trusty persons. The order was precise; but D'Aunay had not at the time force enough to execute it, and the frugal King sent him only six soldiers. Hence he could only show the royal order to La Tour, and offer him a passage to France in one of his vessels if he had the discretion to obey. La Tour refused, on which D'Aunay returned to France to report his rival's contumacy. At about the same time La Tour's French agent sent him a vessel with succors. The King ordered it to be seized; but the order came too late, for the vessel had already sailed from Rochelle bound to Fort St. Jean.

When D'Aunay reported the audacious conduct of his enemy, the royal council ordered that the offender should be brought prisoner to France; [1] and D'Aunay,

[1] *Arrêt du Conseil,* 21 *Fév.,* 1642.

as the King's lieutenant-general in Acadia, was again
required to execute the decree.[1] La Tour was now
in the position of a rebel, and all legality was on the
side of his enemy, who represented royalty itself.

D'Aunay sailed at once for Acadia, and in August,
1642, anchored at the mouth of the St. John,
before La Tour's fort, and sent three gentlemen in a
boat to read to its owner the decree of the council
and the order of the King. La Tour snatched the
papers, crushed them between his hands, abused the
envoys roundly, put them and their four sailors into
prison, and kept them there above a year.[2]

His position was now desperate, for he had placed
himself in open revolt. Alarmed for the consequences, he turned for help to the heretics of Boston.
True Catholics detested them as foes of God and
man; but La Tour was neither true Catholic nor true
Protestant, and would join hands with anybody who
could serve his turn. Twice before he had made
advances to the Boston malignants, and sent to them
first one Rochet, and then one Lestang, with proposals of trade and alliance. The envoys were
treated with courtesy, but could get no promise of
active aid.[3]

La Tour's agent, Desjardins, had sent him from
Rochelle a ship, called the "St. Clement," manned

[1] Menou, *L'Acadie colonisée.*

[2] Menou, *L'Acadie colonisée.* Moreau, *Histoire de l'Acadie,* 169,
170.

[3] Hubbard, *History of New England,* chap. liv. Winthrop, ii.
42, 88.

by a hundred and forty Huguenots, laden with stores and munitions, and commanded by Captain Mouron. In due time La Tour at his Fort St. Jean heard that the "St. Clement" lay off the mouth of the river, unable to get in because D'Aunay blockaded the entrance with two armed ships and a pinnace. On this he resolved to appeal in person to the heretics. He ran the blockade in a small boat under cover of night, and, accompanied by his wife, boarded the "St. Clement" and sailed for Boston.[1]

[1] Menou, *L'Acadie colonisée.*

CHAPTER II.

1643–1645.

LA TOUR AND THE PURITANS.

ON the twelfth of June, 1643, the people of the
infant town of Boston saw with some misgiving a
French ship entering their harbor. It chanced that
the wife of Captain Edward Gibbons, with her
children, was on her way in a boat to a farm belonging to her husband on an island in the harbor. One
of La Tour's party, who had before made a visit to
Boston, and had been the guest of Gibbons, recognized his former hostess; and he, with La Tour and
a few sailors, cast off from the ship and went to
speak to her in a boat that was towed at the stern of
the "St. Clement." Mrs. Gibbons, seeing herself
chased by a crew of outlandish foreigners, took refuge
on the island where Fort Winthrop was afterwards
built, which was then known as the "Governor's
Garden," as it had an orchard, a vineyard, and

"many other conveniences."[1] The islands in the harbor, most of which were at that time well wooded, seem to have been favorite places of cultivation, as sheep and cattle were there safe from those pests of the mainland, the wolves. La Tour, no doubt to the dismay of Mrs. Gibbons and her children, landed after them, and was presently met by the governor himself, who, with his wife, two sons, and a daughter-in-law, had apparently rowed over to their garden for the unwonted recreation of an afternoon's outing.[2] La Tour made himself known to the governor, and, after mutual civilities, told him that a ship bringing supplies from France had been stopped by his enemy, D'Aunay, and that he had come to ask for help to raise the blockade and bring her to his fort. Winthrop replied that, before answering, he must consult the magistrates. As Mrs. Gibbons and her children were anxious to get home, the governor sent them to town in his own boat, promising to follow with his party in that of La Tour, who had placed it at his disposal. Meanwhile, the people of Boston had heard of what was taking place, and were in some anxiety, since, in a truly British distrust of all Frenchmen, they feared lest their governor might be kidnapped and held for ransom. Some of them accordingly took arms, and came in three boats to the rescue. In fact, remarks Winthrop, "if La Tour had been ill-minded towards us, he had such an

---

1 Wood, *New England's Prospect*, part i., chap. x.
2 Winthrop, ii. 127.

opportunity as we hope neither he nor any other shall
ever have the like again."[1] The castle, or fort,
which was on another island hard by, was defenceless,
its feeble garrison having been lately withdrawn, and
its cannon might easily have been turned on the town.

Boston, now in its thirteenth year, was a straggling
village, with houses principally of boards or logs,
gathered about a plain wooden meeting-house which
formed the heart or vital organ of the place. The
rough peninsula on which the infant settlement stood
was almost void of trees, and was crowned by a hill
split into three summits, — whence the name of
Tremont, or Trimount, still retained by a street of
the present city. Beyond the narrow neck of the
peninsula were several smaller villages with outlying
farms; but the mainland was for the most part a
primeval forest, possessed by its original owners, —
wolves, bears, and rattlesnakes. These last unde-
sirable neighbors made their favorite haunt on a high
rocky hill, called Rattlesnake Hill, not far inland,
where, down to the present generation, they were
often seen, and where good specimens may occasionally be found to this day.[2]

Far worse than wolves or rattlesnakes were the
Pequot Indians, — a warlike race who had boasted

[1] Winthrop, ii. 127.

[2] Blue Hill in Milton. "Up into the country is a high hill which
is called rattlesnake hill, where there is great store of these
poysonous creatures." (Wood, *New England's Prospect*.) "They
[the wolves] be the greatest inconveniency the country hath."
(*Ibid.*)

that they would wipe the whites from the face of the earth, but who, by hard marching and fighting, had lately been brought to reason.

Worse than wolves, rattlesnakes, and Indians together were the theological quarrels that threatened to kill the colony in its infancy. Children are taught that the Puritans came to New England in search of religious liberty. The liberty they sought was for themselves alone. It was the liberty to worship in their own way, and to prevent all others from doing the like. They imagined that they held a monopoly of religious truth, and were bound in conscience to defend it against all comers. Their mission was to build up a western Canaan, ruled by the law of God; to keep it pure from error, and, if need were, purge it of heresy by persecution, — to which ends they set up one of the most detestable theocracies on record. Church and State were joined in one. Church-members alone had the right to vote. There was no choice but to remain politically a cipher, or embrace, or pretend to embrace, the extremest dogmas of Calvin. Never was such a premium offered to cant and hypocrisy; yet in the early days hypocrisy was rare, so intense and pervading was the faith of the founders of New England.

It was in the churches themselves, the appointed sentinels and defenders of orthodoxy, that heresy lifted its head and threatened the State with disruption. Where minds different in complexion and character were continually busied with subtle ques-

tions of theology, unity of opinion could not be long
maintained; and innovation found a champion in one
Mrs. Hutchinson, a woman of great controversial
ability and inexhaustible fluency of tongue.   Persons
of a mystical turn of mind, or a natural inclination
to contrariety, were drawn to her preachings; and
the church of Boston, with three or four exceptions,
went over to her in a body.   "Sanctification," "justi-
fication," "revelations," the "covenant of grace,"
and the "covenant of works," mixed in furious battle
with all the subtleties, sophistries, and venom of theological war; while the ghastly spectre of Antinomian-
ism hovered over the fray, carrying terror to the souls
of the faithful.   The embers of the strife still burned
hot when La Tour appeared to bring another firebrand.

As a "papist" or "idolater," though a mild one,
he was sorely prejudiced in Puritan eyes, while his
plundering of the Plymouth trading-house some
years before, and killing two of its five tenants, did
not tend to produce impressions in his favor; but it
being explained that all five were drunk, and had
begun the fray by firing on the French, the ire
against him cooled a little.   Landing with Winthrop,
he was received under the hospitable roof of Captain
Gibbons, whose wife had recovered from her fright
at his approach.   He went to church on Sunday, and
the gravity of his demeanor gave great satisfaction,
— a solemn carriage being of itself a virtue in Puritan
eyes.   Hence he was well treated, and his men were
permitted to come ashore daily in small numbers.

The stated training-day of the Boston militia fell
in the next week, and La Tour asked leave to exercise his soldiers with the rest. This was granted;
and, escorted by the Boston trained band, about
forty of them marched to the muster-field, which
was probably the Common, — a large tract of pasture-
land in which was a marshy pool, the former home
of a colony of frogs, perhaps not quite exterminated
by the sticks and stones of Puritan boys. This pool,
cleaned, paved, and curbed with granite, preserves to
this day the memory of its ancient inhabitants, and
is still the Frog Pond, though bereft of frogs.

The Boston trained band, in steel caps and buff
coats, went through its exercise; and the visitors,
we are told, expressed high approval. When the
drill was finished, the Boston officers invited La
Tour's officers to dine, while his rank and file were
entertained in like manner by the Puritan soldiers.
There were more exercises in the afternoon, and this
time it was the turn of the French, who, says
Winthrop, "were very expert in all their postures
and motions." A certain "judicious minister," in
dread of popish conspiracies, was troubled in spirit
at this martial display, and prophesied that "store of
blood would be spilled in Boston," — a prediction
that was not fulfilled, although an incident took
place which startled some of the spectators. The
Frenchmen suddenly made a sham charge, sword in
hand, which the women took for a real one. The
alarm was soon over; and as this demonstration

ended the performance, La Tour asked leave of the governor to withdraw his men to their ship. The leave being granted, they fired a salute and marched to the wharf where their boat lay, escorted, as before, by the Boston trained band. During the whole of La Tour's visit he and Winthrop went amicably to church together every Sunday, — the governor being attended, on these and all other occasions while the strangers were in town, by a guard of honor of musketeers and halberd men. La Tour and his chief officers had their lodging and meals in the houses of the principal townsmen, and all seemed harmony and good-will.

La Tour, meanwhile, had laid his request before the magistrates, and produced among other papers the commission to Mouron, captain of his ship, dated in the last April, and signed and sealed by the Vice-Admiral of France, authorizing Mouron to bring supplies to La Tour, whom the paper styled Lieutenant-General for the King in Acadia; La Tour also showed a letter, genuine or forged, from the agent of the Company of New France, addressed to him as lieutenant-general, and warning him to beware of D'Aunay: from all which the Boston magistrates inferred that their petitioner was on good terms with the French government,[1] notwithstanding a letter

[1] Count Jules de Menou, in his remarkable manuscript book now before me, expresses his belief that the commission of the Vice-Admiral was genuine, but that the letter of the agent of the Company was a fabrication.

sent them by D'Aunay the year before, assuring them that La Tour was a proclaimed rebel, which in fact he was. Throughout this affair one is perplexed by the French official papers, whose entanglements and contradictions in regard to the Acadian rivals are past unravelling.

La Tour asked only for such help as would enable him to bring his own ship to his own fort; and, as his papers seemed to prove that he was a recognized officer of his King, Winthrop and the magistrates thought that they might permit him to hire such ships and men as were disposed to join him.

La Tour had tried to pass himself as a Protestant; but his professions were distrusted, notwithstanding the patience with which he had listened to the long-winded sermons of the Reverend John Cotton. As to his wife, however, there appears to have been but one opinion. She was approved as a sound Protestant "of excellent virtues;" and her denunciations of D'Aunay no doubt fortified the prejudice which was already strong against him for his seizure of the Plymouth trading-house at Penobscot, and for his aggressive and masterful character, which made him an inconvenient neighbor.

With the permission of the governor and the approval of most of the magistrates, La Tour now made a bargain with his host, Captain Gibbons, and a merchant named Thomas Hawkins. They agreed to furnish him with four vessels; to arm each of these with from four to fourteen small cannon, and

man them with a certain number of sailors, La Tour
himself completing the crews with Englishmen hired
at his own charge. Hawkins was to command the
whole. The four vessels were to escort La Tour and
his ship, the "St. Clement," to the mouth of the St.
John, in spite of D'Aunay and all other opponents.
The agreement ran for two months; and La Tour
was to pay £250 sterling a month for the use of the
four ships, and mortgage to Gibbons and Hawkins
his fort and all his Acadian property as security.
Winthrop would give no commissions to Hawkins or
any others engaged in the expedition, and they were
all forbidden to fight except in self-defence; but the
agreement contained the significant clause that all
plunder was to be equally divided according to rule
in such enterprises. Hence it seems clear that the
contractors had an eye to booty; yet no means were
used to hold them to their good behavior.

Now rose a brisk dispute, and the conduct of
Winthrop was sharply criticised. Letters poured in
upon him concerning "great dangers," "sin upon the
conscience," and the like. He himself was clearly in
doubt as to the course he was taking, and he soon
called another meeting of magistrates, in which the
inevitable clergy were invited to join; and they all
fell to discussing the matter anew. As every man of
them had studied the Bible daily from childhood up,
texts were the chief weapons of the debate. Doubts
were advanced as to whether Christians could law-
fully help idolaters, and Jehoshaphat, Ahab, and

Josias were brought forward as cases in point. Then Solomon was cited to the effect that "he that meddleth with the strife that belongs not to him takes a dog by the ear;" to which it was answered that the quarrel did belong to us, seeing that Providence now offered us the means to weaken our enemy, D'Aunay, without much expense or trouble to ourselves. Besides, we ought to help a neighbor in distress, seeing that Joshua helped the Gibeonites, and Jehoshaphat helped Jehoram against Moab with the approval of Elisha. The opposing party argued that "by aiding papists we advance and strengthen popery;" to which it was replied that the opposite effect might follow, since the grateful papist, touched by our charity, might be won to the true faith and turned from his idols.

Then the debate continued on the more worldly grounds of expediency and statecraft, and at last Winthrop's action was approved by the majority. Still, there were many doubters, and the governor was severely blamed. John Endicott wrote to him that La Tour was not to be trusted, and that he and D'Aunay had better be left to fight it out between them, since if we help the former to put down his enemy he will be a bad neighbor to us.

Presently came a joint letter from several chief men of the colony, — Saltonstall, Bradstreet, Nathaniel Ward, John Norton, and others, — saying in substance: We fear international law has been ill observed; the merits of the case are not clear; we

are not called upon in charity to help La Tour (see
2 Chronicles xix. 2, and Proverbs xxvi. 17); this
quarrel is for England and France, and not for us; if
D'Aunay is not completely put down, we shall have
endless trouble; and "he that loses his life in an
unnecessary quarrel dies the devil's martyr."

This letter, known as the "Ipswich letter," touched
Winthrop to the quick. He thought that it trenched
on his official dignity, and the asperity of his answer
betrays his sensitiveness. He calls the remonstrance
"an act of an exorbitant nature," and says that it
"blows a trumpet to division and dissension." "If
my neighbor is in trouble," he goes on to say, "I
must help him." He maintains that "there is great
difference between giving permission to hire to guard
or transport, and giving commission to fight," and he
adds the usual Bible text, "The fear of man bringeth
a snare; but whoso putteth his trust in the Lord
shall be safe." [1]

In spite of Winthrop's reply, the Ipswich letter
had great effect; and he and the Boston magistrates
were much blamed, especially in the country towns.
The governor was too candid not to admit that he
had been in fault, though he limits his self-accusation
to three points: first, that he had given La Tour an
answer too hastily; next, that he had not sufficiently

---

[1] Winthrop's *Answer to the Ipswich Letter about La Tour* (no date),
in *Hutchinson Papers*, 122. Bradstreet writes to him on the 21st of
June, "Our ayding of Latour was very grievous to many hereabouts,
the design being feared to be unwarrantable by dyvers."

consulted the elders or ministers; and lastly, that he had not opened the discussion with prayer.

The upshot was that La Tour and his allies sailed on the fourteenth of July. D'Aunay's three vessels fled before them to Port Royal. La Tour tried to persuade his Puritan friends to join him in an attack; but Hawkins, the English commander, would give no order to that effect, on which about thirty of the Boston men volunteered for the adventure. D'Aunay's followers had ensconced themselves in a fortified mill, whence they were driven with some loss. After burning the mill and robbing a pinnace loaded with furs, the Puritans returned home, having broken their orders and compromised their colony.

In the next summer, La Tour, expecting a serious attack from D'Aunay, — who had lately been to France, and was said to be on his way back with large reinforcements, — turned again to Massachusetts for help. The governor this time was John Endicott, of Salem. To Salem the suppliant repaired; and as Endicott spoke French, the conference was easy. The rugged bigot had before expressed his disapproval of "having anything to do with these idolatrous French;" but, according to Hubbard, he was so moved with compassion at the woful tale of his visitor that he called a meeting of magistrates and ministers to consider if anything could be done for him. The magistrates had by this time learned caution, and the meeting would do nothing but write a letter to D'Aunay, demanding satisfaction for his seizure of Penobscot and other aggressions, and declaring that the men who escorted La Tour to his fort in the last summer had no commission from Massachusetts, yet that if they had wronged him he should have justice, though if he seized any New England trading vessels they would hold him answerable.   In short, La Tour's petition was not granted.

D'Aunay, when in France, had pursued his litigation against his rival, and the royal council had ordered that the contumacious La Tour should be seized, his goods confiscated, and he himself brought home a prisoner; which decree D'Aunay was empowered to execute, if he could.   He had returned to Acadia the accredited agent of the royal will.   It was reported at Boston that a Biscayan pirate had sunk his ship on the way; but the wish was father to the thought, and the report proved false.   D'Aunay arrived safely, and was justly incensed at the support given by the Puritans in the last year to his enemy. But he too had strong reasons for wishing to be on good terms with his heretic neighbors.   King Louis, moreover, had charged him not to offend them, since, when they helped La Tour, they had done so in the belief that he was commissioned as lieutenant-general for the King, and therefore they should be held blameless.

Hence D'Aunay made overtures of peace and friendship to the Boston Puritans.   Early in October,

1644, they were visited by one Monsieur Marie, "supposed," says the chronicle, "to be a friar, but habited like a gentleman." He was probably one of the Capuchins who formed an important part of D'Aunay's establishment at Port Royal. The governor and magistrates received him with due consideration; and along with credentials from D'Aunay he showed them papers under the great seal of France, wherein the decree of the royal council was set forth in full, La Tour condemned as a rebel and traitor, and orders given to arrest both him and his wife. Henceforth there was no room to doubt which of the rival chiefs had the King and the law on his side. The envoy, while complaining of the aid given to La Tour, offered terms of peace to the governor and magistrates, — who replied to his complaints with their usual subterfuge, that they had given no commission to those who had aided La Tour, declaring at the same time that they could make no treaty without the concurrence of the commissioners of the United Colonies. They then desired Marie to set down his proposals in writing; on which he went to the house of one Mr. Fowle, where he lodged, and drew up in French his plan for a treaty, adding the proposal that the Bostonians should join D'Aunay against La Tour. Then he came back to the place of meeting and discussed the subject for half a day, — sometimes in Latin with the magistrates, and sometimes in French with the governor, that old soldier being probably ill versed in the classic

tongues. In vain they all urged that D'Aunay
should come to terms with La Tour. Marie replied,
that if La Tour would give himself up his life would
be spared, but that if he were caught he would lose
his head as a traitor; adding that his wife was worse
than he, being the mainspring of his rebellion.
Endicott and the magistrates refused active alliance;
but the talk ended in a provisional treaty of peace,
duly drawn up in Latin, Marie keeping one copy and
the governor the other. The agreement needed rati-
fication by the commissioners of the United Colonies
on one part, and by D'Aunay on the other. What
is most curious in the affair is the attitude of Massachusetts, which from first to last figures as an independent State, with no reference to the King under
whose charter it was building up its theocratic
republic, and consulting none but the infant confederacy of the New England colonies, of which it was
itself the head. As the commissioners of the confederacy were not then in session, Endicott and the
magistrates took the matter provisionally into their
own hands.

Marie had made good despatch, for he reached
Boston on a Friday and left it on the next Tuesday,
having finished his business in about three days, or
rather two, as one of the three was "the Sabbath."
He expressed surprise and gratification at the attention and courtesy with which he had been treated.
His hosts supplied him with horses, and some of
them accompanied him to Salem, where he had left

his vessel, and whence he sailed for Port Royal, well pleased.

Just before he came to Boston, that town had received a visit from Madame de la Tour, who, soon after her husband's successful negotiation with Winthrop in the past year, had sailed for France in the ship "St. Clement." She had labored strenuously in La Tour's cause; but the influence of D'Aunay's partisans was far too strong, and, being charged with complicity in her husband's misconduct, she was forbidden to leave France on pain of death. She set the royal command at naught, escaped to England, took passage in a ship bound for America, and after long delay landed at Boston. The English ship-master had bargained to carry her to her husband at Fort St. Jean; but he broke his bond, and was sentenced by the Massachusetts courts to pay her £2,000 as damages. She was permitted to hire three armed vessels then lying in the harbor, to convey her to Fort St. Jean, where she arrived safely and rejoined La Tour.

Meanwhile, D'Aunay was hovering off the coast, armed with the final and conclusive decree of the royal council, which placed both husband and wife under the ban, and enjoined him to execute its sentence. But a resort to force was costly and of doubtful result, and D'Aunay resolved again to try the effect of persuasion. Approaching the mouth of the St. John, he sent to the fort two boats, commanded by his lieutenant, who carried letters from his chief, promising to La Tour's men pardon for their past conduct and payment of all wages due them if they would return to their duty. An adherent of D'Aunay declares that they received these advances with insults and curses. It was a little before this time that Madame de la Tour arrived from Boston. The same writer says that she fell into a transport of fury, "behaved like one possessed with a devil," and heaped contempt on the Catholic faith in the presence of her husband, who approved everything she did; and he further affirms that she so berated and reviled the Récollet friars in the fort that they refused to stay, and set out for Port Royal in the depth of winter, taking with them eight soldiers of the fort who were too good Catholics to remain in such a nest of heresy and rebellion. They were permitted to go, and were provided with an old pinnace and two barrels of Indian corn, with which, unfortunately for La Tour, they safely reached their destination.

On her arrival from Boston, Madame de la Tour had given her husband a piece of politic advice. Her enemies say that she had some time before renounced her faith to gain the favor of the Puritans; but there is reason to believe that she had been a Huguenot from the first. She now advised La Tour to go to Boston, declare himself a Protestant, ask for a minister to preach to his men, and promise that if the Bostonians would help him to master D'Aunay and conquer Acadia, he would share the conquest with them. La Tour admired the sagacious counsels of his wife, and sailed for Boston to put them in practice just before the friars and the eight deserters sailed for Port Royal, thus leaving their departure unopposed.

At Port Royal both friars and deserters found a warm welcome. D'Aunay paid the eight soldiers their long arrears of wages, and lodged the friars in the seminary with his Capuchins. Then he questioned them, and was well rewarded. They told him that La Tour had gone to Boston, leaving his wife with only forty-five men to defend the fort. Here was a golden opportunity. D'Aunay called his officers to council. All were of one mind. He mustered every man about Port Royal and embarked them in the armed ship of three hundred tons that had brought him from France; he then crossed the Bay of Fundy with all his force, anchored in a small harbor a league from Fort St. Jean, and sent the Récollet Père André to try to seduce more of La Tour's men, — an attempt which proved a failure. D'Aunay lay two months at his anchorage, during which time another ship and a pinnace joined him from Port Royal. Then he resolved to make an attack. Meanwhile, La Tour had persuaded a Boston merchant to send one Grafton to Fort St. Jean in a small vessel loaded with provisions, and bringing also a letter to Madame de la Tour containing a promise from her husband that he would join her in a month. When the Boston vessel appeared at the mouth of the St. John, D'Aunay seized it, placed Grafton and the few men with him on an island, and finally supplied them with a leaky sail-boat to make their way home as they best could.

D'Aunay now landed two cannon to batter Fort St. Jean on the land side; and on the seventeenth of April, having brought his largest ship within pistol-shot of the water rampart, he summoned the garrison to surrender.[1] They answered with a volley of cannon-shot, then hung out a red flag, and, according to D'Aunay's reporter, shouted "a thousand insults and blasphemies"![2] Towards evening a breach was made in the wall, and D'Aunay ordered a general assault. Animated by their intrepid mistress, the defenders fought with desperation, and killed or wounded many of the assailants, not without severe loss on their own side. Numbers prevailed at last;

---

[1] The site of Fort St. Jean, or Fort La Tour, has been matter of question. At Carleton, opposite the present city of St. John, are the remains of an earthen fort, by some supposed to be that of La Tour, but which is no doubt of later date, as the place was occupied by a succession of forts down to the Seven Years' War. On the other hand, it has been assumed that Fort La Tour was at Jemsec, which is about seventy miles up the river. Now, in the second mortgage deed of Fort La Tour to Major Gibbons, May 10, 1645, the fort is described as "*situé près de l'embouchure de la rivière de St. Jean.*" Moreover, there is a cataract just above the mouth of the river, which, though submerged at high tide, cannot be passed by heavy ships at any time; and as D'Aunay brought his largest ship of war to within pistol-shot of the fort, it must have been below the cataract. Mr. W. F. Ganong, after careful examination, is convinced that Fort La Tour was at Portland Point, on the east side of the St. John, at its mouth. See his paper on the subject in *Transactions of the Royal Society of Canada*, 1891.

[2] *Procès Verbal d'André Certain*, in Appendix A.

all resistance was overcome; the survivors of the
garrison were made prisoners, and the fort was pil-
laged.   Madame de la Tour, her maid, and another
woman, who were all of their sex in the place, were
among the captives, also Madame de la Tour's son,
a mere child.   D'Aunay pardoned some of his prisoners, but hanged the greater part, "to serve as an
example to posterity," says his reporter.   Nicolas
Denys declares that he compelled Madame de la
Tour to witness the execution with a halter about her
neck; but the more trustworthy accounts say nothing
of this alleged outrage.   On the next day, the eighteenth of April, the bodies of the dead were decently
buried, an inventory was made of the contents of the
fort, and D'Aunay set his men to repair it for his
own use.   These labors occupied three weeks or more,
during a part of which Madame de la Tour was left
at liberty, till, being detected in an attempt to corre-
spond with her husband by means of an Indian, she
was put into confinement; on which, according to
D'Aunay's reporter, "she fell ill with spite and
rage," and died within three weeks, — after, as he
tells us, renouncing her heresy in the chapel of the
fort.

CHAPTER III.

1645–1710.

THE VICTOR VANQUISHED.

D'Aunay's Envoys to the Puritans: their Reception at
Boston. — Winthrop and his "Papist" Guests. — Recon-
ciliation. — Treaty. — Behavior of La Tour. — Royal
Favors to D'Aunay: his Hopes; his Death; his Character.
— Conduct of the Court towards him. — Intrigues of La
Tour. — Madame D'Aunay. — La Tour marries her. — Chil-
dren of D'Aunay. — Descendants of La Tour.

Having triumphed over his rival, D'Aunay was
left free to settle his accounts with the Massachusetts
Puritans, who had offended him anew by sending
provisions to Fort St. Jean, having always insisted
that they were free to trade with either party.
They, on their side, were no less indignant with
him for his seizure of Grafton's vessel and harsh
treatment of him and his men.

After some preliminary negotiation and some rather
sharp correspondence, D'Aunay, in September, 1646,
sent a pinnace to Boston, bearing his former envoy,
Marie, accompanied by his own secretary and by one
Monsieur Louis.

It was Sunday, the Puritan Sabbath, when the
three envoys arrived; and the pious inhabitants were

preparing for the afternoon sermon. Marie and his two colleagues were met at the wharf by two militia officers, and conducted through the silent and dreary streets to the house of Captain, now Major, Gibbons, who seems to have taken upon himself in an especial manner the office of entertaining strangers of consequence.

All was done with much civility, but no ceremony; for the Lord's Day must be kept inviolate. Winthrop, who had again been chosen governor, now sent an officer, with a guard of musketeers, to invite the envoys to his own house. Here he regaled them with wine and sweetmeats, and then informed them of "our manner that all men either come to our publick meetings, or keep themselves quiet in their houses."[1] He then laid before them such books in Latin and French as he had, and told them that they were free to walk in his garden. Though the diversion offered was no doubt of the dullest, — since the literary resources of the colony then included little besides arid theology, and the walk in the garden promised but moderate delights among the bitter pot-herbs provided against days of fasting, — the victims resigned themselves with good grace, and, as the governor tells us, "gave no offence." Sunset came at last, and set the captives free.

On Monday both sides fell to business. The envoys showed their credentials; but, as the commissioners of the United Colonies were not yet in

[1] Winthrop, ii. 273, 275.

session, nothing conclusive could be done till Tuesday. Then, all being assembled, each party made
its complaints of the conduct of the other, and a
long discussion followed. Meals were provided for
the three visitors at the "ordinary," or inn, where
the magistrates dined during the sessions of the
General Court. The governor, as their host, always
sat with them at the board, and strained his Latin to
do honor to his guests. They, on their part, that
courtesies should be evenly divided, went every
morning at eight o'clock to the governor's house,
whence he accompanied them to the place of meeting; and at night he, or some of the commissioners
in his stead, attended them to their lodging at the
house of Major Gibbons.

Serious questions were raised on both sides; but
as both wanted peace, explanations were mutually
made and accepted. The chief difficulty lay in the
undeniable fact, that, in escorting La Tour to his
fort in 1643, the Massachusetts volunteers had
chased D'Aunay to Port Royal, killed some of his
men, burned his mill, and robbed his pinnace, for
which wrongs the envoys demanded heavy damages.
It was true that the governor and magistrates had
forbidden acts of aggression on the part of the volunteers; but on the other hand they had had reason to
believe that their prohibition would be disregarded,
and had taken no measures to enforce it. The
envoys clearly had good ground of complaint; and
here, says Winthrop, "they did stick two days." At

last they yielded so far as to declare that what
D'Aunay wanted was not so much compensation in
money as satisfaction to his honor by an acknowledgment of their fault on the part of the Massachusetts
authorities; and they further declared that he would
accept a moderate present in token of such acknowledgment. The difficulty now was to find such a
present. The representatives of Massachusetts presently bethought themselves of a "very fair new
sedan" which the Viceroy of Mexico had sent to his
sister, and which had been captured in the West
Indies by one Captain Cromwell, a corsair, who
gave it to "our governor." Winthrop, to whom it
was entirely useless, gladly parted with it in such a
cause; and the sedan, being graciously accepted,
ended the discussion.[1] The treaty was signed in
duplicate by the commissioners of the United Colonies
and the envoys of D'Aunay, and peace was at last
concluded.

The conference had been conducted with much
courtesy on both sides. One small cloud appeared,
but soon passed away. The French envoys displayed
the *fleur-de-lys* at the masthead of their pinnace as
she lay in the harbor. The townsmen were incensed;
and Monsieur Marie was told that to fly foreign
colors in Boston harbor was not according to custom.
He insisted for a time, but at length ordered the
offending flag to be lowered.

On the twenty-eighth of September the envoys bade

[1] Winthrop, ii. 274.

farewell to Winthrop, who had accompanied them to their pinnace with a guard of honor. Five cannon saluted them from Boston, five from "the Castle," and three from Charlestown. A supply of mutton and a keg of sherry were sent on board their vessel; and then, after firing an answering salute from their swivels, they stood down the bay till their sails disappeared among the islands.

La Tour had now no more to hope from his late supporters. He had lost his fort, and, what was worse, he had lost his indomitable wife. Throughout the winter that followed his disaster he had been entertained by Samuel Maverick, at his house on Noddle's Island. In the spring he begged hard for further help; and, as he begged in vain, he sailed for Newfoundland to make the same petition to Sir David Kirke, who then governed that island. Kirke refused, but lent him a pinnace and sent him back to Boston. Here some merchants had the good nature or folly to intrust him with goods for the Indian trade, to the amount of four hundred pounds. Thus equipped, he sailed for Acadia in Kirke's pinnace, manned with his own followers and five New England men. On reaching Cape Sable, he conspired with the master of the pinnace and his own men to seize the vessel and set the New England sailors ashore, — which was done, La Tour, it is said, shooting one of them in the face with a pistol. It was winter, and the outcasts roamed along the shore for a fortnight, half frozen and half starved, till they were met by Micmac Indians, who gave them food and a boat, — in which, by rare good fortune, they reached Boston, where their story convinced the most infatuated that they had harbored a knave. "Whereby," solemnly observes the pious but much mortified Winthrop, who had been La Tour's best friend, "it appeared (as the Scripture saith) that there is no confidence in an unfaithful or carnal man."[1]

When the capture of Fort St. Jean was known at court the young King was well pleased, and promised to send D'Aunay the gift of a ship;[2] but he forgot to keep his word, and requited his faithful subject with the less costly reward of praises and honors. After a preamble reciting his merits, and especially his "care, courage, and valor" in "taking, by our express order, and reducing again under our authority the fort on the St. John which La Tour had rebelliously occupied with the aid of foreign sectaries," the King confirms D'Aunay's authority in Acadia, and extends it on paper from the St. Lawrence to Virginia, — empowering him to keep for himself such parts of this broad domain as he might want, and grant out the rest to others, who were to hold of him as vassals. He could build forts and cities, at his own expense; command by land and sea; make war or peace within the limits of his grant; appoint officers of government, justice, and police; and, in short, exercise sovereign power, with the simple

[1] Winthrop, ii. 266.
[2] *Le Roy à M. d'Aunay Charnisay*, 28 *Sept.*, 1645.

reservation of homage to the King, and a tenth part of all gold, silver, and copper to the royal treasury. A full monopoly of the fur-trade throughout his dominion was conferred on him; and any infringement of it was to be punished by confiscation of ships and goods, and thirty thousand livres of damages. On his part he was enjoined to "establish the name, power, and authority of the King; subject the nations to his rule, and teach them the knowledge of the true God and the light of the Christian faith."[1] Acadia, in short, was made an hereditary fief; and D'Aunay and his heirs became lords of a domain as large as a European kingdom.

D'Aunay had spent his substance in the task of civilizing a wilderness.[2] The King had not helped him; and though he belonged to a caste which held commerce in contempt, he must be a fur-trader or a bankrupt. La Tour's Fort St. Jean was a better trading-station than Port Royal, and it had wofully abridged D'Aunay's profits. Hence an ignoble competition in beaver-skins had greatly embittered their quarrel. All this was over; Fort St. Jean, the best trading-stand in Acadia, was now in its conqueror's hands; and his monopoly was no longer a mere name, but a reality.

[1] *Lettre du Roy de Gouverneur et Lieutenant Général es costes de l'Acadie pour Charles de Menou d'Aulnay Charnisay, Février*, 1647. *Lettre de la Reyne régente au même*, 13 *Avril*, 1647.

[2] His heirs estimated his outlays for the colony at 800,000 livres. *Mémoire des filles du feu Seigneur d'Aulnay Charnisay*, 1686. *Placet de Joseph de Menou d'Aunay Charnisay, fils ainé du feu Charles de Menou d'Aunay Charnisay*, 1658.

Everything promised a thriving trade and a growing colony, when the scene was suddenly changed. On the twenty-fourth of May, 1650, a dark and stormy day, D'Aunay and his valet were in a birch canoe in the basin of Port Royal, not far from the mouth of the Annapolis. Perhaps neither master nor man was skilled in the management of the treacherous craft that bore them. The canoe overset. D'Aunay and the valet clung to it and got astride of it, one at each end. There they sat, sunk to the shoulders, the canoe though under water having buoyancy enough to keep them from sinking farther. So they remained an hour and a half; and at the end of that time D'Aunay was dead, not from drowning but from cold, for the water still retained the chill of winter. The valet remained alive; and in this condition they were found by Indians and brought to the north shore of the Annapolis, whither Father Ignace, the Superior of the Capuchins, went to find the body of his patron, brought it to the fort, and buried it in the chapel, in presence of his wife and all the soldiers and inhabitants.[1]

The Father Superior highly praises the dead chief, and is astonished that the earth does not gape and devour the slanderers who say that he died in desperation, as one abandoned of God. He admits that in former times cavillers might have found wherewith to accuse him, but declares that before his death he had amended all his faults. This is the testimony

[1] *Lettre du Rev. P. Ignace, Capucin, 6 Aoust,* 1653.

of a Capuchin, whose fraternity he had always favored. The Récollets, on the other hand, whose patron was La Tour, complained that D'Aunay had ill-used them, and demanded redress.[1] He seems to have been a favorable example of his class; loyal to his faith and his King, tempering pride with courtesy, and generally true to his cherished ideal of the *gentilhomme Français*. In his qualities, as in his birth, he was far above his rival; and his death was the ruin of the only French colony in Acadia that deserved the name.

At the news of his enemy's fate a new hope possessed La Tour. He still had agents in France interested to serve him; while the father of D'Aunay, who acted as his attorney, was feeble with age, and his children were too young to defend their interests.

There is an extraordinary document bearing date February, 1651, or less than a year after D'Aunay's death. It is a complete reversal of the decree of 1647 in his favor. La Tour suddenly appears as the favorite of royalty, and all the graces before lavished on his enemy are now heaped upon him. The lately proscribed "rebel and traitor" is confirmed as governor and lieutenant-general in New France. His services to God and the King are rehearsed "as of our certain knowledge," and he is praised with the same emphasis used towards D'Aunay in the decree

[1] Papers to this effect are among the many pieces cited in the *Arrêt du Conseil d'État à l'égard du Seigneur de la Tour,* 6 *Mars,* **1644.**

of 1647, and almost in the same words. The paper goes on to say that he, La Tour, would have converted the Indians and conquered Acadia for the King if D'Aunay had not prevented him.[1]

Unless this document is a fabrication in the interest of La Tour, as there is some reason to believe, it suggests strange reflections on colonial administration during the minority of Louis XIV. Genuine or not, La Tour profited by it, and after a visit to France, which proved a successful and fruitful one, he returned to Acadia with revived hopes. The widow of D'Aunay had eight children, all minors; and their grandfather, the octogenarian René de Menou, had been appointed their guardian. He sent an incompetent and faithless person to Port Royal to fulfil the wardship of which he was no longer capable.

The unfortunate widow and her children needed better help. D'Aunay had employed as his agent one Le Borgne, a merchant of Rochelle, who now succeeded in getting the old man under his influence, and induced him to sign an acknowledgment, said to be false, that D'Aunay's heirs owed him 260,000

---

[1] *Confirmation de Gouverneur et Lieutenant Général pour le Roy de la Nouvelle France, à la Coste de l'Acadie, au Sr. Charles de St. Étienne, Chevalier de la Tour,* 27 *Fév.,* 1651. A copy of this strange paper is before me. Comte de Menou, and after him, his follower Moreau, doubt the genuineness of the document, which, however, is alluded to without suspicion in the legal paper entitled *Mémoire* in re *Charles de St. Étienne, Seigneur de la Tour* (fils) *et ses frères et sœurs,* 1700. This *Mémoire* is in the interest of the heirs of La Tour, and is to be judged accordingly.

livres.[1] Le Borgne next came to Port Royal to push
his schemes; and here he inveigled or frightened the
widow into signing a paper to the effect that she and
her children owed him 205,286 livres. It was fortunate for his unscrupulous plans that he had to do
with the soft and tractable Madame d'Aunay, and
not with the high-spirited and intelligent Amazon
Madame La Tour. Le Borgne now seized on Port
Royal as security for the alleged debts; while La
Tour on his return from his visit to France induced
the perplexed and helpless widow to restore to him
Fort St. Jean, conquered by her late husband.
Madame d'Aunay, beset with insidious enemies, saw
herself and her children in danger of total ruin. She
applied to the Duc de Vendôme, grand-master, chief,
and superintendent of navigation, and offered to
share all her Acadian claims with him if he would
help her in her distress; but, from the first, Vendôme
looked more to his own interests than to hers. La
Tour was not satisfied with her concessions to him,
and perplexing questions rose between them touching
land claims and the fur-trade. To end these troubles
she took a desperate step, and on the twenty-fourth
of February, 1653, married her tormentor, the foe of
her late husband, who had now been dead not quite
three years.[2] Her chief thought seems to have been
for her children, whose rights are guarded, though

---

[1] *Mémoire* in re *Charles de St. Étienne* (fils de la Tour), etc.

[2] Rameau, i. 120. Menou and Moreau think that this marriage
took place two or three years later.

to little purpose, in the marriage contract. She and La Tour took up their abode at Fort St. Jean. Of the children of her first marriage four were boys and four were girls. They were ruined at last by the harpies leagued to plunder them, and sought refuge in France, where the boys were all killed in the wars of Louis XIV., and at least three of the girls became nuns.[1]

Now follow complicated disputes, without dignity or interest, and turning chiefly on the fur-trade. Le Borgne and his son, in virtue of their claims on the estate of D'Aunay, which were sustained by the French courts, got a lion's share of Acadia; a part fell also to La Tour and his children by his new wife, while Nicolas Denys kept a feeble hold on the shore of the Gulf of St. Lawrence as far north as Cape Rosiers.

War again broke out between France and England, and in 1654 Major Robert Sedgwick of Charlestown, Massachusetts, who had served in the civil war as a major-general of Cromwell, led a small New England force to Acadia under a commission from the Protector, captured Fort St. Jean, Port Royal, and all the other French stations, and conquered the colony for England. It was restored to France by the treaty of Breda, and captured again in 1690 by Sir William Phips. The treaty of Ryswick again restored it to France, till, in 1710, it was finally seized for England by General Nicholson.

[1] Menou, *L'Acadie colonisée.*

When, after Sedgwick's expedition, the English were in possession of Acadia, La Tour, not for the first time, tried to fortify his claims by a British title, and, jointly with Thomas Temple and William Crown, obtained a grant of the colony from Cromwell, — though he soon after sold his share to his copartner, Temple. He seems to have died in 1666.[1] Descendants of his were living in Acadia in 1830, and some may probably still be found there. As for D'Aunay, no trace of his blood is left in the land where he gave wealth and life for France and the Church.

[1] Rameau, i. 122.

SECTION SECOND.

CANADA A MISSION.

———•———

CHAPTER IV.

1653–1658.

THE JESUITS AT ONONDAGA.

THE IROQUOIS WAR. — FATHER PONCET: HIS ADVENTURES. — JESUIT BOLDNESS. — LE MOYNE'S MISSION. — CHAUMONOT AND DABLON. — IROQUOIS FEROCITY. — THE MOHAWK KIDNAPPERS. — CRITICAL POSITION. — THE COLONY OF ONONDAGA. — SPEECH OF CHAUMONOT. — OMENS OF DESTRUCTION. — DEVICE OF THE JESUITS. — THE MEDICINE FEAST. — THE ESCAPE.

IN the summer of 1653 all Canada turned to fasting and penance, processions, vows, and supplications. The saints and the Virgin were beset with unceasing prayer. The wretched little colony was like some puny garrison, starving and sick, compassed with inveterate foes, supplies cut off, and succor hopeless.

At Montreal — the advance guard of the settlements, a sort of Castle Dangerous, held by about fifty Frenchmen, and said by a pious writer of the day to exist only by a continuous miracle — some two

hundred Iroquois fell upon twenty-six Frenchmen.
The Christians were outmatched, eight to one; but,
says the chronicle, the Queen of Heaven was on their
side, and the Son of Mary refuses nothing to his
holy mother.[1] Through her intercession, the Iroquois
shot so wildly that at their first fire every bullet
missed its mark, and they met with a bloody defeat.
The palisaded settlement of Three Rivers, though in
a position less exposed than that of Montreal, was
in no less jeopardy. A noted war-chief of the
Mohawk Iroquois had been captured here the year
before, and put to death; and his tribe swarmed out,
like a nest of angry hornets, to revenge him. Not
content with defeating and killing the commandant,
Du Plessis Bochart, they encamped during the winter
in the neighboring forest, watching for an opportunity to surprise the place. Hunger drove them
off, but they returned in the spring, infesting every
field and pathway; till at length some six hundred
of their warriors landed in secret and lay hidden in
the depths of the woods, silently biding their time.
Having failed, however, in an artifice designed to
lure the French out of their defences, they showed
themselves on all sides, plundering, burning, and
destroying, up to the palisades of the fort.[2]

Of the three settlements which, with their feeble

---

[1] Le Mercier, *Relation*, 1653, 3.

[2] So bent were they on taking the place, that they brought their
families, in order to make a permanent settlement. Marie de
l'Incarnation, *Lettre du 6 Sept.*, 1653.

dependencies, then comprised the whole of Canada, Quebec was least exposed to Indian attacks, being partially covered by Montreal and Three Rivers. Nevertheless, there was no safety this year, even under the cannon of Fort St. Louis. At Cap Rouge, a few miles above, the Jesuit Poncet saw a poor woman who had a patch of corn beside her cabin, but could find nobody to harvest it. The father went to seek aid; met one Mathurin Franchetot, whom he persuaded to undertake the charitable task, and was returning with him, when they both fell into an ambuscade of Iroquois, who seized them and dragged them off. Thirty-two men embarked in canoes at Quebec to follow the retreating savages and rescue the prisoners. Pushing rapidly up the St. Lawrence, they approached Three Rivers, found it beset by the Mohawks, and bravely threw themselves into it, to the great joy of its defenders and discouragement of the assailants.

Meanwhile, the intercession of the Virgin wrought new marvels at Montreal, and a bright ray of hope beamed forth from the darkness and the storm to cheer the hearts of her votaries. It was on the twenty-sixth of June that sixty of the Onondaga Iroquois appeared in sight of the fort, shouting from a distance that they came on an errand of peace, and asking safe-conduct for some of their number. Guns, scalping-knives, tomahawks, were all laid aside; and, with a confidence truly astonishing, a deputation of chiefs, naked and defenceless, came into the midst of those

whom they had betrayed so often. The French had
a mind to seize them, and pay them in kind for past
treachery; but they refrained, seeing in this won-
drous change of heart the manifest hand of Heaven.
Nevertheless, it can be explained without a miracle.
The Iroquois, or at least the western nations of their
league, had just become involved in war with their
neighbors the Eries,[1] and "one war at a time" was
the sage maxim of their policy.

All was smiles and blandishment in the fort at
Montreal; presents were exchanged, and the deputies
departed, bearing home golden reports of the French.
An Oneida deputation soon followed; but the enraged
Mohawks still infested Montreal and beleaguered
Three Rivers, till one of their principal chiefs and
four of their best warriors were captured by a party
of Christian Hurons. Then, seeing themselves
abandoned by the other nations of the league and
left to wage the war alone, they too made overtures
of peace.

A grand council was held at Quebec. Speeches
were made, and wampum-belts exchanged. The
Iroquois left some of their chief men as pledges of
sincerity, and two young soldiers offered themselves
as reciprocal pledges on the part of the French.
The war was over; at least Canada had found a
moment to take breath for the next struggle. The

---

[1] See "Jesuits in North America," 542. The Iroquois, it will be
remembered, consisted of five "nations," or tribes, — the Mohawks,
Oneidas, Onondagas, Cayugas, and Senecas. For an account of
them, see the work just cited, Introduction.

fur-trade was restored again, with promise of plenty; for the beaver, profiting by the quarrels of their human foes, had of late greatly multiplied. It was a change from death to life; for Canada lived on the beaver, and robbed of this, her only sustenance, had been dying slowly since the strife began.[1]

"Yesterday," writes Father Le Mercier, "all was dejection and gloom; to-day, all is smiles and gayety. On Wednesday, massacre, burning, and pillage; on Thursday, gifts and visits, as among friends. If the Iroquois have their hidden designs, so too has God.

"On the day of the Visitation of the Holy Virgin, the chief, Aontarisati,[2] so regretted by the Iroquois, was taken prisoner by our Indians, instructed by our fathers, and baptized; and on the same day, being put to death, he ascended to heaven. I doubt not that he thanked the Virgin for his misfortune and the blessing that followed, and that he prayed to God for his countrymen.

"The people of Montreal made a solemn vow to celebrate publicly the *fête* of this mother of all blessings; whereupon the Iroquois came to ask for peace.

"It was on the day of the Assumption of this Queen of angels and of men that the Hurons took at

[1] According to Le Mercier, beaver to the value of from 200,000 to 300,000 livres was yearly brought down to the colony before the destruction of the Hurons (1649–50). Three years later, not one beaver-skin was brought to Montreal during a twelvemonth, and Three Rivers and Quebec had barely enough to pay for keeping the fortifications in repair.

[2] The chief whose death had so enraged the Mohawks.

Montreal that other famous Iroquois chief, whose
capture caused the Mohawks to seek our alliance.

"On the day when the Church honors the Nativity
of the Holy Virgin, the Iroquois granted Father
Poncet his life; and he, or rather the Holy Virgin
and the holy angels, labored so well in the work of
peace, that on Saint Michael's Day it was resolved in
a council of the elders that the father should be conducted to Quebec, and a lasting treaty made with
the French." [1]

Happy as was this consummation, Father Poncet's
path to it had been a thorny one. He has left us his
own rueful story, written in obedience to the command of his superior. He and his companion in
misery had been hurried through the forests, from
Cap Rouge on the St. Lawrence to the Indian towns
on the Mohawk. He tells us how he slept among
dank weeds, dropping with the cold dew; how frightful colics assailed him as he waded waist-deep through
a mountain stream; how one of his feet was blistered
and one of his legs benumbed; how an Indian snatched
away his reliquary and lost the precious contents.
"I had," he says, "a picture of Saint Ignatius with
our Lord bearing the cross, and another of Our Lady
of Pity surrounded by the five wounds of her Son.
They were my joy and my consolation; but I hid
them in a bush, lest the Indians should laugh at
them." He kept, however, a little image of the
crown of thorns, in which he found great comfort,

[1] *Relation*, 1653, 18.

as well as in communion with his patron saints, Saint Raphael, Saint Martha, and Saint Joseph. On one occasion he asked these celestial friends for something to soothe his thirst, and for a bowl of broth to revive his strength. Scarcely had he framed the petition when an Indian gave him some wild plums; and in the evening, as he lay fainting on the ground, another brought him the coveted broth. Weary and forlorn, he reached at last the lower Mohawk town, where, after being stripped, and with his companion forced to run the gantlet, he was placed on a scaffold of bark, surrounded by a crowd of grinning and mocking savages. As it began to rain, they took him into one of their lodges, and amused themselves by making him dance, sing, and perform various fantastic tricks for their amusement. He seems to have done his best to please them; "but," adds the chronicler, "I will say in passing, that as he did not succeed to their liking in these buffooneries (*singeries*), they would have put him to death if a young Huron prisoner had not offered himself to sing, dance, and make wry faces in place of the father, who had never learned the trade."

Having sufficiently amused themselves, they left him for a time in peace; when an old one-eyed Indian approached, took his hands, examined them, selected the left forefinger, and calling a child four or five years old, gave him a knife, and told him to cut it off, which the imp proceeded to do, his victim meanwhile singing the *Vexilla Regis*. After this preliminary, they would have burned him, like Franchetot, his unfortunate companion, had not a squaw happily adopted him in place, as he says, of a deceased brother. He was installed at once in the lodge of his new relatives, where, bereft of every rag of Christian clothing, and attired in leggins, moccasins, and a greasy shirt, the astonished father saw himself transformed into an Iroquois. But his deliverance was at hand. A special agreement providing for it had formed a part of the treaty concluded at Quebec; and he now learned that he was to be restored to his countrymen. After a march of almost intolerable hardship, he saw himself once more among Christians, — Heaven, as he modestly thinks, having found him unworthy of martyrdom.

"At last," he writes, "we reached Montreal on the twenty-first of October, the nine weeks of my captivity being accomplished, in honor of Saint Michael and all the holy angels. On the sixth of November the Iroquois who conducted me made their presents to confirm the peace; and thus, on a Sunday evening, eighty-and-one days after my capture, — that is to say, nine times nine days, — this great business of the peace was happily concluded, the holy angels showing by this number nine, which is specially dedicated to them, the part they bore in this holy work." [1] This incessant supernaturalism is the key to the early history of New France.

[1] Poncet in *Relation*, 1653, 17. On Poncet's captivity see also *Morale Pratique des Jésuites*, vol. xxxiv. (4to) chap. xii.

Peace was made; but would peace endure? There was little chance of it, and this for several reasons. First, the native fickleness of the Iroquois, who, astute and politic to a surprising degree, were in certain respects, like all savages, mere grown-up children. Next, their total want of control over their fierce and capricious young warriors, any one of whom could break the peace with impunity whenever he saw fit; and, above all, the strong probability that the Iroquois had made peace in order, under cover of it, to butcher or kidnap the unhappy remnant of the Hurons who were living, under French protection, on the island of Orleans, immediately below Quebec. I have already told the story of the destruction of this people and of the Jesuit missions established among them.[1] The conquerors were eager to complete their bloody triumph by seizing upon the refugees of Orleans, killing the elders, and strengthening their own tribes by the adoption of the women, children, and youths. The Mohawks and the Onondagas were competitors for the prize. Each coveted the Huron colony, and each was jealous lest his rival should pounce upon it first.

When the Mohawks brought home Poncet, they covertly gave wampum-belts to the Huron chiefs, and invited them to remove to their villages. It was the wolf's invitation to the lamb. The Hurons, aghast with terror, went secretly to the Jesuits, and told them that demons had whispered in their ears an

[1] See "Jesuits in North America."

invitation to destruction. So helpless were both the Hurons and their French supporters, that they saw no recourse but dissimulation. The Hurons promised to go, and only sought excuses to gain time.

The Onondagas had a deeper plan. Their towns were already full of Huron captives, former converts of the Jesuits, cherishing their memory and constantly repeating their praises. Hence their tyrants conceived the idea that by planting at Onondaga a colony of Frenchmen under the direction of these beloved fathers, the Hurons of Orleans, disarmed of suspicion, might readily be led to join them. Other motives, as we shall see, tended to the same end, and the Onondaga deputies begged, or rather demanded, that a colony of Frenchmen should be sent among them.

Here was a dilemma. Was not this, like the Mohawk invitation to the Hurons, an invitation to butchery? On the other hand, to refuse would probably kindle the war afresh. The Jesuits had long nursed a project bold to temerity. Their great Huron mission was ruined; but might not another be built up among the authors of this ruin, and the Iroquois themselves, tamed by the power of the Faith, be annexed to the kingdoms of Heaven and of France? Thus would peace be restored to Canada, a barrier of fire opposed to the Dutch and English heretics, and the power of the Jesuits vastly increased. Yet the time was hardly ripe for such an attempt. Before thrusting a head into the tiger's jaws, it would be well to try the effect of thrusting in a hand. They resolved to compromise with the danger, and before risking a colony at Onondaga to send thither an envoy who could soothe the Indians, confirm them in pacific designs, and pave the way for more decisive steps. The choice fell on Father Simon Le Moyne.

The errand was mainly a political one; and this sagacious and able priest, versed in Indian languages and customs, was well suited to do it. "On the second day of the month of July, the festival of the Visitation of the Most Holy Virgin, ever favorable to our enterprises, Father Simon Le Moyne set out from Quebec for the country of the Onondaga Iroquois." In these words does Father Le Mercier chronicle the departure of his brother Jesuit. Scarcely was he gone when a band of Mohawks, under a redoubtable half-breed known as the Flemish Bastard, arrived at Quebec; and when they heard that the envoy was to go to the Onondagas without visiting their tribe, they took the imagined slight in high dudgeon, displaying such jealousy and ire that a letter was sent after Le Moyne, directing him to proceed to the Mohawk towns before his return. But he was already beyond reach, and the angry Mohawks were left to digest their wrath.

At Montreal, Le Moyne took a canoe, a young Frenchman, and two or three Indians, and began the tumultuous journey of the Upper St. Lawrence. Nature, or habit, had taught him to love the wilderness life. He and his companions had struggled all

day against the surges of La Chine, and were bivouacked at evening by the Lake of St. Louis, when
a cloud of mosquitoes fell upon them, followed by a
shower of warm rain. The father, stretched under
a tree, seems clearly to have enjoyed himself. "It
is a pleasure," he writes, "the sweetest and most
innocent imaginable, to have no other shelter than
trees planted by Nature since the creation of the
world." Sometimes, during their journey, this
primitive tent proved insufficient, and they would
build a bark hut or find a partial shelter under their
inverted canoe. Now they glided smoothly over the
sunny bosom of the calm and smiling river, and now
strained every nerve to fight their slow way against
the rapids, dragging their canoe upward in the
shallow water by the shore, as one leads an unwilling
horse by the bridle, or shouldering it and bearing it
through the forest to the smoother current above.
Game abounded; and they saw great herds of elk
quietly defiling between the water and the woods,
with little heed of men, who in that perilous region
found employment enough in hunting one another.

At the entrance of Lake Ontario they met a party
of Iroquois fishermen, who proved friendly, and
guided them on their way. Ascending the Onondaga,
they neared their destination; and now all misgivings
as to their reception at the Iroquois capital were dispelled. The inhabitants came to meet them, bringing roasting ears of the young maize and bread made
of its pulp, than which they knew no luxury more

5

exquisite. Their faces beamed welcome. Le Moyne was astonished. "I never," he says, "saw the like among Indians before." They were flattered by his visit, and, for the moment, were glad to see him. They hoped for great advantages from the residence of Frenchmen among them; and having the Erie war on their hands, they wished for peace with Canada. "One would call me brother," writes Le Moyne; "another, uncle; another, cousin. I never had so many relations."

He was overjoyed to find that many of the Huron converts, who had long been captives at Onondaga, had not forgotten the teachings of their Jesuit instructors. Such influence as they had with their conquerors was sure to be exerted in behalf of the French. Deputies of the Senecas, Cayugas, and Oneidas at length arrived, and on the tenth of August the criers passed through the town, summoning all to hear the words of Onontio. The naked dignitaries, sitting, squatting, or lying at full length, thronged the smoky hall of council. The father knelt and prayed in a loud voice, invoking the aid of Heaven, cursing the demons who are spirits of discord, and calling on the tutelar angels of the country to open the ears of his listeners. Then he opened his packet of presents and began his speech. "I was full two hours," he says, "in making it, speaking in the tone of a chief, and walking to and fro, after their fashion, like an actor on a theatre." Not only did he imitate the prolonged accents of the Iroquois

orators, but he adopted and improved their figures of
speech, and addressed them in turn by their respective
tribes, bands, and families, calling their men of note
by name, as if he had been born among them.   They
were delighted; and their ejaculations of approval —
hoh-hoh-hoh — came thick and fast at every pause of
his harangue.   Especially were they pleased with the
eighth, ninth, tenth, and eleventh presents, whereby
the reverend speaker gave to the four upper nations
of the league four hatchets to strike their new enemies, the Eries; while by another present he meta-
phorically daubed their faces with the war-paint.
However it may have suited the character of a Christian priest to hound on these savage hordes to a war
of extermination which they had themselves pro-
voked, it is certain that, as a politician, Le Moyne
did wisely; since in the war with the Eries lay the
best hope of peace for the French.

The reply of the Indian orator was friendly to
overflowing.   He prayed his French brethren to
choose a spot on the lake of Onondaga, where they
might dwell in the country of the Iroquois, as they
dwelt already in their hearts.   Le Moyne promised,
and made two presents to confirm the pledge.   Then,
his mission fulfilled, he set out on his return,
attended by a troop of Indians.   As he approached
the lake, his escort showed him a large spring of
water, possessed, as they told him, by a bad spirit.
Le Moyne tasted it, then boiled a little of it, and
produced a quantity of excellent salt.   He had dis-

covered the famous salt-springs of Onondaga.   Fishing and hunting, the party pursued their way till, at noon of the seventh of September, Le Moyne reached Montreal.[1]

When he reached Quebec, his tidings cheered for a while the anxious hearts of its tenants; but an unwonted incident soon told them how hollow was the ground beneath their feet.   Le Moyne, accompanied by two Onondagas and several Hurons and Algonquins, was returning to Montreal, when he and his companions were set upon by a war-party of Mohawks. The Hurons and Algonquins were killed.   One of the Onondagas shared their fate, and the other, with Le Moyne himself, was seized and bound fast.   The captive Onondaga, however, was so loud in his threats and denunciations that the Mohawks released both him and the Jesuit.[2]   Here was a foreshadowing of civil war, — Mohawk against Onondaga, Iroquois against Iroquois.   The quarrel was patched up, but fresh provocations were imminent.

The Mohawks took no part in the Erie war, and hence their hands were free to fight the French and the tribes allied with them.   Reckless of their promises, they began a series of butcheries, — fell upon the French at Isle aux Oies, killed a lay brother of the Jesuits at Sillery, and attacked Montreal. Here, being roughly handled, they came for a time

---

[1] *Journal du Père Le Moine, Relation,* 1654, chaps. vi. vii.

[2] Compare *Relation,* 1654, 33, and *Lettre de Marie de l'Incarnation,* 18 *Oct.,* 1654.

to their senses, and offered terms, promising to spare
the French, but declaring that they would still wage
war against the Hurons and Algonquins. These
were allies whom the French were pledged to protect;
but so helpless was the colony that the insolent and
humiliating proffer was accepted, and another peace
ensued, as hollow as the last. The indefatigable Le
Moyne was sent to the Mohawk towns to confirm it,
"so far," says the chronicle, "as it is possible to confirm a peace made by infidels backed by heretics."[1]
The Mohawks received him with great rejoicing; yet
his life was not safe for a moment. A warrior,
feigning madness, raved through the town with
uplifted hatchet, howling for his blood; but the
saints watched over him and balked the machinations
of hell. He came off alive and returned to Montreal,
spent with famine and fatigue.

Meanwhile a deputation of eighteen Onondaga
chiefs arrived at Quebec. There was a grand council.
The Onondagas demanded a colony of Frenchmen to
dwell among them. Lauson, the governor, dared
neither to consent nor to refuse. A middle course
was chosen; and two Jesuits, Chaumonot and Dablon,
were sent, like Le Moyne, partly to gain time, partly
to reconnoitre, and partly to confirm the Onondagas
in such good intentions as they might entertain.
Chaumonot was a veteran of the Huron mission, who,
miraculously as he himself supposed, had acquired a

---

[1] *Copie de Deux Lettres envoyées de la Nouvelle France au Père
Procureur des Missions de la Compagnie de Jésus.*

great fluency in the Huron tongue, which is closely allied to that of the Iroquois. Dablon, a new-comer, spoke, as yet, no Indian.

Their voyage up the St. Lawrence was enlivened by an extraordinary bear-hunt, and by the antics of one of their Indian attendants, who, having dreamed that he had swallowed a frog, roused the whole camp by the gymnastics with which he tried to rid himself of the intruder. On approaching Onondaga, they were met by a chief who sang a song of welcome, a part of which he seasoned with touches of humor, — apostrophizing the fish in the river Onondaga, naming each sort, great or small, and calling on them in turn to come into the nets of the Frenchmen and sacrifice life cheerfully for their behoof. Hereupon there was much laughter among the Indian auditors. An unwonted cleanliness reigned in the town; the streets had been cleared of refuse, and the arched roofs of the long houses of bark were covered with red-skinned children staring at the entry of the "black robes."

Crowds followed behind, and all was jubilation. The dignitaries of the tribe met them on the way, and greeted them with a speech of welcome. A feast of bear's meat awaited them; but, unhappily, it was Friday, and the fathers were forced to abstain.

"On Monday, the fifteenth of November, at nine in the morning, after having secretly sent to Paradise a dying infant by the waters of baptism, all the elders and the people having assembled, we opened

the council by public prayer." Thus writes Father
Dablon. His colleague, Chaumonot, a Frenchman
bred in Italy, now rose, with a long belt of wampum
in his hand, and proceeded to make so effective a
display of his rhetorical gifts that the Indians were
lost in admiration, and their orators put to the blush
by his improvements on their own metaphors. "If
he had spoken all day," said the delighted auditors,
"we should not have had enough of it." "The
Dutch," added others, "have neither brains nor
tongues; they never tell us about paradise and hell;
on the contrary, they lead us into bad ways."

On the next day the chiefs returned their answer.
The council opened with a song or chant, which was
divided into six parts, and which, according to
Dablon, was exceedingly well sung. The burden
of the fifth part was as follows:—

"Farewell war! farewell tomahawk! We have
been fools till now; henceforth we will be brothers,
—yes, we will be brothers."

Then came four presents, the third of which
enraptured the fathers. It was a belt of seven thousand beads of wampum. "But this," says Dablon,
"was as nothing to the words that accompanied it."
"It is the gift of the faith," said the orator. "It is
to tell you that we are believers; it is to beg you not
to tire of instructing us. Have patience, seeing that
we are so dull in learning prayer; push it into our
heads and our hearts." Then he led Chaumonot
into the midst of the assembly, clasped him in his

arms, tied the belt about his waist, and protested, with a suspicious redundancy of words, that as he clasped the father, so would he clasp the faith.

What had wrought this sudden change of heart? The eagerness of the Onondagas that the French should settle among them had, no doubt, a large share in it. For the rest, the two Jesuits saw abundant signs of the fierce, uncertain nature of those with whom they were dealing. Erie prisoners were brought in and tortured before their eyes, — one of them being a young stoic of about ten years, who endured his fate without a single outcry. Huron women and children, taken in war and adopted by their captors, were killed on the slightest provocation, and sometimes from mere caprice. For several days the whole town was in an uproar with the crazy follies of the "dream feast," [1] and one of the Fathers nearly lost his life in this Indian Bedlam.

One point was clear: the French must make a settlement at Onondaga, and that speedily, or, despite their professions of brotherhood, the Onondagas would make war. Their attitude became menacing; from urgency they passed to threats; and the two priests felt that the critical posture of affairs must at once be reported at Quebec. But here a difficulty arose. It was the beaver-hunting season; and, eager as were the Indians for a French colony, not one of them would offer to conduct the Jesuits to Quebec in order to fetch one. It was not until

[1] See "Jesuits in North America," 154.

nine masses had been said to Saint John the Baptist, that a number of Indians consented to forego their hunting, and escort Father Dablon home.[1] Chaumonot remained at Onondaga, to watch his dangerous hosts and soothe their rising jealousies.

It was the second of March when Dablon began his journey. His constitution must have been of iron, or he would have succumbed to the appalling hardships of the way. It was neither winter nor spring. The lakes and streams were not yet open, but the half-thawed ice gave way beneath the foot. One of the Indians fell through and was drowned. Swamp and forest were clogged with sodden snow, and ceaseless rains drenched them as they toiled on, knee-deep in slush. Happily, the St. Lawrence was open. They found an old wooden canoe by the shore, embarked, and reached Montreal after a journey of four weeks.

Dablon descended to Quebec. There was long and anxious counsel in the chambers of Fort St. Louis. The Jesuits had information that if the demands of the Onondagas were rejected, they would join the Mohawks to destroy Canada. But why were they so eager for a colony of Frenchmen? Did they want them as hostages, that they might attack the Hurons and Algonquins without risk of French interference; or would they massacre them, and then, like tigers mad with the taste of blood, turn upon

[1] De Quen, *Relation*, 1656, 35. Chaumonot, in his Autobiography ascribes the miracle to the intercession of the deceased Brébeuf.

the helpless settlements of the St. Lawrence? An abyss yawned on either hand. Lauson, the governor, was in an agony of indecision; but at length he declared for the lesser and remoter peril, and gave his voice for the colony. The Jesuits were of the same mind, though it was they, and not he, who must bear the brunt of danger. "The blood of the martyrs is the seed of the Church," said one of them; "and if we die by the fires of the Iroquois, we shall have won eternal life by snatching souls from the fires of hell."

Preparation was begun at once. The expense fell on the Jesuits, and the outfit is said to have cost them seven thousand livres, — a heavy sum for Canada at that day. A pious gentleman, Zachary Du Puys, major of the fort of Quebec, joined the expedition with ten soldiers; and between thirty and forty other Frenchmen also enrolled themselves, impelled by devotion or destitution. Four Jesuits, — Le Mercier, the superior, with Dablon, Ménard, and Frémin, — besides two lay brothers of the order, formed, as it were, the pivot of the enterprise. The governor made them the grant of a hundred square leagues of land in the heart of the Iroquois country, — a preposterous act, which, had the Iroquois known it, would have rekindled the war; but Lauson had a mania for land-grants, and was himself the proprietor of vast domains which he could have occupied only at the cost of his scalp.

Embarked in two large boats and followed by

twelve canoes filled with Hurons, Onondagas, and a few Senecas lately arrived, they set out on the seventeenth of May "to attack the demons," as Le Mercier writes, "in their very stronghold." With shouts, tears, and benedictions, priests, soldiers, and inhabitants waved farewell from the strand. They passed the bare steeps of Cape Diamond and the mission-house nestled beneath the heights of Sillery, and vanished from the anxious eyes that watched the last gleam of their receding oars.[1]

Meanwhile three hundred Mohawk warriors had taken the war-path, bent on killing or kidnapping the Hurons of Orleans. When they heard of the departure of the colonists for Onondaga, their rage was unbounded; for not only were they full of jealousy towards their Onondaga confederates, but they had hitherto derived great profit from the control which their local position gave them over the traffic between this tribe and the Dutch of the Hudson, — upon whom the Onondagas, in common with all the upper Iroquois, had been dependent for their guns, hatchets, scalping-knives, beads, blankets, and brandy. These supplies would now be furnished by the French, and the Mohawk speculators saw their occupation gone. Nevertheless, they had just made peace with the French, and for the moment were not quite in the mood to break it. To wreak their spite, they took a middle course, — crouched in ambush

---

[1] Marie de l'Incarnation, *Lettres*, 1656. Le Mercier, *Relation*, 1657, chap. iv. Chaulmer, *Nouveau Monde*, ii. 265, 322, 319.

among the bushes at Point St. Croix, ten or twelve
leagues above Quebec, allowed the boats bearing the
French to pass unmolested, and fired a volley at the
canoes in the rear, filled with Onondagas, Senecas,
and Hurons. Then they fell upon them with a yell,
and, after wounding a lay brother of the Jesuits
who was among them, bound and flogged such of
the Indians as they could seize. The astonished
Onondagas protested and threatened; whereupon the
Mohawks feigned great surprise, declared that they
had mistaken them for Hurons, called them brothers,
and suffered the whole party to escape without
further injury.[1]

The three hundred marauders now paddled their
large canoes of elm-bark stealthily down the current,
passed Quebec undiscovered in the dark night of the
nineteenth of May, landed in early morning on the
island of Orleans, and ambushed themselves to surprise the Hurons as they came to labor in their cornfields. They were tolerably successful, — killed six,
and captured more than eighty, the rest taking refuge
in their fort, where the Mohawks dared not attack
them.

At noon, the French on the rock of Quebec saw
forty canoes approaching from the island of Orleans,
and defiling, with insolent parade, in front of the
town, all crowded with the Mohawks and their prisoners, among whom were a great number of Huron

[1] Compare Marie de l'Incarnation, *Lettre* 14 *Août*, 1656, Le Jeune,
Relation, 1657, 9.

girls. Their captors, as they passed, forced them
to sing and dance. The Hurons were the allies, or
rather the wards, of the French, who were in every
way pledged to protect them. Yet the cannon of
Fort St. Louis were silent, and the crowd stood gap-
ing in bewilderment and fright. Had an attack been
made, nothing but a complete success and the capture
of many prisoners to serve as hostages could have
prevented the enraged Mohawks from taking their
revenge on the Onondaga colonists. The emergency
demanded a prompt and clear-sighted soldier. The
governor, Lauson, was a gray-haired civilian, who,
however enterprising as a speculator in wild lands,
was in no way matched to the desperate crisis of the
hour. Some of the Mohawks landed above and
below the town, and plundered the houses from
which the scared inhabitants had fled. Not a soldier
stirred and not a gun was fired. The French, bullied
by a horde of naked savages, became an object of
contempt to their own allies.

The Mohawks carried their prisoners home, burned
six of them, and adopted or rather enslaved the
rest.[1]

Meanwhile the Onondaga colonists pursued their
perilous way. At Montreal they exchanged their
heavy boats for canoes, and resumed their journey
with a flotilla of twenty of these sylvan vessels. A
few days after, the Indians of the party had the satisfaction of pillaging a small band of Mohawk hunters,

---

[1] See authorities just cited, and Perrot, *Mœurs des Sauvages*, 106.

in vicarious reprisal for their own wrongs.   On the twenty-sixth of June, as they neared Lake Ontario, they heard a loud and lamentable voice from the edge of the forest; whereupon, having beaten their drum to show that they were Frenchmen, they beheld a spectral figure, lean and covered with scars, which proved to be a pious Huron,— one Joachim Ondakout, captured by the Mohawks in their descent on the island of Orleans, five or six weeks before.   They had carried him to their village and begun to torture him; after which they tied him fast and lay down to sleep, thinking to resume their pleasure on the morrow.   His cuts and burns being only on the surface, he had the good fortune to free himself from his bonds, and, naked as he was, to escape to the woods. He held his course northwestward, through regions even now a wilderness, gathered wild strawberries to sustain life, and in fifteen days reached the St. Lawrence, nearly dead with exhaustion.   The Frenchmen gave him food and a canoe, and the living skeleton paddled with a light heart for Quebec.

The colonists themselves soon began to suffer from hunger.   Their fishing failed on Lake Ontario, and they were forced to content themselves with cranberries of the last year, gathered in the meadows. Of their Indians, all but five deserted them.   The Father Superior fell ill, and when they reached the mouth of the Oswego many of the starving Frenchmen had completely lost heart.   Weary and faint, they dragged their canoes up the rapids, when suddenly they were cheered by the sight of a stranger canoe swiftly descending the current. The Onondagas, aware of their approach, had sent it to meet them, laden with Indian corn and fresh salmon. Two more canoes followed, freighted like the first; and now all was abundance till they reached their journey's end, the Lake of Onondaga. It lay before them in the July sun, a glittering mirror, framed in forest verdure.

They knew that Chaumonot with a crowd of Indians was awaiting them at a spot on the margin of the water, which he and Dablon had chosen as the site of their settlement. Landing on the strand, they fired, to give notice of their approach, five small cannon which they had brought in their canoes. Waves, woods, and hills resounded with the thunder of their miniature artillery. Then re-embarking, they advanced in order, four canoes abreast, towards the destined spot. In front floated their banner of white silk, embroidered in large letters with the name of Jesus. Here were Du Puys and his soldiers, with the picturesque uniforms and quaint weapons of their time; Le Mercier and his Jesuits in robes of black; hunters and bush-rangers; Indians painted and feathered for a festal day. As they neared the place where a spring bubbling from the hillside is still known as the "Jesuits' Well," they saw the edge of the forest dark with the muster of savages whose yells of welcome answered the salvo of their guns. Happily for them, a flood of summer rain saved them from the harangues of the Onondaga

orators, and forced white men and red alike to seek
such shelter as they could find. Their hosts, with
hospitable intent, would fain have sung and danced
all night; but the Frenchmen pleaded fatigue, and
the courteous savages, squatting around their tents,
chanted in monotonous tones to lull them to sleep.
In the morning they woke refreshed, sang *Te Deum*,
reared an altar, and, with a solemn mass, took possession of the country in the name of Jesus.[1]

Three things, which they saw or heard of in their
new home, excited their astonishment. The first
was the vast flight of wild pigeons which in spring
darkened the air around the Lake of Onondaga; the
second was the salt springs of Salina; the third was
the rattlesnakes, which Le Mercier describes with
excellent precision, — adding that, as he learns from
the Indians, their tails are good for toothache and
their flesh for fever. These reptiles, for reasons
best known to themselves, haunted the neighborhood
of the salt-springs, but did not intrude their presence
into the abode of the French.

On the seventeenth of July, Le Mercier and Chaumonot, escorted by a file of soldiers, set out for Onondaga, scarcely five leagues distant. They followed
the Indian trail, under the leafy arches of the woods,
by hill and hollow, still swamp and gurgling brook,
till through the opening foliage they saw the Iroquois
capital, compassed with cornfields and girt with its
rugged palisade. As the Jesuits, like black spectres,

[1] Le Mercier, *Relation*, 1657, 14.

issued from the shadows of the forest, followed by
the plumed soldiers with shouldered arquebuses, the
red-skinned population swarmed out like bees, and
they defiled to the town through gazing and admiring
throngs. All conspired to welcome them. Feast
followed feast throughout the afternoon, till, what
with harangues and songs, bear's meat, beaver-tails,
and venison, beans, corn, and grease, they were
wellnigh killed with kindness. "If, after this, they
murder us," writes Le Mercier, "it will be from
fickleness, not premeditated treachery." But the
Jesuits, it seems, had not sounded the depths of
Iroquois dissimulation.[1]

There was one exception to the real or pretended
joy. Some Mohawks were in the town, and their
orator was insolent and sarcastic; but the ready
tongue of Chaumonot turned the laugh against him
and put him to shame.

Here burned the council-fire of the Iroquois, and
at this very time the deputies of the five tribes were
assembling. The session opened on the twenty-fourth.
In the great council-house, on the earthen floor and the
broad platforms, beneath the smoke-begrimed concave
of the bark roof, stood, sat, or squatted the wisdom
and valor of the confederacy, — Mohawks, Oneidas,

---

[1] The Jesuits were afterwards told by Hurons, captive among
the Mohawks and the Onondagas, that, from the first, it was
intended to massacre the French as soon as their presence had
attracted the remnant of the Hurons of Orleans into the power of
the Onondagas. *Lettre du P. Ragueneau au R. P. Provincial,* 31
Août, 1658.

Onondagas, Cayugas, and Senecas; sachems, counsellors, orators, warriors fresh from Erie victories;
tall, stalwart figures, limbed like Grecian statues.

The pressing business of the council over, it was
Chaumonot's turn to speak. But, first, all the
Frenchmen, kneeling in a row, with clasped hands,
sang the *Veni Creator*, amid the silent admiration
of the auditors. Then Chaumonot rose, with an
immense wampum-belt in his hand, and said:

"It is not trade that brings us here. Do you
think that your beaver-skins can pay us for all our
toils and dangers? Keep them, if you like; or, if
any fall into our hands, we shall use them only for
your service. We seek not the things that perish.
It is for the Faith that we have left our homes to
live in your hovels of bark, and eat food which the
beasts of our country would scarcely touch. We are
the messengers whom God has sent to tell you that
his Son became a man for the love of you; that this
man, the Son of God, is the prince and master of
men; that he has prepared in heaven eternal joys for
those who obey him, and kindled the fires of hell for
those who will not receive his word. If you reject
it, whoever you are, — Onondaga, Seneca, Mohawk,
Cayuga, or Oneida, — know that Jesus Christ, who
inspires my heart and my voice, will plunge you one
day into hell. Avert this ruin; be not the authors
of your own destruction; accept the truth; listen to
the voice of the Omnipotent."

Such, in brief, was the pith of the father's exhorta-

tion.   As he spoke Indian like a native, and as his
voice and gestures answered to his words, we may
believe what Le Mercier tells us, that his hearers
listened with mingled wonder, admiration, and terror.
The work was well begun.   The Jesuits struck while
the iron was hot; built a small chapel for the mass,
installed themselves in the town, and preached and
catechised from morning till night.

The Frenchmen at the lake were not idle.   The
chosen site of their settlement was the crown of a
hill commanding a broad view of waters and forests.
The axemen fell to their work, and a ghastly wound
soon gaped in the green bosom of the woodland.
Here, among the stumps and prostrate trees of the
unsightly clearing, the blacksmith built his forge,
saw and hammer plied their trade; palisades were
shaped and beams squared, in spite of heat, mosquitoes, and fever.   At one time twenty men were ill,
and lay gasping under a wretched shed of bark; but
they all recovered, and the work went on, till at
length a capacious house, large enough to hold the
whole colony, rose above the ruin of the forest.   A
palisade was set around it, and the Mission of Saint
Mary of Gannentaa [1] was begun.

France and the Faith were intrenched on the Lake
of Onondaga.   How long would they remain there?
The future alone could tell.   The mission, it must

---

[1] *Gannentaa* or *Ganuntaah* is still the Iroquois name for Lake
Onondaga.   According to Morgan, it means " Material for Council-
Fire."

not be forgotten, had a double scope, — half ecclesiastical, half political. The Jesuits had essayed a
fearful task, — to convert the Iroquois to God and to
the King, thwart the Dutch heretics of the Hudson,
save souls from hell, avert ruin from Canada, and
thus raise their order to a place of honor and influence both hard-earned and well-earned. The mission at Lake Onondaga was but a base of operations.
Long before they were lodged and fortified here,
Chaumonot and Ménard set out for the Cayugas,
whence the former proceeded to the Senecas, the
most numerous and powerful of the five confederate
nations; and in the following spring another mission
was begun among the Oneidas. Their reception was
not unfriendly; but such was the reticence and dissimulation of these inscrutable savages, that it was
impossible to foretell results. The women proved,
as might be expected, far more impressible than the
men; and in them the fathers placed great hope,
since in this, the most savage people of the continent,
women held a degree of political influence never perhaps equalled in any civilized nation.[1]

1 Women, among the Iroquois, had a council of their own,
which, according to Lafitau, who knew this people well, had the
initiative in discussion, subjects presented by them being settled in
the council of chiefs and elders. In this latter council the women
had an orator, often of their own sex, to represent them. The
matrons had a leading voice in determining the succession of
chiefs. There were also female chiefs, one of whom, with her
attendants, came to Quebec with an embassy in 1655 (Marie de
'Incarnation). In the torture of prisoners, great deference was

But while infants were baptized and squaws converted, the crosses of the mission were many and
great. The devil bestirred himself with more than
his ordinary activity; "for," as one of the fathers
writes, "when in sundry nations of the earth men
are rising up in strife against us [the Jesuits], then
how much more the demons, on whom we continually
wage war!" It was these infernal sprites, as the
priests believed, who engendered suspicions and
calumnies in the dark and superstitious minds of the
Iroquois, and prompted them in dreams to destroy
the apostles of the Faith. Whether the foe was of
earth or hell, the Jesuits were like those who tread
the lava-crust that palpitates with the throes of the
coming eruption, while the molten death beneath
their feet glares white-hot through a thousand
crevices. Yet, with a sublime enthusiasm and a
glorious constancy, they toiled and they hoped,
though the skies around were black with portent.

In the year in which the colony at Onondaga was
begun, the Mohawks murdered the Jesuit Garreau
on his way up the Ottawa. In the following spring,
a hundred Mohawk warriors came to Quebec to carry

paid to the judgment of the women, who, says Champlain, were
thought more skilful and subtle than the men.

The learned Lafitau, whose book appeared in 1724, dwells at
length on the resemblance of the Iroquois to the ancient Lycians,
among whom, according to Grecian writers, women were in the
ascendant. "Gynecocracy, or the rule of women," continues
Lafitau, "which was the foundation of the Lycian government,
was probably common in early times to nearly all the barbarous
people of Greece." *Mœurs des Sauvages,* i 460 (ed. in 4to).

more of the Hurons into slavery, — though the
remnant of that unhappy people, since the catastrophe
of the last year, had sought safety in a palisaded
camp within the limits of the French town, and
immediately under the ramparts of Fort St. Louis.
Here, one might think, they would have been safe;
but Charny, son and successor of Lauson, seems to
have been even more imbecile than his father, and
listened meekly to the threats of the insolent
strangers who told him that unless he abandoned
the Hurons to their mercy, both they and the French
should feel the weight of Mohawk tomahawks.
They demanded, further, that the French should
give them boats to carry their prisoners; but, as
there were none at hand, this last humiliation was
spared. The Mohawks were forced to make canoes,
in which they carried off as many as possible of their
victims.

When the Onondagas learned this last exploit of
their rivals, their jealousy knew no bounds, and a
troop of them descended to Quebec to claim their
share in the human plunder. Deserted by the
French, the despairing Hurons abandoned themselves
to their fate; and about fifty of those whom the
Mohawks had left obeyed the behest of their tyrants,
and embarked for Onondaga. They reached Montreal
in July, and thence proceeded towards their destination in company with the Onondaga warriors. The
Jesuit Ragueneau, bound also for Onondaga, joined
them. Five leagues above Montreal, the warriors

left him behind; but he found an old canoe on the
bank, in which, after abandoning most of his bag-
gage, he contrived to follow with two or three
Frenchmen who were with him.   There was a rumor
that a hundred Mohawk warriors were lying in
wait among the Thousand Islands to plunder the
Onondagas of their Huron prisoners.   It proved a
false report.   A speedier catastrophe awaited these
unfortunates.

Towards evening on the third of August, after the
party had landed to encamp, an Onondaga chief
made advances to a Christian Huron girl, as he had
already done at every encampment since leaving
Montreal.   Being repulsed for the fourth time, he
split her head with his tomahawk.   It was the
beginning of a massacre.   The Onondagas rose upon
their prisoners, killed seven men, all Christians,
before the eyes of the horrified Jesuit, and plundered
the rest of all they had.   When Ragueneau protested, they told him with insolent mockery that
they were acting by direction of the governor and
the superior of the Jesuits.   The priest himself was
secretly warned that he was to be killed during the
night; and he was surprised in the morning to find
himself alive.[1]   On reaching Onondaga, some of the
Christian captives were burned, including several
women and their infant children.[2]

The confederacy was a hornet's nest, buzzing with

---

[1] *Lettre de Ragueneau au R. P. Provincial,* 9 *Août,* 1657 (*Rel.,* 1657).
[2] *Ibid.,* 21 *Août,* 1658 (*Rel.,* 1658).

preparation, and fast pouring out its wrathful swarms. The indomitable Le Moyne had gone again to the Mohawks, whence he wrote that two hundred of them had taken the war-path against the Algonquins of Canada; and, a little later, that all were gone but women, children, and old men. A great war-party of twelve hundred Iroquois from all the five cantons was to advance into Canada in the direction of the Ottawa. The settlements on the St. Lawrence were infested with prowling warriors, who killed the Indian allies of the French, and plundered the French themselves, whom they treated with an insufferable insolence; for they felt themselves masters of the situation, and knew that the Onondaga colony was in their power. Near Montreal they killed three Frenchmen. "They approach like foxes," writes a Jesuit, "attack like lions, and disappear like birds." Charny, fortunately, had resigned the government in despair in order to turn priest, and the brave soldier d'Ailleboust had taken his place. He caused twelve of the Iroquois to be seized and held as hostages. This seemed to increase their fury. An embassy came to Quebec and demanded the release of the hostages, but were met with a sharp reproof and a flat refusal.

At the mission on Lake Onondaga the crisis was drawing near. The unbridled young warriors, whose capricious lawlessness often set at naught the monitions of their crafty elders, killed wantonly at various times thirteen Christian Hurons, captives at

Onondaga.   Ominous reports reached the ears of the
colonists.   They heard of a secret council at which
their death was decreed.   Again, they heard that
they were to be surprised and captured, that the
Iroquois in force were then to descend upon Canada,
lay waste the outlying settlements, and torture them,
the colonists, in sight of their countrymen, by which
they hoped to extort what terms they pleased.   At
length a dying Onondaga, recently converted and
baptized, confirmed the rumors, and revealed the
whole plot.

It was to take effect before the spring opened; but
the hostages in the hands of d'Ailleboust embarrassed
the conspirators and caused delay.   Messengers were
sent in haste to call in the priests from the detached
missions; and all the colonists, fifty-three in number,
were soon gathered at their fortified house on the
lake.   Their situation was frightful.   Fate hung
over them by a hair, and escape seemed hopeless.
Of Du Puys's ten soldiers, nine wished to desert;
but the attempt would have been fatal.   A throng
of Onondaga warriors were day and night on the
watch, bivouacked around the house.   Some of them
had built their huts of bark before the gate, and
here, with calm, impassive faces, they lounged and
smoked their pipes; or, wrapped in their blankets,
strolled about the yards and outhouses, attentive to
all that passed.   Their behavior was very friendly.
The Jesuits, themselves adepts in dissimulation,
were amazed at the depth of their duplicity; for the

conviction had been forced upon them that some of the chiefs had nursed their treachery from the first. In this extremity Du Puys and the Jesuits showed an admirable coolness, and among them devised a plan of escape, critical and full of doubt, but not devoid of hope.

First, they must provide means of transportation; next, they must contrive to use them undiscovered. They had eight canoes, all of which combined would not hold half their company. Over the mission-house was a large loft or garret, and here the carpenters were secretly set at work to construct two large and light flat-boats, each capable of carrying fifteen men. The task was soon finished. The most difficult part of their plan remained.

There was a beastly superstition prevalent among the Hurons, the Iroquois, and other tribes. It consisted of a "medicine" or mystic feast, in which it was essential that the guests should devour everything set before them, however inordinate in quantity, unless absolved from duty by the person in whose behalf the solemnity was ordained, — he, on his part, taking no share in the banquet. So grave was the obligation, and so strenuously did the guests fulfil it, that even their ostrich digestion was sometimes ruined past redemption by the excess of this benevolent gluttony. These *festins à manger tout* had been frequently denounced as diabolical by the Jesuits, during their mission among the Hurons; but now, with a pliancy of conscience as excusable in this case as in any other, they resolved to set aside their scruples, although, judged from their point of view, they were exceedingly well founded.

Among the French was a young man who had been adopted by an Iroquois chief, and who spoke the language fluently. He now told his Indian father that it had been revealed to him in a dream that he would soon die unless the spirits were appeased by one of these magic feasts. Dreams were the oracles of the Iroquois, and woe to those who slighted them. A day was named for the sacred festivity. The fathers killed their hogs to meet the occasion, and, that nothing might be wanting, they ransacked their stores for all that might give piquancy to the entertainment. It took place in the evening of the twentieth of March, apparently in a large enclosure outside the palisade surrounding the mission-house. Here, while blazing fires or glaring pine-knots shed their glow on the wild assemblage, Frenchmen and Iroquois joined in the dance, or vied with each other in games of agility and skill. The politic fathers offered prizes to the winners, and the Indians entered with zest into the sport, the better, perhaps, to hide their treachery and hoodwink their intended victims; for they little suspected that a subtlety, deeper this time than their own, was at work to countermine them. Here too were the French musicians, and drum, trumpet, and cymbal lent their clangor to the din of shouts and laughter. Thus the evening wore on, till at length the serious labors of the feast began.

The kettles were brought in, and their steaming
contents ladled into the wooden bowls which each
provident guest had brought with him. Seated
gravely in a ring, they fell to their work. It was a
point of high conscience not to flinch from duty on
these solemn occasions; and though they might burn
the young man to-morrow, they would gorge themselves like vultures in his behoof to-day.

Meantime, while the musicians strained their lungs
and their arms to drown all other sounds, a band of
anxious Frenchmen, in the darkness of the cloudy
night, with cautious tread and bated breath, carried
the boats from the rear of the mission-house down to
the border of the lake. It was near eleven o'clock.
The miserable guests were choking with repletion.
They prayed the young Frenchman to dispense them
from further surfeit. "Will you suffer me to die?"
he asked, in piteous tones. They bent to their task
again; but Nature soon reached her utmost limit,
and they sat helpless as a conventicle of gorged
turkey-buzzards, without the power possessed by
those unseemly birds to rid themselves of the burden.
"That will do," said the young man; "you have
eaten enough: my life is saved. Now you can sleep
till we come in the morning to waken you for
prayers."[1] And one of his companions played soft
airs on a violin to lull them to repose. Soon all were
asleep, or in a lethargy akin to sleep. The few
remaining Frenchmen now silently withdrew and

[1] *Lettre de Marie de l'Incarnation à son fils*, 4 *Oct.*, 1658.

cautiously descended to the shore, where their comrades, already embarked, lay on their oars anxiously
awaiting them.   Snow was falling fast as they pushed
out upon the murky waters.   The ice of the winter
had broken up, but recent frosts had glazed the surface with a thin crust.   The two boats led the way,
and the canoes followed in their wake, while men in
the bows of the foremost boat broke the ice with
clubs as they advanced.   They reached the outlet
and rowed swiftly down the dark current of the
Oswego.   When day broke, Lake Onondaga was far
behind, and around them was the leafless, lifeless
forest.

When the Indians woke in the morning, dull and
stupefied from their nightmare slumbers, they were
astonished at the silence that reigned in the mission-
house.   They looked through the palisade.   Nothing
was stirring but a bevy of hens clucking and scratch-
ing in the snow, and one or two dogs imprisoned in
the house and barking to be set free.   The Indians
waited for some time, then climbed the palisade,
burst in the doors, and found the house empty.
Their amazement was unbounded.   How, without
canoes, could the French have escaped by water?
And how else could they escape?   The snow which
had fallen during the night completely hid their
footsteps.   A superstitious awe seized the Iroquois.
They thought that the "black-robes" and their flock
had flown off through the air.

Meanwhile the fugitives pushed their flight with

the energy of terror, passed in safety the rapids of the Oswego, crossed Lake Ontario, and descended the St. Lawrence with the loss of three men drowned in the rapids. On the third of April they reached Montreal, and on the twenty-third arrived at Quebec. They had saved their lives; but the mission of Onondaga was a miserable failure.[1]

[1] On the Onondaga mission, the authorities are Marie de l'Incarnation, *Lettres Historiques,* and *Relations des Jésuites,* 1657 and 1658, where the story is told at length, accompanied with several interesting letters and journals. Chaumonot, in his *Autobiographie,* speaks only of the Seneca mission, and refers to the *Relations* for the rest. Dollier de Casson, in his *Histoire du Montréal,* mentions the arrival of the fugitives at that place, the sight of which, he adds complacently, cured them of their fright. The *Journal des Supérieurs des Jésuites* chronicles with its usual brevity the ruin of the mission and the return of the party to Quebec.

The contemporary Jesuits, in their account, say nothing of the superstitious character of the feast. It is Marie de l'Incarnation who lets out the secret. The later Jesuit Charlevoix, much to his credit, repeats the story without reserve.

Since the above chapter was written, the remarkable narratives of Pierre Esprit Radisson have been rescued from the obscurity where they have lain for more than two centuries. Radisson, a native of St. Malo, was a member of the colony at Onondaga; but having passed into the service of England, he wrote in a language which, for want of a fitter name, may be called English. He does not say that the feast was of the kind known as *festin à manger tout,* though he asserts that one of the priests pretended to have broken his arm, and that the Indians believed that the "feasting was to be done for the safe recovery of the father's health." Like the other writers, he says that the feasters gorged themselves like wolves and became completely helpless, "making strange kinds of faces that turned their eyes up and downe," till, when almost bursting, they were forced to cry *Skenon,* which according to Radisson means "enough." Radisson adds that it was proposed that the French, "being three and fifty in number, while the Iroquois were but 100 beasts not able to budge," should fall upon the impotent savages and kill them all, but that the Jesuits would not consent. His account of the embarkation and escape of the colonists agrees with that of the other writers.   See *Second Voyage made in the Upper Country of the Iroquoits*, in *Publications of the Prince Society*, 1885.

The Sulpitian Allet, in the *Morale Pratique des Jésuites*, says that the French placed effigies of soldiers in the fort to deceive the Indians.

CHAPTER V.

1642–1661.

THE HOLY WARS OF MONTREAL.

DAUVERSIÈRE. — MANCE AND BOURGEOYS. — MIRACLE. — A PIOUS
DEFAULTER. — JESUIT AND SULPITIAN. — MONTREAL IN 1659. —
THE HOSPITAL NUNS. — THE NUNS AND THE IROQUOIS. — MORE
MIRACLES. — THE MURDERED PRIESTS. — BRIGEAC AND CLOSSE.
— SOLDIERS OF THE HOLY FAMILY.

On the second of July, 1659, the ship "St. André"
lay in the harbor of Rochelle, crowded with passengers
for Canada. She had served two years as a hospital
for marines, and was infected with a contagious
fever. Including the crew, some two hundred persons
were on board, more than half of whom were bound
for Montreal. Most of these were sturdy laborers,
artisans, peasants, and soldiers, together with a troop
of young women, their present or future partners; a
portion of the company set down on the old record
as "sixty virtuous men and thirty-two pious girls."
There were two priests also, Vignal and Le Maître,
both destined to a speedy death at the hands of the
Iroquois. But the most conspicuous among these
passengers for Montreal were two groups of women
in the habit of nuns, under the direction of Marguerite

Bourgeoys and Jeanne Mance. Marguerite Bourgeoys, whose kind, womanly face bespoke her fitness for the task, was foundress of the school for female children at Montreal; her companion, a tall, austere figure, worn with suffering and care, was directress of the hospital. Both had returned to France for aid, and were now on their way back, each with three recruits, — three being the mystic number, as a type of the Holy Family, to whose worship they were especially devoted.

Amid the bustle of departure, the shouts of sailors, the rattling of cordage, the flapping of sails, the tears and the embracings, an elderly man, with heavy plebeian features, sallow with disease, and in a sober, half-clerical dress, approached Mademoiselle Mance and her three nuns, and, turning his eyes to heaven, spread his hands over them in benediction. It was Le Royer de la Dauversière, founder of the sisterhood of St. Joseph, to which the three nuns belonged. "Now, O Lord," he exclaimed, with the look of one whose mission on earth is fulfilled, "permit thou thy servant to depart in peace!"

Sister Maillet, who had charge of the meagre treasury of the community, thought that something more than a blessing was due from him, and asked where she should apply for payment of the interest of the twenty thousand livres which Mademoiselle Mance had placed in his hands for investment. Dauversière changed countenance, and replied with troubled voice: "My daughter, God will provide

5

for you. Place your trust in Him." [1] He was bankrupt, and had used the money of the sisterhood to
pay a debt of his own, leaving the nuns penniless.

I have related in another place [2] how an association
of devotees, inspired, as they supposed, from heaven,
had undertaken to found a religious colony at
Montreal in honor of the Holy Family. The essen-
tials of the proposed establishment were to be a seminary of priests dedicated to the Virgin, a hospital to
Saint Joseph, and a school to the Infant Jesus; while
a settlement was to be formed around them simply
for their defence and maintenance. This pious purpose had in part been accomplished. It was seventeen years since Mademoiselle Mance had begun
her labors in honor of Saint Joseph. Marguerite
Bourgeoys had entered upon hers more recently; yet
even then the attempt was premature, for she found
no white children to teach. In time, however, this
want was supplied, and she opened her school in a
stable, which answered to the stable of Bethlehem,
lodging with her pupils in the loft, and instructing
them in Roman Catholic Christianity, with such
rudiments of mundane knowledge as she and her
advisers thought fit to impart.

Mademoiselle Mance found no lack of hospital
work, for blood and blows were rife at Montreal,
where the woods were full of Iroquois, and not a

1 Faillon, *Vie de M'lle Mance*, i. 172. This volume is illustrated
with a portrait of Dauversière.

2 The Jesuits in North America.

moment was without its peril.   Though years began
to tell upon her, she toiled patiently at her dreary
task, till, in the winter of 1657, she fell on the ice
of the St. Lawrence, broke her right arm, and dis-
located the wrist. Bonchard, the surgeon of Montreal,
set the broken bones, but did not discover the dis-
location. The arm in consequence became totally
useless, and her health wasted away under incessant
and violent pain.   Maisonneuve, the civil and military chief of the settlement, advised her to go to
France for assistance in the work to which she was
no longer equal; and Marguerite Bourgeoys, whose
pupils, white and red, had greatly multiplied, resolved
to go with her for a similar object.   They set out
in September, 1658, landed at Rochelle, and went
thence to Paris.   Here they repaired to the seminary
of St. Sulpice; for the priests of this community
were joined with them in the work at Montreal, of
which they were afterwards to become the feudal
proprietors.

Now ensued a wonderful event, if we may trust
the evidence of sundry devout persons.   Olier, the
founder of St. Sulpice, had lately died, and the two
pilgrims would fain pay their homage to his heart,
which the priests of his community kept as a precious
relic, enclosed in a leaden box. The box was
brought, when the thought inspired Mademoiselle
Mance to try its miraculous efficacy and invoke the
intercession of the departed founder.   She did so,
touching her disabled arm gently with the leaden

casket. Instantly a grateful warmth pervaded the shrivelled limb, and from that hour its use was restored. It is true that the Jesuits ventured to doubt the Sulpitian miracle, and even to ridicule it; but the Sulpitians will show to this day the attestation of Mademoiselle Mance herself, written with the fingers once paralyzed and powerless.[1] Nevertheless, the cure was not so thorough as to permit her again to take charge of her patients.

Her next care was to visit Madame de Bullion, a devout lady of great wealth, who was usually designated at Montreal as "the unknown benefactress," because, though her charities were the mainstay of the feeble colony, and though the source from which they proceeded was well known, she affected, in the interest of humility, the greatest secrecy, and required those who profited by her gifts to pretend ignorance whence they came. Overflowing with zeal for the pious enterprise, she received her visitor with enthusiasm, lent an open ear to her recital, responded graciously to her appeal for aid, and paid over to her the sum, munificent at that day, of twenty-two thousand francs. Thus far successful, Mademoiselle Mance repaired to the town of La Flèche to visit Le Royer de la Dauversière.

It was this wretched fanatic who, through visions and revelations, had first conceived the plan of a

---

[1] For an account of this miracle, written in perfect good faith and supported by various attestations, see Faillon, *Vie de M'lle Mance*, chap. iv.

hospital in honor of Saint Joseph at Montreal.[1] H
had found in Mademoiselle Mance a zealous and
efficient pioneer; but the execution of his scheme
required a community of hospital nuns, and therefore
he had labored for the last eighteen years to form
one at La Flèche, meaning to despatch its members
in due time to Canada.   The time at length was
come.   Three of the nuns were chosen, — Sisters
Brésoles, Macé, and Maillet, — and sent under the
escort of certain pious gentlemen to Rochelle.   Their
exit from La Flèche was not without its difficulties.
Dauversière was in ill odor, not only from the multi-
plicity of his debts, but because, in his character of
agent of the association of Montreal, he had at
various times sent thither those whom his biographer
describes as "the most virtuous girls to be found at
La Flèche," intoxicating them with religious excitement, and shipping them for the New World against
the will of their parents.   It was noised through the
town that he had kidnapped and sold them; and now
the report spread abroad that he was about to crown
his iniquity by luring away three young nuns.   A
mob gathered at the convent gate, and the escort
were forced to draw their swords to open a way for
the terrified sisters.

Of the twenty-two thousand francs which she had
received, Mademoiselle Mance kept two thousand for
immediate needs, and confided the rest to the hands
of Dauversière, who, hard pressed by his creditors,

[1] See "The Jesuits in North America.".

used it to pay one of his debts; and then, to his horror, found himself unable to replace it. Racked by the gout and tormented by remorse, he betook himself to his bed in a state of body and mind truly pitiable. One of the miracles, so frequent in the early annals of Montreal, was vouchsafed in answer to his prayer, and he was enabled to journey to Rochelle and bid farewell to his nuns. It was but a brief respite; he returned home to become the prey of a host of maladies, and to die at last a lingering and painful death.

While Mademoiselle Mance was gaining recruits in La Flèche, Marguerite Bourgeoys was no less successful in her native town of Troyes; and she rejoined her companions at Rochelle, accompanied by Sisters Châtel, Crolo, and Raisin, her destined assistants in the school at Montreal. Meanwhile, the Sulpitians and others interested in the pious enterprise, had spared no effort to gather men to strengthen the colony, and young women to serve as their wives; and all were now mustered at Rochelle, waiting for embarkation. Their waiting was a long one. Laval, bishop at Quebec, was allied to the Jesuits, and looked on the colonists of Montreal with more than coldness. Sulpitian writers say that his agents used every effort to discourage them, and that certain persons at Rochelle told the master of the ship in which the emigrants were to sail that they were not to be trusted to pay their passage-money. Hereupon ensued a delay of more than two months before means could be found to quiet the scruples of the prudent commander. At length the anchor was weighed, and the dreary voyage begun.

The woe-begone company, crowded in the filthy and infected ship, were tossed for two months more on the relentless sea, buffeted by repeated storms and wasted by a contagious fever, which attacked nearly all of them and reduced Mademoiselle Mance to extremity. Eight or ten died and were dropped overboard, after a prayer from the two priests. At length land hove in sight; the piny odors of the forest regaled their languid senses as they sailed up the broad estuary of the St. Lawrence and anchored under the rock of Quebec.

High aloft, on the brink of the cliff, they saw the *fleur-de-lis* waving above the fort of St. Louis, and, beyond, the cross on the tower of the cathedral traced against the sky, the houses of the merchants on the strand below, and boats and canoes drawn up along the bank. The bishop and the Jesuits greeted them as co-workers in a holy cause, with an unction not wholly sincere. Though a unit against heresy, the pious founders of New France were far from unity among themselves. To the thinking of the Jesuits, Montreal was a government within a government, a wheel within a wheel. This rival Sulpitian settlement was in their eyes an element of disorganization adverse to the disciplined harmony of the Canadian Church, which they would fain have seen, with its focus at Quebec, radiating light unrefracted to the uttermost parts of the colony. That is to say, they wished to control it unchecked, through their ally the bishop.

The emigrants, then, were received with a studious courtesy, which veiled but thinly a stiff and persistent opposition. The bishop and the Jesuits were especially anxious to prevent the La Flèche nuns from establishing themselves at Montreal, where they would form a separate community under Sulpitian influence; and in place of the newly arrived sisters they wished to substitute nuns from the Hôtel Dieu of Quebec, who would be under their own control. That which most strikes the non-Catholic reader throughout this affair is the constant reticence and dissimulation practised, not only between Jesuits and Montrealists, but among the Montrealists themselves. Their self-devotion, great as it was, was fairly matched by their disingenuousness.[1]

All difficulties being overcome, the Montrealists embarked in boats and ascended the St. Lawrence, leaving Quebec infected with the contagion they had brought. The journey now made in a single night cost them fifteen days of hardship and danger. At length they reached their new home. The little settlement lay before them, still gasping betwixt life and death, in a puny, precarious infancy. Some

[1] See, for example, chapter iv. of Faillon's Life of Mademoiselle Mance. The evidence is unanswerable, the writer being the partisan and admirer of most of those whose *pieuse tromperie,* to use the expression of Dollier de Casson, he describes in apparent unconsciousness that anybody will see reason to cavil at it.

forty small, compact houses were ranged parallel to
the river, chiefly along the line of what is now St.
Paul's Street. On the left there was a fort, and on
a rising ground at the right a massive windmill of
stone, enclosed with a wall or palisade pierced for
musketry, and answering the purpose of a redoubt
or block-house.[1] Fields studded with charred and
blackened stumps, between which crops were growing, stretched away to the edges of the bordering
forest; and the green, shaggy back of the mountain
towered over all.

There were at this time a hundred and sixty men
at Montreal, about fifty of whom had families, or at
least wives. They greeted the new-comers with a
welcome which, this time, was as sincere as it was
warm, and bestirred themselves with alacrity to provide them with shelter for the winter. As for the
three nuns from La Flèche, a chamber was hastily
made for them over two low rooms which had served
as Mademoiselle Mance's hospital. This chamber
was twenty-five feet square, with four cells for the
nuns, and a closet for stores and clothing, which for
the present was empty, as they had landed in such
destitution that they were forced to sell all their
scanty equipment to gain the bare necessaries of
existence. Little could be hoped from the colonists,
who were scarcely less destitute than they. Such
was their poverty, — thanks to Dauversière's breach

---

[1] *Lettre du Vicomte d'Argenson, Gouverneur du Canada, 4 Août,*
1659, MS.

of trust, — that when their clothes were worn out, they were unable to replace them, and were forced to patch them with such material as came to hand. Maisonneuve the governor, and the pious Madame d'Ailleboust, being once on a visit to the hospital, amused themselves with trying to guess of what stuff the habits of the nuns had originally been made, and were unable to agree on the point in question.[1]

Their chamber, which they occupied for many years, being hastily built of ill-seasoned planks, let in the piercing cold of the Canadian winter through countless cracks and chinks; and the driving snow sifted through in such quantities that they were sometimes obliged, the morning after a storm, to remove it with shovels. Their food would freeze on the table before them, and their coarse brown bread had to be thawed on the hearth before they could cut it. These women had been nurtured in ease, if not in luxury. One of them, Judith de Brésoles, had in her youth, by advice of her confessor, run away from parents who were devoted to her, and immured herself in a convent, leaving them in agonies of doubt as to her fate. She now acted as superior of the little community. One of her nuns records of her that she had a fervent devotion for the Infant Jesus; and that, along with many more spiritual graces, he inspired her with so transcendent a skill in cookery, that "with a small piece of lean pork and a few herbs

---

[1] *Annales des Hospitalières de Villemarie, par la Sœur Morin,* — a contemporary record, from which Faillon gives long extracts.

she could make soup of a marvellous relish."[1]   Sister
Macé was charged with the care of the pigs and hens,
to whose wants she attended in person, though she
too had been delicately bred.   In course of time, the
sisterhood was increased by additions from without,
— though more than twenty girls who entered the
hospital as novices recoiled from the hardship, and
took husbands in the colony.   Among a few who
took the vows, Sister Jumeau should not pass
unnoticed.   Such was her humility that, though of
a good family and unable to divest herself of the
marks of good breeding, she pretended to be the
daughter of a poor peasant, and persisted in repeating
the pious falsehood till the merchant Le Ber told her
flatly that he did not believe her.

The sisters had great need of a man to do the
heavy work of the house and garden, but found no
means of hiring one, when an incident, in which they
saw a special providence, excellently supplied the
want.   There was a poor colonist named Jouaneaux,
to whom a piece of land had been given at some distance from the settlement.   Had he built a cabin
upon it, his scalp would soon have paid the forfeit;
but, being bold and hardy, he devised a plan by
which he might hope to sleep in safety without
abandoning the farm which was his only possession.
Among the stumps of his clearing there was one hol-

---

[1] " C'était par son recours à l'Enfant Jésus qu'elle trouvait tous
ces secrets et d'autres semblables," writes in our own day the
excellent annalist, Faillon.

low with age.   Under this he dug a sort of cave, the
entrance of which was a small hole carefully hidden by
brushwood.   The hollow stump was easily converted
into a chimney; and by creeping into his burrow at
night, or when he saw signs of danger, he escaped
for some time the notice of the Iroquois.   But though
he could dispense with a house, he needed a barn for
his hay and corn; and while he was building one, he
fell from the ridge of the roof and was seriously hurt.
He was carried to the Hôtel Dieu, where the nuns
showed him every attention, until, after a long confinement, he at last recovered.   Being of a grateful
nature and enthusiastically devout, he was so touched
by the kindness of his benefactors, and so moved by
the spectacle of their piety, that he conceived the
wish of devoting his life to their service.   To this
end a contract was drawn up, by which he pledged
himself to work for them as long as strength
remained; and they, on their part, agreed to maintain him in sickness or old age.

This stout-hearted retainer proved invaluable;
though had a guard of soldiers been added, it would
have been no more than the case demanded.   Montreal
was not palisaded, and at first the hospital was as
much exposed as the rest.   The Iroquois would
skulk at night among the houses, like wolves in a
camp of sleeping travellers on the prairies; though
the human foe was, of the two, incomparably the
bolder, fiercer, and more bloodthirsty.   More than
once one of these prowling savages was known to

have crouched all night in a rank growth of wild mustard in the garden of the nuns, vainly hoping that one of them would come out within reach of his tomahawk. During summer, a month rarely passed without a fight, sometimes within sight of their windows. A burst of yells from the ambushed marksmen, followed by a clatter of musketry, would announce the opening of the fray, and promise the nuns an addition to their list of patients. On these occasions they bore themselves according to their several natures. Sister Morin, who had joined their number three years after their arrival, relates that Sister Brésoles and she used to run to the belfry and ring the tocsin to call the inhabitants together. "From our high station," she writes, "we could sometimes see the combat, which terrified us extremely, so that we came down again as soon as we could, trembling with fright, and thinking that our last hour was come. When the tocsin sounded, my Sister Maillet would become faint with excess of fear; and my Sister Macé, as long as the alarm continued, would remain speechless, in a state pitiable to see. They would both get into a corner of the rood-loft, before the Holy Sacrament, so as to be prepared for death, or else go into their cells. As soon as I heard that the Iroquois were gone, I went to tell them, which comforted them and seemed to restore them to life. My Sister Brésoles was stronger and more courageous; her terror, which she could not help, did not prevent her from attending the sick and receiving the dead and wounded who were brought in."

The priests of St. Sulpice, who had assumed the entire spiritual charge of the settlement, and who were soon to assume its entire temporal charge also, had for some years no other lodging than a room at the hospital, adjoining those of the patients. They caused the building to be fortified with palisades, and the houses of some of the chief inhabitants were placed near it, for mutual defence. They also built two fortified houses, called Ste. Marie and St. Gabriel, at the two extremities of the settlement, and lodged in them a considerable number of armed men, whom they employed in clearing and cultivating the surrounding lands, the property of their community. All other outlying houses were also pierced with loopholes, and fortified as well as the slender means of their owners would permit. The laborers always carried their guns to the field, and often had need to use them. A few incidents will show the state of Montreal and the character of its tenants.

In the autumn of 1657 there was a truce with the Iroquois, under cover of which three or four of them came to the settlement. Nicolas Godé and Jean Saint-Père were on the roof of their house, laying thatch, when one of the visitors aimed his arquebuse at Saint-Père, and brought him to the ground like a wild turkey from a tree. Now ensued a prodigy; for the assassins, having cut off his head and carried it home to their village, were amazed to hear it speak

to them in good Iroquois, scold them for their per-
fidy, and threaten them with the vengeance of
Heaven; and they continued to hear its voice of
admonition even after scalping it and throwing away
the skull.[1] This story, circulated at Montreal on the
alleged authority of the Indians themselves, found believers among the most intelligent men of the colony.

Another miracle, which occurred several years
later, deserves to be recorded. Le Maître, one of
the two priests who had sailed from France with
Mademoiselle Mance and her nuns, being one day at
the fortified house of St. Gabriel, went out with the
laborers in order to watch while they were at their
work. In view of a possible enemy, he had girded
himself with an earthly sword; but seeing no sign of
danger, he presently took out his breviary, and, while
reciting his office with eyes bent on the page, walked
into an ambuscade of Iroquois, who rose before him
with a yell.

He shouted to the laborers, and, drawing his
sword, faced the whole savage crew, in order, probably, to give the men time to snatch their guns.
Afraid to approach, the Iroquois fired and killed
him; then rushed upon the working party, who
escaped into the house, after losing several of their
number. The victors cut off the head of the heroic
priest, and tied it in a white handkerchief which
they took from a pocket of his cassock. It is said
that on reaching their villages they were astonished

[1] Dollier de Casson, *Histoire du Montréal,* 1657–1658.

to find the handkerchief without the slightest stain
of blood, but stamped indelibly with the features of
its late owner, so plainly marked that none who had
known him could fail to recognize them.[1] This not
very original miracle, though it found eager credence
at Montreal, was received coolly, like other Montreal
miracles, at Quebec; and Sulpitian writers complain
that the bishop, in a long letter which he wrote to
the Pope, made no mention of it whatever.

Le Maître, on the voyage to Canada, had been
accompanied by another priest, Guillaume de Vignal,
who met a fate more deplorable than that of his companion, though unattended by any recorded miracle.
Le Maître had been killed in August. In the
October following, Vignal went with thirteen men,
in a flat-boat and several canoes, to Isle à la Pierre,
nearly opposite Montreal, to get stone for the seminary which the priests had recently begun to build.
With him was a pious and valiant gentleman named
Claude de Brigeac, who, though but thirty years of
age, had come as a soldier to Montreal, in the hope
of dying in defence of the true Church, and thus
reaping the reward of a martyr. Vignal and three
or four men had scarcely landed when they were set
upon by a large band of Iroquois who lay among the
bushes waiting to receive them. The rest of the

---

[1] This story is told by Sister Morin, Marguerite Bourgeoys, and
Dollier de Casson, on the authority of one Lavigne, then a prisoner
among the Iroquois, who declared that he had seen the handkerchief in the hands of the returning warriors.

party, who were still in their boats, with a cowardice rare at Montreal, thought only of saving themselves. Claude de Brigeac alone leaped ashore and ran to aid his comrades. Vignal was soon mortally wounded. Brigeac shot the chief dead with his arquebuse, and then, pistol in hand, held the whole troop for an instant at bay; but his arm was shattered by a gunshot, and he was seized, along with Vignal, René Cuillérier, and Jacques Dufresne. Crossing to the main shore, immediately opposite Montreal, the Iroquois made, after their custom, a small fort of logs and branches, in which they ensconced themselves, and then began to dress the wounds of their prisoners. Seeing that Vignal was unable to make the journey to their villages, they killed him, divided his flesh, and roasted it for food.

Brigeac and his fellows in misfortune spent a woful night in this den of wolves; and in the morning their captors, having breakfasted on the remains of Vignal, took up their homeward march, dragging the Frenchmen with them. On reaching Oneida, Brigeac was tortured to death with the customary atrocities. Cuillérier, who was present, declared that they could wring from him no cry of pain, but that throughout he ceased not to pray for their conversion. The witness himself expected the same fate, but an old squaw happily adopted him, and thus saved his life. He eventually escaped to Albany, and returned to Canada by the circuitous but comparatively safe route of New York and Boston.

In the following winter, Montreal suffered an irreparable loss in the death of the brave Major Closse, a man whose intrepid coolness was never known to fail in the direst emergency. Going to the aid of a party of laborers attacked by the Iroquois, he was met by a crowd of savages, eager to kill or capture him. His servant ran off. He snapped a pistol at the foremost assailant, but it missed fire. His remaining pistol served him no better, and he was instantly shot down. "He died," writes Dollier de Casson, "like a brave soldier of Christ and the King." Some of his friends once remonstrating with him on the temerity with which he exposed his life, he replied: "Messieurs, I came here only to die in the service of God; and if I thought I could not die here, I would leave this country to fight the Turks, that I might not be deprived of such a glory."[1]

The fortified house of Ste. Marie, belonging to the priests of St. Sulpice, was the scene of several hot and bloody fights. Here, too, occurred the following nocturnal adventure. A man named Lavigne, who had lately returned from captivity among the Iroquois, chancing to rise at night and look out of the window, saw by the bright moonlight a number of naked warriors stealthily gliding round a corner and crouching near the door, in order to kill the first Frenchman who should go out in the morning. He silently woke his comrades; and, having the rest of the night for consultation, they arranged their plan

[1] Dollier de Casson, *Histoire du Montréal*, 1661, 1662.

so well that some of them, sallying from the rear of
the house, came cautiously round upon the Iroquois,
placed them between two fires, and captured them all.

The summer of 1661 was marked by a series of
calamities scarcely paralleled even in the annals of
this disastrous epoch. Early in February, thirteen
colonists were surprised and captured; next came a
fight between a large band of laborers and two hundred and sixty Iroquois; in the following month, ten
more Frenchmen were killed or taken; and thenceforth, till winter closed, the settlement had scarcely
a breathing space. "These hobgoblins," writes the
author of the *Relation* of this year, "sometimes
appeared at the edge of the woods, assailing us with
abuse; sometimes they glided stealthily into the
midst of the fields, to surprise the men at work;
sometimes they approached the houses, harassing us
without ceasing, and, like importunate harpies or
birds of prey, swooping down on us whenever they
could take us unawares."[1]

Speaking of the disasters of this year, the soldier-
priest, Dollier de Casson, writes: "God, who afflicts
the body only for the good of the soul, made a marvellous use of these calamities and terrors to hold the
people firm in their duty towards Heaven. Vice
was then almost unknown here, and in the midst of
war religion flourished on all sides in a manner very
different from what we now see in time of peace."[2]

[1] Le Jeune, *Relation*, 1661, p. 3 (ed. 1858).
[2] *Histoire du Montréal*, 1660, 1661.

The war was, in fact, a war of religion. The small redoubts of logs, scattered about the skirts of the settlement to serve as points of defence in case of attack, bore the names of saints, to whose care they were commended. There was one placed under a higher protection, and called the " Redoubt of the Infant Jesus." Chomedey de Maisonneuve, the pious and valiant governor of Montreal, to whom its successful defence is largely due, resolved, in view of the increasing fury and persistency of the Iroquois attacks, to form among the inhabitants a military fraternity, to be called " Soldiers of the Holy Family of Jesus, Mary, and Joseph; " and to this end he issued a proclamation, of which the following is the characteristic beginning: —

" We, Paul de Chomedey, governor of the island of Montreal and lands thereon dependent, on information given us from divers quarters that the Iroquois have formed the design of seizing upon this settlement by surprise or force, have thought it our duty, seeing that this island is the property of the Holy Virgin,[1] to invite and exhort those zealous for her service to unite together by squads, each of seven persons; and after choosing a corporal by a plurality of voices, to report themselves to us for enrolment in our garrison, and, in this capacity, to obey our orders, to the end that the country may be saved."

[1] This is no figure of speech. The Associates of Montreal, after receiving a grant of the island from Jean de Lauson, placed it under the protection of the Virgin, and formally declared her to be the proprietor of it from that day forth forever.

Twenty squads, numbering in all one hundred and forty men, whose names, appended to the proclamation, may still be seen on the ancient records of Montreal, answered the appeal and enrolled themselves in the holy cause.

The whole settlement was in a state of religious exaltation. As the Iroquois were regarded as actual myrmidons of Satan in his malign warfare against Mary and her divine Son, those who died in fighting them were held to merit the reward of martyrs, assured of a seat in paradise.

And now it remains to record one of the most heroic feats of arms ever achieved on this continent. That it may be rated as it merits, it will be well to glance for a moment at the condition of Canada, under the portentous cloud of war which constantly overshadowed it.[1]

[1] In all that relates to Montreal, I cannot be sufficiently grateful to the Abbé Faillon, the indefatigable, patient, conscientious chronicler of its early history; an ardent and prejudiced Sulpitian, a priest who three centuries ago would have passed for credulous, and, withal, a kind-hearted and estimable man. His numerous books on his favorite theme, with the vast and heterogeneous mass of facts which they embody, are invaluable, provided their partisan character be well kept in mind. His recent death leaves his principal work unfinished. His *Histoire de la Colonie Française en Canada* — it might more fitly be called *Histoire du Montréal* — is unhappily little more than half complete.

CHAPTER VI.

1660, 1661.

THE HEROES OF THE LONG SAUT.

SUFFERING AND TERROR. — FRANÇOIS HERTEL. — THE CAPTIVE WOLF. — THE THREATENED INVASION. — DAULAC DES ORMEAUX. — THE ADVENTURERS AT THE LONG SAUT. — THE ATTACK. — A DESPERATE DEFENCE. — A FINAL ASSAULT. — THE FORT TAKEN.

CANADA had writhed for twenty years, with little respite, under the scourge of Iroquois war. During a great part of this dark period the entire French population was less than three thousand. What, then, saved them from destruction? In the first place, the settlements were grouped around three fortified posts, — Quebec, Three Rivers, and Montreal, — which in time of danger gave asylum to the fugitive inhabitants. Again, their assailants were continually distracted by other wars, and never, except at a few spasmodic intervals, were fully in earnest to destroy the French colony. Canada was indispensable to them. The four upper nations of the league soon became dependent on her for supplies; and all the nations alike appear, at a very early period, to have conceived the policy on which they afterwards distinctly acted, of balancing the rival settlements of the Hudson and the St. Lawrence, the one against the other. They would torture, but not kill. It was but rarely that, in fits of fury, they struck their hatchets at the brain; and thus the bleeding and gasping colony lingered on in torment.

The seneschal of New France, son of the governor Lauson, was surprised and killed on the island of Orleans, along with seven companions. About the same time, the same fate befell the son of Godefroy, one of the chief inhabitants of Quebec. Outside the fortifications there was no safety for a moment. A universal terror seized the people. A comet appeared above Quebec, and they saw in it a herald of destruction. Their excited imaginations turned natural phenomena into portents and prodigies. A blazing canoe sailed across the sky; confused cries and lamentations were heard in the air; and a voice of thunder sounded from mid-heaven.[1] The Jesuits despaired for their scattered and persecuted flocks. "Everywhere," writes their superior, "we see infants to be saved for heaven, sick and dying to be baptized, adults to be instructed; but everywhere we see the Iroquois. They haunt us like persecuting goblins. They kill our new-made Christians in our arms. If they meet us on the river, they kill us. If they find us in the huts of our Indians, they burn us and them together."[2] And he appeals urgently for troops

[1] Marie de l'Incarnation, *Lettre, Septembre*, 1661.
[2] *Relation,* 1660 (anonymous), 3.

to destroy them, as a holy work inspired by God, and needful for his service.

Canada was still a mission, and the influence of the Church was paramount and pervading. At Quebec, as at Montreal, the war with the Iroquois was regarded as a war with the hosts of Satan. Of the settlers' cabins scattered along the shores above and below Quebec, many were provided with small iron cannon, made probably by blacksmiths in the colony; but they had also other protectors. In each was an image of the Virgin or some patron saint; and every morning the pious settler knelt before the shrine to beg the protection of a celestial hand in his perilous labors of the forest or the farm.

When, in the summer of 1658, the young Vicomte d'Argenson came to assume the thankless task of governing the colony, the Iroquois war was at its height. On the day after his arrival, he was washing his hands before seating himself at dinner in the hall of the Château St. Louis, when cries of alarm were heard, and he was told that the Iroquois were close at hand. In fact, they were so near that their war-whoops and the screams of their victims could plainly be heard. Argenson left his guests, and, with such a following as he could muster at the moment, hastened to the rescue; but the assailants were too nimble for him. The forests, which grew at that time around Quebec, favored them both in attack and in retreat. After a year or two of experience, he wrote urgently to the court for troops. He adds that, what with the demands of the harvest and the unmilitary character of many of the settlers, the colony could not furnish more than a hundred men for offensive operations. A vigorous, aggressive war, he insists, is absolutely necessary, and this not only to save the colony, but to save the only true faith; "for," to borrow his own words, "it is this colony alone which has the honor to be in the communion of the Holy Church. Everywhere else reigns the doctrine of England or Holland, to which I can give no other name, because there are as many creeds as there are subjects who embrace them. They do not care in the least whether the Iroquois and the other savages of this country have or have not a knowledge of the true God, or else they are so malicious as to inject the venom of their errors into souls incapable of distinguishing the truth of the gospel from the falsehoods of heresy; and hence it is plain that religion has its sole support in the French colony, and that, if this colony is in danger, religion is equally in danger." [1]

Among the most interesting memorials of the time are two letters written by François Hertel, a youth of eighteen, captured at Three Rivers, and carried to the Mohawk towns in the summer of 1661. He belonged to one of the best families of Canada, and was the favorite child of his mother, to whom the second of the two letters is addressed. The first is to the Jesuit Le Moyne, who had gone to Onondaga,

---

[1] *Papiers d'Argenson; Mémoire sur le sujet de la guerre des Iroquois,* 1659 (1660 ?). *MS.*

in July of that year, to effect the release of French prisoners in accordance with the terms of a truce.[1] Both letters were written on birch-bark: —

MY REVEREND FATHER, — The very day when you left Three Rivers I was captured, at about three in the afternoon, by four Iroquois of the Mohawk tribe. I would not have been taken alive, if, to my sorrow, I had not feared that I was not in a fit state to die. If you came here, my Father, I could have the happiness of confessing to you ; and I do not think they would do you any harm ; and I think that I could return home with you. I pray you to pity my poor mother, who is in great trouble. You know, my Father, how fond she is of me. I have heard from a Frenchman, who was taken at Three Rivers on the 1st of August, that she is well, and comforts herself with the hope that I shall see you. There are three of us Frenchmen alive here. I commend myself to your good prayers, and particularly to the Holy Sacrifice of the Mass. I pray you, my Father, to say a mass for me. I pray you give my dutiful love to my poor mother, and console her, if it pleases you.

My Father, I beg your blessing on the hand that writes to you, which has one of the fingers burned in the bowl of an Indian pipe, to satisfy the Majesty of God which I have offended. The thumb of the other hand is cut off ; but do not tell my mother of it.

My Father, I pray you to honor me with a word from your hand in reply, and tell me if you shall come here before winter.

Your most humble and most obedient servant,
FRANÇOIS HERTEL.

[1] *Journal des Jésuites*, 300.

The following is the letter to his mother, sent probably, with the other, to the charge of Le Moyne: —

MY MOST DEAR AND HONORED MOTHER, — I know very well that my capture must have distressed you very much. I ask you to forgive my disobedience. It is my sins that have placed me where I am. I owe my life to your prayers, and those of M. de Saint-Quentin, and of my sisters. I hope to see you again before winter. I pray you to tell the good brethren of Notre Dame to pray to God and the Holy Virgin for me, my dear mother, and for you and all my sisters.

Your poor

FANCHON.

This, no doubt, was the name by which she had called him familiarly when a child. And who was this "Fanchon," this devout and tender son of a fond mother? New England can answer to her cost. When, twenty-nine years later, a band of French and Indians issued from the forest and fell upon the fort and settlement of Salmon Falls, it was François Hertel who led the attack; and when the retiring victors were hard pressed by an overwhelming force, it was he who, sword in hand, held the pursuers in check at the bridge of Wooster River, and covered the retreat of his men. He was ennobled for his services, and died at the age of eighty, the founder of one of the most distinguished families of Canada.[1]

---

[1] His letters of nobility, dated 1716, will be found in Daniel's *Histoire des Grandes Familles Françaises du Canada,* 404.

To the New England of old he was the abhorred chief of Popish malignants and murdering savages. The New England of to-day will be more just to the brave defender of his country and his faith.

In May, 1660, a party of French Algonquins captured a Wolf, or Mohegan, Indian, naturalized among the Iroquois, brought him to Quebec, and burned him there with their usual atrocity of torture. A modern Catholic writer says that the Jesuits could not save him; but this is not so. Their influence over the consciences of the colonists was at that time unbounded, and their direct political power was very great. A protest on their part, and that of the newly arrived bishop, who was in their interest, could not have failed of effect. The truth was, they did not care to prevent the torture of prisoners of war, — not solely out of that spirit of compliance with the savage humor of Indian allies which stains so often the pages of French American history, but also, and perhaps chiefly, from motives purely religious. Torture, in their eyes, seems to have been a blessing in disguise. They thought it good for the soul, and in case of obduracy the surest way of salvation. "We have very rarely indeed," writes one of them, "seen the burning of an Iroquois without feeling sure that he was on the path to paradise; and we never knew one of them to be surely on the path to paradise without seeing him pass through this fiery punishment." [1] So they let the Wolf burn; but

[1] *Relation*, 1660, 31.

first, having instructed him after their fashion, they baptized him, and his savage soul flew to heaven out of the fire. "Is it not," pursues the same writer, "a marvel to see a wolf changed at one stroke into a lamb, and enter into the fold of Christ, which he came to ravage?"

Before he died, he requited their spiritual cares with a startling secret. He told them that eight hundred Iroquois warriors were encamped below Montreal; that four hundred more, who had wintered on the Ottawa, were on the point of joining them; and that the united force would swoop upon Quebec, kill the governor, lay waste the town, and then attack Three Rivers and Montreal.[1] This time, at least, the Iroquois were in deadly earnest. Quebec was wild with terror. The Ursulines and the nuns of the Hôtel Dieu took refuge in the strong and extensive building which the Jesuits had just finished, opposite the Parish Church. Its walls and palisades made it easy of defence; and in its yards and court were lodged the terrified Hurons, as well as the fugitive inhabitants of the neighboring settlements. Others found asylum in the fort, and others in the convent of the Ursulines, which, in place of nuns, was occupied by twenty-four soldiers, who fortified it with redoubts, and barricaded the doors and windows. Similar measures of defence were taken at the Hôtel Dieu, and the streets of the Lower Town were strongly barricaded. Everybody was in

[1] Marie de l'Incarnation, *Lettre*, 25 *Juin*, 1660.

arms, and the *Qui vive* of the sentries and patrols resounded all night.[1]

Several days passed, and no Iroquois appeared. The refugees took heart, and began to return to their deserted farms and dwellings. Among the rest was a family consisting of an old woman, her daughter, her son-in-law, and four small children, living near St. Anne, some twenty miles below Quebec. On reaching home, the old woman and the man went to their work in the fields, while the mother and children remained in the house. Here they were pounced upon and captured by eight renegade Hurons, Iroquois by adoption, who placed them in their large canoe, and paddled up the river with their prize. It was Saturday, a day dedicated to the Virgin; and the captive mother prayed to her for aid, "feeling," writes a Jesuit, "a full conviction that, in passing before Quebec on a Saturday, she would be delivered by the power of this Queen of Heaven." In fact, as the marauders and their captives glided in the darkness of night by Point Levi, under the shadow of the shore, they were greeted with a volley of musketry from the bushes, and a band of French and Algonquins dashed into the water to seize them. Five of the eight were taken, and the rest shot or drowned. The governor had heard of the descent at St. Anne, and despatched a

---

[1] On this alarm at Quebec compare Marie de l'Incarnation, 25 *Juin*, 1660; *Relation*, 1660, 5; Juchereau, *Histoire de l'Hôtel-Dieu de Québec*, 125, and *Journal des Jésuites*, 282.

party to lie in ambush for the authors of it. The Jesuits, it is needless to say, saw a miracle in the result. The Virgin had answered the prayer of her votary, — "though it is true," observes the father who records the marvel, "that, in the volley, she received a mortal wound." The same shot struck the infant in her arms. The prisoners were taken to Quebec, where four of them were tortured with even more ferocity than had been shown in the case of the unfortunate Wolf.[1] Being questioned, they confirmed his story, and expressed great surprise that the Iroquois had not come, adding that they must have stopped to attack Montreal or Three Rivers. Again all was terror, and again days passed and no enemy appeared. Had the dying converts, so charitably despatched to heaven through fire, sought an unhallowed consolation in scaring the abettors of their torture with a lie? Not at all. Bating a slight exaggeration, they had told the truth. Where, then, were the Iroquois? As one small point of

---

[1] The torturers were Christian Algonquins, converts of the Jesuits. Chaumonot, who was present to give spiritual aid to the sufferers, describes the scene with horrible minuteness. "I could not," he says, "deliver them from their torments." Perhaps not : but it is certain that the Jesuits as a body, with or without the bishop, could have prevented the atrocity, had they seen fit. They sometimes taught their converts to pray for their enemies. It would have been well had they taught them not to torture them. I can recall but one instance in which they did so. The prayers for enemies were always for a spiritual, not a temporal good. The fathers held the body in slight account, and cared little what happened to it.

steel disarms the lightning of its terrors, so did the heroism of a few intrepid youths divert this storm of war, and save Canada from a possible ruin.

In the preceding April, before the designs of the Iroquois were known, a young officer named Daulac, commandant of the garrison of Montreal, asked leave of Maisonneuve, the governor, to lead a party of volunteers against the enemy. His plan was bold to desperation. It was known that Iroquois warriors in great numbers had wintered among the forests of the Ottawa. Daulac proposed to waylay them on their descent of the river, and fight them without regard to disparity of force. The settlers of Montreal had hitherto acted solely on the defensive, for their numbers had been too small for aggressive war. Of late their strength had been somewhat increased, and Maisonneuve, judging that a display of enterprise and boldness might act as a check on the audacity of the enemy, at length gave his consent.

Adam Daulac, or Dollard, Sieur des Ormeaux, was a young man of good family, who had come to the colony three years before, at the age of twenty-two. He had held some military command in France, though in what rank does not appear. It was said that he had been involved in some affair which made him anxious to wipe out the memory of the past by a noteworthy exploit; and he had been busy for some time among the young men of Montreal, inviting them to join him in the enterprise he meditated. Sixteen of them caught his spirit, struck hands with him, and pledged

their word. They bound themselves by oath to
accept no quarter; and, having gained Maisonneuve's
consent, they made their wills, confessed, and
received the sacraments. As they knelt for the last
time before the altar in the chapel of the Hôtel Dieu,
that sturdy little population of pious Indian-fighters
gazed on them with enthusiasm, not unmixed with
an envy which had in it nothing ignoble. Some of
the chief men of Montreal, with the brave Charles
Le Moyne at their head, begged them to wait till the
spring sowing was over, that they might join them;
but Daulac refused. He was jealous of the glory
and the danger, and he wished to command, which
he could not have done had Le Moyne been present.

The spirit of the enterprise was purely mediæval.
The enthusiasm of honor, the enthusiasm of adventure, and the enthusiasm of faith were its motive
forces. Daulac was a knight of the early crusades
among the forests and savages of the New World.
Yet the incidents of this exotic heroism are definite
and clear as a tale of yesterday. The names, ages,
and occupations of the seventeen young men may
still be read on the ancient register of the parish of
Montreal; and the notarial acts of that year, preserved in the records of the city, contain minute
accounts of such property as each of them possessed.
The three eldest were of twenty-eight, thirty, and
thirty-one years respectively. The age of the rest
varied from twenty-one to twenty-seven. They were
of various callings, — soldiers, armorers, locksmiths,

lime-burners, or settlers without trades. The greater number had come to the colony as part of the reinforcement brought by Maisonneuve in 1653.

After a solemn farewell, they embarked in several canoes well supplied with arms and ammunition. They were very indifferent canoe-men; and it is said that they lost a week in vain attempts to pass the swift current of St. Anne, at the head of the island of Montreal. At length they were more successful, and entering the mouth of the Ottawa, crossed the Lake of Two Mountains, and slowly advanced against the current.

Meanwhile, forty warriors of that remnant of the Hurons who, in spite of Iroquois persecutions, still lingered at Quebec, had set out on a war-party, led by the brave and wily Etienne Annahotaha, their most noted chief. They stopped by the way at Three Rivers, where they found a band of Christian Algonquins under a chief named Mituvemeg. Annahotaha challenged him to a trial of courage, and it was agreed that they should meet at Montreal, where they were likely to find a speedy opportunity of putting their mettle to the test. Thither, accordingly, they repaired, the Algonquin with three followers, and the Huron with thirty-nine.

It was not long before they learned the departure of Daulac and his companions. "For," observes the honest Dollier de Casson, "the principal fault of our Frenchmen is to talk too much." The wish seized them to share the adventure, and to that end the

Huron chief asked the governor for a letter to
Daulac, to serve as credentials. Maisonneuve hesitated. His faith in Huron valor was not great, and
he feared the proposed alliance. Nevertheless, he at
length yielded so far as to give Annahotaha a letter,
in which Daulac was told to accept or reject the
proffered reinforcement as he should see fit. The
Hurons and Algonquins now embarked, and paddled
in pursuit of the seventeen Frenchmen.

They meanwhile had passed with difficulty the
swift current at Carillon, and about the first of May
reached the foot of the more formidable rapid called
the Long Saut, where a tumult of waters, foaming
among ledges and bowlders, barred the onward way.
It was needless to go farther. The Iroquois were
sure to pass the Saut, and could be fought here as
well as elsewhere. Just below the rapid, where the
forests sloped gently to the shore, among the bushes
and stumps of the rough clearing made in constructing it, stood a palisade fort, the work of an
Algonquin war-party in the past autumn. It was a
mere enclosure of trunks of small trees planted in a
circle, and was already ruinous. Such as it was, the
Frenchmen took possession of it. Their first care,
one would think, should have been to repair and
strengthen it; but this they seem not to have done,
— possibly, in the exaltation of their minds, they
scorned such precaution. They made their fires,
and slung their kettles on the neighboring shore;
and here they were soon joined by the Hurons and

Algonquins. Daulac, it seems, made no objection to their company, and they all bivouacked together. Morning and noon and night they prayed in three different tongues; and when at sunset the long reach of forests on the farther shore basked peacefully in the level rays, the rapids joined their hoarse music to the notes of their evening hymn.

In a day or two their scouts came in with tidings that two Iroquois canoes were coming down the Saut. Daulac had time to set his men in ambush among the bushes at a point where he thought the strangers likely to land. He judged aright. The canoes, bearing five Iroquois, approached, and were met by a volley fired with such precipitation that one or more of them escaped the shot, fled into the forest, and told their mischance to their main body, two hundred in number, on the river above. A fleet of canoes suddenly appeared, bounding down the rapids, filled with warriors eager for revenge. The allies had barely time to escape to their fort, leaving their kettles still slung over the fires. The Iroquois made a hasty and desultory attack, and were quickly repulsed. They next opened a parley, hoping, no doubt, to gain some advantage by surprise. Failing in this, they set themselves, after their custom on such occasions, to building a rude fort of their own in the neighboring forest.

This gave the French a breathing-time, and they used it for strengthening their defences. Being provided with tools, they planted a row of stakes within their palisade, to form a double fence, and filled the intervening space with earth and stones to the height of a man, leaving some twenty loop-holes, at each of which three marksmen were stationed. Their work was still unfinished when the Iroquois were upon them again. They had broken to pieces the birch canoes of the French and their allies, and, kindling the bark, rushed up to pile it blazing against the palisade; but so brisk and steady a fire met them that they recoiled, and at last gave way. They came on again, and again were driven back, leaving many of their number on the ground, — among them the principal chief of the Senecas. Some of the French dashed out, and, covered by the fire of their comrades, hacked off his head, and stuck it on the palisade, while the Iroquois howled in a frenzy of helpless rage. They tried another attack, and were beaten off a third time.

This dashed their spirits, and they sent a canoe to call to their aid five hundred of their warriors who were mustered near the mouth of the Richelieu. These were the allies whom, but for this untoward check, they were on their way to join for a combined attack on Quebec, Three Rivers, and Montreal. It was maddening to see their grand project thwarted by a few French and Indians ensconced in a paltry redoubt, scarcely better than a cattle-pen; but they were forced to digest the affront as best they might.

Meanwhile, crouched behind trees and logs, they beset the fort, harassing its defenders day and night with a spattering fire and a constant menace of attack. Thus five days passed. Hunger, thirst, and want of sleep wrought fatally on the strength of the French and their allies, who, pent up together in their narrow prison, fought and prayed by turns. Deprived as they were of water, they could not swallow the crushed Indian corn, or "hominy," which was their only food. Some of them, under cover of a brisk fire, ran down to the river and filled such small vessels as they had; but this pittance only tantalized their thirst. They dug a hole in the fort, and were rewarded at last by a little muddy water oozing through the clay.

Among the assailants were a number of Hurons, adopted by the Iroquois and fighting on their side. These renegades now shouted to their countrymen in the fort, telling them that a fresh army was close at hand; that they would soon be attacked by seven or eight hundred warriors; and that their only hope was in joining the Iroquois, who would receive them as friends. Annahotaha's followers, half dead with thirst and famine, listened to their seducers, took the bait, and, one, two, or three at a time, climbed the palisade and ran over to the enemy, amid the hootings and execrations of those whom they deserted. Their chief stood firm; and when he saw his nephew, La Mouche, join the other fugitives, he fired his pistol at him in a rage. The four Algonquins, who had no mercy to hope for, stood fast, with the courage of despair.

On the fifth day an uproar of unearthly yells from seven hundred savage throats, mingled with a clattering salute of musketry, told the Frenchmen that the expected reinforcement had come; and soon, in the forest and on the clearing, a crowd of warriors mustered for the attack. Knowing from the Huron deserters the weakness of their enemy, they had no doubt of an easy victory. They advanced cautiously, as was usual with the Iroquois before their blood was up, screeching, leaping from side to side, and firing as they came on; but the French were at their posts, and every loophole darted its tongue of fire. Besides muskets, they had heavy musketoons of large calibre, which, scattering scraps of lead and iron among the throng of savages, often maimed several of them at one discharge. The Iroquois, astonished at the persistent vigor of the defence, fell back discomfited. The fire of the French, who were themselves completely under cover, had told upon them with deadly effect. Three days more wore away in a series of futile attacks, made with little concert or vigor; and during all this time Daulac and his men, reeling with exhaustion, fought and prayed as before, sure of a martyr's reward.

The uncertain, vacillating temper common to all Indians now began to declare itself. Some of the Iroquois were for going home. Others revolted at the thought, and declared that it would be an eternal disgrace to lose so many men at the hands of so paltry an enemy, and yet fail to take revenge. It

was resolved to make a general assault, and volunteers were called for to lead the attack. After the
custom on such occasions, bundles of small sticks
were thrown upon the ground, and those picked
them up who dared, thus accepting the gage of
battle, and enrolling themselves in the forlorn hope.
No precaution was neglected. Large and heavy
shields four or five feet high were made by lashing
together three split logs with the aid of cross-bars.
Covering themselves with these mantelets, the chosen
band advanced, followed by the motley throng of
warriors. In spite of a brisk fire, they reached the
palisade, and, crouching below the range of shot,
hewed furiously with their hatchets to cut their way
through. The rest followed close, and swarmed like
angry hornets around the little fort, hacking and
tearing to get in.

Daulac had crammed a large musketoon with
powder, and plugged up the muzzle. Lighting the
fuse inserted in it, he tried to throw it over the
barrier, to burst like a grenade among the crowd of
savages without; but it struck the ragged top of one
of the palisades, fell back among the Frenchmen and
exploded, killing and wounding several of them, and
nearly blinding others. In the confusion that followed, the Iroquois got possession of the loopholes,
and, thrusting in their guns, fired on those within.
In a moment more they had torn a breach in the
palisade; but, nerved with the energy of desperation, Daulac and his followers sprang to defend it.

Another breach was made, and then another. Daulac was struck dead, but the survivors kept up the fight. With a sword or a hatchet in one hand and a knife in the other, they threw themselves against the throng of enemies, striking and stabbing with the fury of madmen; till the Iroquois, despairing of taking them alive, fired volley after volley and shot them down. All was over, and a burst of triumphant yells proclaimed the dear-bought victory.

Searching the pile of corpses, the victors found four Frenchmen still breathing. Three had scarcely a spark of life, and, as no time was to be lost, they burned them on the spot. The fourth, less fortunate, seemed likely to survive, and they reserved him for future torments. As for the Huron deserters, their cowardice profited them little. The Iroquois, regardless of their promises, fell upon them, burned some at once, and carried the rest to their villages for a similar fate. Five of the number had the good fortune to escape; and it was from them, aided by admissions made long afterwards by the Iroquois themselves, that the French of Canada derived all their knowledge of this glorious disaster.[1]

[1] When the fugitive Hurons reached Montreal, they were unwilling to confess their desertion of the French, and declared that they and some others of their people, to the number of fourteen, had stood by them to the last. This was the story told by one of them to the Jesuit Chaumonot, and by him communicated in a letter to his friends at Quebec. The substance of this letter is given by Marie de l'Incarnation, in her letter to her son of June 25, 1660. The Jesuit *Relation* of this year gives another long account of the affair, also derived from the Huron deserters, who this time

To the colony it proved a salvation. The Iroquois
had had fighting enough. If seventeen Frenchmen,
four Algonquins, and one Huron, behind a picket
fence, could hold seven hundred warriors at bay so
long, what might they expect from many such, fight-

only pretended that ten of their number remained with the French.
They afterwards admitted that all had deserted but Annahotaha,
as appears from the account drawn up by Dollier de Casson, in his
Histoire du Montréal. Another contemporary, Belmont, who heard
the story from an Iroquois, makes the same statement. All these
writers, though two of them were not friendly to Montreal, agree
that Daulac and his followers saved Canada from a disastrous
invasion. The governor, Argenson, in a letter written on the fourth
of July following, and in his *Mémoire sur le sujet de la guerre des
Iroquois*, expresses the same conviction. Before me is an extract,
copied from the *Petit Registre de la Cure de Montréal*, giving the
names and ages of Daulac's men.

Radisson, the famous *voyageur*, says that, on his way down the
Ottawa from Lake Superior, he passed the Long Saut eight days
after the destruction of Daulac and his party; and he gives an
account of the fight that answers on the whole to those of the
other writers. He adds, however, that the Hurons remained outside the fort, which was too small to hold them, and that only the
seventeen Frenchmen and four Algonquins — or twenty-one in all
— were under cover. He also says that the reinforcement which
joined the two hundred Iroquois who began the attack consisted of
"five hundred and fifty Iroquoits of the lower nation [Mohawks]
and fifty Orijonot" (Oneidas?), — making with the original assailants eight hundred in all. (*Publications of the Prince Society*, 1885,
233.) Radisson, whose narratives were not written till some years
after the events that they record, forgets the date of the fight at the
Long Saut, which would appear from him to have happened three
years after it really took place.

Abbé Faillon took extreme pains to collect the evidence touching Daulac's heroism, and, though Radisson's writings were
unknown to him, his narrative should be consulted by those interested in the subject. See his anonymous *Histoire de la Colonie
Française au Canada*, ii. chap. xv.

ing behind walls of stone? For that year they thought no more of capturing Quebec and Montreal, but went home dejected and amazed, to howl over their losses, and nurse their dashed courage for a day of vengeance.

CHAPTER VII.

1657–1668.

THE DISPUTED BISHOPRIC.

Domestic Strife. — Jesuit and Sulpitian. — Abbé Queylus. — François de Laval. — The Zealots of Caen. — Gallican and Ultramontane. — The Rival Claimants. — Storm at Quebec. — Laval Triumphant.

Canada, gasping under the Iroquois tomahawk, might, one would suppose, have thought her cup of tribulation full, and, sated with inevitable woe, have sought consolation from the wrath without in a holy calm within. Not so, however; for while the heathen raged at the door, discord rioted at the hearthstone. Her domestic quarrels were wonderful in number, diversity, and bitterness. There was the standing quarrel of Montreal and Quebec, the quarrels of priests with one another, of priests with the governor, and of the governor with the intendant, besides ceaseless wranglings of rival traders and rival peculators.

Some of these disputes were local and of no special significance; while others are very interesting, because, on a remote and obscure theatre, they repre-

sent, sometimes in striking forms, the contending
passions and principles of a most important epoch of
history.   To begin with one which even to this day
has left a root of bitterness behind it.

The association of pious enthusiasts who had
founded Montreal [1] was reduced in 1657 to a remnant
of five or six persons, whose ebbing zeal and over-
taxed purses were no longer equal to the devout but
arduous enterprise.   They begged the priests of the
Seminary of St. Sulpice to take it off their hands.
The priests consented; and, though the conveyance
of the island of Montreal to these its new proprietors
did not take effect till some years later, four of the
Sulpitian fathers — Queylus, Souart, Galinée, and
Allet — came out to the colony and took it in charge.
Thus far Canada had had no bishop, and the
Sulpitians now aspired to give it one from their own
brotherhood.   Many years before, when the Récollets
had a foothold in the colony, they too, or at least
some of them, had cherished the hope of giving
Canada a bishop of their own.   As for the Jesuits,
who for nearly thirty years had of themselves constituted the Canadian church, they had been content
thus far to dispense with a bishop; for having no
rivals in the field, they had felt no need of episcopal
support.

The Sulpitians put forward Queylus as their candi-
date for the new bishopric.   The assembly of French

1 See "Jesuits in North America," chap. xxii.

clergy approved, and Cardinal Mazarin himself seemed to sanction, the nomination. The Jesuits saw that their time of action was come. It was they who had borne the heat and burden of the day, the toils, privations, and martyrdoms, while as yet the Sulpitians had done nothing and endured nothing. If any body of ecclesiastics was to have the nomination of a bishop, it clearly belonged to them, the Jesuits. Their might, too, matched their right. They were strong at court; Mazarin withdrew his assent, and the Jesuits were invited to name a bishop to their liking.

Meanwhile the Sulpitians, despairing of the bishopric, had sought their solace elsewhere. Ships bound for Canada had usually sailed from ports within the jurisdiction of the Archbishop of Rouen, and the departing missionaries had received their ecclesiastical powers from him, till he had learned to regard Canada as an outlying section of his diocese. Not unwilling to assert his claims, he now made Queylus his vicar-general for all Canada, thus clothing him with episcopal powers, and placing him over the heads of the Jesuits. Queylus, in effect though not in name a bishop, left his companion Souart in the spiritual charge of Montreal, came down to Quebec, announced his new dignity, and assumed the curacy of the parish. The Jesuits received him at first with their usual urbanity, an exercise of self-control rendered more easy by their knowledge that one more potent than Queylus would soon arrive to supplant him.[1]

The vicar of the Archbishop of Rouen was a man of many virtues, devoted to good works, as he understood them; rich, for the Sulpitians were under no vow of poverty; generous in almsgiving, busy, indefatigable, overflowing with zeal, vivacious in temperament and excitable in temper, impatient of opposition, and, as it seems, incapable, like his destined rival, of seeing any way of doing good but his own. Though the Jesuits were outwardly courteous, their partisans would not listen to the new curé's sermons, or listened only to find fault; and germs of discord grew vigorously in the parish of Quebec. Prudence was not among the virtues of Queylus. He launched two sermons against the Jesuits, in which he likened himself to Christ and them to the Pharisees. "Who," he supposed them to say, "is this Jesus, so beloved of the people, who comes to cast discredit on us, who for thirty or forty years have governed church and state here, with none to dispute us?"[2] He denounced such of his

---

[1] A detailed account of the experiences of Queylus at Quebec, immediately after his arrival, as related by himself, will be found in a memoir by the Sulpitian Allet, in *Morale Pratique des Jésuites*, xxxiv. chap. xii. In chapter ten of the same volume the writer says that he visited Queylus at Mont St. Valérien, after his return from Canada. "Il me prit à part; nous nous promenâmes assez longtemps dans le jardin et il m'ouvrit son cœur sur la conduite des Jésuites dans le Canada et partout ailleurs. Messieurs de St. Sulpice savent bien ce qu'il m'en a pu dire, et je suis assuré qu'ils ne diront pas que je l'ai dû prendre pour des mensonges."

[2] *Journal des Jésuites, Octobre,* 1657.

hearers as came to pick flaws in his discourse, and told them it would be better for their souls if they lay in bed at home, sick of a "good quartan fever." His ire was greatly kindled by a letter of the Jesuit Pijart, which fell into his hands through a female adherent, the pious Madame d'Ailleboust, and in which that father declared that he, Queylus, was waging war on him and his brethren more savagely than the Iroquois.[1] "He was as crazy at sight of a Jesuit," writes an adverse biographer, "as a mad dog at sight of water."[2] He cooled, however, on being shown certain papers which proved that his position was neither so strong nor so secure as he had supposed; and the governor, Argenson, at length persuaded him to retire to Montreal.[3]

The queen-mother, Anne of Austria, always inclined to the Jesuits, had invited Father Le Jeune, who was then in France, to make choice of a bishop for Canada. It was not an easy task. No Jesuit was eligible, for the sage policy of Loyola had excluded members of the order from the bishopric. The signs of the times portended trouble for the Canadian church, and there was need of a bishop who would assert her claims and fight her battles. Such a man could not be made an instrument of the Jesuits; therefore there was double need that he should be one with them in sympathy and purpose.

[1] *Journal des Jésuites, Octobre,* 1657.
[2] Viger, *Notice Historique sur l'Abbé de Queylus.*
[3] *Papiers d'Argenson.*

They made a sagacious choice.   Le Jeune presented
to the queen-mother the name of François Xavier de
Laval-Montmorency, Abbé de Montigny.

Laval, for by this name he was thenceforth known,
belonged to one of the proudest families of Europe,
and, churchman as he was, there is much in his
career to remind us that in his veins ran the blood
of the stern Constable of France, Anne de Montmorency.   Nevertheless, his thoughts from childhood
had turned towards the Church, or, as his biographers
will have it, all his aspirations were heavenward.
He received the tonsure at the age of nine.   The
Jesuit Bagot confirmed and moulded his youthful
predilections; and at a later period he was one of a
band of young zealots formed under the auspices of
Bernières de Louvigni, royal treasurer at Caen, who,
though a layman, was reputed almost a saint.   It
was Bernières who had borne the chief part in the
pious fraud of the pretended marriage through which
Madame de la Peltrie escaped from her father's roof
to become foundress of the Ursulines of Quebec.[1]
He had since renounced the world, and dwelt at
Caen in a house attached to an Ursuline convent,
and known as the "Hermitage."   Here he lived like
a monk, in the midst of a community of young
priests and devotees, who looked to him as their
spiritual director, and whom he trained in the
maxims and practices of the most extravagant, or, as

[1] See "Jesuits in North America," chap. **xiv.**

his admirers say, the most sublime ultramontane piety.[1]

The conflict between the Jesuits and the Jansenists was then at its height. The Jansenist doctrines of election and salvation by grace, which sapped the power of the priesthood and impugned the authority of the Pope himself in his capacity of holder of the keys of heaven, were to the Jesuits an abomination; while the rigid morals of the Jansenists stood in stern contrast to the pliancy of Jesuit casuistry. Bernières and his disciples were zealous, not to say fanatical, partisans of the Jesuits. There is a long account of the "Hermitage" and its inmates from the pen of the famous Jansenist Nicole, — an opponent, it is true, but one whose qualities of mind and character give weight to his testimony.[2]

"In this famous Hermitage," says Nicole, "the late Sieur de Bernières brought up a number of young men, to whom he taught a sort of sublime and transcendental devotion called *passive prayer*, because in it the mind does not act at all, but merely receives the divine operation; and this devotion is the source of all those visions and revelations in which the Hermitage is so prolific." In short, he and his disciples were mystics of the most exalted type. Nicole pursues: "After having thus subtilized

---

[1] La Tour in his *Vie de Laval* gives his maxims at length.

[2] *Mémoire pour faire connoistre l'esprit et la conduite de la Compagnie établie en la ville de Caen, appellée l'Hermitage* (Bibliothèque Nationale. Imprimés. Partie Réservée). Written in 1660.

their minds, and almost sublimed them into vapor,
he rendered them capable of detecting Jansenists
under any disguise, insomuch that some of his followers said that they knew them by the scent, as
dogs know their game; but the aforesaid Sieur de
Bernières denied that they had so subtile a sense of
smell, and said that the mark by which he detected
Jansenists was their disapproval of his teachings or
their opposition to the Jesuits."

The zealous band at the Hermitage was aided in
its efforts to extirpate error by a sort of external
association in the city of Caen, consisting of merchants, priests, officers, petty nobles, and others, all
inspired and guided by Bernières. They met every
week at the Hermitage, or at the houses of one
another. Similar associations existed in other cities
of France, besides a fraternity in the Rue St.
Dominique at Paris, which was formed by the Jesuit
Bagot, and seems to have been the parent, in a certain sense, of the others. They all acted together
when any important object was in view.

Bernières and his disciples felt that God had
chosen them not only to watch over doctrine and
discipline in convents and in families, but also to
supply the prevalent deficiency of zeal in bishops and
other dignitaries of the Church. They kept, too, a
constant eye on the humbler clergy, and whenever a
new preacher appeared in Caen, two of their number
were deputed to hear his sermon and report upon it.
If he chanced to let fall a word concerning the grace

of God, they denounced him for Jansenistic heresy. Such commotion was once raised in Caen by charges of sedition and Jansenism, brought by the Hermitage against priests and laymen hitherto without attaint, that the Bishop of Bayeux thought it necessary to interpose; but even he was forced to pause, daunted by the insinuations of Bernières that he was in secret sympathy with the obnoxious doctrines.

Thus the Hermitage and its affiliated societies constituted themselves a sort of inquisition in the interest of the Jesuits; "for what," asks Nicole, "might not be expected from persons of weak minds and atrabilious dispositions, dried up by constant fasts, vigils, and other austerities, besides meditations of three or four hours a day, and told continually that the Church is in imminent danger of ruin through the machinations of the Jansenists, who are represented to them as persons who wish to break up the foundations of the Christian faith and subvert the mystery of the Incarnation; who believe neither in transubstantiation, the invocation of saints, nor indulgences; who wish to abolish the sacrifice of the Mass and the sacrament of Penitence, oppose the worship of the Holy Virgin, deny free-will and substitute predestination in its place, and, in fine, conspire to overthrow the authority of the Supreme Pontiff?"

Among other anecdotes, Nicole tells the following: One of the young zealots of the Hermitage took it into his head that all Caen was full of Jansenists,

and that the curés of the place were in league with
them.　He inoculated four others with this notion,
and they resolved to warn the people of their danger.
They accordingly made the tour of the streets, with
out hats or collars, and with coats unbuttoned,
though it was a cold winter day, stopping every
moment to proclaim in a loud voice that all the curés,
excepting two, whom they named, were abettors of
the Jansenists.　A mob was soon following at their
heels, and there was great excitement.　The magistrates chanced to be in session, and hearing of the
disturbance, they sent constables to arrest the authors
of it.　Being brought to the bar of justice and questioned by the judge, they answered that they were
doing the work of God, and were ready to die in the
cause; that Caen was full of Jansenists, and that the
curés had declared in their favor, inasmuch as they
denied any knowledge of their existence.　Four of
the five were locked up for a few days, tried, and
sentenced to a fine of a hundred livres, with a
promise of further punishment should they again
disturb the peace.[1]

The fifth, being pronounced out of his wits by the
physicians, was sent home to his mother, at a village
near Argentan, where two or three of his fellow
zealots presently joined him.　Among them, they
persuaded his mother, who had hitherto been devoted

---

[1] Nicole is not the only authority for this story.　It is also told
by a very different writer.　See *Notice Historique de l'Abbaye de Ste.
Claire d'Argentan*, 124.

to household cares, to exchange them for a life of mystical devotion. "These three or four persons," says Nicole, "attracted others as imbecile as themselves." Among these recruits were a number of women, and several priests. After various acts of fanaticism, "two or three days before last Pentecost," proceeds the narrator, "they all set out, men and women, for Argentan. The priests had drawn the skirts of their cassocks over their heads, and tied them about their necks with twisted straw. Some of the women had their heads bare, and their hair streaming loose over their shoulders. They picked up filth on the road, and rubbed their faces with it; and the most zealous ate it, saying that it was necessary to mortify the taste. Some held stones in their hands, which they knocked together to draw the attention of the passers-by. They had a leader, whom they were bound to obey; and when this leader saw any mud-hole particularly deep and dirty, he commanded some of the party to roll themselves in it, which they did forthwith.[1]

"After this fashion, they entered the town of Argentan, and marched, two by two, through all the streets, crying with a loud voice that the Faith was perishing, and that whoever wished to save it must quit the country and go with them to Canada,

[1] These proceedings were probably intended to produce the result which was the constant object of the mystics of the Hermitage; namely, the "annihilation of self," with a view to a perfect union with God. To become despised of men was an important if not an essential step in this mystical suicide.

whither they were soon to repair. It is said that they still hold this purpose, and that their leaders declare it revealed to them that they will find a vessel ready at the first port to which Providence directs them. The reason why they choose Canada for an asylum is, that Monsieur de Montigny (Laval), Bishop of Petræa, who lived at the Hermitage a long time, where he was instructed in mystical theology by Monsieur de Bernières, exercises episcopal functions there; and that the Jesuits, who are their oracles, reign in that country."

This adventure, like the other, ended in a collision with the police. "The priests," adds Nicole, "were arrested, and are now waiting trial; and the rest were treated as mad, and sent back with shame and confusion to the places whence they had come."

Though these pranks took place after Laval had left the Hermitage, they serve to characterize the school in which he was formed; or, more justly speaking, to show its most extravagant side. That others did not share the views of the celebrated Jansenist, may be gathered from the following passage of the funeral oration pronounced over the body of Laval half a century later: —

"The humble abbé was next transported into the terrestrial paradise of Monsieur de Bernières. It is thus that I call, as it is fitting to call it, that famous Hermitage of Caen, where the seraphic author of the 'Christian Interior' [Bernières] transformed into angels all those who had the happiness to be the companions of his solitude and of his spiritual exercises. It was there that, during four years, the fervent abbé drank the living and abounding waters of grace which have since flowed so benignly over this land of Canada. In this celestial abode his ordinary occupations were prayer, mortification, instruction of the poor, and spiritual readings or conferences; his recreations were to labor in the hospitals, wait upon the sick and poor, make their beds, dress their wounds, and aid them in their most repulsive needs."[1]

In truth, Laval's zeal was boundless, and the exploits of self-humiliation recorded of him were unspeakably revolting.[2] Bernières himself regarded him as a light by which to guide his own steps in ways of holiness. He made journeys on foot about the country, disguised, penniless, begging from door to door, and courting scorn and opprobrium, "in order," says his biographer, "that he might suffer for the love of God." Yet, though living at this time in a state of habitual religious exaltation, he was by nature no mere dreamer; and in whatever heights his spirit might wander, his feet were always planted on the solid earth. His flaming zeal had for its servants a hard, practical nature, perfectly fitted for the battle of life, a narrow intellect, a stiff and

[1] *Eloge funèbre de Messire François Xavier de Laval-Montmorency, par Messire de la Colombière, Vicaire Général.*

[2] See La Tour, *Vie de Laval,* liv. i. Some of them were closely akin to that of the fanatics mentioned above, who ate "immondices d'animaux" to mortify the taste.

persistent will, and, as his enemies thought, the love of domination native to his blood.

Two great parties divided the Catholics of France, — the Gallican or national party, and the ultramontane or papal party. The first, resting on the Scriptural injunction to give tribute to Cæsar, held that to the King, the Lord's anointed, belonged the temporal, and to the Church the spiritual power. It held also that the laws and customs of the Church of France could not be broken at the bidding of the Pope.[1] The ultramontane party, on the other hand, maintained that the Pope, Christ's vicegerent on earth, was supreme over earthly rulers, and should of right hold jurisdiction over the clergy of all Christendom, with powers of appointment and removal. Hence they claimed for him the right of nominating bishops in France. This had anciently been exercised by assemblies of the French clergy, but in the reign of Francis I. the King and the Pope had combined to wrest it from them by the Concordat of Bologna. Under this compact, which was still in force, the Pope appointed French bishops on the nomination of the King, — a plan which displeased the Gallicans, and did not satisfy the ultramontanes.

The Jesuits, then as now, were the most forcible exponents of ultramontane principles. The Church to rule the world; the Pope to rule the Church; the Jesuits to rule the Pope, — such was and is the

---

[1] See the famous *Quatre Articles* of 1682, in which the liberties of the Gallican Church are asserted.

simple programme of the Order of Jesus; and to it they have held fast, except on a few rare occasions of misunderstanding with the Vicegerent of Christ.[1] In the question of papal supremacy, as in most things else, Laval was of one mind with them.

Those versed in such histories will not be surprised to learn that when he received the royal nomination, humility would not permit him to accept it; nor that, being urged, he at length bowed in resignation, still protesting his unworthiness. Nevertheless, the royal nomination did not take effect. The ultramontanes outflanked both the King and the Gallicans, and by adroit strategy made the new prelate completely a creature of the papacy. Instead of appointing him Bishop of Quebec, in accordance with the royal initiative, the Pope made him his vicar apostolic for Canada, — thus evading the King's nomination, and affirming that Canada, a country of infidel savages, was excluded from the concordat, and under his (the Pope's) jurisdiction pure and simple. The Gallicans were enraged. The Archbishop of Rouen vainly opposed, and the parliaments of Rouen and of Paris vainly protested. The papal party prevailed. The King, or rather Mazarin, gave his consent, subject to certain conditions, the chief of which was an oath of allegiance; and Laval, grand vicar apostolic, decorated with the title of Bishop of Petræa, sailed

---

[1] For example, not long after this time, the Jesuits, having a dispute with Innocent XI., threw themselves into the party of opposition.

for his wilderness diocese in the spring of 1659.[1]
He was but thirty-six years of age, but even when a
boy he could scarcely have seemed young.

Queylus, for a time, seemed to accept the situation,
and tacitly admit the claim of Laval as his ecclesiastical superior; but, stimulated by a letter from the
Archbishop of Rouen, he soon threw himself into an
attitude of opposition,[2] in which the popularity which
his generosity to the poor had won for him gave him
an advantage very annoying to his adversary. The
quarrel, it will be seen, was three-sided, — Gallican
against ultramontane, Sulpitian against Jesuit,
Montreal against Quebec. To Montreal the recal-
citrant abbé, after a brief visit to Quebec, had again
retired; but even here, girt with his Sulpitian
brethren and compassed with partisans, the arm
of the vicar apostolic was long enough to reach
him.

By temperament and conviction Laval hated a
divided authority, and the very shadow of a schism
was an abomination in his sight. The young King,
who, though abundantly jealous of his royal power,
was forced to conciliate the papal party, had sent
instructions to Argenson, the governor, to support
Laval, and prevent divisions in the Canadian

[1] Compare La Tour, *Vie de Laval*, with the long statement in
Faillon, *Colonie Française*, ii. 315–335. Faillon gives various documents in full, including the royal letter of nomination and those
in which the King gives a reluctant consent to the appointment of
the vicar apostolic.

[2] *Journal des Jésuites, Septembre*, 1657.

Church.[1] These instructions served as the pretext
of a procedure sufficiently summary. A squad of
soldiers, commanded, it is said, by the governor himself, went up to Montreal, brought the indignant
Queylus to Quebec, and shipped him thence for
France.[2] By these means, writes Father Lalemant,
order reigned for a season in the Church.

It was but for a season. Queylus was not a man
to bide his defeat in tranquillity, nor were his brother
Sulpitians disposed to silent acquiescence. Laval,
on his part, was not a man of half measures. He
had an agent in France, and partisans strong at
court. Fearing, to borrow the words of a Catholic
writer, that the return of Queylus to Canada would
prove "injurious to the glory of God," he bestirred
himself to prevent it. The young King, then at
Aix, on his famous journey to the frontiers of Spain
to marry the Infanta, was induced to write to
Queylus, ordering him to remain in France.[3]
Queylus, however, repaired to Rome; but even
against this movement provision had been made:
accusations of Jansenism had gone before him, and
he met a cold welcome. Nevertheless, as he had
powerful friends near the Pope, he succeeded in
removing these adverse impressions, and even in
obtaining certain bulls relating to the establishment

---

[1] *Lettre du Roi à d'Argenson*, 14 *Mai*, 1659.

[2] Belmont, *Histoire du Canada*, A.D. 1659. Memoir by Abbé
d'Allet, in *Morale Pratique des Jésuites*, xxxiv. 725.

[3] *Lettre du Roi à Queylus*, 27 *Fév.*, 1660.

of the parish of Montreal, and favorable to the
Sulpitians. Provided with these, he set at nought
the King's letter, embarked under an assumed
name, and sailed to Quebec, where he made his
appearance on the third of August, 1661,[1] to the
extreme wrath of Laval.

A ferment ensued. Laval's partisans charged the
Sulpitians with Jansenism and opposition to the will
of the Pope. A preacher more zealous than the rest
denounced them as priests of Antichrist; and as to
the bulls in their favor, it was affirmed that Queylus
had obtained them by fraud from the Holy Father.
Laval at once issued a mandate forbidding him to
proceed to Montreal till ships should arrive with
instructions from the King.[2] At the same time he
demanded of the governor that he should interpose
the civil power to prevent Queylus from leaving
Quebec.[3] As Argenson, who wished to act as peace-
maker between the belligerent fathers, did not at
once take the sharp measures required of him, Laval
renewed his demand on the next day, — calling on
him, in the name of God and the King, to compel
Queylus to yield the obedience due to him, the vicar
apostolic.[4] At the same time he sent another to the
offending abbé, threatening to suspend him from
priestly functions if he persisted in his rebellion.[5]

1 *Journal des Jésuites, Août,* 1661.

2 *Lettre de Laval à Queylus,* 4 *Août,* 1661.

3 *Lettre de Laval à d'Argenson, Ibid.*

4 *Ibid.,* 5 *Août,* 1661.

5 *Lettre de Laval à Queylus, Ibid.*

The incorrigible Queylus, who seems to have lived for some months in a simmer of continual indignation, set at nought the vicar apostolic as he had set at nought the King, took a boat that very night, and set out for Montreal under cover of darkness. Great was the ire of Laval when he heard the news in the morning. He despatched a letter after him, declaring him suspended *ipso facto*, if he did not instantly return and make his submission.[1] This letter, like the rest, failed of the desired effect; but the governor, who had received a second mandate from the King to support Laval and prevent a schism,[2] now reluctantly interposed the secular arm, and Queylus was again compelled to return to France.[3]

His expulsion was a Sulpitian defeat. Laval, always zealous for unity and centralization, had some time before taken steps to repress what he regarded as a tendency to independence at Montreal. In the preceding year he had written to the Pope: "There are some secular priests [Sulpitians] at Montreal, whom the Abbé de Queylus brought out with him in 1657, and I have named for the functions of curé the one among them whom I thought the least disobedient." The bulls which Queylus had obtained from Rome related to this very curacy, and greatly disturbed the mind of the vicar apostolic. He accordingly wrote again to the Pope: "I pray

[1] *Lettre de Laval à Queylus,* 6 *Août,* 1661.

[2] *Lettre du Roi à d'Argenson,* 13 *Mai,* 1660.

[3] For the governor's attitude in this affair, consult the *Papiers d'Argenson,* containing his despatches.

your Holiness to let me know your will concerning
the jurisdiction of the Archbishop of Rouen. M.
l'Abbé de Queylus, who has come out this year as
vicar of this archbishop, has tried to deceive us by
surreptitious letters, and has obeyed neither our
prayers nor our repeated commands to desist. But
he has received orders from the King to return immediately to France, to render an account of his disobedience; and he has been compelled by the governor
to conform to the will of his Majesty. What I now
fear is that on his return to France, by using every
kind of means, employing new artifices, and falsely
representing our affairs, he may obtain from the
Court of Rome powers which may disturb the peace
of our Church; for the priests whom he brought
with him from France, and who live at Montreal,
are animated with the same spirit of disobedience
and division; and I fear, with good reason, that all
belonging to the Seminary of St. Sulpice, who may
come hereafter to join them, will be of the same disposition. If what is said is true, that by means of
fraudulent letters the right of patronage of the pretended parish of Montreal has been granted to the
superior of this seminary, and the right of appointment to the Archbishop of Rouen, then is altar
reared against altar in our Church of Canada; for
the clergy of Montreal will always stand in opposition
to me, the vicar apostolic, and to my successors." [1]

[1] *Lettre de Laval au Pape*, 22 *Oct.*, 1661. Printed by Faillon,
from the original in the archives of the Propaganda.

These dismal forebodings were never realized. The Holy See annulled the obnoxious bulls; the Archbishop of Rouen renounced his claims, and Queylus found his position untenable. Seven years later, when Laval was on a visit to France, a reconciliation was brought about between them. The former vicar of the Archbishop of Rouen made his submission to the vicar of the Pope, and returned to Canada as a missionary. Laval's triumph was complete, to the joy of the Jesuits, — silent, if not idle, spectators of the tedious and complex quarrel.

CHAPTER VIII.

1659, 1660.

LAVAL AND ARGENSON.

FRANÇOIS DE LAVAL: HIS POSITION AND CHARACTER. — ARRIVAL OF ARGENSON. — THE QUARREL.

WE are touching delicate ground. To many excellent Catholics of our own day Laval is an object of veneration. The Catholic university of Quebec glories in bearing his name, and certain modern ecclesiastical writers rarely mention him in terms less reverent than "the virtuous prelate," or "the holy prelate." Nor are some of his contemporaries less emphatic in eulogy. Mother Juchereau de Saint-Denis, Superior of the Hôtel Dieu, wrote immediately after his death: "He began in his tenderest years the study of perfection, and we have reason to think that he reached it, since every virtue which Saint Paul demands in a bishop was seen and admired in him;" and on his first arrival in Canada, Mother Marie de l'Incarnation, Superior of the Ursulines, wrote to her son that the choice of such a prelate was not of man, but of God. "I will not," she adds. "say that he is a saint; but I may say with

11

truth that he lives like a saint and an apostle."
And she describes his austerity of life; how he had
but two servants, a gardener — whom he lent on
occasion to his needy neighbors — and a valet; how
he lived in a small hired house, saying that he would
not have one of his own if he could build it for only
five sous; and how, in his table, furniture, and bed,
he showed the spirit of poverty, even, as she thinks,
to excess.   His servant, a lay brother named Houssart,
testified, after his death, that he slept on a hard
bed, and would not suffer it to be changed even
when it became full of fleas; and, what is more to
the purpose, that he gave fifteen hundred or two
thousand francs to the poor every year.[1] Houssart
also gives the following specimen of his austerities:
"I have seen him keep cooked meat five, six, seven,
or eight days in the heat of summer; and when it
was all mouldy and wormy he washed it in warm
water and ate it, and told me that it was very good."
The old servant was so impressed by these and other
proofs of his master's sanctity, that "I determined,"
he says, "to keep everything I could that had
belonged to his holy person, and after his death to
soak bits of linen in his blood when his body was
opened, and take a few bones and cartilages from his
breast, cut off his hair, and keep his clothes, and
such things, to serve as most precious relics."

[1] *Lettre du Frère Houssart, ancien serviteur de M'g'r de Laval à
M. Tremblay*, 1 *Sept.*, 1708. This letter is printed, though with one
or two important omissions, in the *Abeille*, vol. i. (Quebec, 1848.)

These pious cares were not in vain, for the relics proved greatly in demand.

Several portraits of Laval are extant. A drooping nose of portentous size; a well-formed forehead; a brow strongly arched; a bright, clear eye; scanty hair, half hidden by a black skullcap; thin lips, compressed and rigid, betraying a spirit not easy to move or convince; features of that indescribable cast which marks the priestly type, — such is Laval, as he looks grimly down on us from the dingy canvas of two centuries ago.

He is one of those concerning whom Protestants and Catholics, at least ultramontane Catholics, will never agree in judgment. The task of eulogizing him may safely be left to those of his own way of thinking. It is for us to regard him from the standpoint of secular history. And, first, let us credit him with sincerity. He believed firmly that the princes and rulers of this world ought to be subject to guidance and control at the hands of the Pope, the vicar of Christ on earth. But he himself was the Pope's vicar, and, so far as the bounds of Canada extended, the Holy Father had clothed him with his own authority. The glory of God demanded that this authority should suffer no abatement; and he, Laval, would be guilty before Heaven if he did not uphold the supremacy of the Church over the powers both of earth and of hell.

Of the faults which he owed to nature, the principal seems to have been an arbitrary and domineer-

ing temper. He was one of those who by nature
lean always to the side of authority; and in the
English Revolution he would inevitably have stood
for the Stuarts; or, in the American Revolution, for
the Crown. But being above all things a Catholic
and a priest, he was drawn by a constitutional necessity to the ultramontane party, or the party of centralization. He fought lustily, in his way, against
the natural man; and humility was the virtue to the
culture of which he gave his chief attention; but
soil and climate were not favorable. His life was
one long assertion of the authority of the Church,
and this authority was lodged in himself. In his
stubborn fight for ecclesiastical ascendency, he was
aided by the impulses of a nature that loved to
rule, and could not endure to yield. His principles
and his instinct of domination were acting in perfect
unison, and his conscience was the handmaid of his
fault. Austerities and mortifications, playing at
beggar, sleeping in beds full of fleas, or performing
prodigies of gratuitous dirtiness in hospitals, however fatal to self-respect, could avail little against
influences working so powerfully and so insidiously
to stimulate the most subtle of human vices. The
history of the Roman Church is full of Lavals.

The Jesuits, adepts in human nature, had made a
sagacious choice when they put forward this conscientious, zealous, dogged, and pugnacious priest
to fight their battles. Nor were they ill pleased
that, for the present, he was not Bishop of Canada,

but only vicar apostolic; for such being the case, they could have him recalled if on trial they did not like him, while an unacceptable bishop would be an evil past remedy.

Canada was entering a state of transition. Hitherto ecclesiastical influence had been all in all. The Jesuits, by far the most educated and able body of men in the colony, had controlled it, not alone in things spiritual, but virtually in things temporal also; and the governor may be said to have been little else than a chief of police, under the direction of the missionaries. The early governors were themselves deeply imbued with the missionary spirit. Champlain was earnest above all things for converting the Indians; Montmagny was half-monk, for he was a Knight of Malta; d'Ailleboust was so insanely pious that he lived with his wife like monk and nun. A change was at hand. From a mission and a trading station, Canada was soon to become, in the true sense, a colony; and civil government had begun to assert itself on the banks of the St. Lawrence. The epoch of the martyrs and apostles was passing away, and the man of the sword and the man of the gown — the soldier and the legist — were threatening to supplant the paternal sway of priests: or, as Laval might have said, the hosts of this world were beleaguering the sanctuary, and he was called of Heaven to defend it. His true antagonist, though three thousand miles away, was the great minister Colbert, as purely a statesman as the vicar apostolic was purely a priest. Laval, no doubt, could see behind the statesman's back another adversary, — the Devil.

Argenson was governor when the crozier and the sword began to clash, which is merely another way of saying that he was governor when Laval arrived. He seems to have been a man of education, moderation, and sense, and he was also an earnest Catholic; but if Laval had his duties to God, so had Argenson his duties to the King, of whose authority he was the representative and guardian. If the first collisions seem trivial, they were no less the symptoms of a grave antagonism. Argenson could have purchased peace only by becoming an agent of the Church.

The vicar apostolic, or, as he was usually styled, the bishop, being, it may be remembered, titular Bishop of Petræa in Arabia, presently fell into a quarrel with the governor touching the relative position of their seats in church, — a point which, by the way, was a subject of contention for many years, and under several successive governors. This time the case was referred to the ex-governor, d'Ailleboust, and a temporary settlement took place.[1] A few weeks after, on the fête of Saint Francis Xavier, when the Jesuits were accustomed to ask the dignitaries of the colony to dine in their refectory after mass, a fresh difficulty arose, — Should the governor or the bishop have the higher seat at table? The

[1] Lalemant, in *Journal des Jésuites, Septembre,* 1659.

question defied solution; so the fathers invited neither of them.[1]

Again, on Christmas, at the midnight mass, the deacon offered incense to the bishop, and then, in obedience to an order from him, sent a subordinate to offer it to the governor, instead of offering it himself. Laval further insisted that the priests of the choir should receive incense before the governor received it. Argenson resisted, and a bitter quarrel ensued.[2]

The late governor, d'Ailleboust, had been churchwarden *ex officio;*[3] and in this pious community the office was esteemed as an addition to his honors. Argenson had thus far held the same position; but Laval declared that he should hold it no longer. Argenson, to whom the bishop had not spoken on the subject, came soon after to a meeting of the wardens, and, being challenged, denied Laval's right to dismiss him. A dispute ensued, in which the bishop, according to his Jesuit friends, used language not very respectful to the representative of royalty.[4]

On occasion of the "solemn catechism," the bishop insisted that the children should salute him before saluting the governor. Argenson, hearing of this, declined to come. A compromise was contrived. It was agreed that when the rival dignitaries entered,

---

[1] Lalemant, in *Journal des Jésuites, Decembre,* 1659.

[2] *Ibid.; Lettre d'Argenson à MM. de la Compagnie de St. Sulpice.*

[3] *Livre des Délibérations de la Fabrique de Québec.*

[4] *Journal des Jésuites, Novembre,* 1660.

the children should be busied in some manual exercise which should prevent their saluting either. Nevertheless, two boys, "enticed and set on by their parents," saluted the governor first, to the great indignation of Laval. They were whipped on the next day for breach of orders.[1]

Next there was a sharp quarrel about a sentence pronounced by Laval against a heretic, to which the governor, good Catholic as he was, took exception.[2] Palm Sunday came, and there could be no procession and no distribution of branches, because the governor and the bishop could not agree on points of precedence.[3]

On the day of the Fête Dieu, however, there was a grand procession, which stopped from time to time at temporary altars, or *reposoirs*, placed at intervals along its course. One of these was in the fort, where the soldiers were drawn up, waiting the arrival of the procession. Laval demanded that they should take off their hats. Argenson assented, and the soldiers stood uncovered. Laval now insisted that they should kneel. The governor replied that it was their duty as soldiers to stand; whereupon the bishop refused to stop at the altar, and ordered the procession to move on.[4]

The above incidents are set down in the private journal of the superior of the Jesuits, which was not

1 *Journal des Jésuites, Février*, 1661.
2 *Ibid.*
3 *Ibid., Avril*, 1661.   4 *Ibid., Juin*, 1661.

meant for the public eye. The bishop, it will be
seen, was, by the showing of his friends, in most
cases the aggressor. The disputes in question,
though of a nature to provoke a smile on irreverent
lips, were by no means so puerile as they appear.
It is difficult in a modern democratic society to conceive the substantial importance of the signs and
symbols of dignity and authority at a time and among
a people where they were adjusted with the most
scrupulous precision, and accepted by all classes as
exponents of relative degrees in the social and
political scale. Whether the bishop or the governor
should sit in the higher seat at table thus became a
political question, for it defined to the popular understanding the position of Church and State in their
relations to government.

Hence it is not surprising to find a memorial,
drawn up apparently by Argenson, and addressed to
the council of State, asking for instructions when
and how a governor — lieutenant-general for the
King — ought to receive incense, holy water, and
consecrated bread; whether the said bread should be
offered him with sound of drum and fife; what
should be the position of his seat at church; and
what place he should hold in various religious ceremonies; whether in feasts, assemblies, ceremonies,
and councils of *a purely civil character*, he or the
bishop was to hold the first place; and, finally, if
the bishop could excommunicate the inhabitants or
others for acts of a civil and political character,

when the said acts were pronounced lawful by the governor.

The reply to the memorial denies to the bishop the power of excommunication in civil matters, assigns to him the second place in meetings and ceremonies of a civil character, and is very reticent as to the rest.[1]

Argenson had a brother, a counsellor of State, and a fast friend of the Jesuits. Laval was in corre· spondence with him, and, apparently sure of sympathy, wrote to him touching his relations with the governor. " Your brother," he begins, "received me on my arrival with extraordinary kindness; " but he proceeds to say, that, perceiving with sorrow that he entertained a groundless distrust of those good servants of God, the Jesuit fathers, he, the bishop, thought it his duty to give him in private a candid warning which ought to have done good, but which, to his surprise, the governor had taken amiss, and had conceived, in consequence, a prejudice against his monitor.[2]

Argenson, on his part, writes to the same brother, at about the same time. " The Bishop of Petræa is so stiff in opinion, and so often transported by his zeal beyond the rights of his position, that he makes no difficulty in encroaching on the functions of others; and this with so much heat that he will

---

[1] *Advis et Résolutions demandés sur la Nouvelle France.*

[2] *Lettre de Laval à M. d'Argenson, frère du Gouverneur,* 20 *Oct.,* 1659.

listen to nobody. A few days ago he carried off a servant girl of one of the inhabitants here, and placed her by his own authority in the Ursuline convent, on the sole pretext that he wanted to have her instructed, — thus depriving her master of her services, though he had been at great expense in bringing her from France. This inhabitant is M. Denis, who, not knowing who had carried her off, came to me with a petition to get her out of the convent. I kept the petition three days without answering it, to prevent the affair from being noised abroad. The Reverend Father Lalemant, with whom I communicated on the subject, and who greatly blamed the Bishop of Petræa, did all in his power to have the girl given up quietly, but without the least success, so that I was forced to answer the petition, and permit M. Denis to take his servant wherever he should find her; and if I had not used means to bring about an accommodation, and if M. Denis, on the refusal which was made him to give her up, had brought the matter into court, I should have been compelled to take measures which would have caused great scandal, — and all from the self-will of the Bishop of Petræa, who says that *a bishop can do what he likes*, and threatens nothing but excommunication." [1]

In another letter he speaks in the same strain of this redundancy of zeal on the part of the bishop,

[1] " — Qui dict *quun Evesque peult ce qu'il veult* et ne menace que dexcommunication."—*Lettre d'Argenson à son Frère,* 1659.

which often, he says, takes the shape of obstinacy
and encroachment on the rights of others. "It is
greatly to be wished," he observes, "that the Bishop
of Petræa would give his confidence to the Reverend
Father Lalemant instead of Father Ragueneau;"[1]
and he praises Lalemant as a person of excellent
sense. "It would be well," he adds, "if the rest of
their community were of the same mind; for in that
case they would not mix themselves up with various
matters in the way they do, and would leave the
government to those to whom God has given it in
charge."[2]

One of Laval's modern admirers, the worthy Abbé
Ferland, after confessing that his zeal may now and
then have savored of excess, adds in his defence that
a vigorous hand was needed to compel the infant
colony to enter "the good path," — meaning, of
course, the straitest path of Roman Catholic orthodoxy. We may hereafter see more of this stringent
system of colonial education, its success, and the
results that followed.

[1] *Lettre d'Argenson à son Frère*, 21 *Oct.*, 1659.
[2] *Ibid.*, 7 *July*, 1660.

CHAPTER IX.

1658–1663.

LAVAL AND AVAUGOUR.

WHEN Argenson arrived to assume the government, a curious greeting had awaited him. The Jesuits asked him to dine; vespers followed the repast; and then they conducted him into a hall, where the boys of their school — disguised, one as the Genius of New France, one as the Genius of the Forest, and others as Indians of various friendly tribes — made him speeches by turn, in prose and verse. First, Pierre du Quet, who played the Genius of New France, presented his Indian retinue to the governor, in a complimentary harangue. Then four other boys, personating French colonists, made him four flattering addresses, in French verse. Charles Denis, dressed as a Huron, followed, bewailing the ruin of his people, and appealing to Argenson for aid. Jean François Bourdon, in the character of an Algonquin, next advanced on the platform,

boasted his courage, and declared that he was ashamed
to cry like the Huron. The Genius of the Forest
now appeared, with a retinue of wild Indians from
the interior, who, being unable to speak French,
addressed the governor in their native tongues, which
the Genius proceeded to interpret. Two other boys,
in the character of prisoners just escaped from the
Iroquois, then came forward, imploring aid in piteous
accents; and, in conclusion, the whole troop of
Indians, from far and near, laid their bows and
arrows at the feet of Argenson, and hailed him as
their chief.[1]

Besides these mock Indians, a crowd of genuine
savages had gathered at Quebec to greet the new
"Onontio." On the next day — at his own cost, as
he writes to a friend — he gave them a feast, consisting of "seven large kettles full of Indian corn, peas,
prunes, sturgeons, eels, and fat, which they devoured,
having first sung me a song, after their fashion."[2]

These festivities over, he entered on the serious
business of his government, and soon learned that his
path was a thorny one. He could find, he says, but
a hundred men to resist the twenty-four hundred
warriors of the Iroquois;[3] and he begs the proprietary

[1] *La Reception de Monseigneur le Vicomte d'Argenson par toutes les
nations du pais de Canada à son entrée au gouvernement de la Nouvelle
France; à Quebecq au College de la Compagnie de Jésus, le 28 de
Juillet de l'année* 1658. The speeches, in French and Indian, are
here given *verbatim*, with the names of all the boys who took part
in the ceremony.

[2] *Papiers d'Argenson. Kebec,* 5 *Sept.,* 1658.

[3] *Mémoire sur le subject* (sic) *de la Guerre des Iroquois,* 1659.

company which he represented to send him a hundred
more, who could serve as soldiers or laborers, according to the occasion.

The company turned a deaf ear to his appeals.
They had lost money in Canada, and were grievously
out of humor with it.   In their view, the first duty
of a governor was to collect their debts, which, for
more reasons than one, was no easy task.   While
they did nothing to aid the colony in its distress,
they beset Argenson with demands for the thousand
pounds of beaver-skins, which the inhabitants had
agreed to send them every year in return for the
privilege of the fur-trade, — a privilege which the
Iroquois war made for the present worthless.   The
perplexed governor vents his feelings in sarcasm.
"They [the company] take no pains to learn the
truth; and when they hear of settlers carried off and
burned by the Iroquois, they will think it a punishment for not settling old debts, and paying over the
beaver-skins." [1]   "I wish," he adds, "they would
send somebody to look after their affairs here.   I
would gladly give him the same lodging and
entertainment as my own."

Another matter gave him great annoyance.   This
was the virtual independence of Montreal; and here,
if nowhere else, he and the bishop were of the same
mind.   On one occasion he made a visit to the place
in question, where he expected to be received as governor-general; but the local governor, Maisonneuve,

[1] *Papiers d'Argenson*, 21 *Oct.*, 1659.

declined, or at least postponed, to take his orders and give him the keys of the fort. Argenson accordingly speaks of Montreal as "a place which makes so much noise, but which is of such small account."[1] He adds that, besides wanting to be independent, the Montrealists want to monopolize the fur-trade, which would cause civil war; and that the King ought to interpose to correct their obstinacy.

In another letter he complains of d'Ailleboust, who had preceded him in the government, though himself a Montrealist. Argenson says that, on going out to fight the Iroquois, he left d'Ailleboust at Quebec, to act as his lieutenant; that, instead of doing so, he had assumed to govern in his own right; that he had taken possession of his absent superior's furniture, drawn his pay, and in other respects behaved as if he never expected to see him again. "When I returned," continues the governor, "I made him director in the council, without pay, as there was none to give him. It was this, I think, that made him remove to Montreal; for which I do not care, provided the glory of our Master suffer no prejudice thereby."[2]

These extracts may, perhaps, give an unjust impression of Argenson, who, from the general tenor of his letters, appears to have been a temperate and reasonable person. His patience and his nervous

---

[1] *Papiers d'Argenson, 4 Août*, 1659.

[2] *Ibid. Double de la lettre escripte par le Vaisseau du Gaigneur, parti le 6 Septembre* (1658).

system seem, however, to have been taxed to the utmost. His pay could not support him. "The costs of living here are horrible," he writes. "I have only two thousand crowns a year for all my expenses, and I have already been forced to run into debt to the company to an equal amount."[1] Part of his scanty income was derived from a fishery of eels, on which sundry persons had encroached, to his great detriment.[2] "I see no reason," he adds, "for staying here any longer. When I came to this country, I hoped to enjoy a little repose, but I am doubly deprived of it, — on one hand by enemies without, and incessant petty disputes within; and, on the other, by the difficulty I find in subsisting. The profits of the fur-trade have been so reduced that all the inhabitants are in the greatest poverty. They are all insolvent, and cannot pay the merchants their advances."

His disgust at length reached a crisis. "I am resolved to stay here no longer, but to go home next year. My horror of dissension, and the manifest certainty of becoming involved in disputes with certain persons with whom I am unwilling to quarrel, oblige me to anticipate these troubles, and seek some way of living in peace. These excessive fatigues are far too much for my strength. I am writing to Monsieur the President, and to the gentlemen of the Company of New France, to choose some other man

---

[1] *Papiers d'Argenson. Lettre à M. de Morangi, 5 Sept., 1658.*
[2] *Délibérations de la Compagnie de la Nouvelle France.*

for this government." [1]   And again, "If you take any interest in this country, see that the person chosen to command here has, besides the true piety necessary to a Christian in every condition of life, great firmness of character and strong bodily health.   I assure you that without these qualities he cannot succeed. Besides, it is absolutely necessary that he should be a man of property and of some rank, so that he will not be despised for humble birth, or suspected of coming here to make his fortune; for in that case he can do no good whatever." [2]

His constant friction with the head of the Church distressed the pious governor, and made his recall doubly a relief.   According to a contemporary writer, Laval was the means of delivering him from the burden of government, having written to the President Lamoignon to urge his removal. [3]   Be this as it may, it is certain that the bishop was not sorry to be rid of him.

The Baron Dubois d'Avaugour arrived to take his place.   He was an old soldier of forty years' service, [4] blunt, imperative, and sometimes obstinate to perverseness, but full of energy, and of a probity which even his enemies confessed.   "He served a long time in Germany while you were there," writes the minis-

[1] *Papiers d'Argenson.   Lettre à son Frère,* 1659.

[2] *Ibid.   Lettre (à son Frère?),* 4 *Nov.,* 1660. The originals of Argenson's letters were destroyed in the burning of the library of the Louvre by the Commune.

[3] Lachenaye, *Mémoire sur le Canada.*

[4] Avaugour, *Mémoire,* 4 *Août,* 1663.

ter Colbert to the Marquis de Tracy, "and you must have known his talents, as well as his *bizarre* and somewhat impracticable temper." On landing, he would have no reception, being, as Father Lalemant observes, "an enemy of all ceremony." He went, however, to see the Jesuits, and "took a morsel of food in our refectory."[1] Laval was prepared to receive him with all solemnity at the Church; but the governor would not go. He soon set out on a tour of observation as far as Montreal, whence he returned delighted with the country, and immediately wrote to Colbert in high praise of it, observing that the St. Lawrence was the most beautiful river he had ever seen.[2]

It was clear from the first that, while he had a prepossession against the bishop, he wished to be on good terms with the Jesuits. He began by placing some of them on the council; but they and Laval were too closely united; and if Avaugour thought to separate them, he signally failed. A few months only had elapsed when we find it noted in Father Lalemant's private journal that the governor had dissolved the council and appointed a new one, and that other "changes and troubles" had befallen. The inevitable quarrel had broken out; it was a complex one, but the chief occasion of dispute was fortunate for the ecclesiastics, since it placed them, to a certain degree, morally in the right.

[1] Lalemant, *Journal des Jésuites, Septembre,* 1661.
[2] *Lettre d'Avaugour au Ministre,* 1661.

The question at issue was not new. It had agitated the colony for years, and had been the spring
of some of Argenson's many troubles. Nor did it
cease with Avaugour, for we shall trace its course
hereafter, tumultuous as a tornado. It was simply
the temperance question, — not as regards the
colonists, though here, too, there was great room for
reform, but as regards the Indians.

Their inordinate passion for brandy had long been
the source of excessive disorders. They drank
expressly to get drunk, and when drunk they were
like wild beasts. Crime and violence of all sorts
ensued; the priests saw their teachings despised and
their flocks ruined. On the other hand, the sale of
brandy was a chief source of profit, direct or indirect,
to all those interested in the fur-trade, including the
principal persons of the colony.   In Argenson's time,
Laval launched an excommunication against those
engaged in the abhorred traffic; for nothing less
than total prohibition would content the clerical
party, and besides the spiritual penalty, they demanded
the punishment of death against the contumacious
offender. Death, in fact, was decreed. Such was
the posture of affairs when Avaugour arrived; and,
willing as he was to conciliate the Jesuits, he permitted the decree to take effect, although, it seems,
with great repugnance. A few weeks after his
arrival, two men were shot and one whipped, for
selling brandy to Indians.[1] An extreme though

[1] *Journal des Jésuites, Octobre,* 1661.

partially suppressed excitement shook the entire settlement; for most of the colonists were, in one degree or another, implicated in the offence thus punished. An explosion soon followed; and the occasion of it was the humanity or good-nature of the Jesuit Lalemant.

A woman had been condemned to imprisonment for the same cause, and Lalemant, moved by compassion, came to the governor to intercede for her. Avaugour could no longer contain himself, and answered the reverend petitioner with characteristic bluntness. "You and your brethren were the first to cry out against the trade, and now you want to save the traders from punishment. I will no longer be the sport of your contradictions. Since it is not a crime for this woman, it shall not be a crime for anybody." [1] And in this posture he stood fast, with an inflexible stubbornness.

Henceforth there was full license to liquor-dealers. A violent reaction ensued against the past restriction, and brandy flowed freely among French and Indians alike. The ungodly drank to spite the priests and revenge themselves for the "constraint of consciences," of which they loudly complained. The utmost confusion followed, and the principles on which the pious colony was built seemed upheaved from the foundation. Laval was distracted with grief and anger. He outpoured himself from the pulpit in threats of divine wrath, and launched fresh excommunications

[1] La Tour, *Vie de Laval*, liv. v.

against the offenders; but such was the popular fury
that he was forced to yield and revoke them.[1]

Disorder grew from bad to worse. "Men gave
no heed to bishop, preacher, or confessor," writes
Father Charlevoix. "The French have despised the
remonstrances of our prelate, because they are supported by the civil power," says the superior of the
Ursulines. "He is almost dead with grief, and
pines away before our eyes."

Laval could bear it no longer, but sailed for
France, to lay his complaints before the court, and
urge the removal of Avaugour. He had, besides,
two other important objects, as will appear hereafter.
His absence brought no improvement. Summer and
autumn passed, and the commotion did not abate.
Winter was drawing to a close, when, at length,
outraged Heaven interposed an awful warning to the
guilty colony.

Scarcely had the bishop left his flock when the
skies grew portentous with signs of the chastisement
to come. "We beheld," gravely writes Father
Lalemant, "blazing serpents which flew through the
air, borne on wings of fire. We beheld above Quebec
a great globe of flame, which lighted up the night,
and threw out sparks on all sides. This same meteor
appeared above Montreal, where it seemed to issue

---

[1] *Journal des Jésuites, Février*, 1662. The sentence of excommunication is printed in the Appendix to the *Esquisse de la Vie de
Laval*. It bears date February 24. It was on this very day that
he was forced to revoke it.

from the bosom of the moon, with a noise as loud as cannon or thunder; and after sailing three leagues through the air, it disappeared behind the mountain whereof this island bears the name." [1]

Still greater marvels followed. First, a Christian Algonquin squaw, described as "innocent, simple, and sincere," being seated erect in bed, wide awake, by the side of her husband, in the night between the fourth and fifth of February, distinctly heard a voice saying, "Strange things will happen to-day; the earth will quake!" In great alarm she whispered the prodigy to her husband, who told her that she lied. This silenced her for a time; but when, the next morning, she went into the forest with her hatchet to cut a fagot of wood, the same dread voice resounded through the solitude, and sent her back in terror to her hut. [2]

These things were as nothing compared with the marvel that befell a nun of the hospital, Mother Catherine de Saint-Augustin, who died five years later, in the odor of sanctity. On the night of the fourth of February, 1663, she beheld in the spirit four furious demons at the four corners of Quebec, shaking it with a violence which plainly showed their purpose of reducing it to ruins; "and this they would have done," says the story, "if a personage of admirable beauty and ravishing majesty [Christ], whom she saw in the midst of them, and who from

[1] Lalemant, *Relation*, 1663, 2.
[2] *Ibid.*, 1663, 6.

time to time gave rein to their fury, had not restrained them when they were on the point of accomplishing their wicked design." She also heard the conversation of these demons, to the effect that people were now well frightened, and many would be converted; but this would not last long, and they, the demons, would have them in time. "Let us keep on shaking," they cried, encouraging one another, "and do our best to upset everything." [1]

Now, to pass from visions to facts: "At half-past five o'clock on the morning of the fifth," writes Father Lalemant, "a great roaring sound was heard at the same time through the whole extent of Canada. This sound, which produced an effect as if the houses were on fire, brought everybody out of doors; but instead of seeing smoke and flame, they were amazed to behold the walls shaking, and all the stones moving as if they would drop from their places. The houses seemed to bend first to one side and then to the other. Bells sounded of themselves; beams, joists, and planks cracked; the ground heaved, making the pickets of the palisades dance in a way that would have seemed incredible had we not seen it in divers places.

"Everybody was in the streets; animals ran wildly about; children cried; men and women, seized with

---

[1] Ragueneau, *Vie de Catherine de St. Augustin*, liv. iv. chap. i. The same story is told by Juchereau, Lalemant, and Marie de l'Incarnation, to whom Charlevoix erroneously ascribes the vision, as does also the Abbé La Tour.

fright, knew not where to take refuge, expecting every moment to be buried under the ruins of the houses, or swallowed up in some abyss opening under their feet. Some, on their knees in the snow, cried for mercy, and others passed the night in prayer; for the earthquake continued without ceasing, with a motion much like that of a ship at sea, insomuch that sundry persons felt the same qualms of stomach which they would feel on the water. In the forests the commotion was far greater. The trees struck one against the other as if there were a battle between them; and you would have said that not only their branches, but even their trunks, started out of their places and leaped on one another with such noise and confusion that the Indians said that the whole forest was drunk."

Mary of the Incarnation gives a similar account, as does also Frances Juchereau de Saint-Ignace; and these contemporary records are sustained to some extent by the evidence of geology.[1] A remarkable effect was produced on the St. Lawrence, which was so charged with mud and clay that for many weeks the water was unfit to drink. Considerable hills and large tracts of forest slid from their places, some into

[1] Professor Sterry Hunt, whose intimate knowledge of Canadian geology is well known, tells me that the shores of the St. Lawrence are to a great extent formed of beds of gravel and clay resting on inclined strata of rock, so that earth-slides would be the necessary result of any convulsion like that of 1663. He adds that the evidence that such slides have taken place on a great scale is very distinct at various points along the river, especially at Les Eboulemens, on the north shore.

the river, and some into adjacent valleys. A number of men in a boat near Tadoussac stared aghast at a large hill covered with trees, which sank into the water before their eyes; streams were turned from their courses; water-falls were levelled; springs were dried up in some places, while in others new springs appeared. Nevertheless, the accounts that have come down to us seem a little exaggerated, and sometimes ludicrously so; as when, for example, Mother Mary of the Incarnation tells us of a man who ran all night to escape from a fissure in the earth which opened behind him and chased him as he fled.

It is perhaps needless to say that "spectres and phantoms of fire, bearing torches in their hands," took part in the convulsion. "The fiery figure of a man vomiting flames" also appeared in the air, with many other apparitions too numerous to mention. It is recorded that three young men were on their way through the forest to sell brandy to the Indians, when one of them, a little in advance of the rest, was met by a hideous spectre which nearly killed him with fright. He had scarcely strength enough to rejoin his companions, who, seeing his terror, began to laugh at him. One of them, however, presently came to his senses, and said: "This is no laughing matter; we are going to sell liquor to the Indians against the prohibitions of the Church, and perhaps God means to punish our disobedience." On this they all turned back. That night they had scarcely lain down to sleep when the earthquake roused

them, and they ran out of their hut just in time to
escape being swallowed up along with it.[1]

With every allowance, it is clear that the convulsion must have been a severe one, and it is remarkable that in all Canada not a life was lost. The
writers of the day see in this a proof that God meant
to reclaim the guilty and not destroy them. At
Quebec there was for the time an intense revival of
religion. The end of the world was thought to be
at hand, and everybody made ready for the last judgment. Repentant throngs beset confessionals and
altars; enemies were reconciled; fasts, prayers, and
penances filled the whole season of Lent. Yet, as
we shall see, the Devil could still find wherewith to
console himself.

It was midsummer before the shocks wholly ceased
and the earth resumed her wonted calm. An extreme
drought was followed by floods of rain, and then
Nature began her sure work of reparation. It was
about this time that the thorn which had plagued the
Church was at length plucked out. Avaugour was
summoned home. He took his recall with magna-
nimity, and on his way wrote at Gaspé a memorial to
Colbert, in which he commends New France to the
attention of the King. "The St. Lawrence," he
says, "is the entrance to what may be made the

---

[1] Marie de l'Incarnation, *Lettre du* 20 *Août*, 1663. It appears
from Morton, Josselyn, and other writers, that the earthquake
extended to New England and New Netherlands, producing similar
effects on the imagination of the people.

greatest state in the world;" and, in his purely military way, he recounts the means of realizing this grand possibility. Three thousand soldiers should be sent to the colony, to be discharged and turned into settlers after three years of service. During these three years they may make Quebec an impregnable fortress, subdue the Iroquois, build a strong fort on the river where the Dutch have a miserable wooden redoubt, called Fort Orange (Albany), and finally open a way by that river to the sea. Thus the heretics will be driven out, and the King will be master of America, at a total cost of about four hundred thousand francs yearly for ten years. He closes his memorial by a short allusion to the charges against him, and to his forty years of faithful service; and concludes, speaking of the authors of his recall, Laval and the Jesuits: "By reason of the respect I owe their cloth, I will rest content, Monseigneur, with assuring you that I have not only served the King with fidelity, but also, by the grace of God, with very good success, considering the means at my disposal."[1] He had, in truth, borne himself as a brave and experienced soldier; and he soon after died a soldier's death, while defending the fortress of Zrin, in Croatia, against the Turks.[2]

---

[1] Avaugour, *Mémoire, Gaspé,* 4 *Août,* 1663.

[2] *Lettre de Colbert au Marquis de Tracy,* 1664. *Mémoire du Roy, pour servir d'instruction au Sieur Talon.*

CHAPTER X.

1661–1664.

LAVAL AND DUMESNIL.

Péronne Dumesnil. — The Old Council. — Alleged Murder. — The New Council. — Bourdon and Villeray. — Strong Measures. — Escape of Dumesnil. — Views of Colbert.

Though the proposals of Avaugour's memorial were not adopted, it seems to have produced a strong impression at court. For this impression the minds of the King and his minister had already been prepared. Two years before, the inhabitants of Canada had sent one of their number, Pierre Boucher, to represent their many grievances and ask for aid.[1] Boucher had had an audience of the young King, who listened with interest to his statements; and when in the following year he returned to Quebec, he was accompanied by an officer named Dumont, who had under his command a hundred soldiers for the colony, and was commissioned to report its con-

---

[1] To promote the objects of his mission, Boucher wrote a little book, *Histoire Véritable et Naturelle des Mœurs et Productions du Pays de la Nouvelle France.* He dedicates it to Colbert.

dition and resources.[1] The movement seemed to betoken that the government was wakening at last from its long inaction.

Meanwhile the Company of New France, feudal lord of Canada, had also shown signs of returning life. Its whole history had been one of mishap, followed by discouragement and apathy; and it is difficult to say whether its ownership of Canada had been more hurtful to itself or to the colony. At the eleventh hour it sent out an agent invested with powers of controller-general, intendant, and supreme judge, to inquire into the state of its affairs. This agent, Péronne Dumesnil, arrived early in the autumn of 1660, and set himself with great vigor to his work. He was an advocate of the Parliament of Paris, an active, aggressive, and tenacious person, of a temper well fitted to rip up an old abuse or probe a delinquency to the bottom. His proceedings quickly raised a storm at Quebec.

It may be remembered that, many years before, the company had ceded its monopoly of the fur-trade to the inhabitants of the colony, in consideration of that annual payment in beaver-skins which had been so tardily and so rarely made. The direction of the trade had at that time been placed in the hands of a council composed of the governor, the superior of the Jesuits, and several other members. Various changes had since taken place, and the trade was

---

[1] A long journal of Dumont is printed anonymously in the *Relation* of 1663.

now controlled by another council, established without the consent of the company,[1] and composed of the principal persons in the colony. The members of this council, with certain prominent merchants in league with them, engrossed all the trade, so that the inhabitants at large profited nothing by the right which the company had ceded;[2] and as the councillors controlled not only the trade, but all the financial affairs of Canada, while the remoteness of their scene of operations made it difficult to supervise them, they were able, with little risk, to pursue their own profit, to the detriment both of the company and the colony. They and their allies formed a petty trading oligarchy, as pernicious to the prosperity of Canada as the Iroquois war itself.

The company, always anxious for its beaver-skins, made several attempts to control the proceedings of the councillors and call them to account, but with little success, till the vigorous Dumesnil undertook the task; when, to their wrath and consternation, they and their friends found themselves attacked by wholesale accusations of fraud and embezzlement. That these charges were exaggerated there can be little doubt; that they were unfounded is incredible, in view of the effect they produced.

The councillors refused to acknowledge Dumesnil's

---

[1] *Registres du Conseil du Roy; Reponse à la requeste presentée au Roy.*

[2] *Arrêt du Conseil d'État,* 7 *Mars,* 1657. Also *Papiers d'Argenson,* and *Extrait des Registres du Conseil d'État,* 15 *Mars,* 1656.

powers as controller, intendant, and judge, and declared his proceedings null. He retorted by charging them with usurpation. The excitement increased, and Dumesnil's life was threatened.

He had two sons in the colony. One of them, Péronne de Mazé, was secretary to Avaugour, then on his way up the St. Lawrence to assume the government. The other, Péronne des Touches, was with his father at Quebec. Towards the end of August this young man was attacked in the street in broad daylight, and received a kick which proved fatal. He was carried to his father's house, where he died on the twenty-ninth. Dumesnil charges four persons, all of whom were among those into whose affairs he had been prying, with having taken part in the outrage; but it is very uncertain who was the immediate cause of Des Touches's death. Dumesnil, himself the supreme judicial officer of the colony, made complaint to the judge in ordinary of the company; but he says that justice was refused, the complaint suppressed by authority, his allegations torn in pieces, and the whole affair hushed.[1]

At the time of the murder, Dumesnil was confined

---

[1] Dumesnil, *Mémoire*. Under date August 31 the *Journal des Jésuites* makes this brief and guarded mention of the affair: "Le fils de Mons. du Mesnil . . . fut enterré le mesme iour, tué d'vn coup de pié par N." Who is meant by N. it is difficult to say. The register of the parish church records the burial as follows:—

"L'an 1661. Le 30 Aoust a esté enterré au Cemetiere de Quebec Michel peronne dit Sr. des Touches fils de Mr. du Mesnil decedé le Jour precedent a sa Maison."

to his house by illness. An attempt was made to rouse the mob against him, by reports that he had come to the colony for the purpose of laying taxes; but he sent for some of the excited inhabitants, and succeeded in convincing them that he was their champion rather than their enemy. Some Indians in the neighborhood were also instigated to kill him, and he was forced to conciliate them by presents.

He soon renewed his attacks, and in his quality of intendant called on the councillors and their allies to render their accounts, and settle the long arrears of debt due to the company. They set his demands at naught. The war continued month after month. It is more than likely that when in the spring of 1662 Avaugour dissolved and reconstructed the council, his action had reference to these disputes; and it is clear that when in the following August Laval sailed for France, one of his objects was to restore the tranquillity which Dumesnil's proceedings had disturbed. There was great need; for, what with these proceedings and the quarrel about brandy, Quebec was a little hell of discord, the earthquake not having as yet frightened it into propriety.

The bishop's success at court was triumphant. Not only did he procure the removal of Avaugour, but he was invited to choose a new governor to replace him.[1] This was not all; for he succeeded in effecting a complete change in the government of the colony. The Company of New France was called

---

[1] La Tour, *Vie de Laval*, liv. v.

upon to resign its claims;[1] and by a royal edict of April, 1663, all power, legislative, judicial, and executive, was vested in a council composed of the governor whom Laval had chosen, of Laval himself, and of five councillors, an attorney-general, and a secretary, to be chosen by Laval and the governor jointly.[2] Bearing with them blank commissions to be filled with the names of the new functionaries, Laval and his governor sailed for Quebec, where they landed on the fifteenth of September. With them came one Gaudais-Dupont, a royal commissioner instructed to inquire into the state of the colony.

No sooner had they arrived than Laval and Mézy, the new governor, proceeded to construct the new council. Mézy knew nobody in the colony, and was, at this time, completely under Laval's influence. The nominations, therefore, were virtually made by the bishop alone, in whose hands, and not in those of the governor, the blank commissions had been placed.[3] Thus for the moment he had complete control of the government; that is to say, the Church was mistress of the civil power.

[1] See the deliberations and acts to this end in *Édits et Ordonnances concernant le Canada,* i. 30–32.

[2] *Édit de Création du Conseil Supérieur de Quebec.*

[3] *Commission actroyée au Sieur Gaudais. Mémoire pour servir d'Instruction au Sieur Gaudais.* A sequel to these instructions, marked "secret," shows that, notwithstanding Laval's extraordinary success in attaining his objects, he and the Jesuits were somewhat distrusted. Gaudais is directed to make, with great discretion and caution, careful inquiry into the bishop's conduct, and with equal secrecy to ascertain why the Jesuits had asked for Avaugour's recall.

Laval formed his council as follows: Jean Bourdon for attorney-general; Rouer de Villeray, Juchereau de la Ferté, Ruette d'Auteuil, Le Gardeur de Tilly, and Matthieu D'Amours for Councellors; and Peuvret de Mesnu for secretary. The royal commissioner, Gaudais, also took a prominent place at the board.[1] This functionary was on the point of marrying his niece to a son of Robert Giffard, who had a strong interest in suppressing Dumesnil's accusations.[2] Dumesnil had laid his statements before the commissioner, who quickly rejected them, and took part with the accused.

Of those appointed to the new council, their enemy Dumesnil says that they were "incapable persons;" and their associate Gaudais, in defending them against worse charges, declares that they were "unlettered, of little experience, and nearly all unable to deal with affairs of importance." This was, perhaps, unavoidable; for except among the ecclesiastics, education was then scarcely known in Canada. But if Laval may be excused for putting

[1] As substitute for the *intendant*, an officer who had been appointed but who had not arrived.

[2] Dumesnil here makes one of the few mistakes I have been able to detect in his long memorials. He says that the name of the niece of Gaudais was *Marie Nau*. It was, in fact, *Michelle-Thérèse Nau*, who married Joseph, son of Robert Giffard, on the 22d of October, 1663. Dumesnil had forgotten the bride's first name. The elder Giffard was surety for Repentigny, whom Dumesnil charged with liabilities to the company, amounting to 644,700 livres. Giffard was also father-in-law of Juchereau de la Ferté, one of the accused.

incompetent men in office, nothing can excuse him
for making men charged with gross public offences
the prosecutors and judges in their own cause; and
his course in doing so gives color to the assertion of
Dumesnil that he made up the council expressly to
shield the accused and smother the accusation.[1]

The two persons under the heaviest charges
received the two most important appointments, —
Bourdon, attorney-general; and Villeray, keeper of
the seals.   La Ferté was also one of the accused.[2]
Of Villeray, the governor Argenson had written in
1659: "Some of his qualities are good enough, but
confidence cannot be placed in him on account of his
instability."[3]   In the same year he had been ordered
to France, "to purge himself of sundry crimes where-

[1] Dumesnil goes further than this, for he plainly intimates that
the removing from power of the company, to whom the accused
were responsible, and the placing in power of a council formed of
the accused themselves, was a device contrived from the first by
Laval and the Jesuits to get their friends out of trouble.

[2] Bourdon is charged with not having accounted for an immense
quantity of beaver-skins which had passed through his hands
during twelve years or more, and which are valued at more than
300,000 livres.   Other charges are made against him in connection
with large sums borrowed in Lauson's time on account of the
colony.   In a memorial addressed to the King in council, Dumesnil
says that in 1662 Bourdon, according to his own accounts, had in
his hands 37,516 livres belonging to the company, which he still
retained.

Villeray's liabilities arose out of the unsettled accounts of his
father-in-law, Charles Sevestre, and are set down at more than
600,000 livres.   La Ferté's are of a smaller amount.   Others of the
council were indirectly involved in the charges.

[3] *Lettre d'Argenson*, 20 *Nov.*, 1659.

with he stands charged."[1] He was not yet free of
suspicion, having returned to Canada under an order
to make up and render his accounts, which he had
not yet done. Dumesnil says that he first came to
the colony in 1651, as valet of the governor Lauson,
who had taken him from the jail at Rochelle, where
he was imprisoned for a debt of seventy-one francs,
"as appears by the record of the jail of date July
eleventh in that year." From this modest beginning
he became in time the richest man in Canada.[2] He
was strong in orthodoxy, and an ardent supporter of
the bishop and the Jesuits. He is alternately praised
and blamed, according to the partisan leanings of the
writer.

Bourdon, though of humble origin, was, perhaps,
the most intelligent man in the council. He was
chiefly known as an engineer, but he had also been a
baker, a painter, a syndic of the inhabitants, chief
gunner at the fort, and collector of customs for the
company. Whether guilty of embezzlement or not,
he was a zealous devotee, and would probably have
died for his creed. Like Villeray, he was one of
Laval's stanchest supporters, while the rest of the
council were also sound in doctrine and sure in
allegiance.

In virtue of their new dignity, the accused now
claimed exemption from accountability; but this was
not all. The abandonment of Canada by the com-

---

[1] *Édit du Roy*, 13 *Mai*, 1659.
[2] *Lettre de Colbert à Frontenac*, 17 *Mai*, 1674.

pany, in leaving Dumesnil without support, and depriving him of official character, had made his charges far less dangerous. Nevertheless, it was thought best to suppress them altogether, and the first act of the new government was to this end.

On the twentieth of September, the second day after the establishment of the council, Bourdon, in his character of attorney-general, rose and demanded that the papers of Jean Péronne Dumesnil should be seized and sequestered. The council consented; and, to complete the scandal, Villeray was commissioned to make the seizure in the presence of Bourdon. To color the proceeding, it was alleged that Dumesnil had obtained certain papers unlawfully from the *greffe*, or record office. "As he was thought," says Gaudais, "to be a violent man," Bourdon and Villeray took with them ten soldiers, well armed, together with a locksmith and the secretary of the council. Thus prepared for every contingency, they set out on their errand, and appeared suddenly at Dumesnil's house between seven and eight o'clock in the evening. "The aforesaid Sieur Dumesnil," further says Gaudais, "did not refute the opinion entertained of his violence; for he made a great noise, shouted *robbers!* and tried to rouse the neighborhood, outrageously abusing the aforesaid Sieur de Villeray and the attorney-general, in great contempt of the authority of the council, which he even refused to recognize."

They tried to silence him by threats, but without

effect; upon which they seized him and held him fast in a chair,— "me," writes the wrathful Dumesnil, "who had lately been their judge." The soldiers stood over him and stopped his mouth, while the others broke open and ransacked his cabinet, drawers, and chest, from which they took all his papers, refusing to give him an inventory, or to permit any witness to enter the house. Some of these papers were private; among the rest were, he says, the charges and specifications, nearly finished, for the trial of Bourdon and Villeray, together with the proofs of their "peculations, extortions, and malversations." The papers were enclosed under seal, and deposited in a neighboring house, whence they were afterwards removed to the council-chamber, and Dumesnil never saw them again. It may well be believed that this, the inaugural act of the new council, was not allowed to appear on its records.[1]

On the twenty-first, Villeray made a formal report of the seizure to his colleagues; upon which, "by reason of the insults, violences, and irreverences therein set forth against the aforesaid Sieur de Villeray, commissioner, as also against the authority of the council," it was ordered that the offending Dumesnil should be put under arrest; but Gaudais, as he declares, prevented the order from being carried into effect.

[1] The above is drawn from the two memorials of Gaudais and of Dumesnil. They do not contradict each other as to the essential facts.

Dumesnil, who says that during the scene at his house he had expected to be murdered like his son, now, though unsupported and alone, returned to the attack, demanded his papers, and was so loud in threats of complaint to the King that the council were seriously alarmed. They again decreed his arrest and imprisonment, but resolved to keep the decree secret till the morning of the day when the last of the returning ships was to sail for France. In this ship Dumesnil had taken his passage, and they proposed to arrest him unexpectedly on the point of embarkation, that he might have no time to prepare and despatch a memorial to the court. Thus a full year must elapse before his complaints could reach the minister, and seven or eight months more before a reply could be returned to Canada. During this long delay the affair would have time to cool. Dumesnil received a secret warning of this plan, and accordingly went on board another vessel, which was to sail immediately. The council caused the six cannon of the battery in the Lower Town to be pointed at her, and threatened to sink her if she left the harbor; but she disregarded them, and proceeded on her way.

On reaching France, Dumesnil contrived to draw the attention of the minister Colbert to his accusations, and to the treatment they had brought upon him. On this Colbert demanded of Gaudais, who had also returned in one of the autumn ships, why he had not reported these matters to him. Gaudais made a lame attempt to explain his silence, gave his statement of the seizure of the papers, answered in vague terms some of Dumesnil's charges against the Canadian financiers, and said that he had nothing to do with the rest. In the following spring Colbert wrote as follows to his relative Terron, intendant of marine: —

"I do not know what report M. Gaudais has made to you, but family interests and the connections which he has at Quebec should cause him to be a little distrusted. On his arrival in that country, having constituted himself chief of the council, he despoiled an agent of the Company of Canada of all his papers, in a manner very violent and extraordinary; and this proceeding leaves no doubt whatever that these papers contained matters the knowledge of which it was wished absolutely to suppress. I think it will be very proper that you should be informed of the statements made by this agent, in order that, through him, an exact knowledge may be acquired of everything that has taken place in the management of affairs." [1]

Whether Terron pursued the inquiry does not appear. Meanwhile new quarrels had arisen at

---

[1] *Lettre de Colbert à Terron Rochelle,* 8 *Fév.,* 1664. "Il a spolié un agent de la Compagnie de Canada de tous ses papiers d'une manière fort violente et extraordinaire, et ce procédé ne laisse point à douter que dans ces papiers il n'y eût des choses dont on a voulu absolument supprimer la connaissance." Colbert seems to have received an exaggerated impression of the part borne by Gaudais in the seizure of the papers.

Quebec, and the questions of the past were obscured in the dust of fresh commotions. Nothing is more noticeable in the whole history of Canada, after it came under the direct control of the Crown, than the helpless manner in which this absolute government was forced to overlook and ignore the disobedience and rascality of its functionaries in this distant transatlantic dependency.

As regards Dumesnil's charges, the truth seems to be, that the financial managers of the colony, being ignorant and unpractised, had kept imperfect and confused accounts, which they themselves could not always unravel; and that some, if not all of them, had made illicit profits under cover of this confusion. That their stealings approached the enormous sum at which Dumesnil places them is not to be believed. But, even on the grossly improbable assumption of their entire innocence, there can be no apology for the means, subversive of all justice, by which Laval enabled his partisans and supporters to extricate themselves from embarrassment.

NOTE. — Dumesnil's principal memorial, preserved in the archives of the Marine and Colonies, is entitled *Mémoire concernant les Affaires du Canada, qui montre et fait voir que sous prétexte de la Gloire de Dieu, d'Instruction des Sauvages, de servir le Roy et de faire la nouvelle Colonie, il a été pris et diverti trois millions de livres ou environ.* It forms in the copy before me thirty-eight pages of manuscript, and bears no address, but seems meant for Colbert, or the council of state. There is a second memorial, which is little else than an abridgment of the first. A third, bearing the address *Au Roy et à nos Seigneurs du Conseil (d'État),* and signed *Péronne Dumesnil,* is a petition for the payment of 10,132 livres due to him by the company for his services in Canada, "ou il a perdu son fils assassiné par les comptables du dit pays, qui n'ont voulu rendre compte au dit suppliant, Intendant, et ont pillé sa maison, ses meubles et papiers le 20 du mois de Septembre dernier, dont il y a acte."

Gaudais, in compliance with the demands of Colbert, gives his statement in a long memorial, *Le Sieur Gaudais Dupont à Monseigneur de Colbert*, 1664.

Dumesnil, in his principal memorial, gives a list of the alleged defaulters, with the special charges against each, and the amounts for which he reckons them liable. The accusations cover a period of ten or twelve years, and sometimes more. Some of them are curiously suggestive of more recent "rings." Thus Jean Gloria makes a charge of thirty-one hundred livres (francs) for fireworks to celebrate the King's marriage, when the actual cost is said to have been about forty livres. Others are alleged to have embezzled the funds of the company, under cover of pretended payments to imaginary creditors; and Argenson himself is said to have eked out his miserable salary by drawing on the company for the pay of soldiers who did not exist.

The records of the Council preserve a guarded silence about this affair. I find, however, under date 20 Sept., 1663, "Pouvoir à M. de Villeray de faire recherche dans la maison *d'un nommé du Mesnil* des papiers appartenans au Conseil concernant Sa Majesté;" and under date 18 March, 1664, "Ordre pour l'ouverture du coffre contenant les papiers de Dumesnil," and also an "Ordre pour mettre l'Inventaire des biens du Sr. Dumesnil entre les mains du Sr. Fillion."

CHAPTER XI.

1657–1665.

LAVAL AND MÉZY.

The Bishop's Choice. — A Military Zealot. — Hopeful Beginnings. — Signs of Storm. — The Quarrel. — Distress of Mézy:
he Refuses to Yield; his Defeat and Death.

WE have seen that Laval, when at court, had
been invited to choose a governor to his liking. He
soon made his selection. There was a pious officer,
Saffray de Mézy, major of the town and citadel of
Caen, whom he had well known during his long
stay with Bernières at the Hermitage. Mézy was the
principal member of the company of devotees formed
at Caen under the influence of Bernières and his
disciples. In his youth he had been headstrong and
dissolute. Worse still, he had been, it is said, a
Huguenot; but both in life and doctrine his conversion had been complete, and the fervid mysticism of
Bernières acting on his vehement nature had transformed him into a red-hot zealot. Towards the
hermits and their chief he showed a docility in
strange contrast with his past history, and followed

their inspirations with an ardor which sometimes overleaped its mark.

Thus a Jacobin monk, a doctor of divinity, once came to preach at the church of St. Paul at Caen; on which, according to their custom, the brotherhood of the Hermitage sent two persons to make report concerning his orthodoxy. Mézy and another military zealot, "who," says the narrator, "hardly know how to read, and assuredly do not know their catechism," were deputed to hear his first sermon; wherein this Jacobin, having spoken of the necessity of the grace of Jesus Christ in order to the doing of good deeds, these two wiseacres thought that he was preaching Jansenism; and thereupon, after the sermon, the Sieur de Mézy went to the proctor of the ecclesiastical court and denounced him."[1]

His zeal, though but moderately tempered with knowledge, sometimes proved more useful than on this occasion. The Jacobin convent at Caen was divided against itself. Some of the monks had embraced the doctrines taught by Bernières, while the rest held dogmas which he declared to be contrary to those of the Jesuits, and therefore heterodox. A prior was to be elected, and with the help of Bernières his partisans gained the victory, choosing one Father Louis, through whom the Hermitage gained a complete control in the convent. But the adverse party presently resisted, and com-

---

[1] Nicole, *Mémoire pour faire connoistre l'esprit et la conduite de la Compagnie appellée l'Hermitage.*

plained to the provincial of their order, who came to
Caen to close the dispute by deposing Father Louis.
Hearing of his approach, Bernières asked aid from
his military disciple, and De Mézy sent him a squad
of soldiers, who guarded the convent doors and barred
out the provincial.[1]

Among the merits of Mézy, his humility and
charity were especially admired; and the people of
Caen had more than once seen the town major stag-
gering across the street with a beggar mounted on
his back, whom he was bearing dry-shod through the
mud in the exercise of those virtues.[2] In this he
imitated his master Bernières, of whom similar acts
are recorded.[3] However dramatic in manifestation,
his devotion was not only sincere but intense. Laval
imagined that he knew him well. Above all others,
Mézy was the man of his choice; and so eagerly did
he plead for him that the King himself paid certain
debts which the pious major had contracted, and
thus left him free to sail for Canada.

His deportment on the voyage was edifying, and
the first days of his accession were passed in harmony.
He permitted Laval to form the new council, and
supplied the soldiers for the seizure of Dumesnil's
papers. A question arose concerning Montreal, a
subject on which the governors and the bishop rarely

[1] Nicole, *Mémoire pour faire connoistre l'esprit et la conduite de la
Compagnie appellée l'Hermitage.*

[2] Juchereau, *Histoire de l'Hôtel-Dieu,* 149.

[3] See the laudatory notice of Bernières de Louvigny in the
Nouvelle Biographie Universelle.

differed in opinion. The present instance was no
exception to the rule. Mézy removed Maisonneuve,
the local governor, and immediately replaced him, —
the effect being, that whereas he had before derived
his authority from the seigniors of the island, he now
derived it from the governor-general. It was a
movement in the interest of centralized power, and
as such was cordially approved by Laval.

The first indication to the bishop and the Jesuits
that the new governor was not likely to prove in
their hands as clay in the hands of the potter, is said
to have been given on occasion of an interview with
an embassy of Iroquois chiefs, to whom Mézy, aware
of their duplicity, spoke with a decision and haughtiness that awed the savages and astonished the ecclesiastics. He seems to have been one of those natures
that run with an engrossing vehemence along any
channel into which they may have been turned. At
the Hermitage he was all devotee; but climate and
conditions had changed, and he or his symptoms
changed with them. He found himself raised suddenly to a post of command, or one which was meant
to be such. The town major of Caen was set to rule
over a region far larger than France. The royal
authority was trusted to his keeping, and his honor
and duty forbade him to break the trust. But when
he found that those who had procured for him his
new dignities had done so that he might be an instrument of their will, his ancient pride started again
into life, and his headstrong temper broke out like a

long-smothered fire. Laval stood aghast at the transformation. His lamb had turned wolf.

What especially stirred the governor's dudgeon was the conduct of Bourdon, Villeray, and Auteuil, those faithful allies whom Laval had placed on the council, and who, as Mézy soon found, were wholly in the bishop's interest. On the thirteenth of February he sent his friend Angoville, major of the fort, to Laval, with a written declaration to the effect that he had ordered them to absent themselves from the council, because, having been appointed "on the persuasion of the aforesaid Bishop of Petræa, who knew them to be wholly his creatures, they wish to make themselves masters in the aforesaid council, and have acted in divers ways against the interests of the King and the public for the promotion of personal and private ends, and have formed and fomented cabals, contrary to their duty and their oath of fidelity to his aforesaid Majesty."[1] He further declares that advantage had been taken of the facility of his disposition and his ignorance of the country to surprise him into assenting to their nomination; and he asks the bishop to acquiesce in their expulsion, and join him in calling an assembly of the people to choose others in their place. Laval refused; on which Mézy caused his declaration to be placarded about Quebec and proclaimed by sound of drum.

[1] *Ordre de M. de Mézy de faire sommation à l'Evêque de Petrée,* 13 *Fév.,* 1664. *Notification du dit Ordre, même date.* (Registre du Conseil Supérieur.)

The proposal of a public election, contrary as it was to the spirit of the government, opposed to the edict establishing the council, and utterly odious to the young autocrat who ruled over France, gave Laval a great advantage. "I reply," he wrote, "to the request which Monsieur the Governor makes me to consent to the interdiction of the persons named in his declaration, and proceed to the choice of other councillors or officers by an assembly of the people, that neither my conscience nor my honor, nor the respect and obedience which I owe to the will and commands of the King, nor my fidelity and affection to his service, will by any means permit me to do so." [1]

Mézy was dealing with an adversary armed with redoubtable weapons. It was intimated to him that the sacraments would be refused, and the churches closed against him. This threw him into an agony of doubt and perturbation; for the emotional religion which had become a part of his nature, though overborne by gusts of passionate irritation, was still full of life within him. Tossing between the old feeling and the new, he took a course which reveals the trouble and confusion of his mind. He threw himself for counsel and comfort on the Jesuits, though he knew them to be one with Laval against him, and though, under cover of denouncing sin in general, they had lashed him sharply in their sermons. There is something pathetic in the appeal

[1] *Réponse de l'Évêque de Petrée*, 16 *Fév.*, 1664.

14

he makes to them. For the glory of God and the service of the King, he had come, he says, on Laval's solicitation, to seek salvation in Canada; and being under obligation to the bishop, who had recommended him to the King, he felt bound to show proofs of his gratitude on every occasion. Yet neither gratitude to a benefactor nor the respect due to his character and person should be permitted to interfere with duty to the King, "since neither conscience nor honor permit us to neglect the requirements of our office and betray the interests of his Majesty, after receiving orders from his lips, and making oath of fidelity between his hands." He proceeds to say that, having discovered practices of which he felt obliged to prevent the continuance, he had made a declaration expelling the offenders from office; that the bishop and all the ecclesiastics had taken this declaration as an offence; that, regardless of the King's service, they had denounced him as a calumniator, an unjust judge, without gratitude, and perverted in conscience; and that one of the chief among them had come to warn him that the sacraments would be refused and the churches closed against him. "This," writes the unhappy governor, "has agitated our soul with scruples; and we have none from whom to seek light save those who are our declared opponents, pronouncing judgment on us without knowledge of cause. Yet as our salvation and the duty we owe the King are the things most important to us on earth, and as we hold them to be

inseparable the one from the other; and as nothing
is so certain as death, and nothing so uncertain as
the hour thereof; and as there is no time to inform
his Majesty of what is passing and to receive his
commands; and as our soul, though conscious of
innocence, is always in fear, — we feel obliged, despite
their opposition, to have recourse to the reverend
father casuists of the House of Jesus, to tell us in
conscience what we can do for the fulfilment of our
duty at once to God and to the King." [1]

The Jesuits gave him little comfort. Lalemant,
their superior, replied by advising him to follow the
directions of his confessor, a Jesuit, so far as the
question concerned spiritual matters, adding that in
temporal matters he had no advice to give. [2] The
distinction was illusory. The quarrel turned wholly
on temporal matters, but it was a quarrel with a
bishop. To separate in such a case the spiritual
obligation from the temporal was beyond the skill of
Mézy, nor would the confessor have helped him.

Perplexed and troubled as he was, he would not
reinstate Bourdon and the two councillors. The
people began to clamor at the interruption of justice,
for which they blamed Laval, whom a recent impo-
sition of tithes had made unpopular. Mézy thereupon issued a proclamation, in which, after mentioning
his opponents as the most subtle and artful persons

[1] *Mézy aux PP. Jésuites, Fait au Château de Québec ce dernier
jour de Février*, 1664.

[2] *Lettre du P. H. Lalemant à Mr. le Gouverneur.*

in Canada, he declares that, in consequence of petitions sent him from Quebec and the neighboring settlements, he had called the people to the council-chamber, and by their advice had appointed the Sieur de Chartier as attorney-general in place of Bourdon.[1]

Bourdon replied by a violent appeal from the governor to the remaining members of the council;[2] on which Mézy declared him excluded from all public functions whatever, till the King's pleasure should be known.[3] Thus Church and State still frowned on each other, and new disputes soon arose to widen the breach between them. On the first establishment of the council, an order had been passed for the election of a mayor and two aldermen (*échevins*) for Quebec, which it was proposed to erect into a city, though it had only seventy houses and less than a thousand inhabitants. Repentigny was chosen mayor, and Madry and Charron aldermen; but the choice was not agreeable to the bishop, and the three functionaries declined to act, influence having probably been brought to bear on them to that end. The council now resolved that a mayor was needless, and the people were permitted to choose a syndic in his stead. These municipal elections were always so controlled by the authorities that the element of liberty which they seemed to represent was little but

[1] *Declaration du Sieur de Mézy*, 10 *Mars*, 1664.
[2] *Bourdon au Conseil*, 13 *Mars*, 1664.
[3] *Ordre du Gouverneur*, 13 *Mars*, 1664.

a mockery. On the present occasion, after an unac-
countable delay of ten months, twenty-two persons
cast their votes in presence of the council, and the
choice fell on Charron. The real question was
whether the new syndic should belong to the governor or to the bishop. Charron leaned to the
governor's party. The ecclesiastics insisted that the
people were dissatisfied, and a new election was
ordered, but the voters did not come. The governor
now sent messages to such of the inhabitants as he
knew to be in his interest, who gathered in the
council-chamber, voted under his eye, and again
chose a syndic agreeable to him. Laval's party
protested in vain.[1]

The councillors held office for a year, and the year
had now expired. The governor and the bishop, it
will be remembered, had a joint power of appointment; but agreement between them was impossible.
Laval was for replacing his partisans, Bourdon,
Villeray, Auteuil, and La Ferté. Mézy refused;
and on the eighteenth of September he reconstructed
the council by his sole authority, retaining of the
old councillors only Amours and Tilly, and replacing
the rest by Denis, La Tesserie, and Péronne de Mazé,
the surviving son of Dumesnil. Again Laval protested; but Mézy proclaimed his choice by sound of
drum, and caused placards to be posted, full, according to Father Lalemant, of abuse against the bishop.
On this he was excluded from confession and absolu-

[1] *Registre du Conseil Supérieur.*

tion. He complained loudly; "but our reply was," says the father, "that God knew everything."[1]

This unanswerable but somewhat irrelevant response failed to satisfy him, and it was possibly on this occasion that an incident occurred which is recounted by the bishop's eulogist, La Tour. He says that Mézy, with some unknown design, appeared before the church at the head of a band of soldiers, while Laval was saying mass. The service over, the bishop presented himself at the door, on which, to the governor's confusion, all the soldiers respectfully saluted him.[2] The story may have some foundation, but it is not supported by contemporary evidence.

On the Sunday after Mézy's *coup d'état*, the pulpits resounded with denunciations. The people listened, doubtless, with becoming respect; but their sympathies were with the governor; and he, on his part, had made appeals to them at more than one crisis of the quarrel. He now fell into another indiscretion. He banished Bourdon and Villeray, and ordered them home to France.

They carried with them the instruments of their revenge, — the accusations of Laval and the Jesuits against the author of their woes. Of these accusations one alone would have sufficed. Mézy had appealed to the people. It is true that he did so

[1] *Journal des Jésuites, Octobre,* 1664.

[2] La Tour, *Vie de Laval,* liv. vii. It is charitable to ascribe this writer's many errors to carelessness.

from no love of popular liberty, but simply to make head against an opponent; yet the act alone was enough, and he received a peremptory recall. Again Laval had triumphed. He had made one governor and unmade two, if not three. The modest Levite, as one of his biographers calls him in his earlier days, had become the foremost power in Canada.

Laval had a threefold strength at court, — his high birth, his reputed sanctity, and the support of the Jesuits. This was not all, for the permanency of his position in the colony gave him another advantage. The governors were named for three years, and could be recalled at any time; but the vicar apostolic owed his appointment to the Pope, and the Pope alone could revoke it. Thus he was beyond reach of the royal authority, and the court was in a certain sense obliged to conciliate him. As for Mézy, a man of no rank or influence, he could expect no mercy. Yet, though irritable and violent, he seems to have tried conscientiously to reconcile conflicting duties, or what he regarded as such. The governors and intendants, his successors, received, during many years, secret instructions from the court to watch Laval, and cautiously prevent him from assuming powers which did not belong to him. It is likely that similar instructions had been given to Mézy,[1]

[1] The royal commissioner, Gaudais, who came to Canada with Mézy, had, as before mentioned, orders to inquire with great secrecy into the conduct of Laval. The intendant, Talon, who followed immediately after, had similar instructions.

and that the attempt to fulfil them had aided to embroil him with one who was probably the last man on earth with whom he would willingly have quarrelled.

An inquiry was ordered into his conduct; but a voice more potent than the voice of the King had called him to another tribunal. A disease, the result perhaps of mental agitation, seized upon him and soon brought him to extremity. As he lay gasping between life and death, fear and horror took possession of his soul. Hell yawned before his fevered vision, peopled with phantoms which long and lonely meditations, after the discipline of Loyola, made real and palpable to his thought. He smelt the fumes of infernal brimstone, and heard the howlings of the damned. He saw the frown of the angry Judge, and the fiery swords of avenging angels, hurling wretches like himself, writhing in anguish and despair, into the gulf of unutterable woe. He listened to the ghostly counsellors who besieged his bed, bowed his head in penitence, made his peace with the Church, asked pardon of Laval, confessed to him, and received absolution at his hands; and his late adversaries, now benign and bland, soothed him with promises of pardon, and hopes of eternal bliss.

Before he died, he wrote to the Marquis de Tracy, newly appointed viceroy, a letter which indicates that even in his penitence he could not feel himself wholly in the wrong.[1] He also left a will in which the

[1] *Lettre de Mézy au Marquis de Tracy, 26 Avril,* 1665.

pathetic and the quaint are curiously mingled. After praying his patron, Saint Augustine, with Saint John, Saint Peter, and all the other saints, to intercede for the pardon of his sins, he directs that his body shall be buried in the cemetery of the poor at the hospital, as being unworthy of more honored sepulture. He then makes various legacies of piety and charity. Other bequests follow, — one of which is to his friend Major Angoville, to whom he leaves two hundred francs, his coat of English cloth, his camlet mantle, a pair of new shoes, eight shirts with sleeve-buttons, his sword and belt, and a new blanket for the major's servant. Felix Aubert is to have fifty francs, with a gray jacket, a small coat of gray serge, "which," says the testator, "has been worn for a while," and a pair of long white stockings. And in a codicil he further leaves to Angoville his best black coat, in order that he may wear mourning for him.[1]

His earthly troubles closed on the night of the sixth of May. He went to his rest among the paupers; and the priests, serenely triumphant, sang requiems over his grave.

NOTE. — Mézy sent home charges against the bishop and the Jesuits which seem to have existed in Charlevoix's time, but for which, as well as for those made by Laval, I have sought in vain.

The substance of these mutual accusations is given thus by the minister Colbert, in a memorial addressed to the Marquis de Tracy, in 1665: " Les Jésuites l'accusent d'avarice et de violences; et lui

---

[1] *Testament du Sieur de Mézy.* This will, as well as the letter, is engrossed in the registers of the council.

qu'ils voulaient entreprendre sur l'autorité qui lui a été commise par le Roy, en sorte que n'ayant que de leurs créatures dans le Conseil Souverain, toutes les résolutions s'y prenaient selon leurs sentiments."

The papers cited are drawn partly from the *Registres du Conseil Supérieur*, still preserved at Quebec, and partly from the Archives of the Marine and Colonies. Laval's admirer, the Abbé La Tour, in his eagerness to justify the bishop, says that the quarrel arose from a dispute about precedence between Mézy and the intendant, and from the ill-humor of the governor because the intendant shared the profits of his office. The truth is, that there was no intendant in Canada during the term of Mézy's government. One Robert had been appointed to the office, but he never came to the colony. The commissioner Gaudais, during the two or three months of his stay at Quebec, took the intendant's place at the council-board; but harmony between Laval and Mézy was unbroken till after his departure. Other writers say that the dispute arose from the old question about brandy. Towards the end of the quarrel there was some disorder from this source, but even then the brandy question was subordinate to other subjects of strife.

CHAPTER XII.

1662–1680.

LAVAL AND THE SEMINARY.

Laval's Visit to Court. — The Seminary. — Zeal of the Bishop: his Eulogists. — Church and State. — Attitude of Laval.

THAT memorable journey of Laval to court, which caused the dissolution of the Company of New France, the establishment of the Supreme Council, the recall of Avaugour, and the appointment of Mézy, had yet other objects and other results. Laval, vicar apostolic and titular Bishop of Petræa, wished to become in title, as in fact, Bishop of Quebec. Thus he would gain an increase of dignity and authority, necessary, as he thought, in his conflicts with the civil power; "for," he wrote to the cardinals of the Propaganda, "I have learned from long experience how little security my character of vicar apostolic gives me against those charged with political affairs: I mean the officers of the Crown, perpetual rivals and contemners of the authority of the Church." [1]

[1] For a long extract from this letter, copied from the original in the archives of the Propaganda at Rome, see Faillon, *Colonie Français*, iii. 432.

This reason was for the Pope and the cardinals. It may well be believed that he held a different language to the King. To him he urged that the bishopric was needed to enforce order, suppress sin, and crush heresy. Both Louis XIV. and the Queen Mother favored his wishes;[1] but difficulties arose, and interminable disputes ensued on the question whether the proposed bishopric should depend immediately on the Pope or on the Archbishop of Rouen. It was a revival of the old quarrel of Gallican and ultramontane. Laval, weary of hope deferred, at length declared that he would leave the colony if he could not be its bishop in title; and in 1674, after eleven years of delay, the King yielded to the Pope's demands, and the vicar apostolic became first Bishop of Quebec.

If Laval had to wait for his mitre, he found no delay and no difficulty in attaining another object no less dear to him. He wished to provide priests for Canada, drawn from the Canadian population, fed with sound and wholesome doctrine, reared under his eye, and moulded by his hand. To this end he proposed to establish a seminary at Quebec. The plan found favor with the pious King, and a decree signed by his hand sanctioned and confirmed it. The new seminary was to be a corporation of priests under a superior chosen by the bishop; and, besides

[1] *Anne d'Autriche à Laval,* 23 *Avril,* 1662; *Louis XIV. au Pape,* 28 *Jan.* 1664; *Louis XIV. au Duc de Créquy, Ambassadeur à Rome,* 28 *June,* 1664.

its functions of instruction, it was vested with distinct and extraordinary powers. Laval, an organizer
and a disciplinarian by nature and training, would
fain subject the priests of his diocese to a control as
complete as that of monks in a convent. In France,
the curé or parish priest was, with rare exceptions, a
fixture in his parish, whence he could be removed
only for grave reasons, and through prescribed forms
of procedure. Hence he was to a certain degree
independent of the bishop. Laval, on the contrary,
demanded that the Canadian curé should be removable at his will, and thus placed in the position of a
missionary, to come and go at the order of his
superior. In fact, the Canadian parishes were for a
long time so widely scattered, so feeble in population, and so miserably poor, that, besides the disciplin-
ary advantages of this plan, its adoption was at first
almost a matter of necessity. It added greatly to
the power of the Church; and, as the colony
increased, the King and the minister conceived an
increasing distrust of it. Instructions for the "fixa-
tion" of the curés were repeatedly sent to the colony,
and the bishop, while professing to obey, repeatedly
evaded them. Various fluctuations and changes
took place; but Laval had built on strong foundations, and at this day the system of removable curés
prevails in most of the Canadian parishes.[1]

---

[1] On the establishment of the seminary. *Mandement de l'Évêque
de Petrée, pour l'Établissement du Séminaire de Québec; Approbation
du Roy* (*Édits et Ordonnances*, i. 33, 35); La Tour, *Vie de Laval,* liv.

Thus he formed his clergy into a family with himself at its head. His seminary, the mother who had reared them, was further charged to maintain them, nurse them in sickness, and support them in old age. Under her maternal roof the tired priest found repose among his brethren; and thither every year he repaired from the charge of his flock in the wilderness, to freshen his devotion and animate his zeal by a season of meditation and prayer.

The difficult task remained to provide the necessary funds. Laval imposed a tithe of one-thirteenth on all products of the soil, or, as afterwards settled, on grains alone. This tithe was paid to the seminary, and by the seminary to the priests. The people, unused to such a burden, clamored and resisted; and Mézy, in his disputes with the bishop, had taken advantage of their discontent. It became necessary to reduce the tithe to a twenty-sixth, which, as there was little or no money among the inhabitants, was paid in kind. Nevertheless, the scattered and impoverished settlers grudged even this contribution to the support of a priest whom many of them rarely saw; and the collection of it became a matter of the greatest difficulty and uncertainty. How the King came to the rescue, we shall hereafter see.

Besides the great seminary where young men were trained for the priesthood, there was the lesser semi-

---

vi. ; *Esquisse de la Vie de Laval,* Appendix. Various papers bearing on the subject are printed in the Canadian *Abeille,* from originals in the archives of the seminary.

nary where boys were educated in the hope that they would one day take orders. This school began in 1668, with eight French and six Indian pupils, in the old house of Madame Couillard; but so far as the Indians were concerned it was a failure. Sooner or later they all ran wild in the woods, carrying with them as fruits of their studies a sufficiency of prayers, offices, and chants learned by rote, along with a feeble smattering of Latin and rhetoric, which they soon dropped by the way. There was also a sort of farm-school attached to the seminary, for the training of a humbler class of pupils. It was established at the parish of St. Joachim, below Quebec, where the children of artisans and peasants were taught farming and various mechanical arts, and thoroughly grounded in the doctrine and discipline of the Church.[1]   The Great and Lesser Seminary still subsist, and form one of the most important Roman Catholic institutions on this continent. To them has recently been added the Laval University, resting on the same foundation, and supported by the same funds.

Whence were these funds derived? Laval, in order to imitate the poverty of the apostles, had divested himself of his property before he came to Canada; otherwise there is little doubt that in the fulness of his zeal he would have devoted it to his

---

[1] *Annales du Petit Séminaire de Quebec,* see *Abeille,* vol. i.; *Notice Historique sur le Petit Séminaire de Quebec, Ibid.,* vol. ii.; *Notice Historique sur la Paroisse de St. Joachim, Ibid.,* vol. i. The *Abeille* is a journal published by the seminary.

favorite object. But if he had no property he had influence, and his family had both influence and wealth. He acquired vast grants of land in the best parts of Canada. Some of these he sold or exchanged; others he retained till the year 1680, when he gave them, with nearly all else that he then possessed, to his seminary at Quebec. The lands with which he thus endowed it included the seigniories of the Petite Nation, the Island of Jesus, and Beaupré. The last is of great extent, and at the present day of immense value. Beginning a few miles below Quebec, it borders the St. Lawrence for a distance of sixteen leagues, and is six leagues in depth, measured from the river. From these sources the seminary still draws an abundant revenue, though its seigniorial rights were commuted on the recent extinction of the feudal tenure in Canada.

Well did Laval deserve that his name should live in that of the university which a century and a half after his death owed its existence to his bounty. This father of the Canadian Church, who has left so deep an impress on one of the communities which form the vast population of North America, belonged to a type of character to which an even justice is rarely done. With the exception of the Canadian Garneau, a liberal Catholic, those who have treated of him have seen him through a medium intensely Romanist, coloring, hiding, and exaggerating by turns both his actions and the traits of his character. Tried by the Romanist standard, his merits were great; though the extraordinary influence which he exercised in the affairs of the colony were, as already observed, by no means due to his spiritual graces alone. To a saint sprung from the *haute noblesse*, Earth and Heaven were alike propitious. When the vicar-general Colombière pronounced his funeral eulogy in the sounding periods of Bossuet, he did not fail to exhibit him on the ancestral pedestal where his virtues would shine with redoubled lustre. "The exploits of the heroes of the House of Montmorency," exclaims the reverend orator, "form one of the fairest chapters in the annals of Old France; the heroic acts of charity, humility, and faith achieved by a Montmorency form one of the fairest in the annals of New France. The combats, victories, and conquests of the Montmorency in Europe would fill whole volumes; and so, too, would the triumphs won by a Montmorency in America over sin, passion, and the Devil." Then he crowns the high-born prelate with a halo of fourfold saintship: "It was with good reason that Providence permitted him to be called Francis, for the virtues of all the saints of that name were combined in him, — the zeal of Saint Francis Xavier, the charity of Saint Francis of Sales, the poverty of Saint Francis of Assisi, the self-mortification of Saint Francis Borgia; but poverty was the mistress of his heart, and he loved her with incontrollable transports."

The stories which Colombière proceeds to tell of Laval's asceticism are confirmed by other evidence,

15

and are, no doubt, true. Nor is there any reasonable doubt that, had the bishop stood in the place of Brébeuf or Charles Lalemant, he would have suffered torture and death like them. But it was his lot to strive, not against infidel savages, but against country-men and Catholics, who had no disposition to burn him, and would rather have done him reverence than wrong.

To comprehend his actions and motives, it is neces-sary to know his ideas in regard to the relations of Church and State. They were those of the extreme ultramontanes, which a recent Jesuit preacher has expressed with tolerable distinctness. In a sermon uttered in the Church of Notre Dame, at Montreal, on the first of November, 1872, he thus announced them: "The supremacy and infallibility of the Pope; the independence and liberty of the Church; *the subordination and submission of the State to the Church ;* in case of conflict between them, the Church to decide, the State to submit: for whoever follows and defends these principles, life and a bless-ing; for whoever rejects and combats them, death and a curse." [1]

These were the principles which Laval and the

[1] This sermon was preached by Father Braun, S. J., on occasion of the "Golden Wedding," or fiftieth anniversary of Bishop Bourget of Montreal. A large body of the Canadian clergy were present, some of whom thought his expressions too emphatic. A translation by another Jesuit is published in the "Montreal Weekly Herald" of Nov. 2, 1872; and the above extract is copied *verbatim.*

Jesuits strove to make good. Christ was to rule in Canada through his deputy the bishop, and God's law was to triumph over the laws of man. As in the halcyon days of Champlain and Montmagny, the governor was to be the right hand of the Church, to wield the earthly sword at her bidding; and the council was to be the agent of her high behests.

France was drifting toward the triumph of the *parti dévot*, the sinister reign of petticoat and cassock, the era of Maintenon and Tellier, and the fatal atrocities of the dragonnades. Yet the advancing tide of priestly domination did not flow smoothly. The unparalleled prestige which surrounded the throne of the young King, joined to his quarrels with the Pope and divisions in the Church itself, disturbed, though they could not check, its progress. In Canada it was otherwise. The colony had been ruled by priests from the beginning, and it only remained to continue in her future the law of her past. She was the fold of Christ; the wolf of civil government was among the flock, and Laval and the Jesuits, watchful shepherds, were doing their best to chain and muzzle him.

According to Argenson, Laval had said, " A bishop can do what he likes;" and his action answered reasonably well to his words. He thought himself above human law. In vindicating the assumed rights of the Church, he invaded the rights of others, and used means from which a healthy conscience would have shrunk. All his thoughts and sympathies had run from childhood in ecclesiastical channels, and he cared for nothing outside the Church. Prayer, meditation, and asceticism had leavened and moulded him. During four years he had been steeped in the mysticism of the Hermitage, which had for its aim the annihilation of self, and through self-annihilation the absorption into God.[1] He had passed from a life of visions to a life of action. Earnest to fanaticism, he saw but one great object, — the glory of God on earth. He was penetrated by the poisonous casuistry of the Jesuits, based on the assumption that all means are permitted when the end is the service of God; and as Laval, in his own opinion, was always doing the service of God, while his opponents were always doing that of the Devil, he enjoyed, in the use of means, a latitude of which we have seen him avail himself.

[1] See the maxims of Bernières published by La Tour.

SECTION THIRD.

THE COLONY AND THE KING.

———◆———

CHAPTER XIII.

1661–1665.

ROYAL INTERVENTION.

Fontainebleau. — Louis XIV. — Colbert. — The Company of the West. — Evil Omens. — Action of the King. — Tracy, Courcelle, and Talon. — The Regiment of Carignan-Salières. — Tracy at Quebec. — Miracles. — A Holy War.

Leave Canada behind; cross the sea, and stand, on an evening in June, by the edge of the forest of Fontainebleau. Beyond the broad gardens, above the long ranges of moonlit trees, rise the walls and pinnacles of the vast château, — a shrine of history, the gorgeous monument of lines of vanished kings, haunted with memories of Capet, Valois, and Bourbon.

There was little thought of the past at Fontainebleau in June, 1661. The present was too dazzling and too intoxicating; the future, too radiant with hope and promise. It was the morning of a new reign;

the sun of Louis XIV. was rising in splendor, and the rank and beauty of France were gathered to pay it homage. A youthful court, a youthful king; a pomp and magnificence such as Europe had never seen; a delirium of ambition, pleasure, and love, — all this wrought in many a young heart an enchantment destined to be cruelly broken. Even old courtiers felt the fascination of the scene, and tell us of the music at evening by the borders of the lake; of the gay groups that strolled under the shadowing trees, floated in gilded barges on the still water, or moved slowly in open carriages around its borders. Here was Anne of Austria, the King's mother, and Marie Thérèse, his tender and jealous queen; his brother, the Duke of Orleans, with his bride of sixteen, Henriette of England; and his favorite, that vicious butterfly of the court, the Count de Guiche. Here, too, were the humbled chiefs of the civil war, Beaufort and Condé, obsequious before their triumphant master. Louis XIV., the centre of all eyes, in the flush of health and vigor, and the pride of new-fledged royalty, stood, as he still stands on the canvas of Philippe de Champagne, attired in a splendor which would have been effeminate but for the stately port of the youth who wore it.[1]

Fortune had been strangely bountiful to Louis

---

[1] On the visit of the court at Fontainebleau in the summer of 1661, see *Mémoires de Madame de Motteville, Mémoires de Madame de La Fayette, Mémoires de l'Abbé de Choisy,* and Walckenaer's *Mémoires sur Madame de Sévigné.*

XIV. The nations of Europe, exhausted by wars and dissensions, looked upon him with respect and fear. Among weak and weary neighbors, he alone was strong. The death of Mazarin had released him from tutelage; feudalism in the person of Condé was abject before him; he had reduced his parliaments to submission; and in the arrest of the ambitious prodigal Fouquet, he was preparing a crushing blow to the financial corruption which had devoured France.

Nature had formed him to act the part of King. Even his critics and enemies praise the grace and majesty of his presence, and he impressed his courtiers with an admiration which seems to have been to an astonishing degree genuine. He carried airs of royalty even into his pleasures; and while his example corrupted all France, he proceeded to the apartments of Montespan or Fontanges with the majestic gravity of Olympian Jove. He was a devout observer of the forms of religion; and as the buoyancy of youth passed away, his zeal was stimulated by a profound fear of the Devil. Mazarin had reared him in ignorance; but his faculties were excellent in their way, and in a private station would have made him an efficient man of business. The vivacity of his passions and his inordinate love of pleasure were joined to a persistent will and a rare power of labor. The vigorous mediocrity of his understanding delighted in grappling with details. His astonished courtiers saw him take on himself the burden of administration, and work at it without

relenting for more than half a century. Great as
was his energy, his pride was far greater. As king
by divine right, he felt himself raised immeasurably
above the highest of his subjects; but while vindicating with unparalleled haughtiness his claims to
supreme authority, he was, at the outset, filled with
a sense of the duties of his high place, and fired by
an ambition to make his reign beneficent to France
as well as glorious to himself.

Above all rulers of modern times, Louis XIV. was
the embodiment of the monarchical idea. The
famous words ascribed to him, "I am the State,"
were probably never uttered; but they perfectly
express his spirit. "It is God's will," he wrote in
1666, "that whoever is born a subject should not
reason, but obey;"[1] and those around him were of
his mind. "The State is in the King," said Bossuet,
the great mouthpiece of monarchy; "the will of the
people is merged in his will. O Kings! put forth
your power boldly, for it is divine and salutary to
humankind."[2]

For a few brief years, this King's reign was indeed
salutary to France. His judgment of men, when
not obscured by his pride and his passion for flattery,
was good; and he had at his service the generals and
statesmen formed in the freer and bolder epoch that
had ended with his accession. Among them was
Jean Baptiste Colbert, formerly the intendant of

---

[1] *Œuvres de Louis XIV.*, ii. 283.
[2] Bossuet, *Politique tirée de l'Écriture sainte*, 670 (1843).

Mazarin's household, — a man whose energies matched his talents, and who had preserved his rectitude in the midst of corruption. It was a hard task that Colbert imposed on his proud and violent nature to serve the imperious King, morbidly jealous of his authority, and resolved to accept no initiative but his own. He must counsel while seeming to receive counsel, and lead while seeming to follow. The new minister bent himself to the task, and the nation reaped the profit. A vast system of reform was set in action amid the outcries of nobles, financiers, churchmen, and all who profited by abuses. The methods of this reform were trenchant and sometimes violent, and its principles were not always in accord with those of modern economic science; but the good that resulted was incalculable. The burdens of the laboring classes were lightened, the public revenues increased, and the wholesale plunder of the public money was arrested with a strong hand. Laws were reformed and codified; feudal tyranny, which still subsisted in many quarters, was repressed; agriculture and productive industry of all kinds were encouraged, roads and canals opened, trade was stimulated, a commercial marine created, and a powerful navy formed as if by magic.[1]

It is in his commercial, industrial, and colonial policy that the profound defects of the great minis-

[1] On Colbert, see Clément, *Histoire de Colbert*; Clément, *Lettres et Mémoires de Colbert*; Chéruel, *Administration monarchique en France*, ii. chap. vi.; Henri Martin, *Histoire de France*, xiii., etc.

ter's system are most apparent. It was a system of
authority, monopoly, and exclusion, in which the
government, and not the individual, acted always
the foremost part. Upright, incorruptible, ardent for
the public good, inflexible, arrogant, and domineer-
ing, he sought to drive France into paths of prosperity, and create colonies by the energy of an imperial
will. He feared, and with reason, that the want of
enterprise and capital among the merchants would
prevent the broad and immediate results at which he
aimed; and to secure these results he established a
series of great trading corporations, in which the
principles of privilege and exclusion were pushed to
their utmost limits. Prominent among them was
the Company of the West. The King signed the
edict creating it on the twenty-fourth of May, 1664.
Any person in the kingdom or out of it might become
a partner by subscribing, within a certain time, not
less than three thousand francs. France was a mere
patch on the map, compared to the vast domains of
the new association. Western Africa from Cape
Verd to the Cape of Good Hope, South America
between the Amazon and the Orinoco, Cayenne, the
Antilles, and all New France, from Hudson's Bay to
Virginia and Florida, were bestowed on it forever, to
be held of the Crown on the simple condition of
faith and homage. As, according to the edict, the
glory of God was the chief object in view, the company was required to supply its possessions with a
sufficient number of priests, and diligently to exclude

all teachers of false doctrine. It was empowered to build forts and war-ships, cast cannon, wage war, make peace, establish courts, appoint judges, and otherwise to act as sovereign within its own domains. A monopoly of trade was granted it for forty years.[1] Sugar from the Antilles and furs from Canada were the chief source of expected profit; and Africa was to supply the slaves to raise the sugar. Scarcely was the grand machine set in motion, when its directors betrayed a narrowness and blindness of policy which boded the enterprise no good. Canada was a chief sufferer. Once more, bound hand and foot, she was handed over to a selfish league of merchants, — monopoly in trade, monopoly in religion, monopoly in government. Nobody but the company had a right to bring her the necessaries of life; and nobody but the company had a right to exercise the traffic which alone could give her the means of paying for these necessaries. Moreover, the supplies which it brought were insufficient, and the prices which it demanded were exorbitant. It was throttling its wretched victim. The Canadian merchants remonstrated.[2] It was clear that if the colony was to live, the system must be changed; and a change was accordingly ordered. The company gave up its monopoly of the fur-trade, but reserved the right to levy a duty of one-fourth of the beaver-skins, and one-tenth of the moose-skins; and it also reserved

[1] *Édit d'Établissement de la Compagnie des Indes Occidentales.*
[2] *Lettre du Conseil Souverain à Colbert,* 1668.

the entire trade of Tadoussac, — that is to say, the trade of all the tribes between the lower St. Lawrence and Hudson's Bay. It retained, besides, the exclusive right of transporting furs in its own ships, — thus controlling the commerce of Canada, and discouraging, or rather extinguishing, the enterprise of Canadian merchants. On its part, it was required to pay governors, judges, and all the colonial officials out of the duties which it levied.[1]

Yet the King had the prosperity of Canada at heart; and he proceeded to show his interest in her after a manner hardly consistent with his late action in handing her over to a mercenary guardian. In fact, he acted as if she had still remained under his paternal care. He had just conferred the right of naming a governor and intendant upon the new company; but he now assumed it himself, the company, with a just sense of its own unfitness, readily consenting to this suspension of one of its most important privileges. Daniel de Rémy, Sieur de Courcelle, was appointed governor, and Jean Baptiste Talon intendant.[2] The nature of this duplicate

[1] *Arrêt du Conseil du Roy qui accorde à la Compagnie le quart des castors, le dixième des orignaux et la traite de Tadoussac : Instruction de Monseigneur de Tracy et à Messieurs le Gouverneur et l'Intendant.*

This company prospered as little as the rest of Colbert's trading companies. Within ten years it lost 3,523,000 livres, besides blighting the colonies placed under its control. (*Recherches sur les Finances*, cited by Clément, *Histoire de Colbert*.)

[2] *Commission de Lieutenant Général en Canada, etc., pour M. de Courcelle*, 23 *Mars*, 1665; *Commission d'Intendant de la Justice, Police, et Finances en Canada, etc., pour M. Talon*, 23 *Mars*, 1665.

government will appear hereafter. But before appointing rulers for Canada, the King had appointed a representative of the Crown for all his American domains. The Maréchal d'Estrades had for some time held the title of viceroy for America; and as he could not fulfil the duties of that office, being at the time ambassador in Holland, the Marquis de Tracy was sent in his place, with the title of lieutenant-general.[1]

Canada at this time was an object of very considerable attention at court, and especially in what was known as the *parti dévot*. The *Relations* of the Jesuits, appealing equally to the spirit of religion and the spirit of romantic adventure, had for more than a quarter of a century been the favorite reading of the devout, and the visit of Laval at court had greatly stimulated the interest they had kindled. The letters of Argenson, and especially of Avaugour, had shown the vast political possibilities of the young colony, and opened a vista of future glories alike for Church and for King.

So, when Tracy set sail he found no lack of followers. A throng of young nobles embarked with him, eager to explore the marvels and mysteries of the western world. The King gave him two hundred soldiers of the regiment of Carignan-Salières, and promised that a thousand more should follow. After spending more than a year in the West Indies,

---

[1] *Commission de Lieutenant Général de l'Amérique Méridionale et Septentrionale pour M. Prouville de Tracy*, 19 Nov., 1663.

where, as Mother Mary of the Incarnation expresses it, "he performed marvels and reduced everybody to obedience," he at length sailed up the St. Lawrence, and on the thirtieth of June, 1665, anchored in the basin of Quebec. The broad, white standard, blazoned with the arms of France, proclaimed the representative of royalty; and Point Levi and Cape Diamond and the distant Cape Tourmente roared back the sound of the saluting cannon. All Quebec was on the ramparts or at the landing-place, and all eyes were strained at the two vessels as they slowly emptied their crowded decks into the boats alongside. The boats at length drew near, and the lieutenant-general and his suite landed on the quay with a pomp such as Quebec had never seen before.

Tracy was a veteran of sixty-two, portly and tall, "one of the largest men I ever saw," writes Mother Mary; but he was sallow with disease, for fever had seized him, and it had fared ill with him on the long voyage. The Chevalier de Chaumont walked at his side, and young nobles surrounded him, gorgeous in lace and ribbons and majestic in leonine wigs. Twenty-four guards in the King's livery led the way, followed by four pages and six valets;[1] and thus, while the Frenchmen shouted and the Indians stared, the august procession threaded the streets of the Lower Town, and climbed the steep pathway that scaled the cliffs above. Breathing hard, they reached

---

[1] Juchereau says that this was his constant attendance when he went abroad.

the top, passed on the left the dilapidated walls of
the fort and the shed of mingled wood and masonry
which then bore the name of the Castle of St. Louis;
passed on the right the old house of Couillard and
the site of Laval's new seminary, and soon reached
the square betwixt the Jesuit college and the cathedral. The bells were ringing in a frenzy of welcome. Laval in pontificals, surrounded by priests and
Jesuits, stood waiting to receive the deputy of the
King; and as he greeted Tracy and offered him the
holy water, he looked with anxious curiosity to see
what manner of man he was. The signs were auspicious. The deportment of the lieutenant-general left
nothing to desire. A *prie-dieu* had been placed for
him. He declined it. They offered him a cushion,
but he would not have it; and, fevered as he was,
he knelt on the bare pavement with a devotion that
edified every beholder. *Te Deum* was sung, and a
day of rejoicing followed.

There was good cause. Canada, it was plain, was
not to be wholly abandoned to a trading company.
Louis XIV. was resolved that a new France should
be added to the old. Soldiers, settlers, horses, sheep,
cattle, young women for wives, were all sent out in
abundance by his paternal benignity. Before the
season was over, about two thousand persons had
landed at Quebec at the royal charge. "At length,"
writes Mother Juchereau, "our joy was completed by
the arrival of two vessels with Monsieur de Courcelle,
our governor; Monsieur Talon, our intendant, and

the last companies of the regiment of Carignan."
More state and splendor, more young nobles, more
guards and valets: for Courcelle, too, says the same
chronicler, "had a superb train; and Monsieur
Talon, who naturally loves glory, forgot nothing
which could do honor to the King." Thus a sun-
beam from the court fell for a moment on the rock of
Quebec. Yet all was not sunshine; for the voyage
had been a tedious one, and disease had broken out
in the ships. That which bore Talon had been a
hundred and seventeen days at sea,[1] and others were
hardly more fortunate. The hospital was crowded
with the sick; so, too, were the Church and the
neighboring houses; and the nuns were so spent with
their labors that seven of them were brought to the
point of death. The priests were busied in convert
ing the Huguenots, a number of whom were detected
among the soldiers and emigrants. One of them
proved refractory, declaring with oaths that he would
never renounce his faith. Falling dangerously ill,
he was carried to the hospital, where Mother
Catherine de Saint-Augustin bethought her of a plan
of conversion. She ground to powder a small piece
of a bone of Father Brébeuf, the Jesuit martyr, and
secretly mixed the sacred dust with the patient's
gruel; whereupon, says Mother Juchereau, "this
intractable man forthwith became gentle as an angel,
begged to be instructed, embraced the faith, and

[1] *Talon au Ministre*, 4 *Oct.*, 1665.

abjured his errors publicly with an admirable fervor." [1]

Two or three years before, the Church of Quebec had received as a gift from the Pope the bodies or bones of two saints, — Saint Flavian and Saint Félicité. They were enclosed in four large coffers or reliquaries, and a grand procession was now ordered in their honor. Tracy, Courcelle, Talon, and the agent of the company bore the canopy of the Host. Then came the four coffers on four decorated litters, carried by the principal ecclesiastics. Laval followed in pontificals. Forty-seven priests, and a long file of officers, nobles, soldiers, and inhabitants, followed the precious relics amid the sound of music and the roar of cannon. [2]

"It is a ravishing thing," says Mother Mary, "to see how marvellously exact is Monsieur de Tracy at all these holy ceremonies, where he is always the first to come, for he would not lose a single moment of them. He has been seen in church for six hours together, without once going out." But while the lieutenant-general thus edified the colony, he betrayed no lack of qualities equally needful in his position. In Canada, as in the West Indies, he showed both vigor and conduct. First of all, he had been ordered to subdue or destroy the Iroquois; and the regiment of Carignan-Salières was the weapon

---

[1] Le Mercier tells the same story in the *Relation* of 1665.

[2] Compare Marie de l'Incarnation, *Lettre* 16 *Oct.*, 1666, with La Tour, *Vie de Laval*, chap. x.

16

placed in his hands for this end. Four companies
of this corps had arrived early in the season; four
more came with Tracy, more yet with Salières,
their colonel, — and now the number was complete.
As with slouched hat and plume, bandoleer, and
shouldered firelock, these bronzed veterans of the
Turkish wars marched at the tap of drum through
the narrow street, or mounted the rugged way that
led up to the fort, the inhabitants gazed with a sense
of profound relief. Tame Indians from the neighboring missions, wild Indians from the woods, stared
in silent wonder at their new defenders. Their
numbers, their discipline, their uniform, and their
martial bearing filled the savage beholders with
admiration.

Carignan-Salières was the first regiment of regular
troops ever sent to America by the French government. It was raised in Savoy by the Prince of
Carignan in 1644, but was soon employed in the
service of France; where, in 1652, it took a conspicuous part, on the side of the King, in the battle
with Condé and the Fronde at the Porte St. Antoine.
After the peace of the Pyrenees, the Prince of
Carignan, unable to support the regiment, gave it to
the King, and it was, for the first time, incorporated
into the French armies. In 1664 it distinguished
itself, as part of the allied force of France, in the
Austrian war against the Turks. In the next year
it was ordered to America, along with the fragment
of a regiment formed of Germans, the whole being

placed under the command of Colonel de Salières. Hence its double name.[1]

Fifteen heretics were discovered in its ranks, and quickly converted.[2] Then the new crusade was preached, — the crusade against the Iroquois, enemies of God and tools of the Devil. The soldiers and the people were filled with a zeal half warlike and half religious. "They are made to understand," writes Mother Mary, "that this is a holy war, all for the glory of God and the salvation of souls. The fathers are doing wonders in inspiring them with true sentiments of piety and devotion. Fully five hundred soldiers have taken the scapulary of the Holy Virgin. It is we [the Ursulines], who make them; it is a real pleasure to do such work;" and she proceeds to relate a "beau miracle," by which God made known his satisfaction at the fervor of his military servants.

[1] For a long notice of the regiment of Carignan-Salières (Lorraine), see Susane, *Ancienne Infanterie Française*, v. 236. The portion of it which returned to France from Canada formed a nucleus for the reconstruction of the regiment, which, under the name of the regiment of Lorraine, did not cease to exist as a separate organization till 1794. When it came to Canada it consisted, says Susane, of about a thousand men, besides about two hundred of the other regiment incorporated with it. Compare *Mémoire du Roy pour servir d'instruction au Sieur Talon*, which corresponds very nearly with Susane's statement.

[2] Besides these, there was Berthier, a captain. "Voilà," writes Talon to the King, "le 16me converti; ainsi votre Majesté moissonne déjà à pleines mains de la gloire pour Dieu, et pour elle bien de la renommée dans toute l'étendue de la Chrétienté." (*Lettre d* 7 *Oct.*, 1665.)

The secular motives for the war were in themselves strong enough; for the growth of the colony absolutely demanded the cessation of Iroquois raids, and the French had begun to learn the lesson that in the case of hostile Indians no good can come of attempts to conciliate, unless respect is first imposed by a sufficient castigation. It is true that the writers of the time paint Iroquois hostilities in their worst colors. In the innumerable letters which Mother Mary of the Incarnation sent home every autumn, by the returning ships, she spared no means to gain the sympathy and aid of the devout; and, with similar motives, the Jesuits in their printed *Relations* took care to extenuate nothing of the miseries which the pious colony endured. Avaugour too, in urging the sending out of a strong force to fortify and hold the country, had advised that, in order to furnish a pretext and disarm the jealousy of the English and Dutch, exaggerated accounts should be given of danger from the side of the savage confederates. Yet, with every allowance, these dangers and sufferings were sufficiently great.

The three upper nations of the Iroquois were comparatively pacific; but the two lower nations, the Mohawks and Oneidas, were persistently hostile; making inroads into the colony by way of Lake Champlain and the Richelieu, murdering and scalping, and then vanishing like ghosts. Tracy's first step was to send a strong detachment to the Richelieu to build a picket fort below the rapids of Chambly,

which take their name from that of the officer in
command. An officer named Sorel soon afterwards
built a second fort on the site of the abandoned
palisade work built by Montmagny, at the mouth of
the river, where the town of Sorel now stands; and
Salières, colonel of the regiment, added a third fort,
two or three leagues above Chambly.[1] These forts
could not wholly bar the passage against the nimble
and wily warriors who might pass them in the night,
shouldering their canoes through the woods. A
blow, direct and hard, was needed, and Tracy
prepared to strike it.

Late in the season an embassy from the three
upper nations — the Onondagas, Cayugas, and
Senecas — arrived at Quebec, led by Garacontié, a
famous chief whom the Jesuits had won over, and
who proved ever after a stanch friend of the French.
They brought back the brave Charles Le Moyne of
Montreal, whom they had captured some three
months before, and now restored as a peace-offering,
taking credit to themselves that "not even one of his
nails had been torn out, nor any part of his body
burnt."[2] Garacontié made a peace speech, which, as
rendered by the Jesuits, was an admirable specimen of
Iroquois eloquence; but while joining hands with him
and his companions, the French still urged on their
preparations to chastise the contumacious Mohawks.

[1] See the map in the *Relation* of 1665. The accompanying text
of the *Relation* is incorrect.

[2] *Explanation of the eleven Presents of the Iroquois Ambassadors,*
N. Y. Colonial Docs., ix. 37.

CHAPTER XIV.

1666, 1667.

THE MOHAWKS CHASTISED.

Courcelle's March: his Failure and Return. — Courcelle and the Jesuits. — Mohawk Treachery. — Tracy's Expedition. — Burning of the Mohawk Towns. — French and English. — Dollier de Casson at St. Anne. — Peace. — The Jesuits and the Iroquois.

The governor, Courcelle, says Father Le Mercier, "breathed nothing but war," and was bent on immediate action. He was for the present subordinate to Tracy, who, however, forbore to cool his ardor, and allowed him to proceed. The result was an enterprise bold to rashness. Courcelle, with about five hundred men, prepared to march in the depth of a Canadian winter to the Mohawk towns, — a distance estimated at three hundred leagues. Those who knew the country vainly urged the risks and difficulties of the attempt. The adventurous governor held fast to his purpose, and only waited till the St. Lawrence should be well frozen. Early in January, it was a solid floor; and on the ninth the march began. Officers and men stopped at Sillery, and knelt in the little mission chapel before the shrine of

Saint Michael, to ask the protection and aid of the warlike archangel; then they resumed their course, and, with their snow-shoes tied at their backs, walked with difficulty and toil over the bare and slippery ice. A keen wind swept the river, and the fierce cold gnawed them to the bone. Ears, noses, fingers, hands, and knees were frozen; some fell in torpor, and were dragged on by their comrades to the shivering bivouac. When, after a march of ninety miles, they reached Three Rivers, a considerable number were disabled, and had to be left behind; but others joined them from the garrison, and they set out again. Ascending the Richelieu, and passing the new forts at Sorel and Chambly, they reached at the end of the month the third fort, called Ste. Thérèse. On the thirtieth they left it, and continued their march up the frozen stream.

About two hundred of them were Canadians, and of these seventy were old Indian-fighters from Montreal, versed in wood-craft, seasoned to the climate, and trained among dangers and alarms. Courcelle quickly learned their value, and his "Blue Coats," as he called them, were always placed in the van.[1] Here, wrapped in their coarse blue capotes, with blankets and provisions strapped at their backs, they strode along on snow-shoes, which recent storms had made indispensable. The regulars followed as they could. They were not yet the tough and experienced woodsmen that they and their descend-

[1] Dollier de Casson, *Histoire du Montréal*, A. D. 1665, 1666.

ants afterwards became; and their snow-shoes embarrassed them, burdened as they were with the heavy loads which all carried alike, from Courcelle to the lowest private.

Lake Champlain lay glaring in the winter sun, a sheet of spotless snow; and the wavy ridges of the Adirondacks bordered the dazzling landscape with the cold gray of their denuded forests. The long procession of weary men crept slowly on under the lee of the shore; and when night came they bivouacked by squads among the trees, dug away the snow with their snow-shoes, piled it in a bank around them, built their fire in the middle, and crouched about it on beds of spruce or hemlock,[1] — while, as they lay close packed for mutual warmth, the winter sky arched them like a vault of burnished steel, sparkling with the cold diamond lustre of its myriads of stars. This arctic serenity of the elements was varied at times by heavy snow-storms, and before they reached their journey's end the earth and the ice were buried to the unusual depth of four feet. From Lake Champlain they passed to Lake George[2] and the frigid glories of its snow-wrapped mountains, thence crossed to the Hudson, and groped their way through the woods in search of the Mohawk towns. They

[1] One of the men, telling the story of their sufferings to Daniel Gookin, of Massachusetts, indicated this as their mode of encamping. See Mass. Hist. Coll. first series, i. 161.

[2] *Carte des grands lacs, Ontario et autres . . . et des pays traversez par MM. de Tracy et Courcelle pour aller attaquer les agniés* [Mohawks], 1666.

soon went astray; for thirty Algonquins, whom they
had taken as guides, had found the means of a grand
debauch at Fort Ste. Thérèse, drunk themselves into
helplessness, and lingered behind. Thus Courcelle
and his men mistook the path, and, marching by way
of Saratoga Lake and Long Lake,[1] found themselves,
on Saturday the twentieth of February, close to the
little Dutch hamlet of Corlaer, or Schenectady.
Here the chief man in authority told them that most
of the Mohawks and Oneidas had gone to war with
another tribe. They however caught a few strag-
glers, and had a smart skirmish with a party of
warriors, losing an officer and several men. Half
frozen and half starved, they encamped in the neighboring woods, where, on Sunday, three envoys
appeared from Albany, to demand why they had
invaded the territories of his Royal Highness the
Duke of York. It was now that they learned for the
first time that the New Netherlands had passed into
English hands, a change which boded no good to
Canada. The envoys seemed to take their explanations in good part, made them a present of wine and
provisions, and allowed them to buy further supplies
from the Dutch of Schenectady. They even invited
them to enter the village, but Courcelle declined, —
partly because the place could not hold them all, and
partly because he feared that his men, once seated in
a chimney-corner, could never be induced to leave it.

Their position was cheerless enough; for the vast

[1] *Carte . . . des pays traversez par MM. de Tracy et Courcelle, etc*

beds of snow around them were soaking slowly under
a sullen rain, and there was danger that the lakes
might thaw and cut off their retreat. "Ye Mohaukes,"
says the old English report of the affair, "were all
gone to their Castles with resolution to fight it out
against the french, who, being refresht and supplyed
wth the aforesaid provisions, made a shew of marching
towards the Mohaukes Castles, but with faces about,
and great sylence and dilligence, return'd towards
Cannada." "Surely," observes the narrator, "so
bould and hardy an attempt hath not hapned in any
age." [1] The end hardly answered to the beginning.
The retreat, which began on Sunday night, was
rather precipitate. The Mohawks hovered about
their rear, and took a few prisoners, but famine and
cold proved more deadly foes, and sixty men perished
before they reached the shelter of Fort Ste. Thérèse.
On the eighth of March, Courcelle came to the
neighboring fort of St. Louis or Chambly. Here he
found the Jesuit Albanel acting as chaplain; and,
being in great ill humor, he charged him with caus-
ing the failure of the expedition by detaining the
Algonquin guides. This singular notion took such
possession of him, that, when a few days after he
met the Jesuit Frémin at Three Rivers, he embraced
him ironically, saying, at the same time, "My father,
I am the unluckiest gentleman in the world; and

---

[1] *A Relation of the Govern^r. of Cannada, his March with* 600 *Volun-
eirs into* y^e *Territoryes of His Royall Highnesse the Duke of Yorke in
America.* See Doc. Hist. N. Y. i. 71.

you, and the rest of you, are the cause of it." [1]   The
pious Tracy and the prudent Talon tried to disarm
his suspicions, and with such success that he gave up
an intention he had entertained of discarding his
Jesuit confessor, and forgot or forgave the imagined
wrong.

Unfortunate as this expedition was, it produced
a strong effect on the Iroquois by convincing them
that their forest homes were no safe asylum from
French attacks. In May, the Senecas sent an embassy
of peace; and the other nations, including the
Mohawks, soon followed. Tracy, on his part, sent
the Jesuit Bêchefer to learn on the spot the real
temper of the savages, and ascertain whether peace
could safely be made with them. The Jesuit was
scarcely gone when news came that a party of officers
hunting near the outlet of Lake Champlain had been
set upon by the Mohawks, and that seven of them
had been captured or killed. Among the captured
was Leroles, a cousin of Tracy; and among the
killed was a young gentleman named Chasy, his
nephew.

On this the Jesuit envoy was recalled; twenty-
four Iroquois deputies were seized and imprisoned;
and Sorel, captain in the regiment of Carignan, was
sent with three hundred men to chastise the perfidious Mohawks. If, as it seems, he was expected
to attack their fortified towns or "castles," as the
English call them, his force was too small. This

[1] *Journal des Jésuites, Mars,* 1666.

time, however, there was no fighting. At two days from his journey's end, Sorel met the famous chief called the Flemish Bastard, bringing back Leroles and his fellow-captives, and charged, as he alleged, to offer full satisfaction for the murder of Chasy. Sorel believed him, retraced his course, and with the Bastard in his train returned to Quebec.

Quebec was full of Iroquois deputies, all bent on peace or pretending to be so. On the last day of August there was a grand council in the garden of the Jesuits. Some days later, Tracy invited the Flemish Bastard and a Mohawk chief named Agariata to his table, when allusion was made to the murder of Chasy. On this the Mohawk, stretching out his arm, exclaimed in a braggart tone, "This is the hand that split the head of that young man." The indignation of the company may be imagined. Tracy told his insolent guest that he should never kill anybody else; and he was led out and hanged in presence of the Bastard.[1] There was no more talk of peace. Tracy prepared to march in person against the Mohawks with all the force of Canada.

On the day of the Exaltation of the Cross, "for whose glory," says the chronicler, "this expedition

---

[1] This story rests chiefly on the authority of Nicholas Perrot, *Mœurs des Sauvages*, 113. La Potherie also tells it, with the addition of the chief's name. Colden follows him. The *Journal des Jésuites* mentions that the chief who led the murderers of Chasy arrived at Quebec on the sixth of September. Marie de l'Incarnation mentions the hanging of an Iroquois at Quebec, late in the autumn, for violating the peace.

is undertaken," Tracy and Courcelle left Quebec
with thirteen hundred men. They crossed Lake
Champlain, and launched their boats again on the
waters of St. Sacrament, now Lake George. It was
the first of the warlike pageants that have made that
fair scene historic. October had begun, and the
romantic wilds breathed the buoyant life of the most
inspiring of American seasons, when the blue-jay
screams from the woods, the wild duck splashes
along the lake, and the echoes of distant mountains
prolong the quavering cry of the loon; when weather-
stained rocks are plumed with the fiery crimson of
the sumach, the claret hues of young oaks, the amber
and scarlet of the maple, and the sober purple of the
ash; or when gleams of sunlight, shot aslant through
the rents of cool autumnal clouds, chase fitfully along
the glowing sides of painted mountains. Amid this
gorgeous euthanasia of the dying season, the three
hundred boats and canoes trailed in long procession
up the lake, threaded the labyrinth of the Narrows,
— that sylvan fairy-land of tufted islets and quiet
waters, — and landed at length where Fort William
Henry was afterwards built.[1]

About a hundred miles of forests, swamps, rivers,
and mountains still lay between them and the
Mohawk towns. There seems to have been an
Indian path, for this was the ordinary route of the
Mohawk and Oneida war-parties; but the path was
narrow, broken, full of gullies and pitfalls, crossed

[1] *Carte . . . des pays traversez par MM. de Tracy et Courcelle, etc*

by streams, and in one place interrupted by a lake which they passed on rafts. A hundred and ten "Blue Coats," of Montreal, led the way, under Charles Le Moyne; Repentigny commanded the levies from Quebec. In all there were six hundred Canadians, six hundred regulars, and a hundred Indians from the missions, who ranged the woods in front, flank, and rear, like hounds on the scent. Red or white, Canadians or regulars, all were full of zeal. "It seems to them," writes Mother Mary, "that they are going to lay siege to Paradise, and win it and enter in, because they are fighting for religion and the faith."[1] Their ardor was rudely tried. Officers as well as men carried loads at their backs, whence ensued a large blister on the shoulders of the Chevalier de Chaumont, in no way used to such burdens. Tracy, old, heavy, and infirm, was inopportunely seized with the gout. A Swiss soldier tried to carry him on his shoulders across a rapid stream; but midway his strength failed, and he was barely able to deposit his ponderous load on a rock. A Huron came to his aid, and bore Tracy safely to the farther bank. Courcelle was attacked with cramps, and had to be carried for a time like his commander. Provisions gave out, and men and officers grew faint with hunger. The Montreal soldiers had for chaplain a sturdy priest, Dollier de Casson, as large as Tracy and far stronger; for the incredible story is told of him that when in good

[1] Marie de l'Incarnation, *Lettre du* 16 *Oct.*, 1666.

condition he could hold two men seated on his
extended hands.[1]　Now, however, he was equal to
no such exploit, being not only deprived of food, but
also of sleep, by the necessity of listening at night to
the confessions of his pious flock; and his shoes, too,
had failed him, nothing remaining but the upper
leather, which gave him little comfort among the
sharp stones.　He bore up manfully, being by nature
brave and light-hearted; and when a servant of the
Jesuits fell into the water, he threw off his cassock
and leaped after him.　His strength gave out, and
the man was drowned; but a grateful Jesuit led
him aside, and requited his efforts with a morsel of
bread.[2]　A wood of chestnut-trees full of nuts at
length stayed the hunger of the famished troops.

It was Saint Theresa's day when they approached
the lower Mohawk town.　A storm of wind and rain
set in; but, anxious to surprise the enemy, they
pushed on all night amid the moan and roar of the
forest, — over slippery logs, tangled roots, and oozy
mosses, under dripping boughs and through saturated
bushes.　This time there was no want of good
guides; and when in the morning they issued from
the forest, they saw, amid its cornfields, the palisades
of the Indian stronghold.　They had two small pieces
of cannon brought from the lake by relays of men,
but they did not stop to use them.　Their twenty

---

[1] Grandet, *Notice manuscrite sur Dollier de Casson*, extract given
by J. Viger in appendix to *Histoire du Montréal* (Montreal, 1868).

[2] Dollier de Casson, *Histoire du Montréal*, A. D. 1665, 1666.

drums beat the charge, and they advanced to seize
the place by *coup-de-main*. Luckily for them, a
panic had seized the Indians: not that they were
taken by surprise, for they had discovered the
approaching French, and, two days before, had sent
away their women and children in preparation for a
desperate fight; but the din of the drums, which
they took for so many devils in the French service,
and the armed men advancing from the rocks and
thickets in files that seemed interminable, so wrought
on the scared imagination of the warriors that they
fled in terror to their next town, a short distance
above. Tracy lost no time, but hastened in pursuit.
A few Mohawks were seen on the hills, yelling and
firing too far for effect. Repentigny, at the risk of his
scalp, climbed a neighboring height, and looked down
on the little army, which seemed so numerous as it
passed beneath, "that," writes the superior of the Ursulines, "he told me that he thought the good angels
must have joined with it: whereat he stood amazed."

The second town or fort was taken as easily as
the first; so, too, were the third and the fourth.
The Indians yelled, and fled without killing a man;
and still the troops pursued, following the broad
trail which led from town to town along the valley
of the Mohawk. It was late in the afternoon when
the fourth town was entered,[1] and Tracy thought

---

[1] Marie de l'Incarnation says that there were four towns in all.
I follow the *Acte de prise de possession*, made on the spot Five are
here mentioned.

that his work was done; but an Algonquin squaw
who had followed her husband to the war, and who
had once been a prisoner among the Mohawks, told
him that there was still another above. The sun
was near its setting, and the men were tired with
their pitiless marching; but again the order was
given to advance. The eager squaw showed the
way, holding a pistol in one hand and leading
Courcelle with the other; and they soon came in
sight of Andaraqué, the largest and strongest of the
Mohawk forts. The drums beat with fury, and the
troops prepared to attack; but there were none to
oppose them. The scouts sent forward reported that
the warriors had fled. The last of the savage strong-
holds was in the hands of the French.

"God has done for us," says Mother Mary, "what
he did in ancient days for his chosen people, — striking terror into our enemies, insomuch that we were
victors without a blow. Certain it is that there is
miracle in all this; for if the Iroquois had stood fast,
they would have given us a great deal of trouble
and caused our army great loss, seeing how they
were fortified and armed, and how haughty and bold
they are."

The French were astonished as they looked about
them. These Iroquois forts were very different
from those that Jogues had seen here twenty years
before, or from that which in earlier times set
Champlain and his Hurons at defiance. The Mohawks
had had counsel and aid from their Dutch friends,

17

and adapted their savage defences to the rules of European art. Andaraqué was a quadrangle formed of a triple palisade, twenty feet high, and flanked by four bastions. Large vessels of bark filled with water were placed on the platforms of the palisade for defence against fire. The dwellings which these fortifications enclosed were in many cases built of wood, though the form and arrangement of the primitive bark-lodge of the Iroquois seems to have been preserved. Some of the wooden houses were a hundred and twenty feet long, with fires for eight or nine families. Here, and in subterranean *caches*, was stored a prodigious quantity of Indian-corn and other provisions; and all the dwellings were supplied with carpenters' tools, domestic utensils, and many other appliances of comfort.

The only living things in Andaraqué, when the French entered, were two old women, a small boy, and a decrepit old man, who, being frightened by the noise of the drums, had hidden himself under a canoe. From them the victors learned that the Mohawks, retreating from the other towns, had gathered here, resolved to fight to the last; but at sight of the troops their courage failed, and the chief was first to run, crying out, "Let us save ourselves, brothers! the whole world is coming against us!"

A cross was planted, and at its side the royal arms. The troops were drawn up in battle array, when Jean Baptiste du Bois, an officer deputed by

Tracy, advancing sword in hand to the front, proclaimed in a loud voice that he took possession in the name of the King of all the country of the Mohawks; and the troops shouted three times, *Vive le Roi*.[1]

That night a mighty bonfire illumined the Mohawk forests; and the scared savages from their hiding-places among the rocks saw their palisades, their dwellings, their stores of food, and all their possessions turned to cinders and ashes. The two old squaws captured in the town threw themselves in despair into the flames of their blazing homes. When morning came, there was nothing left of Andaraqué but smouldering embers, rolling their pale smoke against the painted background of the October woods. *Te Deum* was sung and mass said; and then the victors began their backward march, — burning, as they went, all the remaining forts, with all their hoarded stores of corn, except such as they needed for themselves. If they had failed to destroy their enemies in battle, they hoped that winter and famine would do the work of shot and steel.

While there was distress among the Mohawks, there was trouble among their English neighbors, who claimed as their own the country which Tracy had invaded. The English authorities were the more disquieted, because they feared that the lately conquered Dutch might join hands with the French

---

[1] *Acte de prise de possession*, 17 *Oct.*, 1666.

against them. When Nicolls, governor of New York, heard of Tracy's advance, he wrote to the governors of the New England colonies, begging them to join him against the French invaders, and urging that if Tracy's force were destroyed or captured, the conquest of Canada would be an easy task. There was war at the time between the two Crowns; and the British court had already entertained this project of conquest, and sent orders to its colonies to that effect. But the New England governors — ill prepared for war, and fearing that their Indian neighbors, who were enemies of the Mohawks, might take part with the French — hesitated to act, and the affair ended in a correspondence, civil if not sincere, between Nicolls and Tracy.[1] The treaty of Bréda, in the following year, secured peace for a time between the rival colonies.

The return of Tracy was less fortunate than his advance. The rivers, swollen by autumn rains, were difficult to pass; and in crossing Lake Champlain two canoes were overset in a storm, and eight men were drowned. From St. Anne, a new fort built early in the summer on Isle La Motte, near the northern end of the lake, he sent news of his success to Quebec, where there was great rejoicing and a solemn thanksgiving. Signs and prodigies had not been wanting to attest the interest of the upper and nether powers in the crusade against the myrmidons

---

[1] See the correspondence in *N. Y. Col. Docs.*, iii. 118–156. Compare *Hutchinson Collection,* 407 and *Mass. Hist. Coll.*, xviii. 102.

of hell. At one of the forts on the Richelieu, "the soldiers," says Mother Mary, "were near dying of fright. They saw a great fiery cavern in the sky, and from this cavern came plaintive voices mixed with frightful howlings. Perhaps it was the demons, enraged because we had depopulated a country where they had been masters so long, and had said mass and sung the praises of God in a place where there had never before been anything but foulness and abomination."

Tracy had at first meant to abandon Fort St. Anne; but he changed his mind after returning to Quebec. Meanwhile the season had grown so late that there was no time to send proper supplies to the garrison. Winter closed, and the place was not only ill-provisioned, but was left without a priest. Tracy wrote to the superior of the Sulpitians at Montreal to send one without delay; but the request was more easily made than fulfilled, for he forgot to order an escort, and the way was long and dangerous. The stout-hearted Dollier de Casson was told, however, to hold himself ready to go at the first opportunity. His recent campaigning had left him in no condition for braving fresh hardships, for he was nearly disabled by a swelling on one of his knees. By way of cure he resolved to try a severe bleeding, and the Sangrado of Montreal did his work so thoroughly that his patient fainted under his hands. As he returned to consciousness, he became aware that two soldiers had entered the room. They told him that they were going in the morning to Chambly, which was on the way to St. Anne; and they invited him to go with them. "Wait till the day after to-morrow," replied the priest, "and I will try." The delay was obtained; and on the day fixed the party set out by the forest path to Chambly, a distance of about four leagues. When they reached it, Dollier de Casson was nearly spent; but he concealed his plight from the commanding officer, and begged an escort to St. Anne, some twenty leagues farther. As the officer would not give him one, he threatened to go alone, on which ten men and an ensign were at last ordered to conduct him. Thus attended, he resumed his journey after a day's rest. One of the soldiers fell through the ice, and none of his comrades dared help him. Dollier de Casson, making the sign of the cross, went to his aid, and, more successful than on the former occasion, caught him and pulled him out. The snow was deep; and the priest, having arrived in the preceding summer, had never before worn snow-shoes, while a sack of clothing, and his portable chapel which he carried at his back, joined to the pain of his knee and the effects of his late bleeding, made the march a purgatory.

He was sorely needed at Fort St. Anne. There was pestilence in the garrison. Two men had just died without absolution, while more were at the point of death, and praying for a priest. Thus it happened that when the sentinel descried far off, on the ice of Lake Champlain, a squad of soldiers

approaching, and among them a black cassock, every
officer and man not sick or on duty came out with
one accord to meet the new-comer. They overwhelmed him with welcome and with thanks. One
took his sack, another his portable chapel, and they
led him in triumph to the fort. First he made a
short prayer, then went his rounds among the sick,
and then came to refresh himself with the officers.
Here was La Motte de la Lucière, the commandant;
La Durantaye, a name destined to be famous in
Canadian annals; and a number of young subalterns.
The scene was no strange one to Dollier de Casson,
for he had been an officer of cavalry in his time, and
fought under Turenne;[1] a good soldier, without
doubt, at the mess table or in the field, and none the
worse a priest that he had once followed the wars.
He was of a lively humor, given to jests and mirth;
as pleasant a father as ever said *Benedicite*. The
soldier and the gentleman still lived under the cassock of the priest. He was greatly respected and
beloved; and his influence as a peace-maker, which
he often had occasion to exercise, is said to have been
remarkable. When the time demanded it, he could
use arguments more cogent than those of moral
suasion. Once, in a camp of Algonquins, when, as
he was kneeling in prayer, an insolent savage came
to interrupt him, the father, without rising, knocked
the intruder flat by a blow of his fist; and the other

---

[1] Grandet, *Notice manuscrite sur Dollier de Casson*, extracts from
copy in possession of the late Jacques Viger.

Indians, far from being displeased, were filled with admiration at the exploit.[1]

His cheery temper now stood him in good stead; for there was dreary work before him, and he was not the man to flinch from it. The garrison of St. Anne had nothing to live on but salt pork and half-spoiled flour. Their hogshead of vinegar had sprung a leak, and the contents had all oozed out. They had rejoiced in the supposed possession of a reasonable stock of brandy; but they soon discovered that the sailors, on the voyage from France, had emptied the casks and filled them again with salt-water. The scurvy broke out with fury. In a short time, forty out of the sixty men became victims of the loathsome malady. Day or night, Dollier de Casson and Forestier, the equally devoted young surgeon, had no rest. The surgeon's strength failed, and the priest was himself slightly attacked with the disease. Eleven men died; and others languished for want of help, for their comrades shrank from entering the infected dens where they lay. In their extremity some of them devised an ingenious expedient. Though they had nothing to bequeath, they made wills in which they left imaginary sums of money to those who had befriended them; and thenceforth they found no lack of nursing.

In the intervals of his labors, Dollier de Casson would run to and fro for warmth and exercise on a

---

[1] Grandet, *Notice manuscrite sur Dollier de Casson*, cited by Faillon, *Colonie Française*, iii. 395, 396.

certain track of beaten snow, between two of the bastions, reciting his breviary as he went, so that those who saw him might have thought him out of his wits. One day La Motte called out to him as he was thus engaged, "Eh, Monsieur le curé, if the Iroquois should come, you must defend that bastion. My men are all deserting me, and going over to you and the doctor." To which the father replied, "Get me some litters with wheels, and I will bring them out to man my bastion. They are brave enough now; no fear of their running away." With banter like this, they sought to beguile their miseries; and thus the winter wore on at Fort St. Anne.[1]

Early in spring they saw a troop of Iroquois approaching, and prepared as well as they could to make fight; but the strangers proved to be ambassadors of peace. The destruction of the Mohawk towns had produced a deep effect, not on that nation alone, but also on the other four members of the league. They were disposed to confirm the promises of peace which they had already made; and Tracy had spurred their good intentions by sending them a message that unless they quickly presented themselves at Quebec, he would hang all the chiefs whom he had kept prisoners after discovering their treach-

---

[1] The above curious incidents are told by Dollier de Casson, in his *Histoire du Montréal*, preserved in manuscript in the Mazarin Library at Paris. He gives no hint that the person in question was himself, but speaks of him as *un ecclésiastique*. His identity is, however, made certain by internal evidence, by a passage in the *Notice* of Grandet, and by other contemporary allusions.

ery in the preceding summer. The threat had its
effect: deputies of the Oneidas, Onondagas, Cayugas,
and Senecas presently arrived in a temper of befitting
humility. The Mohawks were at first afraid to
come, but in April they sent the Flemish Bastard
with overtures of peace, and in July a large deputation of their chiefs appeared at Quebec. They and
the rest left some of their families as hostages, and
promised that if any of their people should kill a
Frenchman, they would give them up to be hanged.[1]

They begged, too, for blacksmiths, surgeons, and
Jesuits to live among them. The presence of the
Jesuits in their towns was in many ways an advantage to them; while to the colony it was of the
greatest importance. Not only was conversion to
the Church justly regarded as the best means of
attaching the Indians to the French and alienating
them from the English; but the Jesuits living in the
midst of them could influence even those whom they
could not convert, soothe rising jealousies, counter-
act English intrigues, and keep the rulers of the
colony informed of all that was passing in the
Iroquois towns. Thus, half Christian missionaries,
half political agents, the Jesuits prepared to resume
the hazardous mission of the Iroquois. Frémin and
Pierron were ordered to the Mohawks, Bruyas to
the Oneidas, and three others were named for the

---

[1] *Lettre du Père Jean Pierron, de la Compagnie de Jésus, escripte
de la Motte* [Fort Ste. Anne] *sur le lac Champlain, le* 12*me d'aoust,*
1667.

remaining three nations of the league. The troops had made the peace; the Jesuits were the rivets to hold it fast, — and peace endured without absolute rupture for nearly twenty years. Of all the French expeditions against the Iroquois, that of Tracy was the most productive of good.

Note. — On Tracy's expedition against the Mohawks compare Faillon, *Histoire de la Colonie Française au Canada*, iii.

CHAPTER XV.

1665–1672.

PATERNAL GOVERNMENT.

Talon. — Restriction and Monopoly. — Views of Colbert. — Political Galvanism. — A Father of the People.

Tracy's work was done, and he left Canada with the glittering *noblesse* in his train. Courcelle and Talon remained to rule alone; and now the great experiment was begun. Paternal royalty would try its hand at building up a colony, and Talon was its chosen agent. His appearance did him no justice. The regular contour of his oval face, about which fell to his shoulders a cataract of curls, natural or supposititious; the smooth lines of his well-formed features, brows delicately arched, and a mouth more suggestive of feminine sensibility than of masculine force, — would certainly have misled the disciple of Lavater.[1] Yet there was no want of manhood in him. He was most happily chosen for the task placed in his hands, and from first to last approved himself a vigorous executive officer. He was a true

[1] His portrait is at the Hôtel Dieu of Quebec. An engraving from it will be found in the third volume of Shea's Charlevoix.

disciple of Colbert, formed in his school and animated by his spirit.

Being on the spot, he was better able than his master to judge the working of the new order of things. With regard to the company, he writes that it will profit by impoverishing the colony; that its monopolies dishearten the people and paralyze enterprise; that it is thwarting the intentions of the King, who wishes trade to be encouraged; and that if its exclusive privileges are maintained, Canada in ten years will be less populous than now.[1] But Colbert clung to his plan, though he wrote in reply that to satisfy the colonists he had persuaded the company to forego the monopolies for a year.[2] As this proved insufficient, the company was at length forced to give up permanently its right of exclusive trade, still exacting its share of beaver and moose skins. This was its chief source of profit; it begrudged every sou deducted from it for charges of government, and the King was constantly obliged to do at his own cost that which the company should have done. In one point it showed a ceaseless activity; and this was the levying of duties, in which it was never known to fail.

Trade, even after its exercise was permitted, was continually vexed by the hand of authority. One of Tracy's first measures had been to issue a decree reducing the price of wheat one half. The council

---

[1] *Talon à Colbert*, 4 *Oct.*, 1665.
[2] *Colbert à Talon*, 5 *Avril*, 1666.

took up the work of regulation, and fixed the price
of all imported goods in three several tariffs, — one
for Quebec, one for Three Rivers, and one for
Montreal.[1] It may well be believed that there was
in Canada little capital and little enterprise. Indus-
trially and commercially, the colony was almost
dead. Talon set himself to galvanize it; and if one
man could have supplied the intelligence and energy
of a whole community, the results would have been
triumphant.

He had received elaborate instructions, and they
indicate an ardent wish for the prosperity of Canada.
Colbert had written to him that the true means to
strengthen the colony was to "cause justice to reign,
establish a good police, protect the inhabitants, discipline them against enemies, and procure for them
peace, repose, and plenty."[2]   "And as," the minister
further says, "the King regards his Canadian subjects, from the highest to the lowest, almost as his
own children, and wishes them to enjoy equally with
the people of France the mildness and happiness of
his reign, the Sieur Talon will study to solace them
in all things, and encourage them to trade and
industry.   And, seeing that nothing can better promote this end than entering into the details of their
households and of all their little affairs, it will not be
amiss that he visit all their settlements one after the
other in order to learn their true condition, provide

---

[1] Tariff of Prices, in *N. Y. Colonial Docs.* ix. 36.
[2] *Colbert à Talon*, 5 *Avril*, 1666.

as much as possible for their wants, and, performing
the duty of a good head of a family, put them in the
way of making some profit." The intendant was
also told to encourage fathers to inspire their children
with piety, together with "profound love and respect
for the royal person of his Majesty."[1]

Talon entered on his work with admirable zeal.
Sometimes he used authority, sometimes persuasion,
sometimes promises of reward. Sometimes, again, he
tried the force of example. Thus he built a ship to
show the people how to do it, and rouse them to
imitation.[2] Three or four years later, the experiment was repeated. This time it was at the cost of
the King, who applied the sum of forty thousand
livres[3] to the double purpose of promoting the art of
ship-building, and saving the colonists from vagrant
habits by giving them employment. Talon wrote
that three hundred and fifty men had been supplied
that summer with work at the charge of government.[4]

He despatched two engineers to search for coal,
lead, iron, copper, and other minerals. Important
discoveries of iron were made; but three generations
were destined to pass before the mines were successfully worked.[5] The copper of Lake Superior raised

---

[1] *Instruction au Sieur Talon*, 27 *Mars*, 1665.

[2] *Talon à Colbert, Octobre*, 1667; *Colbert à Talon*, 20 *Fév.*, 1668.

[3] *Dépêche de Colbert*, 11 *Fév.*, 1671.

[4] *Talon à Colbert*, 2 *Nov.*, 1671.

[5] Charlevoix speaks of these mines as having been forgotten for
seventy years, and rediscovered in his time. After passing through
various hands, they were finally worked on the King's account.

the intendant's hopes for a time, but he was soon forced to the conclusion that it was too remote to be of practical value.   He labored vigorously to develop arts and manufactures; made a barrel of tar, and sent it to the King as a specimen; caused some of the colonists to make cloth of the wool of the sheep which the King had sent out; encouraged others to establish a tannery, and also a factory of hats and of shoes.   The Sieur Follin was induced by the grant of a monopoly to begin the making of soap and potash.[1] The people were ordered to grow hemp,[2] and urged to gather the nettles of the country as material for cordage; and the Ursulines were supplied with flax and wool, in order that they might teach girls to weave and spin.

Talon was especially anxious to establish trade between Canada and the West Indies; and, to make a beginning, he freighted the vessel he had built with salted cod, salmon, eels, pease, fish-oil, staves, and planks, and sent her thither to exchange her cargo for sugar, which she was in turn to exchange in France for goods suited for the Canadian market.[3] Another favorite object with him was the fishery of seals and white porpoises for the sake of their oil; and some of the chief merchants were urged to undertake it, as well as the establishment of stationary cod-fisheries along the Lower St. Lawrence.   But, with every

[1] *Régistre du Conseil Souverain.*

[2] Marie de l'Incarnation, *Choix des Lettres de*, 371.

[3] Le Mercier, *Rel.* 1667, 3; *Dépêches de Talon.*

encouragement, many years passed before this valuable industry was placed on a firm basis.

Talon saw with concern the huge consumption of wine and brandy among the settlers, costing them, as he wrote to Colbert, a hundred thousand livres a year; and to keep this money in the colony, he declared his intention of building a brewery. The minister approved the plan, not only on economic grounds, but because "the vice of drunkenness would thereafter cause no more scandal by reason of the cold nature of beer, the vapors whereof rarely deprive men of the use of judgment."[1] The brewery was accordingly built, to the great satisfaction of the poorer colonists.

Nor did the active intendant fail to acquit himself of the duty of domiciliary visits, enjoined upon him by the royal instructions, — a point on which he was of one mind with his superiors, for he writes that "those charged in this country with his Majesty's affairs are under a strict obligation to enter into the detail of families."[2] Accordingly, we learn from Mother Juchereau that "he studied with the affection of a father how to succor the poor and cause the colony to grow; entered into the minutest particulars; visited the houses of the inhabitants, and caused them to visit him; learned what crops each one was raising; taught those who had wheat to sell it at a profit, helped those who had none, and encouraged everybody." And Dollier de Casson

[1] *Colbert à Talon*, 20 *Fév.*, 1668.
[2] *Mémoire de* 1667.

18

represents him as visiting in turn every house at
Montreal, and giving aid from the King to such as
needed it.[1] Horses, cattle, sheep, and other domestic
animals were sent out at the royal charge in considerable numbers, and distributed gratuitously, with an
order that none of the young should be killed till the
country was sufficiently stocked. Large quantities
of goods were also sent from the same high quarter.
Some of these were distributed as gifts, and the rest
bartered for corn to supply the troops. As the
intendant perceived that the farmers lost much time
in coming from their distant clearings to buy necessaries at Quebec, he caused his agents to furnish
them with the King's goods at their own houses, —
to the great annoyance of the merchants of Quebec,
who complained that their accustomed trade was thus
forestalled.[2]

These were not the only cares which occupied the
mind of Talon. He tried to open a road across the
country to Acadia, — an almost impossible task, in
which he and his successors completely failed.
Under his auspices, Albanel penetrated to Hudson's
Bay, and Saint-Lusson took possession in the King's
name of the country of the Upper Lakes. It was
Talon, in short, who prepared the way for the
remarkable series of explorations described in another
work.[3] Again and again he urged upon Colbert and

---

[1] *Histoire du Montréal*, A. D. 1666, 1667.

[2] *Talon à Colbert*, 10 *Nov.*, 1670.

[3] La Salle, and the Discovery of the Great West.

the King a measure from which, had it taken effect, momentous consequences must have sprung.　This was the purchase or seizure of New York, — involving the isolation of New England, the subjection of the Iroquois, and the undisputed control of half the continent.

Great as were his opportunities of abusing his trust, it does not appear that he took advantage of them.　He held lands and houses in Canada,[1] owned the brewery which he had established, and embarked in various enterprises of productive industry; but, so far as I can discover, he is nowhere accused of making illicit gains, and there is reason to believe that he acquitted himself of his charge with entire fidelity.[2]　His health failed in 1668, and for this and other causes he asked for his recall.　Colbert granted it with strong expressions of regret; and when, two years later, he resumed the intendancy, the colony seems to have welcomed his return.

[1] In 1682, the Intendant Meules, in a despatch to the minister, makes a statement of Talon's property in Quebec.　The chief items are the brewery and a house of some value on the descent of Mountain Street.　He owned, also, the valuable seigniory, afterwards barony, Des Islets, in the immediate neighborhood.

[2] Some imputations against him, not of much weight, are, however, made in a memorial of Aubert de la Chesnaye, a merchant of Quebec.

CHAPTER XVI.

1661–1673.

MARRIAGE AND POPULATION.

Shipment of Emigrants. — Soldier Settlers. — Importation of Wives. — Wedlock. — Summary Methods. — The Mothers of Canada. — Bounties on Marriage. — Celibacy Punished. — Bounties on Children. — Results.

THE peopling of Canada was due in the main to the King. Before the accession of Louis XIV. the entire population — priests, nuns, traders, and settlers — did not exceed twenty-five hundred;[1] but scarcely had he reached his majority when the shipment of men to the colony was systematically begun. Even in Argenson's time, loads of emigrants sent out by the Crown were landed every year at Quebec. The Sulpitians of Montreal also brought over colonists to people their seigniorial estate; the same was true on a small scale of one or two other proprietors, and once at least the company sent a considerable number: yet the government was the chief agent of emigration. Colbert did the work, and the King paid for it.

In 1661, Laval wrote to the cardinals of the Propaganda that during the past two years the King had spent two hundred thousand livres on the colony;

[1] Le Clerc, *Établissement de la Foy*, ii. 4.

that since 1659 he had sent out three hundred men a
year; and that he had promised to send an equal
number every summer during ten years.[1] These
men were sent by squads in merchant-ships, each
one of which was required to carry a certain number.
In many instances, emigrants were bound on their
arrival to enter into the service of colonists already
established. In this case the employer paid them
wages, and after a term of three years they became
settlers themselves.[2]

The destined emigrants were collected by agents
in the provinces, conducted to Dieppe or Rochelle,
and thence embarked. At first men were sent from
Rochelle itself, and its neighborhood; but Laval
remonstrated, declaring that he wanted none from
that ancient stronghold of heresy.[3] The people of
Rochelle, indeed, found no favor in Canada. Another
writer describes them as "persons of little conscience,
and almost no religion," — adding that the Normans,
Percherons, Picards, and peasants of the neighborhood of Paris are docile, industrious, and far more
pious. "It is important," he concludes, "in beginning a new colony, to sow good seed."[4] It was,
accordingly, from the northwestern provinces that
most of the emigrants were drawn.[5] They seem in

[1] *Lettre de Laval envoyée à Rome*, 21 *Oct.*, 1661 (extract in Faillon
from Archives of the Propaganda).

[2] Marie de l'Incarnation, 18 *Août*, 1664. These *engagés* were
sometimes also brought over by private persons.

[3] *Colbert à Laval*, 18 *Mars*, 1664.

[4] *Mémoire de* 1664 (anonymous).

[5] See a paper by Garneau in *Le National* of Quebec, 28 Oct.,

the main to have been a decent peasantry, though writers who from their position should have been well informed have denounced them in unmeasured terms.[1] Some of them could read and write, and some brought with them a little money.

Talon was constantly begging for more men, till Louis XIV. at length took alarm. Colbert replied to the over-zealous intendant that the King did not think it expedient to depopulate France in order to people Canada; that he wanted men for his armies; and that the colony must rely chiefly on increase from within. Still the shipments did not cease; and, even while tempering the ardor of his agent, the

1856, embodying the results of research among the papers of the early notaries of Quebec. The chief emigration was from Paris, Normandy, Poitou, Pays d'Aunis, Brittany, and Picardy. Nearly all those from Paris were sent by the King from houses of charity.

1 "Une foule d'aventuriers, ramassés au hazard en France, presque tous de la lie du peuple, la plupart oberés de dettes ou chargés de crimes," etc. (La Tour, *Vie de Laval*, liv. iv.) "Le vice a obligé la plupart de chercher ce pays comme un asile pour se mettre à couvert de leurs crimes." (Meules, *Dépêche de* 1682.) Meules was intendant in that year. Marie de l'Incarnation, after speaking of the emigrants as of a very mixed character, says that it would have been far better to send a few who were good Christians, rather than so many who give so much trouble. *Lettre du — Octobre*, 1669.

Le Clerc, on the other hand, is emphatic in praise, calling the early colonists "très honnêtes gens, ayant de la probité, de la droiture, et de la religion. . . . L'on a examiné et choisi les habitants, et renvoyé en France les personnes vicieuses." If, he adds, any such were left, "ils effaçaient glorieusement par leur pénitence les taches de leur première condition." Charlevoix is almost as strong in praise as La Tour in censure. Both of them wrote in the next century. We shall have means hereafter of judging between these conflicting statements.

King gave another proof how much he had the growth of Canada at heart.[1]

The regiment of Carignan-Salières had been ordered home, with the exception of four companies kept in garrison,[2] and a considerable number discharged in order to become settlers. Of those who returned, six companies were a year or two later sent back, discharged in their turn, and converted into colonists. Neither men nor officers were positively constrained to remain in Canada; but the officers were told that if they wished to please his Majesty this was the way to do so; and both they and the men were stimulated by promises and rewards. Fifteen hundred livres were given to La Motte, because he had married in the country and meant to remain there. Six thousand livres were assigned to other officers because they had followed, or were about to follow, La Motte's example; and twelve thousand were set apart to be distributed to the soldiers under similar conditions.[3] Each soldier who consented to remain and settle was promised a grant of land and a hundred livres in money; or, if he preferred it, fifty livres with provisions for a year. This military colonization had a strong and lasting influence on the character of the Canadian people.

[1] The King had sent out more emigrants than he had promised, to judge from the census reports during the years 1666, 1667, and 1668. The total population for those years is 3418, 4312, and 5870, respectively. A small part of this growth may be set down to emigration not under government auspices, and a large part to natural increase, — which was enormous at this time, from causes which will soon appear.

[2] *Colbert à Talon*, 20 *Fév.*, 1668.   [3] *Ibid.*

But if the colony was to grow from within, the new settlers must have wives. For some years past the Sulpitians had sent out young women for the supply of Montreal; and the King, on a larger scale, continued the benevolent work. Girls for the colony were taken from the hospitals of Paris and of Lyons, which were not so much hospitals for the sick as houses of refuge for the poor. Mother Mary writes in 1665 that a hundred had come that summer, and were nearly all provided with husbands, and that two hundred more were to come next year. The case was urgent, for the demand was great. Complaints, however, were soon heard that women from cities made indifferent partners; and peasant girls, healthy, strong, and accustomed to field-work, were demanded in their place. Peasant girls were therefore sent; but this was not all. Officers as well as men wanted wives; and Talon asked for a consignment of young ladies. His request was promptly answered. In 1667, he writes: "They send us eighty-four girls from Dieppe and twenty-five from Rochelle; among them are fifteen or twenty of pretty good birth; several of them are really *demoiselles*, and tolerably well brought up." They complained of neglect and hardship during the voyage. "I shall do what I can to soothe their discontent," adds the intendant; "for if they write to their correspondents at home how ill they have been treated, it would be an obstacle to your plan of sending us next year a number of select young ladies." [1]

---

[1] "Des demoiselles bien choisies." — *Talon à Colbert*, 27 *Oct.*, 1667.

Three years later we find him asking for three or four more in behalf of certain bachelor officers. The response surpassed his utmost wishes; and he wrote again: "It is not expedient to send more *demoiselles*. I have had this year fifteen of them, instead of the four I asked for." [1]

As regards peasant girls, the supply rarely equalled the demand. Count Frontenac, Courcelle's successor, complained of the scarcity: "If a hundred and fifty girls and as many servants," he says, "had been sent out this year, they would all have found husbands and masters within a month." [2]

The character of these candidates for matrimony has not escaped the pen of slander. The caustic La Hontan, writing fifteen or twenty years after, draws the following sketch of the mothers of Canada: "After the regiment of Carignan was disbanded, ships were sent out freighted with girls of indifferent virtue, under the direction of a few pious old duennas, who divided them into three classes. These vestals were, so to speak, piled one on the other in three different halls, where the bridegrooms

[1] *Talon à Colbert,* 2 *Nov.,* 1671.

[2] *Frontenac à Colbert,* 2 *Nov.,* 1672. This year only eleven girls had been sent. The scarcity was due to the indiscretion of Talon, who had written to the minister, that, as many of the old settlers had daughters just becoming marriageable, it would be well, in order that they might find husbands, to send no more girls from France at present.

The next year, 1673, the King writes, that, though he is involved in a great war, which needs all his resources, he has nevertheless sent sixty more girls.

chose their brides as a butcher chooses his sheep out of the midst of the flock.   There was wherewith to content the most fantastical in these three harems; for here were to be seen the tall and the short, the blond and the brown, the plump and the lean; everybody, in short, found a shoe to fit him.   At the end of a fortnight not one was left.   I am told that the plumpest were taken first, because it was thought that, being less active, they were more likely to keep at home, and that they could resist the winter cold better.   Those who wanted a wife applied to the directresses, to whom they were obliged to make known their possessions and means of livelihood before taking from one of the three classes the girl whom they found most to their liking.   The marriage was concluded forthwith, with the help of a priest and a notary; and the next day the governor-general caused the couple to be presented with an ox, a cow, a pair of swine, a pair of fowls, two barrels of salted meat, and eleven crowns in money."[1]

As regards the character of the girls, there can be no doubt that this amusing sketch is, in the main, maliciously untrue.   Since the colony began, it had been the practice to send back to France women of the class alluded to by La Hontan, as soon as they became notorious.[2]   Those who were not taken from

[1] La Hontan, *Nouveaux Voyages*, i. 11 (1709).   In some of the other editions the same account is given in different words, equally lively and scandalous.

[2] This is the statement of Boucher, a good authority.   A case of the sort in 1658 is mentioned in the correspondence of Argenson.

institutions of charity usually belonged to the families of peasants overburdened with children, and glad to find the chance of establishing them.[1] How some of them were obtained appears from a letter of Colbert to Harlay, Archbishop of Rouen. "As in the parishes about Rouen," he writes, "fifty or sixty girls might be found who would be very glad to go to Canada to be married, I beg you to employ your credit and authority with the curés of thirty or forty of these parishes, to try to find in each of them one or two girls disposed to go voluntarily for the sake of a settlement in life."[2]

Mistakes nevertheless occurred. "Along with

Boucher says further, that an assurance of good character was required from the relations or friends of the girl who wished to embark. This refers to a period anterior to 1663, when Boucher wrote his book. Colbert evidently cared for no qualification except the capacity of maternity.

[1] *Témoignage de la Mère du Plessis de Sainte-Helène* (extract in Faillon).

[2] *Colbert à l'Archevêque de Rouen*, 27 *Fév.*, 1670.

That they were not always destitute may be gathered from a passage in one of Talon's letters : "Entre les filles qu'on fait passer ici il y en a qui ont de légitimes et considérables prétentions aux successions de leurs parents, même entre celles qui sont tirées de l'Hôpital Général." The General Hospital of Paris had recently been established (1656) as a house of refuge for the "Bohemians," or vagrants of Paris. The royal edict creating it says that "les pauvres mendiants et invalides des deux sexes y seraient enfermés pour estre employés aux manufactures et aultres travaux selon leur pouvoir." They were gathered by force in the streets by a body of special police, called "Archers de l'Hôpital." They resisted at first, and serious riots ensued. In 1662, the General Hospital of Paris contained 6262 paupers. See Clément, *Histoire de Colbert*, 113. Mother de Sainte-Helène says that the girls sent from this asylum had been there from childhood in charge of nuns.

the honest people," complains Mother Mary, "comes
a great deal of *canaille* of both sexes, who cause a
great deal of scandal."[1] After some of the young
women had been married at Quebec, it was found
that they had husbands at home. The priests became
cautious in tying the matrimonial knot, and Colbert
thereupon ordered that each girl should provide herself with a certificate from the curé or magistrate of
her parish to the effect that she was free to marry.
Nor was the practical intendant unmindful of other
precautions to smooth the path to the desired goal.
"The girls destined for this country," he writes,
"besides being strong and healthy, ought to be
entirely free from any natural blemish or anything
personally repulsive."[2]

Thus qualified canonically and physically, the
annual consignment of young women was shipped to
Quebec, in charge of a matron employed and paid by
the King. Her task was not an easy one, for the
troop under her care was apt to consist of what
Mother Mary in a moment of unwonted levity calls
"mixed goods."[3] On one occasion the office was

---

[1] "Beaucoup de canaille de l'un et l'autre sexe qui causent beaucoup de scandale." — *Lettre du — Octobre*, 1669.

[2] *Talon à Colbert*, 10 *Nov.*, 1670.

[3] "Une marchandise mêlée." — *Lettre du — *1668. In that year,
1668, the King spent 40,000 livres in the shipment of men and girls.
In 1669, a hundred and fifty girls were sent; in 1670, a hundred and
sixty-five; and Talon asks for a hundred and fifty or two hundred
more to supply the soldiers who had got ready their houses and
clearings, and were now prepared to marry. The total number of
girls sent from 1665 to 1673, inclusive, was about a thousand.

undertaken by the pious widow of Jean Bourdon. Her flock of a hundred and fifty girls, says Mother Mary, "gave her no little trouble on the voyage; for they are of all sorts, and some of them are very rude and hard to manage." Madame Bourdon was not daunted. She not only saw her charge distributed and married, but she continued to receive and care for the subsequent ship-loads as they arrived summer after summer. She was indeed chief among the pious duennas of whom La Hontan irreverently speaks. Marguerite Bourgeoys did the same good offices for the young women sent to Montreal. Here the "King's girls," as they were called, were all lodged together in a house to which the suitors repaired to make their selection. "I was obliged to live there myself," writes the excellent nun, "because families were to be formed;"[1] that is to say, because it was she who superintended these extemporized unions. Meanwhile she taught the girls their catechism, and, more fortunate than Madame Bourdon, inspired them with a confidence and affection which they retained long after.

At Quebec, where the matrimonial market was on a larger scale, a more ample bazaar was needed. That the girls were assorted into three classes, each penned up for selection in a separate hall, is a statement probable enough in itself, but resting on no better authority than that of La Hontan. Be this as it may, they were submitted together to the inspec-

[1] Extract in Faillon, *Colonie Française,* iii. 214.

tion of the suitor; and the awkward young peasant
or the rugged soldier of Carignan was required to
choose a bride without delay from among the anxious
candidates. They, on their part, were permitted to
reject any applicant who displeased them; and the
first question, we are told, which most of them asked
was whether the suitor had a house and a farm.

Great as was the call for wives, it was thought
prudent to stimulate it. The new settler was at
once enticed and driven into wedlock. Bounties
were offered on early marriages. Twenty livres were
given to each youth who married before the age of
twenty, and to each girl who married before the age
of sixteen.[1] This, which was called the "King's
gift," was exclusive of the dowry given by him to
every girl brought over by his orders. The dowry
varied greatly in form and value; but, according to
Mother Mary, it was sometimes a house with provisions for eight months. More often it was fifty
livres in household supplies, besides a barrel or two
of salted meat. The royal solicitude extended also
to the children of colonists already established. "I
pray you," writes Colbert to Talon, "to commend it
to the consideration of the whole people, that their
prosperity, their subsistence, and all that is dear to
them depend on a general resolution, never to be
departed from, to marry youths at eighteen or nine-
teen years and girls at fourteen or fifteen; since
abundance can never come to them except through

---

[1] *Arrêt du Conseil d'État du Roy* (see *Édits et Ordonnances*, i. 67)

the abundance of men."[1] This counsel was followed by appropriate action. Any father of a family who, without showing good cause, neglected to marry his children when they had reached the ages of twenty and sixteen was fined;[2] and each father thus delinquent was required to present himself every six months to the local authorities to declare what reason, if any, he had for such delay.[3] Orders were issued, a little before the arrival of the yearly ships from France, that all single men should marry within a fortnight after the landing of the prospective brides. No mercy was shown to the obdurate bachelor. Talon issued an order forbidding unmarried men to hunt, fish, trade with the Indians, or go into the woods under any pretence whatsoever.[4] In

[1] *Colbert à Talon*, 20 *Fév.*, 1668.

[2] *Arrêts du Conseil d'État*, 1669 (cited by Faillon); *Arrêt du Conseil d'État*, 1670 (see *Édits et Ordonnances*, i. 67); *Ordonnance du Roy*, 5 *Avril*, 1669. See Clément, *Instructions, etc. de Colbert*, iii. 2me Partie, 657.

[3] *Régistre du Conseil Souverain*.

[4] *Talon au Ministre*, 10 *Oct.*, 1670. Colbert highly approves this order. Faillon found a case of its enforcement among the ancient records of Montreal. In December, 1670, François Le Noir, an inhabitant of La Chine, was summoned before the judge, because, though a single man, he had traded with Indians at his own house He confessed the fact, but protested that he would marry within three weeks after the arrival of the vessels from France, or, failing to do so, that he would give a hundred and fifty livres to the church of Montreal, and an equal sum to the hospital. On this condition he was allowed to trade, but was still forbidden to go into the woods. The next year he kept his word, and married Marie Magdeleine Charbonnier, late of Paris.

The prohibition to go into the woods was probably intended to prevent the bachelor from finding a temporary Indian substitute for a French wife.

short, they were made as miserable as possible.
Colbert goes further.   He writes to the intendant,
"Those who may seem to have absolutely renounced
marriage should be made to bear additional burdens,
and be excluded from all honors; it would be well
even to add some marks of infamy."[1]   The success
of these measures was complete.   "No sooner," says
Mother Mary, "have the vessels arrived than the
young men go to get wives; and, by reason of the
great number, they are married by thirties at a time."
Throughout the length and breadth of Canada, Hymen, if not Cupid, was whipped into a frenzy of activity.   Dollier de Casson tells us of a widow who was
married afresh before her late husband was buried.[2]

Nor was the fatherly care of the King confined to
the humbler classes of his colonists.   He wished to
form a Canadian *noblesse*, to which end early marriages were thought needful among officers and others
of the better sort.   The progress of such marriages
was carefully watched and reported by the intendant.
We have seen the reward bestowed upon La Motte
for taking to himself a wife, and the money set apart
for the brother officers who imitated him.   In his
despatch of October, 1667, the intendant announces
that two captains are already married to two damsels
of the country; that a lieutenant has espoused a
daughter of the governor of Three Rivers; and that

[1] "Il serait à propos de leur augmenter les charges, de les priver
de tous honneurs, même d'y ajouter quelque marque d'infamie."
Lettre du 20 Fév., 1668.

[2] *Histoire du Montréal*, A. D. 1671, 1672.

"four ensigns are in treaty with their mistresses, and are already half engaged."[1] The paternal care of government, one would think, could scarcely go further.

It did, however, go further. Bounties were offered on children. The King, in council, passed a decree "that in future all inhabitants of the said country of Canada who shall have living children to the number of ten, born in lawful wedlock, not being priests, monks, or nuns, shall each be paid out of the moneys sent by his Majesty to the said country a pension of three hundred livres a year, and those who shall have twelve children, a pension of four hundred livres; and that, to this effect, they shall be required to declare the number of their children every year in the months of June or July to the intendant of justice, police, and finance, established in the said country, who, having verified the same, shall order the payment of said pensions, one-half in cash, and the other half at the end of each year."[2] This was

---

[1] " Quatre enseignes sont en pourparler avec leurs maîtresses et sont déjà à demi engagés." (*Dépêche du* 27 *Oct.*, 1667.) The lieutenant was René Gaultier de Varennes, who on the 26th September, 1667, married Marie Bochart, daughter of the governor of Three Rivers, *aged twelve years.* One of the children of this marriage was Varennes de la Vérendrye, whose son discovered the Rocky Mountains.

[2] *Édits et Ordonnances*, i. 67. It was thought at this time that the Indians, mingled with the French, might become a valuable part of the population. The reproductive qualities of Indian women, therefore, became an object of Talon's attention, and he reports that they impair their fertility by nursing their children longer than is necessary; "but," he adds, "this obstacle to the speedy building up of the colony can be overcome by a police regulation." *Mémoire sur l'État Présent du Canada*, 1667.

19

applicable to all. Colbert had before offered a reward, intended specially for the better class, of twelve hundred livres to those who had fifteen children, and eight hundred to those who had ten.

These wise encouragements, as the worthy Faillon calls them, were crowned with the desired result. A despatch of Talon in 1670 informs the minister that most of the young women sent out last summer are pregnant already; and in 1671 he announces that from six hundred to seven hundred children have been born in the colony during the year, — a prodigious number in view of the small population. The climate was supposed to be particularly favorable to the health of women, which is somewhat surprising in view of recent American experience. "The first reflection I have to make," says Dollier de Casson, "is on the advantage that women have in this place [Montreal] over men; for though the cold is very wholesome to both sexes, it is incomparably more so to the female, who is almost immortal here." Her fecundity matched her longevity, and was the admiration of Talon and his successors, accustomed as they were to the scanty families of France.

Why with this great natural increase joined to an immigration which, though greatly diminishing, did not entirely cease, was there not a corresponding increase in the population of the colony? Why, more than half a century after the King took Canada in charge, did the census show a total of less than twenty-five thousand souls? The reasons will appear hereafter.

It is a peculiarity of Canadian immigration, at this
its most flourishing epoch, that it was mainly an
immigration of single men and single women. The
cases in which entire families came over were comparatively few.[1] The new settler was found by the
King, sent over by the King, and supplied by the
King with a wife, a farm, and sometimes with a
house. Well did Louis XIV. earn the title of
Father of New France. But the royal zeal was spasmodic. The King was diverted to other cares; and
soon after the outbreak of the Dutch war in 1672
the regular despatch of emigrants to Canada wellnigh ceased, — though the practice of disbanding
soldiers in the colony, giving them lands, and turning them into settlers, was continued in some degree,
even to the last.

[1] The principal emigration of families seems to have been in
1669, when, at the urgency of Talon, then in France, a considerable
number were sent out. In the earlier period the emigration of
families was, relatively, much greater. Thus, in 1634, the physician
Giffard brought over seven to people his seigniory of Beauport.
Before 1663, when the King took the colony in hand, the emigrants
were for the most part apprenticed laborers.

The zeal with which the King entered into the work of stocking
his colony is shown by numberless passages in his letters, and
those of his minister. "The end and the rule of all your conduct,"
says Colbert to the intendant Bouteroue, "should be the increase
of the colony; and on this point you should never be satisfied, but
labor without ceasing to find every imaginable expedient for pre-
serving the inhabitants, attracting new ones, and multiplying them
by marriage." — *Instruction pour M. Bouteroue*, 1668.

CHAPTER XVII.

1665–1672.

THE NEW HOME.

MILITARY FRONTIER. — THE CANADIAN SETTLER. — SEIGNIOR AND VASSAL. — EXAMPLE OF TALON. — PLAN OF SETTLEMENT. — ASPECT OF CANADA. — QUEBEC. — THE RIVER SETTLEMENTS. — MONTREAL. — THE PIONEERS.

WE have seen the settler landed and married; let us follow him to his new home. At the end of Talon's administration, the head of the colony — that is to say, the island of Montreal and the borders of the Richelieu — was the seat of a peculiar colonization, the chief object of which was to protect the rest of Canada against Iroquois incursions. The lands along the Richelieu, from its mouth to a point above Chambly, were divided in large seigniorial grants among several officers of the regiment of Carignan, who in their turn granted out the land to the soldiers, reserving a sufficient portion as their own. The officer thus became a kind of feudal chief, and the whole settlement a permanent military cantonment admirably suited to the object in view. The disbanded soldier was practically a soldier still, but he was also a farmer and a landholder.

Talon had recommended this plan as being in accordance with the example of the Romans. "The practice of that politic and martial people," he wrote, "may, in my opinion, be wisely adopted in a country a thousand leagues distant from its monarch. And as the peace and harmony of peoples depend above all things on their fidelity to their sovereign, our first kings, better statesmen than is commonly supposed, introduced into newly conquered countries men of war, of approved trust, in order at once to hold the inhabitants to their duty within, and repel the enemy from without." [1]

The troops were accordingly discharged, and settled not alone on the Richelieu, but also along the St. Lawrence, between Lake St. Peter and Montreal, as well as at some other points. The Sulpitians, feudal owners of Montreal, adopted a similar policy, and surrounded their island with a border of fiefs large and small, granted partly to officers and partly to humbler settlers, bold, hardy, and practised in bush-fighting. Thus a line of sentinels was posted around their entire shore, ready to give the alarm whenever an enemy appeared. About Quebec the settlements, covered as they were by those above, were for the most part of a more pacific character.

To return to the Richelieu. The towns and villages which have since grown upon its banks and along the adjacent shores of the St. Lawrence owe their names to these officers of Carignan, ancient

[1] *Projets de Réglemens*, 1667 (see *Édits et Ordonnances*, ii. 29).

lords of the soil, — Sorel, Chambly, Saint Ours, Contrecœur, Varennes, Verchères. Yet let it not be supposed that villages sprang up at once. The military seignior, valiant and poor as Walter the Penniless, was in no condition to work such magic. His personal possessions usually consisted of little but his sword and the money which the King had paid him for marrying a wife. A domain varying from half a league to six leagues in front on the river, and from half a league to two leagues in depth, had been freely given him. When he had distributed a part of it in allotments to the soldiers, a variety of tasks awaited him, — to clear and cultivate his land; to build his seigniorial mansion, often a log hut; to build a fort; to build a chapel; and to build a mill. To do all this at once was impossible. Chambly, the chief proprietor on the Richelieu, was better able than the others to meet the exigency. He built himself a good house, where, with cattle and sheep furnished by the King, he lived in reasonable comfort.[1] The King's fort, close at hand, spared him and his tenants the necessity of building one for themselves, and furnished, no doubt, a mill, a chapel, and a chaplain. His brother officers, Sorel excepted, were less fortunate. They and their tenants were forced to provide defence as well as shelter. Their houses were all built together, and surrounded by a palisade, so as to form a little fortified village. The

[1] *Frontenac au Ministre*, 2 *Nov.*, 1672. Marie de l'Incarnation speaks of these officers on the Richelieu as *très honnêtes gens*.

ever-active benevolence of the King had aided them
in the task, for the soldiers were still maintained by
him while clearing the lands and building the houses
destined to be their own; nor was it till this work
was done that the provident government despatched
them to Quebec with orders to bring back wives.
The settler, thus lodged and wedded, was required
on his part to aid in clearing lands for those who
should come after him.[1]

It was chiefly in the more exposed parts of the
colony that the houses were gathered together in
palisaded villages, thus forcing the settler to walk or
paddle some distance to his farm. He naturally
preferred to build when he could on the front of his
farm itself, near the river, which supplied the place
of a road. As the grants of land were very narrow,
his house was not far from that of his next neighbor;
and thus a line of dwellings was ranged along the
shore, forming what in local language was called a
côte, — a use of the word peculiar to Canada, where
it still prevails.

The impoverished seignior rarely built a chapel.
Most of the early Canadian churches were built with

---

[1] "Sa Majesté semble prétendre faire la dépense entière pour
former le commencement des habitations par l'abattis du bois, la
culture et semence de deux arpens de terre, l'avance de quelques
farines aux familles venantes," etc. (*Projets de Réglemens*, 1667.)
This applied to civil and military settlers alike. The established
settler was allowed four years to clear two arpents of land for
a new-comer. The soldiers were maintained by the King during
a year, while preparing their farms and houses. Talon asks that
two years more be given them. *Talon au Roy*, 10 *Nov.*, 1670.

funds furnished by the seminaries of Quebec or of Montreal, aided by contributions of material and labor from the parishioners.[1]   Meanwhile mass was said in some house of the neighborhood by a missionary priest, paddling his canoe from village to village, or from *côte* to *côte*.

The mill was an object of the last importance.   It was built of stone and pierced with loopholes, to serve as a blockhouse in case of attack.   The great mill at Montreal was one of the chief defences of the place.   It was at once the duty and the right of the seignior to supply his tenants, or rather vassals, with this essential requisite; and they on their part were required to grind their grain at his mill, leaving the fourteenth part in payment.   But for many years there was not a seigniory in Canada where this fraction would pay the wages of a miller; and, except the ecclesiastical corporations, there were few seigniors who could pay the cost of building.   The first settlers were usually forced to grind for themselves after the tedious fashion of the Indians.

Talon, in his capacity of counsellor, friend, and father to all Canada, arranged the new settlements near Quebec in the manner which he judged best, and which he meant to serve as an example to the rest of the colony.   It was his aim to concentrate population around this point, so that, should an enemy appear, the sound of a cannon-shot from the Château St. Louis might summon a numerous body

[1] La Tour, *Vie de Laval*, chap. x.

of defenders to this the common point of rendezvous.[1]
He bought a tract of land near Quebec, laid it out,
and settled it as a model seigniory, hoping, as he
says, to kindle a spirit of emulation among the new-
made seigniors to whom he had granted lands from
the King. He also laid out at the royal cost three
villages in the immediate neighborhood, planning
them with great care, and peopling them partly with
families newly arrived, partly with soldiers, and
partly with old settlers, in order that the new-comers
might take lessons from the experience of these
veterans. That each village might be complete in
itself, he furnished it as well as he could with the
needful carpenter, mason, blacksmith, and shoe-
maker. These inland villages, called respectively
Bourg Royal, Bourg la Reine, and Bourg Talon, did
not prove very thrifty.[2] Wherever the settlers were
allowed to choose for themselves, they ranged their
dwellings along the watercourses. With the exception of Talon's villages, one could have seen nearly
every house in Canada, by paddling a canoe up the
St. Lawrence and the Richelieu. The settlements
formed long thin lines on the edges of the rivers, — a
convenient arrangement, but one very unfavorable
to defence, to ecclesiastical control, and to strong
government. The King soon discovered this; and
repeated orders were sent to concentrate the inhab-

---

[1] *Projets de Réglemens,* 1667.
[2] In 1672 the King, as a mark of honor, attached these villages
to Talon's seigniory. See Documents on Seigniorial Tenure.

itants and form Canada into villages, instead of *côtes*.
To do so would have involved a general revocation
of grants and abandonment of houses and clearings,
— a measure too arbitrary and too wasteful, even for
Louis XIV., and one extremely difficult to enforce.
Canada persisted in attenuating herself, and the royal
will was foiled.

As you ascended the St. Lawrence, the first harboring place of civilization was Tadoussac, at the
mouth of the Saguenay, where the company had its
trading station, where its agents ruled supreme, and
where, in early summer, all was alive with canoes
and wigwams, and troops of Montagnais savages,
bringing their furs to market. Leave Tadoussac
behind, and, embarked in a sail-boat or a canoe,
follow the northern coast. Far on the left, twenty
miles away, the southern shore lies pale and dim, and
mountain ranges wave their faint outline along the
sky. You pass the beetling rocks of Mal Bay, a
solitude but for the bark hut of some wandering
Indian beneath the cliff, the Eboulements with their
wild romantic gorge and foaming waterfalls, and the
Bay of St. Paul with its broad valley and its woody
mountains, rich with hidden stores of iron. Vast
piles of savage verdure border the mighty stream, till
at length the mountain of Cape Tourmente upheaves
its huge bulk from the bosom of the water, shadowed
by lowering clouds, and dark with forests. Just
beyond, begin the settlements of Laval's vast seigniory of Beaupré, which had not been forgotten in the

distribution of emigrants, and which, in 1667, contained more inhabitants than Quebec itself.[1] The ribbon of rich meadow land that borders that beautiful shore was yellow with wheat in harvest time; and on the woody slopes behind, the frequent clearings and the solid little dwellings of logs continued for a long distance to relieve the sameness of the forest. After passing the cataract of Montmorenci, there was another settlement, much smaller, at Beauport, the seigniory of the ex-physician Giffard, one of the earliest proprietors in Canada. The neighboring shores of the Island of Orleans were also edged with houses and clearings. The promontory of Quebec now towered full in sight, crowned with church, fort, château, convents, and seminary. There was little else on the rock. Priests, nuns, government officials, and soldiers were the denizens of the Upper Town; while commerce and the trades were cabined along the strand beneath.[2] From the gallery of the château, you might toss a pebble far down on their shingled roofs. In the midst of them was the magazine of the company, with its two round towers and two projecting wings. It was here that

---

[1] The census of 1667 gives to Quebec only 448 souls; Côte de Beaupré, 656; Beauport, 123; Island of Orleans, 529; other settlements included under the government of Quebec, 1,011; Côte de Lauzon (south shore), 113; Trois Rivières and its dependencies, 666; Montreal, 766. Both Beaupré and Isle d'Orleans belonged at this time to the bishop.

[2] According to Juchereau, there were seventy houses at Quebec about the time of Tracy's arrival.

all the beaver-skins of the colony were collected,
assorted, and shipped for France. The so-called
Château St. Louis was an indifferent wooden structure planted on a site truly superb, — above the
Lower Town, above the river, above the ships, gazing abroad on a majestic panorama of waters, forests,
and mountains.[1] Behind it was the area of the fort,
of which it formed one side. The governor lived in
the château, and soldiers were on guard night and
day in the fort. At some little distance was the
convent of the Ursulines, ugly but substantial,[2]
where Mother Mary of the Incarnation ruled her
pupils and her nuns; and a little farther on, towards
the right, was the Hôtel Dieu. Between them were
the massive buildings of the Jesuits, then as now
facing the principal square. At one side was their
church, newly finished; and opposite, across the
square, stood and still stands the great church of
Notre Dame. Behind the church was Laval's seminary, with the extensive enclosures belonging to it.
The *sénéchaussée* or court-house, the tavern of one
Jacques Boisdon on the square near the church, and
a few houses along the line of what is now St. Louis
Street comprised nearly all the civil part of the Upper
Town. The ecclesiastical buildings were of stone,
and the church of Notre Dame and the Jesuit

---

[1] In 1660, an exact inventory was taken of the contents of the
fort and château, — a beggarly account of rubbish. The château
was then a long low building roofed with shingles.

[2] There is an engraving of it in Abbe Casgrain's interesting *Vie
de Marie de l'Incarnation.* It was burned in 1686.

College were marvels of size and solidity in view of
the poverty and weakness of the colony.[1]

Proceeding upward along the north shore of the
St. Lawrence, one found a cluster of houses at Cap
Rouge, and, farther on, the frequent rude beginnings of a seigniory. The settlements thickened on
approaching Three Rivers, a fur-trading hamlet
enclosed with a square palisade. Above this place,
a line of incipient seigniories bordered the river,
most of them granted to officers, — Laubia, a captain;
Labadie, a sergeant; Moras, an ensign; Berthier, a
captain; Raudin, an ensign; La Valterie, a lieutenant.[2] Under their auspices, settlers, military and
civilian, were ranging themselves along the shore,
and ugly gaps in the forest thickly set with stumps
bore witness to their toils. These settlements rapidly
extended, till in a few years a chain of houses
and clearings reached with little interruption from
Quebec to Montreal. Such was the fruit of Tracy's
chastisement of the Mohawks, and the influx of
immigrants that followed.

As you approached Montreal, the fortified mill

[1] The first stone of Notre Dame de Quebec was laid in September, 1647, and the first mass was said in it on the 24th of
December, 1650. The side walls still remain as part of the present
structure. The Jesuit College was also begun in 1647. The walls
and roof were finished in 1649. The church connected with it,
since destroyed, was begun in 1666. See *Journal des Jésuites.*

[2] See Documents on the Seigniorial Tenure; Abstracts of Titles.
Most of these grants, like those on the Richelieu, were made by
Talon in 1672; but the land had, in many cases, been occupied and
cleared in anticipation of the title.

built by the Sulpitians at Point aux Trembles towered above the woods; and soon after the newly built chapel of the Infant Jesus. More settlements followed, till at length the great fortified mill of Montreal rose in sight; then the long row of compact wooden houses, the Hôtel Dieu, and the rough masonry of the Seminary of St. Sulpice. Beyond the town, the clearings continued at intervals till you reached Lake St. Louis, where young Cavelier de la Salle had laid out his seigniory of La Chine, and abandoned it to begin his hard career of western exploration. Above the island of Montreal, the wilderness was broken only by a solitary trading station on the neighboring Isle Pérot.

Now cross Lake St. Louis, shoot the rapids of La Chine, and follow the southern shore downward. Here the seigniories of Longueuil, Boucherville, Varennes, Verchères, and Contrecœur were already begun. From the fort of Sorel one could visit the military seigniories along the Richelieu or descend towards Quebec, passing on the way those of Lussaudière, Becancour, Lotbinière, and others still in a shapeless infancy. Even far below Quebec, at St. Anne de la Pocatière, River Ouelle, and other points, cabins and clearings greeted the eye of the passing canoeman.

For a year or two the settler's initiation was a rough one; but when he had a few acres under tillage he could support himself and his family on the produce, aided by hunting, if he knew how to use a gun, and by the bountiful profusion of eels which the St. Lawrence never failed to yield in their season, and which, smoked or salted, supplied his larder for months. In winter he hewed timber, sawed planks, or split shingles for the market of Quebec, obtaining in return such necessaries as he required. With thrift and hard work he was sure of comfort at last; but the former habits of the military settlers and of many of the others were not favorable to a routine of dogged industry. The sameness and solitude of their new life often became insufferable; nor, married as they had been, was the domestic hearth likely to supply much consolation. Yet, thrifty or not, they multiplied apace. "A poor man," says Mother Mary, "will have eight children and more, who run about in winter with bare heads and bare feet, and a little jacket on their backs, live on nothing but bread and eels, and on that grow fat and stout." With such treatment the weaker sort died, but the strong survived; and out of this rugged nursing sprang the hardy Canadian race of bush-rangers and bush-fighters.

CHAPTER XVIII.

1663–1763.

CANADIAN FEUDALISM.

TRANSPLANTATION OF FEUDALISM. — PRECAUTIONS. — FAITH AND HOMAGE. — THE SEIGNIOR. — THE CENSITAIRE. — ROYAL INTERVENTION. — THE GENTILHOMME. — CANADIAN NOBLESSE.

CANADIAN society was beginning to form itself, and at its base was the feudal tenure. European feudalism was the indigenous and natural growth of political and social conditions which preceded it. Canadian feudalism was an offshoot of the feudalism of France, modified by the lapse of centuries, and further modified by the royal will.

In France, as in the rest of Europe, the system had lost its vitality. The warrior-nobles who placed Hugh Capet on the throne, and began the feudal monarchy, formed an aristocratic republic; and the King was one of their number, whom they chose to be their chief. But through the struggles and vicissitudes of many succeeding reigns royalty had waxed and oligarchy had waned. The fact had changed, and the theory had changed with it. The King, once powerless among a host of turbulent nobles,

was now a king indeed. Once a chief, because his
equals had made him so, he was now the anointed of
the Lord. This triumph of royalty had culminated
in Louis XIV. The stormy energies and bold indi-
vidualism of the old feudal nobles had ceased to
exist. They who had held his predecessors in awe
had become his obsequious servants. He no longer
feared his nobles: he prized them as gorgeous decora-
tions of his court and satellites of his royal person.

It was Richelieu who first planted feudalism in
Canada.[1] The King would preserve it there, because
with its teeth drawn he was fond of it; and because,
as the feudal tenure prevailed in Old France, it was
natural that it should prevail also in the New. But
he continued as Richelieu had begun, and moulded it
to the form that pleased him. Nothing was left
which could threaten his absolute and undivided
authority over the colony. In France, a multitude
of privileges and prescriptions still clung, despite its
fall, about the ancient ruling class. Few of these
were allowed to cross the Atlantic, while the old
lingering abuses, which had made the system odious,
were at the same time lopped away. Thus retrenched,
Canadian feudalism was made to serve a double
end, — to produce a faint and harmless reflection of
French aristocracy, and simply and practically to
supply agencies for distributing land among the
settlers.

[1] By the charter of the Company of the Hundred Associates,
1627.

20

The nature of the precautions which it was held to require appear in the plan of administration which Talon and Tracy laid before the minister. They urge that, in view of the distance from France, special care ought to be taken to prevent changes and revolutions, aristocratic or otherwise, in the colony, whereby in time sovereign jurisdictions might grow up, as formerly occurred in various parts of France.[1] And in respect to grants already made an inquiry was ordered, to ascertain "if seigniors in distributing lands to their vassals have exacted any conditions injurious to the rights of the Crown and the subjection due solely to the King." In the same view the seignior was denied any voice whatever in the direction of government; and it is scarcely necessary to say that the essential feature of feudalism in the day of its vitality, the requirement of military service by the lord from the vassal, was utterly unknown in Canada. The royal governor called out the militia whenever he saw fit, and set over it what officers he pleased.

The seignior was usually the immediate vassal of the Crown, from which he had received his land gratuitously. In a few cases he made grants to other seigniors inferior in the feudal scale, and they, his vassals, granted in turn to their vassals, — the *habitants*, or cultivators of the soil.[2] Sometimes the

[1] *Projet de Réglement fait par MM. de Tracy et Talon pour la justice et la distribution des terres du Canada, Jan.* 24, 1667.

[2] Most of the seigniories of Canada were simple fiefs; but there wef ; some exceptions. In 1671, the King, as a mark of honor to

habitant held directly of the Crown, in which case there was no step between the highest and lowest degrees of the feudal scale. The seignior held by the tenure of faith and homage, the *habitant* by the inferior tenure *en censive*. Faith and homage were rendered to the Crown or other feudal superior whenever the seigniory changed hands, or, in the case of seigniories held by corporations, after long stated intervals. The following is an example, drawn from the early days of the colony, of the performance of this ceremony by the owner of a fief to the seignior who had granted it to him. It is that of Jean Guion, vassal of Giffard, seignior of Beauport.

The act recounts how, in presence of a notary, Guion presented himself at the principal door of the manor-house of Beauport; how, having knocked, one Boullé, farmer of Giffard, opened the door, and in reply to Guion's question if the seignior was at home, replied that he was not, but that he, Boullé, was empowered to receive acknowledgments of faith and homage from the vassals in his name. "After the which reply," proceeds the act, "the said Guion, being at the principal door, placed himself on his

Talon, erected his seigniory Des Islets into a barony; and it was soon afterwards made an earldom, *comté*. In 1676, the seigniory of St. Laurent, on the island of Orleans, once the property of Laval, and then belonging to François Berthelot, councillor of the King, was erected into an earldom. In 1681, the seigniory of Portneuf, belonging to Réné Robineau, chevalier, was made a barony. In 1700, three seigniories on the south side of the St. Lawrence were united into the barony of Longueuil. (See Papers on the Feudal Tenure in Canada, Abstract of Titles.)

knees on the ground, with head bare, and without
sword or spurs, and said three times these words:
' Monsieur de Beauport, Monsieur de Beauport,
Monsieur de Beauport! I bring you the faith and
homage which I am bound to bring you on account
of my fief Du Buisson, which I hold as a man of
faith of your seigniory of Beauport, declaring that I
offer to pay my seigniorial and feudal dues in their
season, and demanding of you to accept me in faith
and homage as aforesaid.' " [1]

The following instance is the more common one of a
seignior holding directly of the Crown.   It is widely
separated from the first in point of time, having occurred a year after the army of Wolfe entered Quebec.

Philippe Noël had lately died, and Jean Noël, his
son, inherited his seigniory of Tilly and Bonsecours.
To make the title good, faith and homage must be
renewed.   Jean Noël was under the bitter necessity
of rendering this duty to General Murray, governor
for the King of Great Britain.   The form is the
same as in the case of Guion, more than a century
before.   Noël repairs to the Government House at
Quebec, and knocks at the door.   A servant opens
it.   Noël asks if the governor is there.   The servant
replies that he is.   Murray, informed of the visitor's object, comes to the door, and Noël then and
there, "without sword or spurs, with bare head,

---

[1] Ferland, *Notes sur les Registres de Notre Dame de Québec*, 65.
This was a *fief en roture*, as distinguished from a *fief noble*, to which
judicial powers and other privileges were attached.

Goupil & Cᵒ Paris.

and one knee on the ground," repeats the acknowledgment of faith and homage for his seigniory. He
was compelled, however, to add a detested innovation, — the oath of fidelity to his Britannic Majesty,
coupled with a pledge to keep his vassals in obedience to the new sovereign.[1]

The seignior was a proprietor holding that relation
to the feudal superior which, in its pristine character,
has been truly described as servile in form, proud
and bold in spirit.   But in Canada this bold spirit
was very far from being strengthened by the changes
which the policy of the Crown had introduced into
the system.   The reservation of mines and minerals,
oaks for the royal navy, roadways, and a site (if
needed) for royal forts and magazines, had in it
nothing extraordinary.   The great difference between
the position of the Canadian seignior and that of the
vassal proprietor of the Middle Ages lay in the extent
and nature of the control which the Crown and its
officers held over him.   A decree of the King, an
edict of the council, or an ordinance of the intendant,
might at any moment change old conditions, impose
new ones, interfere between the lord of the manor
and his grantees, and modify or annul his bargains,
past or present.   He was never sure whether or not
the government would let him alone; and against its
most arbitrary intervention he had no remedy.

One condition was imposed on him which may be

---

[1] See the act in *Observations de Sir L. H. Lafontaine, Bart., sur
la Tenure Seigneuriale*, 217, *note*.

said to form the distinctive feature of Canadian
feudalism, — that of clearing his land within a
limited time on pain of forfeiting it. The object
was the excellent one of preventing the lands of the
colony from lying waste. As the seignior was often
the penniless owner of a domain three or four leagues
wide and proportionably deep, he could not clear it
all himself, and was therefore under the necessity of
placing the greater part in the hands of those who
could. But he was forbidden to sell any part of it
which he had not cleared. He must grant it without
price, on condition of a small perpetual rent; and
this brings us to the cultivator of the soil, the *censitaire*, the broad base of the feudal pyramid.[1]

The tenure *en censive*, by which the *censitaire* held
of the seignior, consisted in the obligation to make

---

[1] The greater part of the grants made by the old Company of
New France were resumed by the Crown for neglect to occupy and
improve the land, which was granted out anew under the administration of Talon. The most remarkable of these forfeited grants
is that of the vast domain of La Citière, large enough for a
kingdom. Lauson, afterwards governor, had obtained it from the
company, but had failed to improve it. Two or three sub-grants
which he had made from it were held valid; the rest was reunited
to the royal domain. On repeated occasions at later dates, negli-
gent seigniors were threatened with the loss of half or the whole
of their land, and various cases are recorded in which the threat
took effect. In 1741, an ordinance of the governor and intendant
reunited to the royal domain seventeen seigniories at one stroke;
but the former owners were told that if within a year they cleared
and settled a reasonable part of the forfeited estates, the titles
should be restored to them. (*Édits et Ordonnances*, ii. 555.) In the
case of the *habitant* or *censitaire*, forfeitures for neglect to improve
the land and live on it are very numerous.

annual payments in money, produce, or both. In Canada these payments, known as *cens et rente*, were strangely diverse in amount and kind; but in all the early period of the colony they were almost ludicrously small. A common charge at Montreal was half a sou and half a pint of wheat for each arpent. The rate usually fluctuated in the early times between half a sou and two sous; so that a farm of a hundred and sixty arpents would pay from four to sixteen francs, of which a part would be in money and the rest in live capons, wheat, eggs, or all three together, in pursuance of contracts as amusing in their precision as they are bewildering in their variety. Live capons, estimated at twenty sous each, though sometimes not worth ten, form a conspicuous feature in these agreements; so that on pay-day the seignior's barnyard presented an animated scene. Later in the history of the colony grants were at somewhat higher rates. Payment was commonly made on St. Martin's day, when there was a general muster of tenants at the seigniorial mansion, with a prodigious consumption of tobacco and a corresponding retail of neighborhood gossip, joined to the outcries of the captive fowls bundled together for delivery, with legs tied, but throats at full liberty.

A more considerable but a very uncertain source of income to the seignior were the *lods et ventes*, or mutation fines. The land of the *censitaire* passed freely to his heirs; but if he sold it, a twelfth part of the purchase-money must be paid to the seignior. The seignior, on his part, was equally liable to pay a mutation fine to his feudal superior if he sold his seigniory; and for him the amount was larger, — being a *quint*, or a fifth of the price received, of which, however, the greater part was deducted for immediate payment. This heavy charge, constituting as it did a tax on all improvements, was a principal cause of the abolition of the feudal tenure in 1854.

The obligation of clearing his land and living on it was laid on seignior and *censitaire* alike; but the latter was under a variety of other obligations to the former, partly imposed by custom and partly established by agreement when the grant was made. To grind his grain at the seignior's mill, bake his bread in the seignior's oven, work for him one or more days in the year, and give him one fish in every eleven, for the privilege of fishing in the river before his farm, — these were the most annoying of the conditions to which the *censitaire* was liable. Few of them were enforced with much regularity. That of baking in the seignior's oven was rarely carried into effect, though occasionally used for purposes of extortion. It is here that the royal government appears in its true character, so far as concerns its relations with Canada, — that of a well-meaning despotism. It continually intervened between *censitaire* and seignior, on the principle that "as his Majesty gives the land for nothing, he can make what conditions he pleases, and change them when he pleases."[1]

These interventions were usually favorable to the *censitaire*. On one occasion an intendant reported to the minister, that in his opinion all rents ought to be reduced to one sou and one live capon for every arpent of front, equal in most cases to forty superficial arpents.[2] Everything, he remarks, ought to be brought down to the level of the first grants "made in days of innocence," — a happy period which he does not attempt to define. The minister replies that the diversity of the rent is, in fact, vexatious, and that for his part he is disposed to abolish it altogether.[3] Neither he nor the intendant gives the slightest hint of any compensation to the seignior.

Though these radical measures were not executed, many changes were decreed from time to time in the relations between seignior and *censitaire*, — sometimes as a simple act of sovereign power, and sometimes on the ground that the grants had been made with conditions not recognized by the *Coutume de Paris*. This was the code of law assigned to Canada; but most of the contracts between seignior and *censitaire* had been agreed upon in good faith by men who knew as much of the *Coutume de Paris* as of the Capitularies of Charlemagne, and their conditions

---

[1] This doctrine is laid down in a letter of the Marquis de Beauharnois, governor, to the minister, 1734.

[2] *Lettre de Raudot, père, au Ministre,* 10 *Nov.,* 1707.

[3] *Lettre de Ponchartrain à Raudot, père,* 13 *Juin,* 1708.

had remained in force unchallenged for generations. These interventions of government sometimes contradicted one another, and often proved a dead letter. They are more or less active through the whole period of the French rule.

The seignior had judicial powers, which, however, were carefully curbed and controlled. His jurisdiction, when exercised at all, extended in most cases only to trivial causes. He very rarely had a prison, and seems never to have abused it. The dignity of a seigniorial gallows with *high justice* or jurisdiction over heinous offences was granted only in three or four instances.[1]

Four arpents in front by forty in depth were the ordinary dimensions of a grant *en censive*. These ribbons of land, nearly a mile and a half long, with one end on the river and the other on the uplands behind, usually combined the advantages of meadows for cultivation, and forests for timber and firewood. So long as the *censitaire* brought in on Saint Martin's day his yearly capons and his yearly handful of copper, his title against the seignior was perfect. There are farms in Canada which have passed from father to son for two hundred years. The condition of the cultivator was incomparably better than that of the French peasant, crushed by taxes, and oppressed by feudal burdens far heavier than those of Canada.

---

[1] Baronies and *comtés* were empowered to set up gallows and pillories, to which the arms of the owner were affixed. See, for example, the edict creating the Barony des Islets.

In fact, the Canadian settler scorned the name of peasant, and then, as now, was always called the *habitant*. The government held him in wardship, watched over him, interfered with him, but did not oppress him or allow others to oppress him. Canada was not governed to the profit of a class; and if the King wished to create a Canadian *noblesse*, he took care that it should not bear hard on the country.[1]

Under a genuine feudalism, the ownership of land conferred nobility; but all this was changed. The King and not the soil was now the parent of honor. France swarmed with landless nobles, while *roturier* land-holders grew daily more numerous. In Canada half the seigniories were in *roturier* or plebeian hands, and in course of time some of them came into possession of persons on very humble degrees of the social scale. A seigniory could be bought and sold, and a trader or a thrifty *habitant* might, and often did, become the buyer.[2] If the Canadian noble

[1] On the seigniorial tenure, I have examined the entire mass of papers printed at the time when the question of its abolition was under discussion. A great deal of legal research and learning was then devoted to the subject. The argument of Mr. Dunkin in behalf of the seigniors, and the observations of Judge Lafontaine are especially instructive, as is also the collected correspondence of the governors and intendants with the central government on matters relating to the seigniorial system.

[2] In 1712, the engineer Catalogne made a very long and elaborate report on the condition of Canada, with a full account of all the seigniorial estates. Of ninety-one seigniories, fiefs, and baronies, described by him, ten belonged to merchants, twelve to husband-men, and two to masters of small river craft. The rest belonged to religious corporations, members of the council, judges, officials of the Crown, widows, and discharged officers or their sons.

was always a seignior, it is far from being true that the Canadian seignior was always a noble.

In France, it will be remembered, nobility did not in itself imply a title. Besides its titled leaders, it had its rank and file, numerous enough to form a considerable army. Under the later Bourbons, the penniless young nobles were, in fact, enrolled into regiments, — turbulent, difficult to control, obeying officers of high rank, but scorning all others, and conspicuous by a fiery and impetuous valor which on more than one occasion turned the tide of victory. The *gentilhomme*, or untitled noble, had a distinctive character of his own, — gallant, punctilious, vain; skilled in social and sometimes in literary and artistic accomplishments, but usually ignorant of most things except the handling of his rapier. Yet there were striking exceptions; and to say of him, as has been said, that "he knew nothing but how to get himself killed," is hardly just to a body which has produced some of the best writers and thinkers of France. Sometimes the origin of his nobility was lost in the mists of time; sometimes he owed it to a patent from the King. In either case, the line of demarcation between him and the classes below him was perfectly distinct; and in this lies an essential difference between the French *noblesse* and the English gentry, a class not separated from others by a definite barrier. The French *noblesse*, unlike the English gentry, constituted a caste.

The *gentilhomme* had no vocation for emigrating.

He liked the army and he liked the court. If he could not be of it, it was something to live in its shadow. The life of a backwoods settler had no charm for him. He was not used to labor; and he could not trade, at least in retail, without becoming liable to forfeit his nobility. When Talon came to Canada, there were but four noble families in the colony.[1] Young nobles in abundance came out with Tracy; but they went home with him. Where, then, should be found the material of a Canadian *noblesse?* First, in the regiment of Carignan, of which most of the officers were *gentilshommes;* secondly, in the issue of patents of nobility to a few of the more prominent colonists. Tracy asked for four such patents; Talon asked for five more;[2] and such requests were repeated at intervals by succeeding governors and intendants, in behalf of those who had gained their favor by merit or otherwise. Money smoothed the path to advancement, so far had *noblesse* already fallen from its old estate. Thus Jacques Le Ber, the merchant, who had long kept a shop at Montreal, got himself made a "gentleman" for six thousand livres.[3]

All Canada soon became infatuated with *noblesse;*

[1] Talon, *Mémoire sur l'Etat présent du Canada*, 1667. The families of Repentigny, Tilly, Potherie, and Ailleboust appear to be meant.

[2] Tracy's request was in behalf of Bourdon, Boucher, Auteuil, and Juchereau. Talon's was in behalf of Godefroy, Le Moyne, Denis, Amiot, and Couillard.

[3] Faillon, *Vie de Mademoiselle Le Ber*, 325.

and country and town, merchant and seignior, vied
with each other for the quality of *gentilhomme*. If
they could not get it, they often pretended to have
it, and aped its ways with the zeal of Monsieur
Jourdain himself. "Everybody here," writes the
intendant Meules, "calls himself *Esquire*, and ends
with thinking himself a gentleman." Successive
intendants repeat this complaint. The case was
worst with *roturiers* who had acquired seigniories.
Thus Noël Langlois was a good carpenter till he
became owner of a seigniory, on which he grew lazy
and affected to play the gentleman. The real
gentilshommes, as well as the spurious, had their
full share of official stricture. The governor Denonville speaks of them thus: "Several of them have
come out this year with their wives, who are very
much cast down; but they play the fine lady, nevertheless. I had much rather see good peasants; it
would be a pleasure to me to give aid to such,
knowing, as I should, that within two years their
families would have the means of living at ease; for
it is certain that a peasant who can and will work is
well off in this country, while our nobles with nothing to do can never be anything but beggars. Still
they ought not to be driven off or abandoned. The
question is how to maintain them."[1]

The intendant Duchesneau writes to the same
effect: "Many of our *gentilshommes*, officers, and
other owners of seigniories, lead what in France is

[1] *Lettre de Denonville au Ministre*, 10 *Nov.*, 1686.

called the life of a country gentleman, and spend
most of their time in hunting and fishing. As their
requirements in food and clothing are greater than
those of the simple *habitants*, and as they do not
devote themselves to improving their land, they mix
themselves up in trade, run in debt on all hands,
incite their young *habitants* to range the woods, and
send their own children there to trade for furs in the
Indian villages and in the depths of the forest, in
spite of the prohibition of his Majesty. Yet, with
all this, they are in miserable poverty." [1]

Their condition, indeed, was often deplorable.
"It is pitiful," says the intendant Champigny, "to
see their children, of which they have great numbers,
passing all summer with nothing on them but a shirt,
and their wives and daughters working in the
fields." [2]   In another letter he asks aid from the King
for Repentigny with his thirteen children, and for
Tilly with his fifteen. "We must give them some
corn at once," he says, "or they will starve." [3]
These were two of the original four noble families
of Canada. The family of Ailleboust, another of the
four, is described as equally destitute. "Pride and
sloth," says the same intendant, "are the great faults
of the people of Canada, and especially of the nobles
and those who pretend to be such. I pray you grant

[1] *Lettre de Duchesneau au Ministre,* 10 *Nov.,* 1679.
[2] *Lettre de Champigny au Ministre,* 26 *Août,* 1687.
   Ibid., 6 *Nov.,* 1687.

no more letters of nobility, unless you want to multiply beggars." [1]

The governor Denonville is still more emphatic: "Above all things, Monseigneur, permit me to say that the nobles of this new country are everything that is most beggarly, and that to increase their number is to increase the number of do-nothings. A new country requires hard workers, who will handle the axe and mattock. The sons of our councillors are no more industrious than the nobles; and their only resource is to take to the woods, trade a little with the Indians, and, for the most part, fall into the disorders of which I have had the honor to inform you. I shall use all possible means to induce them to engage in regular commerce; but as our nobles and councillors are all very poor and weighed down with debt, they could not get credit for a single crown piece." [2] "Two days ago," he writes in another letter, "Monsieur de Saint-Ours, a gentleman of Dauphiny, came to me to ask leave to go back to France in search of bread. He says that he will put his ten children into the charge of any who will give them a living, and that he himself will go into the army again. His wife and he are in despair; and yet they do what they can. I have seen two of his girls reaping grain and holding the plough. Other families are in the same condition. They

---

[1] *Mémoire instructif sur le Canada, joint à la lettre de M. de Champigny du 10 Mai,* 1691.

[2] *Lettre de Denonville au Ministre,* 13 *Nov.,* 1685.

come to me with tears in their eyes. All our married officers are beggars; and I entreat you to send them aid. There is need that the King should provide support for their children, or else they will be tempted to go over to the English."[1] Again he writes that the sons of the councillor D'Amours have been arrested as *coureurs de bois*, or outlaws in the bush; and that if the minister does not do something to help them, there is danger that all the sons of the *noblesse*, real or pretended, will turn bandits, since they have no other means of living.

The King, dispenser of charity for all Canada, came promptly to the rescue. He granted an alms of a hundred crowns to each family, coupled with a warning to the recipients of his bounty that "their misery proceeds from their ambition to live as persons of quality and without labor."[2] At the same time, the minister announced that no more letters of nobility would be granted in Canada; adding, "to relieve the country of some of the children of those who are really noble, I send you [the governor] six commissions of *Gardes de la Marine*, and recommend you to take care not to give them to any who are not actually *gentilshommes*." The *Garde de la Marine* answered to the midshipman of the English or American service. As the six commissions could

---

[1] *Lettre de Denonville au Ministre*, 10 *Nov.*, 1686. (Condensed in the translation.)

[2] Abstract of Denonville's Letters, and of the Minister's Answers, in *N. Y. Colonial Docs.*, ix. 317, 318.

bring little relief to the crowd of needy youths, it was further ordained that sons of nobles or persons living as such should be enrolled into companies at eight sous a day for those who should best conduct themselves, and six sous a day for the others. Nobles in Canada were also permitted to trade, even at retail, without derogating from their rank.[1]

They had already assumed this right, without waiting for the royal license; but thus far it had profited them little. The *gentilhomme* was not a good shopkeeper, nor, as a rule, was the shopkeeper's vocation very lucrative in Canada. The domestic trade of the colony was small; and all trade was exposed to such vicissitudes from the intervention of intendants, ministers, and councils, that at one time it was almost banished. At best, it was carried on under conditions auspicious to a favored few and withering to the rest. Even when most willing to work, the position of the *gentilhomme* was a painful one. Unless he could gain a post under the Crown, which was rarely the case, he was as complete a political cipher as the meanest *habitant*. His rents were practically nothing, and he had no capital to improve his seigniorial estate. By a peasant's work he could gain a peasant's living, and this was all. The prospect was not inspiring. His long initiation of misery was the natural result of his position and surroundings; and it is no matter of wonder that he threw himself into the only field of action

---

[1] *Lettre de Meules au Ministre,* 1685.

which in time of peace was open to him.   It was
trade, but trade seasoned by adventure and ennobled
by danger, defiant of edict and ordinance, outlawed,
conducted in arms among forests and savages; in
short, it was the Western fur-trade.   The tyro was
likely to fail in it at first, but time and experience
formed him to the work.   On the Great Lakes, in
the wastes of the Northwest, on the Mississippi and
the plains beyond, we find the roving *gentilhomme*,
chief of a gang of bush-rangers, often his own *habitants*, — sometimes proscribed by the government,
sometimes leagued in contraband traffic with its
highest officials; a hardy vidette of civilization,
tracing unknown streams, piercing unknown forests,
trading, fighting, negotiating, and building forts.
Again we find him on the shores of Acadia or Maine,
surrounded by Indian retainers, a menace and a
terror to the neighboring English colonist.   Saint-
Castin, Du Lhut, La Durantaye, La Salle, La Mothe-
Cadillac, Iberville, Bienville, La Vérendrye, are
names that stand conspicuous on the page of half-
savage romance that refreshes the hard and practical
annals of American colonization.   But a more substantial debt is due to their memory.   It was they,
and such as they, who discovered the Ohio, explored
the Mississippi to its mouth, discovered the Rocky
Mountains, and founded Detroit, St. Louis, and New
Orleans.

Even in his earliest day, the *gentilhomme* was not
always in the evil plight where we have found him.

There were a few exceptions to the general misery,
and the chief among them is that of the Le Moynes
of Montreal.   Charles Le Moyne, son of an innkeeper of Dieppe and founder of a family the most
truly eminent in Canada, was a man of sterling
qualities who had been long enough in the colony to
learn how to live there.[1]   Others learned the same
lesson at a later day, adapted themselves to soil and
situation, took root, grew, and became more Canadian
than French.   As population increased, their seigniories began to yield appreciable returns, and their
reserved domains became worth cultivating.   A
future dawned upon them; they saw in hope their
names, their seigniorial estates, their manor-houses,
their tenantry, passing to their children and their
children's children.   The beggared noble of the early
time became a sturdy country gentleman, — poor,
but not wretched; ignorant of books, except possibly
a few scraps of rusty Latin picked up in a Jesuit
school; hardy as the hardiest woodsman, yet never
forgetting his quality of *gentilhomme ;* scrupulously
wearing its badge, the sword, and copying as well as
he could the fashions of the court, which glowed on
his vision across the sea in all the effulgence of

[1] Berthelot, proprietor of the *comté* of St. Laurent, and Robineau,
of the barony of Portneuf, may also be mentioned as exceptionally
prosperous.   Of the younger Charles Le Moyne, afterwards Baron
de Longueuil, Frontenac the governor says, " son fort et sa maison
nous donnent une idée des châteaux de France fortifiez."   His fort
was of stone and flanked with four towers.   It was nearly opposite
Montreal, on the south shore

Versailles, and beamed with reflected ray from the
Château of Quebec. He was at home among his
tenants, at home among the Indians, and never more
at home than when, a gun in his hand and a crucifix
on his breast, he took the war-path with a crew of
painted savages and Frenchmen almost as wild, and
pounced like a lynx from the forest on some lonely
farm or outlying hamlet of New England. How
New England hated him, let her records tell. The
reddest blood-streaks on her old annals mark the
track of the Canadian *gentilhomme.*

CHAPTER XIX.

1663–1763.

THE RULERS OF CANADA.

Nature of the Government. — The Governor. — The Council. — Courts and Judges. — The Intendant: his Grievances. — Strong Government. — Sedition and Blasphemy. — Royal Bounty. — Defects and Abuses.

THE government of Canada was formed in its chief features after the government of a French province. Throughout France the past and the present stood side by side. The kingdom had a double administration; or, rather, the shadow of the old administration and the substance of the new. The government of provinces had long been held by the high nobles, often kindred to the Crown; and hence, in former times, great perils had arisen, amounting during the civil wars to the danger of dismemberment. The high nobles were still governors of provinces; but here, as elsewhere, they had ceased to be dangerous. Titles, honors, and ceremonial they had in abundance; but they were deprived of real power. Close beside them was the royal intendant, an obscure figure, lost amid the vainglories of the feudal sunset, but in the name of the King holding the reins of government, —

a check and a spy on his gorgeous colleague. He
was the King's agent; of modest birth, springing
from the legal class; owing his present to the King,
and dependent on him for his future; learned in the
law and trained to administration. It was by such
instruments that the powerful centralization of the
monarchy enforced itself throughout the kingdom,
and, penetrating beneath the crust of old prescriptions, supplanted without seeming to supplant them.
The courtier noble looked down in the pride of rank
on the busy man in black at his side; but this man
in black, with the troop of officials at his beck, controlled finance, the royal courts, public works, and
all the administrative business of the province.

The governor-general and the intendant of Canada
answered to those of a French province. The governor, excepting in the earliest period of the colony,
was a military noble, — in most cases bearing a title
and sometimes of high rank. The intendant, as in
France, was usually drawn from the *gens de robe*, or
legal class.[1] The mutual relations of the two officers
were modified by the circumstances about them. The
governor was superior in rank to the intendant; he
commanded the troops, conducted relations with
foreign colonies and Indian tribes, and took precedence on all occasions of ceremony. Unlike a

---

[1] The governor was styled in his commission, *Gouverneur et Lieu-
tenant-Général en Canada, Acadie, Isle de Terreneuve, et autres pays
de la France Septentrionale ;* and the intendant, *Intendant de la Justice,
Police, et Finances en Canada, Acadie, Terreneuve, et autres pays de la
France Septentrionale.*

provincial governor in France, he had great and substantial power. The King and the minister, his sole masters, were a thousand leagues distant, and he controlled the whole military force. If he abused his position, there was no remedy but in appeal to the court, which alone could hold him in check. There were local governors at Montreal and Three Rivers; but their power was carefully curbed, and they were forbidden to fine or imprison any person without authority from Quebec.[1]

The intendant was virtually a spy on the governor-general, of whose proceedings and of everything else that took place he was required to make report. Every year he wrote to the minister of state one, two, three, or four letters, often forty or fifty pages long, filled with the secrets of the colony, political and personal, great and small, set forth with a minuteness often interesting, often instructive, and often excessively tedious.[2] The governor, too, wrote letters of pitiless length; and each of the colleagues was jealous of the letters of the other. In truth, their relations to each other were so critical, and perfect harmony so rare, that they might almost be described as natural enemies. The court, it is certain, did not

[1] The Sulpitian seigniors of Montreal claimed the right of appointing their own local governor. This was denied by the court, and the excellent Sulpitian governor, Maisonneuve, was removed by De Tracy, to die in patient obscurity at Paris. Some concessions were afterwards made in favor of the Sulpitian claims.

[2] I have carefully read about two thousand pages of these letters.

desire their perfect accord; nor, on the other hand, did it wish them to quarrel: it aimed to keep them on such terms that, without deranging the machinery of administration, each should be a check on the other.[1]

The governor, the intendant, and the supreme council or court were absolute masters of Canada under the pleasure of the King. Legislative, judicial, and executive power, all centred in them. We have seen already the very unpromising beginnings of the supreme council. It had consisted at first of the governor, the bishop, and five councillors chosen by them. The intendant was soon added, to form the ruling triumvirate; but the appointment of the councillors, the occasion of so many quarrels, was afterwards exercised by the King himself.[2] Even the name of the council underwent a change in the interest of his autocracy, and he commanded that it should no longer be called the *Supreme*, but only the *Superior* Council. The same change had just been imposed on all the high tribunals of France.[3] Under the shadow of the *fleur-de-lis*, the King alone was to be supreme.

---

[1] The governor and intendant made frequent appeals to the court to settle questions arising between them. Several of these appeals are preserved. The King wrote replies on the margin of the paper, but they were usually too curt and general to satisfy either party.

[2] *Déclaration du Roi du* 16 *Juin*, 1703. Appointments were made by the King many years earlier. As they were always made on the recommendation of the governor and intendant, the practical effect of the change was merely to exclude the bishop from a share in them. The West India Company made the nominations during the ten years of its ascendancy.

[3] Cheruel, *Administration Monarchique en France*, ii 100.

In 1675 the number of councillors was increased to seven, and in 1703 it was again increased to twelve; but the character of the council or court remained the same. It issued decrees for the civil, commercial, and financial government of the colony, and gave judgment in civil and criminal causes according to the royal ordinances and the *Coutume de Paris*. It exercised also the function of registration borrowed from the parliament of Paris. That body, it will be remembered, had no analogy whatever with the English parliament. Its ordinary functions were not legislative, but judicial; and it was composed of judges hereditary under certain conditions. Nevertheless, it had long acted as a check on the royal power through its right of registration. No royal edict had the force of law till entered upon its books, and this custom had so deep a root in the monarchical constitution of France, that even Louis XIV., in the flush of his power, did not attempt to abolish it. He did better; he ordered his decrees to be registered, and the humbled parliament submissively obeyed. In like manner all edicts, ordinances, or declarations relating to Canada were entered on the registers of the superior council at Quebec. The order of registration was commonly affixed to the edict or other mandate, and nobody dreamed of disobeying it.[1]

---

[1] Many general edicts relating to the whole kingdom are also registered on the books of the council; but the practice in this respect was by no means uniform.

The council or court had its attorney-general, who heard complaints, and brought them before the tribunal if he thought necessary; its secretary, who kept its registers, and its *huissiers* or attendant officers. It sat once a week; and, though it was the highest court of appeal, it exercised at first original jurisdiction in very trivial cases.[1] It was empowered to establish subordinate courts or judges throughout the colony. Besides these, there was a judge appointed by the King for each of the three districts into which Canada was divided, — those of Quebec, Three Rivers, and Montreal. To each of the three royal judges were joined a clerk and an attorney-general, under the supervision and control of the attorney-general of the superior court, to which tribunal appeal lay from all the subordinate jurisdictions. The jurisdiction of the seigniors within their own limits has already been mentioned. They were entitled by the terms of their grants to the exercise of "high, middle, and low justice;" but most of them were practically restricted to the last of the three, — that is, to petty disputes between the *habitants*, involving not more than sixty sous, or offences for which the fine did not exceed ten sous.[2] Thus limited, their judgments were often useful in saving

[1] See the *Registres du Conseil Supérieur*, preserved at Quebec. Between 1663 and 1673 are a multitude of judgments on matters great and small, — from murder, rape, and infanticide, down to petty nuisances, misbehavior of servants, and disputes about the price of a sow.

[2] Doutre et Lareau, *Histoire du Droit Canadien*, 135.

time, trouble, and money to the disputants. The corporate seigniors of Montreal long continued to hold a feudal court in form, with attorney-general, clerk, and *huissier ;* but very few other seigniors were in a condition to imitate them. Added to all these tribunals was the bishop's court at Quebec, to try causes held to be within the province of the Church.

The office of judge in Canada was no sinecure. The people were of a litigious disposition, — partly from their Norman blood; partly, perhaps, from the idleness of the long and tedious winter, which gave full leisure for gossip and quarrel; and partly from the very imperfect manner in which titles had been drawn and the boundaries of grants marked out, whence ensued disputes without end between neighbor and neighbor.

"I will not say," writes the satirical La Hontan, "that Justice is more chaste and disinterested here than in France; but, at least, if she is sold, she is sold cheaper. We do not pass through the clutches of advocates, the talons of attorneys, and the claws of clerks. These vermin do not infest Canada yet. Everybody pleads his own cause. Our Themis is prompt, and she does not bristle with fees, costs, and charges. The judges have only four hundred francs a year, — a great temptation to look for law in the bottom of the suitor's purse. Four hundred francs! Not enough to buy a cap and gown; so these gentry never wear them."[1]

Thus far La Hontan. Now let us hear the King

---

[1] La Hontan, i. 21 (ed. 1705). In some editions, the above is expressed in different language.

himself. "The greatest disorder which has hitherto existed in Canada," writes Louis XIV. to the intendant Meules, "has come from the small degree of liberty which the officers of justice have had in the discharge of their duties, by reason of the violence to which they have been subjected, and the part they have been obliged to take in the continual quarrels between the governor and the intendant; insomuch that justice having been administered by cabal and animosity, the inhabitants have hitherto been far from the tranquillity and repose which cannot be found in a place where everybody is compelled to take side with one party or another." [1]

Nevertheless, on ordinary local questions between the *habitants*, justice seems to have been administered on the whole fairly; and judges of all grades often interposed in their personal capacity to bring parties to an agreement without a trial. From head to foot, the government kept its attitude of paternity.

Beyond and above all the regular tribunals, beyond and above the council itself, was the independent jurisdiction lodged in the person of the King's man, the intendant. His commission empowered him, if he saw fit, to call any cause whatever before himself for judgment; and he judged exclusively the cases which concerned the King, and those involving the relations of seignior and vassal. [2]   He appointed sub-

---

[1] *Instruction du Roy pour le Sieur de Meules*, 1682.
[2] See the commissions of various intendants, in *Édits et Ordonnances* iii.

ordinate judges, from whom there was appeal to him; but from his decisions, as well as from those of the superior council, there was no appeal but to the King in his council of state.

On any Monday morning one would have found the superior council in session in the antechamber of the governor's apartment, at the Château St. Louis. The members sat at a round table. At the head was the governor, with the bishop on his right, and the intendant on his left. The councillors sat in the order of their appointment, and the attorney-general also had his place at the board. As La Hontan says, they were not in judicial robes, but in their ordinary dress, and all but the bishop wore swords.[1] The want of the cap and gown greatly disturbed the intendant Meules; and he begs the minister to consider how important it is that the councillors, in order to inspire respect, should appear in public in long black robes, which on occasions of ceremony they should exchange for robes of red. He thinks that the principal persons of the colony would thus be induced to train up their children to so enviable a dignity; "and," he concludes, "as none of the councillors can afford to buy red robes, I hope that the King will vouchsafe to send out nine such. As for the black robes, they can furnish those themselves."[2] The King did not respond, and the nine robes never arrived.

[1] Compare La Potherie, i. 260; and La Tour, *Vie de Laval*, liv. vii.
[2] *Meules au Ministre*, 28 *Sept.*, 1685.

The official dignity of the council was sometimes exposed to trials against which even red gowns might have proved an insufficient protection. The same intendant urges that the tribunal ought to be provided immediately with a house of its own. "It is not decent," he says, "that it should sit in the governor's antechamber any longer. His guards and valets make such a noise that we cannot hear one another speak. I have continually to tell them to keep quiet, which causes them to make a thousand jokes at the councillors as they pass in and out."[1] As the governor and the council were often on ill terms, the official head of the colony could not always be trusted to keep his attendants on their good behavior. The minister listened to the complaint of Meules, and adopted his suggestion that the government should buy the old brewery of Talon, — a large structure of mingled timber and masonry on the banks of the St. Charles. It was at an easy distance from the château; passing the Hôtel Dieu and descending the rock, one reached it by a walk of a few minutes. It was accordingly repaired, partly rebuilt, and fitted up to serve the double purpose of a lodging for the intendant and a court-house. Henceforth the transformed brewery was known as the Palace of the Intendant, or the Palace of Justice; and here the council and inferior courts long continued to hold their sessions.

Some of these inferior courts appear to have needed

[1] *Meules au Ministre,* 12 *Nov.,* 1684.

a lodging quite as much as the council. The watchful Meules informs the minister that the royal judge for the district of Quebec was accustomed in winter, with a view to saving fuel, to hear causes and pronounce judgment by his own fireside, in the midst of his children, whose gambols disturbed the even distribution of justice.[1]

The superior council was not a very harmonious body. As its three chiefs — the man of the sword, the man of the church, and the man of the law — were often at variance, the councillors attached themselves to one party or the other, and hot disputes sometimes ensued. The intendant, though but third in rank, presided at the sessions, took votes, pronounced judgment, signed papers, and called special meetings. This matter of the presidency was for some time a source of contention between him and the governor, till the question was set at rest by a decree of the King.

The intendants in their reports to the minister do not paint the council in flattering colors. One of them complains that the councillors, being busy with their farms, neglect their official duties. Another says that they are all more or less in trade. A third calls them uneducated persons of slight account, allied to the chief families and chief merchants in Canada, in whose interest they make laws; and he adds, that, as a year and a half or even two years usually elapse before the answer to a complaint is

---

1 *Meules au Ministre,* 12 *Nov.,* 1684.

received from France, they take advantage of this long interval to the injury of the King's service.[1] These and other similar charges betray the continual friction between the several branches of the government.

The councillors were rarely changed, and they usually held office for life. In a few cases the King granted to the son of a councillor yet living the right of succeeding his father when the charge should become vacant.[2] It was a post of honor and not of profit, at least of direct profit. The salaries were very small, and coupled with a prohibition to receive fees.

Judging solely by the terms of his commission, the intendant was the ruling power in the colony. He controlled all expenditure of public money, and not only presided at the council, but was clothed in his own person with independent legislative as well as judicial power. He was authorized to issue ordinances having the force of law whenever he thought necessary, and, in the words of his commission, "to order everything as he shall see just and proper."[3] He was directed to be present at councils of war, though war was the special province of his colleague,

---

[1] *Meules au Ministre*, 12 *Nov.*, 1684.

[2] A son of Amours was named in his father's lifetime to succeed him, as was also a son of the attorney-general Auteuil. There are several other cases. A son of Tilly, to whom the right of succeeding his father had been granted, asks leave to sell it to the merchant La Chesnaye.

[3] Commissions of Bouteroue, Duchesneau, Meules, etc.

and to protect soldiers and all others from official extortion and abuse; that is, to protect them from the governor. Yet there were practical difficulties in the way of his apparent power. The King, his master, was far away; but official jealousy was busy around him, and his patience was sometimes put to the proof. Thus the royal judge of Quebec had fallen into irregularities. "I can do nothing with him," writes the intendant; "he keeps on good terms with the governor and council, and sets me at naught." The governor had, as he thought, treated him amiss. "You have told me," he writes to the minister, "to bear everything from him and report to you;" and he proceeds to recount his grievances. Again, "the attorney-general is bold to insolence, and needs to be repressed. The King's interposition is necessary." He modestly adds that the intendant is the only man in Canada whom his Majesty can trust, and that he ought to have more power.[1]

These were far from being his only troubles. The enormous powers with which his commission clothed him were sometimes retrenched by contradictory instructions from the King;[2] for this government, not of laws but of arbitrary will, is marked by frequent inconsistencies. When he quarrelled with the governor, and the governor chanced to have strong

[1] *Meules au Ministre,* 12 *Nov.,* 1684.

[2] Thus, Meules is flatly forbidden to compel litigants to bring causes before him (*Instruction pour le Sieur de Meules,* 1682) ; and this prohibition is nearly of the same date with the commission in which the power to do so is expressly given him.

friends at court, his position became truly pitiable.
He was berated as an imperious master berates an
offending servant. "Your last letter is full of nothing but complaints." "You have exceeded your
authority." "Study to know yourself, and to understand clearly the difference there is between a governor and an intendant." "Since you failed to
comprehend the difference between you and the
officer who represents the King's person, you are in
danger of being often condemned, or rather of being
recalled; for his Majesty cannot endure so many
petty complaints, founded on nothing but a certain
quasi equality between the governor and you, which
you assume, but which does not exist." "Meddle
with nothing beyond your functions." "Take good
care to tell me nothing but the truth." "You ask
too many favors for your adherents." "You must
not spend more than you have authority to spend, or
it will be taken out of your pay." In short, there
are several letters from the minister Colbert to his
colonial man-of-all-work, which, from beginning to
end, are one continued scold.[1]

The luckless intendant was liable to be held to
account for the action of natural laws. "If the
population does not increase in proportion to the
pains I take," writes the King to Duchesneau, "you
are to lay the blame on yourself for not having exe-

---

[1] The above examples are all taken from the letters of Colbert
to the intendant Duchesneau. It is an extreme case, but other intendants are occasionally treated with scarcely more ceremony.

cuted my principal order [to promote marriages], and
for having failed in the principal object for which I
sent you to Canada." [1]

A great number of ordinances of intendants are
preserved. They were usually read to the people at
the doors of churches after mass, or sometimes by
the curé from his pulpit. They relate to a great
variety of subjects, — regulation of inns and markets,
poaching, preservation of game, sale of brandy, rent
of pews, stray hogs, mad dogs, tithes, matrimonial
quarrels, fast driving, wards and guardians, weights
and measures, nuisances, value of coinage, trespass
on lands, building churches, observance of Sunday,
preservation of timber, seignior and vassal, settlement of boundaries, and many other matters. If a
curé with some of his parishioners reported that his
church or his house needed repair or rebuilding, the
intendant issued an ordinance requiring all the
inhabitants of the parish, "both those who have
consented and those who have not consented," to
contribute materials and labor, on pain of fine or
other penalty.[2] The militia captain of the *côte* was
to direct the work and see that each parishioner did
his due part, which was determined by the extent of
his farm; so, too, if the *grand voyer*, an officer
charged with the superintendence of highways,
reported that a new road was wanted or that an old

---

[1] *Le Roi à Duchesneau*, 11 *Juin*, 1680.
[2] See, among many examples, the ordinance of 24th December,
1715. *Édits et Ordonnances*, ii. 443.

one needed mending, an ordinance of the intendant set the whole neighborhood at work upon it, directed, as in the other case, by the captain of militia. If children were left fatherless, the intendant ordered the curé of the parish to assemble their relations or friends for the choice of a guardian. If a *censitaire* did not clear his land and live on it, the intendant took it from him and gave it back to the seignior.[1]

Chimney-sweeping having been neglected at Quebec, the intendant commands all householders promptly to do their duty in this respect, and at the same time fixes the pay of the sweep at six sous a chimney. Another order forbids quarrelling in church. Another assigns pews in due order of precedence to the seignior, the captain of militia, and the wardens. The intendant Raudot, who seems to have been inspired even more than the others with the spirit of paternal intervention, issued a mandate to the effect, that, whereas the people of Montreal raise too many horses, which prevents them from raising cattle and sheep, "being therein ignorant of their true interest. . . . Now, therefore, we command that each inhabitant of the *côtes* of this government shall hereafter own no more than two horses, or mares, and one foal, — the same to take effect after the sowing-season of the ensuing year, 1710, giving them time to rid themselves of their horses in excess of said number, after which they will be required to

[1] Compare the numerous ordinances printed in the second and third volumes of *Édits et Ordonnances*.

kill any of such excess that may remain in their possession."[1]   Many other ordinances, if not equally preposterous, are equally stringent; such, for example, as that of the intendant Bigot, in which, with a view of promoting agriculture, and protecting the morals of the farmers by saving them from the temptations of cities, he proclaims to them: "We prohibit and forbid you to remove to this town [Quebec] under any pretext whatever, without our permission in writing, on pain of being expelled and sent back to your farms, your furniture and goods confiscated, and a fine of fifty livres laid on you for the benefit of the hospitals.   And, furthermore, we forbid all inhabitants of the city to let houses or rooms to persons coming from the country, on pain of a fine of a hundred livres, also applicable to the hospitals."[2]   At about the same time a royal edict, designed to prevent the undue subdivision of farms, forbade the country people, except such as were authorized to live in villages, to build a house or barn on any piece of land less than one and a half arpents wide and thirty arpents long;[3] while a subsequent ordinance of the intendant commands the immediate demolition of certain houses built in contravention of the edict.[4]

The spirit of absolutism is everywhere apparent. "It is of very great consequence," writes the intendant Meules, "that the people should not be left at

---

[1] *Édits et Ordonnances*, ii. 273.   [2] *Ibid.*, ii. 399.
[3] *Ibid.*, i. 585.   [4] *Ibid.*, ii. 400.

liberty to speak their minds."[1]   Hence public meetings were jealously restricted.   Even those held by parishioners under the eye of the curé to estimate the cost of a new church seem to have required a special license from the intendant.   During a number of years a meeting of the principal inhabitants of Quebec was called in spring and autumn by the council to discuss the price and quality of bread, the supply of firewood, and other similar matters.   The council commissioned two of its members to preside at these meetings, and on hearing their report took what action it thought best.   Thus, after the meeting held in February, 1686, it issued a decree, in which, after a long and formal preamble, it solemnly ordained "that besides white-bread and light brown-bread, all bakers shall hereafter make dark brown-bread whenever the same shall be required."[2]   Such assemblies, so controlled, could scarcely, one would think, wound the tenderest susceptibilities of authority; yet there was evident distrust of them, and after a few years this modest shred of self-government is seen no more.   The syndic, too, that functionary whom the people of the towns were at first allowed to choose, under the eye of the authorities, was conjured out of existence by a word from the King.   Seignior, *censitaire*, and citizen were prostrate alike

---

[1] "Il ne laisse pas d'être de très grande conséquence de ne pas laisser la liberté au peuple de dire son sentiment."—*Meules au Ministre*, 1685.

[2] *Édits et Ordonnances*, ii. 112.

in flat subjection to the royal will. They were not
free even to go home to France. No inhabitant of
Canada, man or woman, could do so without leave;
and several intendants express their belief that without this precaution there would soon be a falling off
in the population.

In 1671 the council issued a curious decree. One
Paul Dupuy had been heard to say that there is nothing like righting one's self, and that when the
English cut off the head of Charles I. they did a
good thing, with other discourse to the like effect.
The council declared him guilty of speaking ill of
royalty in the person of the King of England, and
uttering words tending to sedition. He was condemned to be dragged from prison by the public exe-
cutioner, and led in his shirt, with a rope about his
neck and a torch in his hand, to the gate of the
Château St. Louis, there to beg pardon of the King;
thence to the pillory of the Lower Town to be
branded with a *fleur-de-lis* on the cheek, and set in
the stocks for half an hour; then to be led back to
prison, and put in irons "till the information against
him shall be completed." [1]

If irreverence to royalty was thus rigorously chastised, irreverence to God was threatened with still
sharper penalties. Louis XIV., ever haunted with
the fear of the Devil, sought protection against him
by his famous edict against swearing, duly registered
on the books of the council at Quebec. "It is our

[1] *Jugements et Délibérations du Conseil Supérieur.*

will and pleasure," says this pious mandate, "that all persons convicted of profane swearing or blaspheming the name of God, the most Holy Virgin his mother, or the saints, be condemned for the first offence to a pecuniary fine according to their possessions and the greatness and enormity of the oath and blasphemy; and if those thus punished repeat the said oaths, then for the second, third, and fourth time they shall be condemned to a double, triple, and quadruple fine; and for the fifth time, they shall be set in the pillory on Sunday or other festival days, there to remain from eight in the morning till one in the afternoon, exposed to all sorts of opprobrium and abuse, and be condemned besides to a heavy fine; and for the sixth time, they shall be led to the pillory, and there have the upper lip cut with a hot iron; and for the seventh time, they shall be led to the pillory and have the lower lip cut; and if, by reason of obstinacy and inveterate bad habit, they continue after all these punishments to utter the said oaths and blasphemies, it is our will and command that they have the tongue completely cut out, so that thereafter they cannot utter them again." [1] All those who should hear anybody swear were further required to report the fact to the nearest judge within twenty-four hours, on pain of fine.

This is far from being the only instance in which the temporal power lends aid to the spiritual.

---

[1] *Édit du Roy contre les Jureurs et Blasphémateurs, du 30me Juillet,* 1666. See *Édits et Ordonnances,* i. 62.

Among other cases, the following is worth mentioning: Louis Gaboury, an inhabitant of the island of Orleans, charged with eating meat in Lent without asking leave of the priest, was condemned by the local judge to be tied three hours to a stake in public, and then led to the door of the chapel, there on his knees, with head bare and hands clasped, to ask pardon of God and the King. The culprit appealed to the council, which revoked the sentence and imposed only a fine.[1]

The due subordination of households had its share of attention. Servants who deserted their masters were to be set in the pillory for the first offence, and whipped and branded for the second; while any person harboring them was to pay a fine of twenty francs.[2] On the other hand, nobody was allowed to employ a servant without a license.[3]

In case of heinous charges, torture of the accused was permitted under the French law; and it was sometimes practised in Canada. Condemned murderers and felons were occasionally tortured before being strangled; and the dead body, enclosed in a kind of iron cage, was left hanging for months at the top of Cape Diamond, a terror to children and a warning to evil-doers. Yet, on the whole, Canadian justice, tried by the standard of the time, was neither vindictive nor cruel.

[1] Doutre et Lareau, *Histoire du Droit Canadien*, 163.
[2] *Réglement de Police*, 1676.
[3] *Édits et Ordonnances*, ii. 53.

In reading the voluminous correspondence of governors and intendants, the minister and the King, nothing is more apparent than the interest with which, in the early part of his reign, Louis XIV. regarded his colony. One of the faults of his rule is the excess of his benevolence; for not only did he give money to support parish priests, build churches, and aid the seminary, the Ursulines, the missions, and the hospitals; but he established a fund destined, among other objects, to relieve indigent persons, subsidized nearly every branch of trade and industry, and in other instances did for the colonists what they would far better have learned to do for themselves.

Meanwhile, the officers of government were far from suffering from an excess of royal beneficence. La Hontan says that the local governor of Three Rivers would die of hunger if, besides his pay, he did not gain something by trade with the Indians; and that Perrot, local governor of Montreal, with one thousand crowns of salary, traded to such purpose that in a few years he made fifty thousand crowns. This trade, it may be observed, was in violation of the royal edicts. The pay of the governor-general varied from time to time. When La Potherie wrote, it was twelve thousand francs a year, besides three thousand which he received in his capacity of local governor of Quebec.[1] This would hardly tempt a

[1] In 1674, the governor-general received 20,718 francs, out of which he was to pay 8,718 to his guard of twenty men and officers.

Frenchman of rank to expatriate himself; and yet
some at least of the governors came out to the colony
for the express purpose of mending their fortunes.
Indeed, the higher nobility could scarcely, in time of
peace, have other motives for going there; the court
and the army were their element, and to be elsewhere was banishment. We shall see hereafter by
what means they sought compensation for their exile
in Canadian forests.

Loud complaints sometimes found their way to
Versailles. A memorial addressed to the regent duke
of Orleans, immediately after the King's death,
declares that the ministers of state, who have been
the real managers of the colony, have made their
creatures and relations governors and intendants, and
set them free from all responsibility. High colonial
officers, pursues the writer, come home rich, while
the colony languishes almost to perishing.[1] As for
lesser offices, they were multiplied to satisfy needy
retainers, till lean and starving Canada was covered

(*Ordonnnance du Roy*, 1675.)   Yet in 1677, in the *État de la Dépense
que le Roy veut et ordonne estre faite*, etc., the total pay of the governor-general is set down at 3,000 francs, and so also in 1681, 1682,
and 1687. The local governor of Montreal was to have 1,800
francs, and the governor of Three Rivers 1,200. It is clear, however, that this *État de dépense* is not complete, as there is no provision for the intendant. The first councillor received 500 francs,
and the rest 300 francs each, equal in Canadian money to 400. An
ordinance of 1676 gives the intendant 12,000 francs. It is tolerably
clear that the provision of 3,000 francs for the governor-general was
meant only to apply to his capacity of local governor of Quebec.

[1] *Mémoire addressé au Régent*, 1715.

with official leeches, sucking, in famished desperation, at her bloodless veins.

The whole system of administration centred in the
King, who, to borrow the formula of his edicts, "in
the fulness of our power and our certain knowledge,"
was supposed to direct the whole machine, from its
highest functions to its pettiest intervention in private
affairs. That this theory, like all extreme theories
of government, was an illusion, is no fault of Louis
XIV. Hard-working monarch as he was, he spared
no pains to guide his distant colony in the paths of
prosperity. The prolix letters of governors and
intendants were carefully studied; and many of the
replies, signed by the royal hand, enter into details
of surprising minuteness. That the King himself
wrote these letters is incredible; but in the early part
of his reign he certainly directed and controlled
them. At a later time, when more absorbing interests engrossed him, he could no longer study in
person the long-winded despatches of his Canadian
officers. They were usually addressed to the minister
of state, who caused abstracts to be made from them
for the King's use, and perhaps for his own.[1] The
minister, or the minister's secretary, could suppress
or color as he or those who influenced him saw fit.

In the latter half of his too long reign, when cares,
calamities, and humiliations were thickening around
the King, another influence was added to make the

[1] Many of these abstracts are still preserved in the Archives of
the Marine and Colonies.

theoretical supremacy of his royal will more than ever
a mockery.   That prince of annalists, Saint-Simon,
has painted Louis XIV. ruling his realm from the
bedchamber of Madame de Maintenon, — seated with
his minister at a small table beside the fire, the King
in an arm-chair, the minister on a stool, with his bag
of papers on a second stool near him.   In another
arm-chair, at another table on the other side of the
fire, sat the sedate favorite, busy to all appearance
with a book or a piece of tapestry, but listening to
everything that passed.   "She rarely spoke," says
Saint-Simon, "except when the King asked her
opinion, which he often did; and then she answered
with great deliberation and gravity.   She never, or
very rarely, showed a partiality for any measure, still
less for any person; but she had an understanding
with the minister, who never dared do otherwise
than she wished.   Whenever any favor or appointment was in question, the business was settled
between them beforehand.   She would send to the
minister that she wanted to speak to him, and he did
not dare bring the matter on the carpet till he had
received her orders."   Saint-Simon next recounts the
subtle methods by which Maintenon and the minister,
her tool, beguiled the King to do their will, while
never doubting that he was doing his own.   "He
thought," concludes the annalist, "that it was he
alone who disposed of all appointments; while in
reality he disposed of very few indeed, except on the
rare occasions when he had taken a fancy to some-

body, or when somebody whom he wanted to favor had spoken to him in behalf of somebody else." [1]

Add to all this the rarity of communication with the distant colony. The ships from France arrived at Quebec in July, August, or September, and returned in November. The machine of Canadian government, wound up once a year, was expected to run unaided at least a twelvemonth. Indeed, it was often left to itself for two years, such was sometimes the tardiness of the overburdened government in answering the despatches of its colonial agents. It is no matter of surprise that a writer well versed in its affairs calls Canada the "country of abuses." [2]

[1] *Mémoires du Duc de Saint-Simon*, xiii. 38, 39 (Cheruel, 1857). Saint-Simon, notwithstanding the independence of his character and his violent prejudices, held a high position at court; and his acute and careful observation, joined to his familiar acquaintance with ministers and other functionaries, both in and out of office, gives a rare value to his matchless portraitures, and makes him indispensable to the annalist of his time.

[2] *État présent du Canada*, 1758.

CHAPTER XX.

1663–1763.

TRADE AND INDUSTRY.

TRADE IN FETTERS. — THE HUGUENOT MERCHANTS. — ROYAL PAT-
RONAGE. — THE FISHERIES. — CRIES FOR HELP. — AGRICULTURE.
— MANUFACTURES. — ARTS OF ORNAMENT. — FINANCE. — CARD
MONEY. — REPUDIATION. — IMPOSTS. — THE BEAVER TRADE. —
THE FAIR AT MONTREAL. — CONTRABAND TRADE. — A FATAL
SYSTEM. — TROUBLE AND CHANGE. — THE COUREURS DE BOIS.
— THE FOREST. — LETTER OF CARHEIL.

WE have seen the head of the colony, its guiding
intellect and will: it remains to observe its organs
of nutrition. Whatever they might have been under
a different treatment, they were perverted and
enfeebled by the regimen to which they were
subjected.

The spirit of restriction and monopoly had ruled
from the beginning. The old governor Lauson,
seignior for a while of a great part of the colony,
held that Montreal had no right to trade directly with
France, but must draw all her supplies from Quebec;[1]
and this preposterous claim was revived in the time
of Mézy. The successive companies to whose hands
the colony was consigned had a baneful effect on

[1] Faillon, *Colonie Française*, ii. 244.

:ndividual enterprise. In 1674 the charter of the West India Company was revoked, and trade was declared open to all subjects of the King; yet commerce was still condemned to wear the ball and chain. New restrictions were imposed, meant for good, but resulting in evil. Merchants not resident in the colony were forbidden all trade, direct or indirect, with the Indians.[1] They were also forbidden to sell any goods at retail except in August, September, and October;[2] to trade anywhere in Canada above Quebec, and to sell clothing or domestic articles ready made. This last restriction was designed to develop colonial industry. No person, resident or not, could trade with the English colonies, or go thither without a special passport, and rigid examination by the military authorities.[3] Foreign trade of any kind was stiffly prohibited. In 1719, after a new company had engrossed the beaver-trade, its agents were empowered to enter all houses in Canada, whether ecclesiastical or secular, and search them for foreign goods, which when found were publicly burned.[4] In the next year the royal council ordered that vessels engaged in foreign trade should be captured by force of arms, like pirates, and confiscated along with their cargoes;[5] while anybody having an article of foreign manufacture in his possession was subjected to a heavy fine.[6]

---

[1] *Réglement de Police*, 1676. Art. xl.
[2] *Édits et Ordonnances*, ii. 100.   [3] *Ibid.*, i. 489.
[4] *Ibid.*, i. 402.   [5] *Ibid.*, i. 425.   [6] *Ibid.*, i. 505.

Attempts were made to fix the exact amount of profit which merchants from France should be allowed to make in the colony; one of the first acts of the superior council was to order them to bring their invoices immediately before that body, which thereupon affixed prices to each article. The merchant who sold and the purchaser who bought above this tariff were alike condemned to heavy penalties; and so, too, was the merchant who chose to keep his goods rather than sell them at the price ordained.[1] Resident merchants, on the other hand, were favored to the utmost: they could sell at what price they saw fit; and, according to La Hontan, they made great profit by the sale of laces, ribbons, watches, jewels, and similar superfluities to the poor but extravagant colonists.

A considerable number of the non-resident merchants were Huguenots, for most of the importations were from the old Huguenot city of Rochelle. No favor was shown them; they were held under rigid restraint, and forbidden to exercise their religion, or to remain in the colony during winter without special license.[2] This sometimes bore very hard upon them. The governor, Denonville, an ardent Catholic, states the case of one Bernon, who had done great service to the colony, and whom La Hontan mentions as the principal French merchant in the Canadian trade. "It is a pity," says Denonville, "that he

---

[1] *Édits et Ordonnances*, ii. 17, 19.
[2] *Réglement de Police*, 1676.   Art. xxxvii.

cannot be converted. As he is a Huguenot, the bishop wants me to order him home this autumn, — which I have done, though he carries on a large business, and a great deal of money remains due to him here." [1]

For a long time the ships from France went home empty, except a favored few which carried furs, or occasionally a load of dried pease or of timber. Payment was made in money when there was any in Canada, or in bills of exchange. The colony, drawing everything from France and returning little besides beaver-skins, remained under a load of debt. French merchants were discouraged, and shipments from France languished. As for the trade with the West Indies, which Talon had tried by precept and example to build up, the intendant reports in 1680 that it had nearly ceased; though six years later it grew again to the modest proportions of three vessels loaded with wheat. [2]

The besetting evil of trade and industry in Canada was the habit they contracted, and were encouraged to contract, of depending on the direct aid of government. Not a new enterprise was set on foot without a petition to the King to lend a helping hand. Sometimes the petition was sent through the governor, sometimes through the intendant; and it was rarely refused. Denonville writes that the merchants

[1] *Denonville au Ministre*, 1685.

[2] *Ibid.*, 1686. The year before, about 18,000 *minots* of grain were sent hither. In 1736 the shipments reached 80,000 *minots*.

of Quebec, by a combined effort, had sent a vessel
of sixty tons to France with colonial produce; and
he asks that the royal commissaries at Rochefort be
instructed to buy the whole cargo, in order to
encourage so deserving an enterprise. One Hazeur
set up a saw-mill at Mal Bay. Finding a large
stock of planks and timber on his hands, he begs the
King to send two vessels to carry them to France;
and the King accordingly did so. A similar request
was made in behalf of another saw-mill at St. Paul's
Bay. Denonville announces that one Riverin wishes
to embark in the whale and cod fishery, and that
though strong in zeal he is weak in resources. The
minister replies that he is to be encouraged, and that
his Majesty will favorably consider his enterprise.[1]
Various gifts were soon after made him. He now
took to himself a partner, the Sieur Chalons; whereupon the governor writes to ask the minister's protection for them. "The Basques," he says, "formerly
carried on this fishery, but some monopoly or other
put a stop to it." The remedy he proposes is homœo-
pathic. He asks another monopoly for the two
partners. Louis Joliet, the discoverer of the Missis-

---

[1] The interest felt by the King in these matters is shown in a
letter signed by his hand in which he enters with considerable detail
into the plans of Riverin. (*Le Roy à Denonville et Champigny*, 1
Mai, 1689.) He afterwards ordered boats, harpooners, and cordage
to be sent him, for which he was to pay at his convenience. Four
years later he complains that, though Riverin had been often
helped, his fisheries were of slight account. "Let him take care,"
pursues the King, "that he does not use his enterprises as a pretext
to obtain favors." *Mémoire du Roy à Frontenac et Champigny*, 1693.

sippi, made a fishing-station on the island of Anticosti; and he begs help from the King, on the ground that his fishery will furnish a good and useful employment to young men. The Sieur Vitry wished to begin a fishery of white porpoises, and he begs the King to give him two thousand pounds of cod-line and two thousand pounds of one and two inch rope. His request was granted, on which he asked for five hundred livres. The money was given him; and the next year he asked to have the gift renewed.[1]

The King was very anxious to develop the fisheries of the colony. "His Majesty," writes the minister, "wishes you to induce the inhabitants to unite with the merchants for this object, and to incite them by all sorts of means to overcome their natural laziness, since there is no other way of saving them from the misery in which they now are."[2] "I wish," says the zealous Denonville, "that fisheries could be well established to give employment to our young men, and prevent them from running wild in the woods;" and he adds mournfully, "they [the fisheries] are

[1] All the above examples are drawn from the correspondence of the governor and intendant with the minister, between 1680 and 1699, together with a memorial of Hazeur and another of Riverin, addressed to the minister.

Vitry's porpoise-fishing appears to have ended in failure. In 1707 the intendant Raudot granted the porpoise-fishery of the seigniory of Rivière Ouelle to six of the *habitants*. This fishery is carried on here successfully at the present day. A very interesting account of it was published in the *Opinion Publique*, 1873, by my friend Abbé Casgrain, whose family residence is the seigniorial mansion of Rivière Ouelle.

[2] *Mémoire pour Denonville et Champigny*, 8 *Mars*, 1688.

enriching Boston at our expense." "They are our true mines," urges the intendant Meules; "but the English of Boston have got possession of those of Acadia, which belong to us, and we ought to prevent it." It was not prevented; and the Canadian fisheries, like other branches of Canadian industry, remained in a state of almost hopeless languor.[1]

The government applied various stimulants. One of these, proposed by the intendant Duchesneau, is characteristic. He advises the formation of a company which should have the exclusive right of exporting fish; but which on its part should be required to take, at a fixed price, all that the inhabitants should bring them. This notable plan did not find favor with the King.[2] It was practised, however, in the case of beaver-skins, and also in that of wood-ashes. The farmers of the revenue were required to take this last commodity at a fixed price, on their own risk, and in any quantity offered. They remonstrated, saying that it was unsalable, — adding, that, if the inhabitants would but take the trouble to turn it into

[1] The Canadian fisheries must not be confounded with the French fisheries of Newfoundland, which were prosperous, but were carried on wholly from French ports.

In a memorial addressed by the partners Chalons and Riverin to the minister Seignelay, they say: "Baston [Boston] et toute sa colonie nous donne un exemple qui fait honte à nostre nation, puisqu'elle s'augmente tous les jours par cette pesche (de la morue) qu'elle fait la plus grande partie sur nos costes pendant que les François ne s'occupent à rien." Meules urges that the King should undertake the fishing business himself, since his subjects cannot or will not.

[2] Ministre à Duchesneau, 15 Mai, 1678.

potash, it might be possible to find a market for it. The King released them entirely, coupling his order to that effect with a eulogy of free-trade.[1]

In all departments of industry the appeals for help are endless. Governors and intendants are so many sturdy beggars for the languishing colony. "Send us money to build storehouses, to which the *habitants* can bring their produce and receive goods from the government in exchange." "Send us a teacher to make sailors of our young men: it is a pity the colony should remain in such a state for want of instruction for youth."[2] "We want a surgeon: there is none in Canada who can set a bone."[3] "Send us some tilers, brick-makers, and potters."[4] "Send us iron-workers to work our mines."[5] "It is to be wished that his Majesty would send us all sorts of artisans, especially potters and glass-workers."[6] "Our Canadians need aid and instruction in their fisheries; they need pilots."[7]

In 1688 the intendant reported that Canada was entirely without either pilots or sailors; and as late as 1712 the engineer Catalogne informed the government, that, though the St. Lawrence was dangerous, a pilot was rarely to be had. "There ought to be

[1] *Le Roy à Duchesneau*, 11 *Juin*, 1680.

[2] *Mémoire à Monseigneur le Marquis de Seignelay, présenté par es Sieurs Chalons et Riverin*, 1686.

[3] *Champigny au Ministre*, 1688.

[4] *Ibid.*

[5] *Denonville au Ministre*, 1686.

[6] *Mémoire de Catalogne*, 1712.

[7] *Denonville au Ministre*, 1686.

trade with the West Indies and other places," urges another writer. "Everybody says it is best, but nobody will undertake it. Our merchants are too poor, or else are engrossed by the fur-trade." [1]

The languor of commerce made agriculture languish. "It is of no use now," writes Meules, in 1682, "to raise any crops except what each family wants for itself." In vain the government sent out seeds for distribution; in vain intendants lectured the farmers, and lavished well-meant advice. Tillage remained careless and slovenly. "If," says the all-observing Catalogne, "the soil were not better cultivated in Europe than here, three-fourths of the people would starve." He complains that the festivals of the Church are so numerous that not ninety working-days are left during the whole working season. The people, he says, ought to be compelled to build granaries to store their crops, instead of selling them in autumn for almost nothing, and every *habitant* should be required to keep two or three sheep. The intendant Champigny calls for seed of hemp and flax, and promises to visit the farms, and show the people the lands best suited for their culture. He thinks that favors should be granted to those who raise hemp and flax as well as to those who marry. Denonville is of opinion that each *habitant* should be compelled to raise a little hemp every year, and that the King should then buy it of him at a high price. [2]

---

[1] *Mémoire de Chalons et Riverin présenté au Marquis de Seignelay.*

[2] *Denonville au Ministre*, 13 *Nov.*, 1685.

It will be well, he says, to make use of severity, while at the same time holding out a hope of gain; and he begs that weavers be sent out to teach the women and girls, who spend the winter in idleness, how to weave and spin. Weaving and spinning, however, as well as the culture of hemp and flax, were neglected till 1705, when the loss of a ship laden with goods for the colony gave the spur to home industry; and Madame de Repentigny set the example of making a kind of coarse blanket of nettle and linden bark.[1]

The jealousy of colonial manufactures shown by England appears but rarely in the relations of France with Canada. According to its light, the French government usually did its best to stimulate Canadian industry, with what results we have just seen. There was afterwards some improvement. In 1714 the intendant Bégon reported that coarse fabrics of wool and linen were made; that the sisters of the congregation wove cloth for their own habits as good as the same stuffs in France; that black cloth was made for priests, and blue cloth for the pupils of the colleges. The inhabitants, he says, have been taught these arts by necessity. They were naturally adroit at handiwork of all kinds; and during the last half-century of the French rule, when the population had settled into comparative stability, many of the mechanic arts were practised with success, notwithstanding the assertion of the Abbé La Tour that everything but

[1] *Beauharnois et Raudot au Ministre,* 1705.

bread and meat had still to be brought from France. This change may be said to date from the peace of Utrecht, or a few years before it. At that time one Duplessis had a new vessel on the stocks. Catalogne, who states the fact, calls it the beginning of ship-building in Canada, — evidently ignorant that Talon had made a fruitless beginning more than forty years before.

Of the arts of ornament not much could have been expected; but, strangely enough, they were in some-what better condition than the useful arts. The nuns of the Hôtel-Dieu made artificial flowers for altars and shrines, under the direction of Mother Juchereau;[1] and the boys of the seminary were taught to make carvings in wood for the decoration of churches.[2] Pierre, son of the merchant Le Ber, had a turn for painting, and made religious pictures, described as very indifferent.[3] His sister Jeanne, an enthusiastic devotee, made embroideries for vest-ments and altars, and her work was much admired.

The colonial finances were not prosperous. In the absence of coin, beaver-skins long served as currency. In 1669 the council declared wheat a legal tender, at four francs the *minot* or three French bushels;[4] and, five years later, all creditors were ordered to receive moose-skins in payment at the market rate.[5] Coin would not remain in the colony: if the company or

[1] Juchereau, *Hist. de l'Hôtel-Dieu*, 244.   [2] *Abeille*, ii. 13.

[3] Faillon, *Vie de Mlle. Le Ber*, 331.   [4] *Édits et Ord.*, ii. 47.

[5] *Ibid.*, ii. 55.

the King sent any thither, it went back in the returning ships.　The government devised a remedy.　A
coinage was ordered for Canada one-fourth less in
value than that of France.　Thus the Canadian livre
or franc was worth, in reality, fifteen sous instead of
twenty.[1]　This shallow expedient produced only a
nominal rise of prices, and coin fled the colony as
before.　Trade was carried on for a time by means
of negotiable notes, payable in furs, goods, or farm
produce.　In 1685 the intendant Meules issued a
card currency.　He had no money to pay the soldiers,
"and not knowing," he informs the minister, "to
what saint to make my vows, the idea occurred to me
of putting in circulation notes made of cards, each
cut into four pieces; and I have issued an ordinance
commanding the inhabitants to receive them in
payment."[2]　The cards were common playing-cards,
and each piece was stamped with a *fleur-de-lis* and a
crown, and signed by the governor, the intendant,
and the clerk of the treasury at Quebec.[3]　The
example of Meules found ready imitation.　Governors
and intendants made card-money whenever they saw
fit; and, being worthless everywhere but in Canada,
it showed no disposition to escape the colony.　It
was declared convertible not into coin, but into bills
of exchange; and this conversion could only take
place at brief specified periods.　"The currency used

[1] This device was of very early date.　See Boucher, *Hist. Véritable*, chap. xiv.

[2] *Meules au Ministre*, 24 *Sept.*, 1685.

[3] *Mémoire addressé au Régent*, 1715.

in Canada," says a writer in the last years of the French rule, "has no value as a representative of money. It is the sign of a sign."[1] It was card representing paper, and this paper was very often dishonored. In 1714 the amount of card rubbish had risen to two million livres. Confidence was lost, and trade was half dead. The minister Ponchartrain came to the rescue, and promised to redeem it at half its nominal value. The holders preferred to lose half rather than the whole, and accepted the terms. A few of the cards were redeemed at the rate named; then the government broke faith, and payment ceased. "This afflicting news," says a writer of the time, "was brought out by the vessel which sailed from France last July."

In 1717 the government made another proposal, and the cards were converted into bills of exchange. At the same time a new issue was made, which it was declared should be the last.[2] This issue was promptly redeemed; but twelve years later another followed it. In the interval, a certain quantity of coin circulated in the colony; but it underwent fluctuations through the intervention of government, and within eight years at least four edicts were issued affecting its value.[3] Then came more promises to pay, till, in the last bitter years of its existence, the colony floundered in drifts of worthless paper.

One characteristic grievance was added to the

---

[1] *Considérations sur l'État du Canada,* 1758.

[2] *Édits et Ordonnances,* i. 370.   [3] *Ibid.,* 400, 432, 436, 484.

countless woes of Canadian commerce. The government was so jealous of popular meetings of all kinds, that for a long time it forbade merchants to meet together for discussing their affairs; and it was not till 1717 that the establishment of a *bourse*, or exchange, was permitted at Quebec and Montreal.[1]

In respect of taxation, Canada, as compared with France, had no reason to complain. If the King permitted governors and intendants to make card-money, he permitted nobody to impose taxes but himself. The Canadians paid no direct civil tax, except in a few instances where temporary and local assessments were ordered for special objects. It was the fur-trade on which the chief burden fell. One-fourth of the beaver-skins, and one-tenth of the moose-hides belonged to the King; and wine, brandy, and tobacco contributed a duty of ten per cent. During a long course of years these were the only imposts. The King also retained the exclusive right of the fur-trade at Tadoussac. A vast tract of wilderness extending from St. Paul's Bay to a point eighty leagues down the St. Lawrence, and stretching indefinitely northward towards Hudson's Bay, formed a sort of royal preserve, whence every settler was rigidly excluded. The farmers of the revenue had their trading-houses at Tadoussac, whither the northern tribes, until war, pestilence, and brandy consumed them, brought every summer a large quantity of furs.

[1] Doutre et Lareau, *Hist. du Droit Canadien*, 254.

When, in 1674, the West India Company, to whom these imposts had been granted, was extinguished, the King resumed possession of them. The various duties, along with the trade of Tadoussac, were now farmed out to one Oudiette and his associates, who paid the Crown three hundred and fifty thousand livres for their privilege.[1]

We come now to a trade far more important than all the others together, one which absorbed the enterprise of the colony, drained the life-sap from other branches of commerce, and, even more than a vicious system of government, kept them in a state of chronic debility, — the hardy, adventurous, lawless, fascinating fur-trade. In the eighteenth century, Canada exported a moderate quantity of timber, wheat, the herb called ginseng, and a few other commodities; but from first to last she lived chiefly on beaver-skins. The government tried without ceasing to control and regulate this traffic; but it never succeeded. It aimed, above all things, to bring the trade home to the colonists; to prevent them from

---

[1] The annual return to the King from the *ferme du Canada* was, for some years, 119,000 francs (livres). Out of this were paid from 35,000 to 40,000 francs a year for "ordinary charges." The governor, intendant, and all troops, except the small garrisons of Quebec, Montreal, and Three Rivers, were paid from other sources. There was a time when the balance must have been in the King's favor; but profit soon changed to loss, owing partly to wars, partly to the confusion into which the beaver-trade soon fell. "His Majesty," writes the minister to the governor in 1698, "may soon grow tired of a colony which, far from yielding him any profit, costs him immense sums every year."

going to the Indians, and induce the Indians to come
to them.   To this end a great annual fair was established by order of the King at Montreal.   Thither
every summer a host of savages came down from the
lakes in their bark canoes.   A place was assigned
them at a little distance from the town.   They
landed, drew up their canoes in a line on the bank,
took out their packs of beaver-skins, set up their
wigwams, slung their kettles, and encamped for the
night.   On the next day there was a grand council
on the common, between St. Paul Street and the
river.   Speeches of compliment were made amid a
solemn smoking of pipes.   The governor-general was
usually present, seated in an arm-chair, while the
visitors formed a ring about him, ranged in the order
of their tribes.   On the next day the trade began in
the same place.   Merchants of high and low degree
brought up their goods from Quebec, and every
inhabitant of Montreal, of any substance, sought a
share in the profit.   Their booths were set along the
palisades of the town, and each had an interpreter,
to whom he usually promised a certain portion of his
gains.   The scene abounded in those contrasts — not
always edifying, but always picturesque — which
mark the whole course of French-Canadian history.
Here was a throng of Indians armed with bows and
arrows, war-clubs, or the cheap guns of the trade,
— some of them being completely naked, except for
the feathers on their heads and the paint on their
faces; French bush-rangers tricked out with savage

finery; merchants and *habitants* in their coarse and plain attire, and the grave priests of St. Sulpice robed in black. Order and sobriety were their watchwords; but the wild gathering was beyond their control. The prohibition to sell brandy could rarely be enforced; and the fair ended at times in a pandemonium of drunken frenzy. The rapacity of trade, and the license of savages and *coureurs de bois*, had completely transformed the pious settlement.

A similar fair was established at Three Rivers, for the Algonquin tribes north of that place. These yearly markets did not fully answer the desired object. There was a constant tendency among the inhabitants of Canada to form settlements above Montreal, in order to intercept the Indians on their way down, drench them with brandy, and get their furs from them at low rates in advance of the fair. Such settlements were forbidden, but not prevented. The audacious "squatter" defied edict and ordinance and the fury of drunken savages, and boldly planted himself in the path of the descending trade. Nor is this a matter of surprise; for he was usually the secret agent of some high colonial officer, — an intendant, the local governor, or the governor-general, who often used his power to enforce the law against others, and to violate it himself.

This was not all; for the more youthful and vigorous part of the male population soon began to escape into the woods, and trade with the Indians far beyond the limits of the remotest settlements.

Here, too, many of them were in league with the authorities, who denounced the abuse while secretly favoring the portion of it in which they themselves were interested. The home government, unable to prevent the evil, tried to regulate it. Licenses were issued for the forest-trade.[1] Their number was limited to twenty-five, and the privileges which they conferred varied at different periods. In La Hontan's time, each license authorized the departure of two canoes loaded with goods. One canoe only was afterwards allowed, bearing three men with about four hundred pounds of freight. The licenses were sometimes sold for the profit of government; but many were given to widows of officers and other needy persons, to the hospitals, or to favorites and retainers of the governor. Those who could not themselves use them sold them to merchants or *voyageurs*, at a price varying from a thousand to eighteen hundred francs. They were valid for a year and a half; and each canoeman had a share in the profits, which, if no accident happened, were very large. The license system was several times suppressed and renewed again; but, like the fair at Montreal, it failed completely to answer its purpose, and restrain the young men of Canada from a general exodus into the wilderness.[2]

The most characteristic features of the Canadian

---

[1] *Ordres du Roy au sujet de la Traite du Canada*, 1681.

[2] Before me is one of these licenses, signed by the governor Denonville. A condition of carrying no brandy is appended to it.

fur-trade still remain to be seen. Oudiette and his associates were not only charged with collecting the revenue, but were also vested with an exclusive right of transporting all the beaver-skins of the colony to France. On their part they were compelled to receive all beaver-skins brought to their magazines, and, after deducting the fourth belonging to the King, to pay for the rest at a fixed price. This price was graduated to the different qualities of the fur; but the average cost to the collectors was a little more than three francs a pound. The inhabitants could barter their furs with merchants; but the merchants must bring them all to the magazines of Oudiette, who paid in receipts convertible into bills of exchange. He soon found himself burdened with such a mass of beaver-skins that the market was completely glutted. The French hatters refused to take them all; and for the part which they consented to take they paid chiefly in hats, which Oudiette was not allowed to sell in France, but only in the French West Indies, where few people wanted them. An unlucky fashion of small hats diminished the con sumption of fur and increased his embarrassments, as did also a practice common among the hatters of mixing rabbit fur with the beaver. In his extremity he bethought him of setting up a hat factory for himself, under the name of a certain licensed hatter, thinking thereby to alarm his customers into buying his stock.[1] The other hatters rose in wrath, and

[1] *Mémoire touchant le Commerce du Canada,* 1687.

petitioned the minister. The new factory was
suppressed, and Oudiette soon became bankrupt.
Another company of farmers of the revenue took his
place with similar results. The action of the law of
supply and demand was completely arrested by the
peremptory edict which, with a view to the prosperity of the colony and the profit of the King, required
the company to take every beaver-skin offered.

All Canada, thinking itself sure of its price, rushed
into the beaver-trade, and the accumulation of unsalable furs became more and more suffocating. The
farmers of the revenue could not meet their engage-
ments. Their bills of exchange were unpaid, and
Canada was filled with distress and consternation.
In 1700 a change of system was ordered. The
monopoly of exporting beaver was placed in the
hands of a company formed of the chief inhabitants of
Canada. Some of them hesitated to take the risk;
but the government was not to be trifled with, and
the minister, Ponchartrain, wrote in terms so peremptory, and so menacing to the recusants, that, in
the words of a writer of the time, he "shut everybody's mouth." About a hundred and fifty merchants accordingly subscribed to the stock of the new
company, and immediately petitioned the King for
a ship and a loan of seven hundred thousand francs.
They were required to take off the hands of the
farmers of the revenue an accumulation of more than
six hundred thousand pounds of beaver, for which,
however, they were to pay but half its usual price.

The market of France absolutely refused it, and the directors of the new company saw no better course than to burn three-fourths of the troublesome and perishable commodity; nor was this the first resort to this strange expedient. One cannot repress a feeling of indignation at the fate of the interesting and unfortunate animals uselessly sacrificed to a false economic system. In order to rid themselves of what remained, the directors begged the King to issue a decree, requiring all hatters to put at least three ounces of genuine beaver-fur into each hat.

All was in vain. The affairs of the company fell into a confusion which was aggravated by the bad faith of some of its chief members. In 1707 it was succeeded by another company, to whose magazines every *habitant* or merchant was ordered to bring every beaver-skin in his possession within forty-eight hours; and the company, like its predecessors, was required to receive it, and pay for it in written promises. Again the market was overwhelmed with a surfeit of beaver. Again the bills of exchange were unpaid, and all was confusion and distress. Among the memorials and petitions to which this state of things gave birth, there is one conspicuous by the presence of good sense and the absence of self-interest. The writer proposes that there should be no more monopoly, but that everybody should be free to buy beaver-skins and send them to France, subject only to a moderate duty of entry. The proposal was not accepted. In 1721 the monopoly of

exporting beaver-skins was given to the new West
India Company; but this time it was provided that
the government should direct from time to time,
according to the capacities of the market, the quantity of furs which the company should be forced to
receive.[1]

Out of the beaver-trade rose a huge evil, baneful
to the growth and the morals of Canada. All that
was most active and vigorous in the colony took to
the woods, and escaped from the control of intendants, councils, and priests, to the savage freedom of
the wilderness. Not only were the possible profits
great; but, in the pursuit of them, there was a fascinating element of adventure and danger. The bush-
rangers, or *coureurs de bois*, were to the King an
object of horror. They defeated his plans for the
increase of the population, and shocked his native
instinct of discipline and order. Edict after edict
was directed against them; and more than once the
colony presented the extraordinary spectacle of the
greater part of its young men turned into forest out-

[1] On the fur-trade the documents consulted are very numerous.
The following are the most important: *Mémoire sur ce qui concerne
le Commerce du Castor et ses dépendances*, 1715; *Mémoire concernant
le Commerce de Traite entre les François et les Sauvages*, 1691; *Mémoire sur le Canada addressé au Régent*, 1715; *Mémoire sur les Affaires
de Canada dans leur Estat présent*, 1696; *Mémoire des Négotiants de
la Rochelle qui font Commerce en Canada sur la Proposition de ne plus
recevoir les Castors et d'engager les Habitants à la Culture des Terres
et Pesche de la Molue*, 1696; *Mémoire du Sr. Riverin sur la Traite et
la Ferme du Castor*, 1696; *Mémoire touchant le Commerce du Canada*,
1687, *etc.*

laws. But severity was dangerous. The offenders
might be driven over to the English, or converted
into a lawless banditti, — renegades of civilization
and the faith. Therefore, clemency alternated with
rigor, and declarations of amnesty with edicts of pro-
scription. Neither threats nor blandishments were
of much avail. We hear of seigniories abandoned;
farms turning again into forests; wives and children
left in destitution. The exodus of the *coureurs de
bois* would take, at times, the character of an organ-
ized movement. The famous Du Lhut is said to
have made a general combination of the young men
of Canada to follow him into the woods. Their plan
was to be absent four years, in order that the edicts
against them might have time to relent. The intendant Duchesneau reported that eight hundred men
out of a population of less than ten thousand souls
had vanished from sight in the immensity of a boundless wilderness. Whereupon the King ordered that
any person going into the woods without a license
should be whipped and branded for the first offence,
and sent for life to the galleys for the second.[1] The
order was more easily given than enforced. "I must
not conceal from you, Monseigneur," again writes
Duchesneau, "that the disobedience of the *coureurs
de bois* has reached such a point that everybody
boldly contravenes the King's interdictions; that
there is no longer any concealment; and that parties

---

[1] *Le Roy à Frontenac,* 30 *Avril,* 1681. On another occasion, it was
ordered that any person thus offending should suffer death.

are collected with astonishing insolence to go and trade in the Indian country. I have done all in my power to prevent this evil, which may cause the ruin of the colony. I have enacted ordinances against the *coureurs de bois;* against the merchants who furnish them with goods; against the gentlemen and others who harbor them; and even against those who have any knowledge of them, and will not inform the local judges. All has been in vain; inasmuch as some of the most considerable families are interested with them, and the governor lets them go on and even shares their profits."[1] "You are aware, Monseigneur," writes Denonville, some years later, "that the *coureurs de bois* are a great evil, but you are not aware how great this evil is. It deprives the country of its effective men; makes them indocile, debauched, and incapable of discipline, and turns them into pretended nobles, — wearing the sword and decked out with lace, both they and their relations, who all affect to be gentlemen and ladies. As for cultivating the soil, they will not hear of it. This, along with the scattered condition of the settlements, causes their children to be as unruly as Indians, being brought up in the same manner. Not that there are not some very good people here, but they are in a minority."[2] In another despatch he enlarges on their vagabond and lawless ways, their indiffer-

---

[1] *N. Y. Colonial Docs.,* ix. 131.

[2] Denonville, *Mémoire sur l'Estat des Affaires de la Nouvelle France.*

ence to marriage, and the mischief caused by their example; describes how, on their return from the woods, they swagger like lords, spend all their gains in dress and drunken revelry, and despise the peasants, whose daughters they will not deign to marry, though they are peasants themselves.

It was a curious scene when a party of *coureurs de bois* returned from their rovings. Montreal was their harboring place, and they conducted themselves much like the crew of a man-of-war paid off after a long voyage. As long as their beaver-skins lasted, they set no bounds to their riot. Every house in the place, we are told, was turned into a drinking-shop. The new-comers were bedizened with a strange mixture of French and Indian finery; while some of them, with instincts more thoroughly savage, stalked about the streets as naked as a Pottawattamie or a Sioux. The clamor of tongues was prodigious, and gambling and drinking filled the day and the night. When at last they were sober again, they sought absolution for their sins; nor could the priests venture to bear too hard on their unruly penitents, lest they should break wholly with the Church and dispense thenceforth with her sacraments.

Under such leaders as Du Lhut, the *coureurs de bois* built forts of palisades at various points throughout the West and Northwest. They had a post of this sort at Detroit some time before its permanent settlement, as well as others on Lake Superior and in the valley of the Mississippi. They occupied them as

long as it suited their purposes, and then abandoned
them to the next comer. Michilimackinac was,
however, their chief resort; and thence they would
set out, two or three together, to roam for hundreds
of miles through the endless mesh-work of inter-
locking lakes and rivers which seams the northern
wilderness.

No wonder that a year or two of bush-ranging
spoiled them for civilization. Though not a very
valuable member of society, and though a thorn in
the side of princes and rulers, the *coureur de bois* had
his uses, at least from an artistic point of view; and
his strange figure, sometimes brutally savage, but
oftener marked with the lines of a dare-devil courage, and a reckless, thoughtless gayety, will always
be joined to the memories of that grand world of
woods which the nineteenth century is fast civilizing
out of existence. At least, he is picturesque, and
with his red-skin companion serves to animate forest
scenery. Perhaps he could sometimes feel, without
knowing that he felt them, the charms of the savage
nature that had adopted him. Rude as he was, her
voice may not always have been meaningless for one
who knew her haunts so well, — deep recesses where,
veiled in foliage, some wild shy rivulet steals with
timid music through breathless caves of verdure;
gulfs where feathered crags rise like castle walls,
where the noonday sun pierces with keen rays
athwart the torrent, and the mossed arms of fallen
pines cast wavering shadows on the illumined foam;

pools of liquid crystal turned emerald in the reflected
green of impending woods; rocks on whose rugged
front the gleam of sunlit waters dances in quivering
light; ancient trees hurled headlong by the storm, to
dam the raging stream with their forlorn and savage
ruin; or the stern depths of immemorial forests, dim
and silent as a cavern, columned with innumerable
trunks, each like an Atlas upholding its world of
leaves, and sweating perpetual moisture down its
dark and channelled rind, — some strong in youth,
some grisly with decrepit age, nightmares of strange
distortion, gnarled and knotted with wens and goitres;
roots intertwined beneath like serpents petrified in
an agony of contorted strife; green and glistening
mosses carpeting the rough ground, mantling the
rocks, turning pulpy stumps to mounds of verdure,
and swathing fallen trunks as, bent in the impotence
of rottenness, they lie outstretched over knoll and
hollow, like mouldering reptiles of the primeval
world, while around, and on and through them,
springs the young growth that battens on their decay,
— the forest devouring its own dead; or, to turn from
its funereal shade to the light and life of the open
woodland, the sheen of sparkling lakes, and mountains basking in the glory of the summer noon,
flecked by the shadows of passing clouds that sail
on snowy wings across the transparent azure.[1]

[1] An adverse French critic gives as his opinion that the sketch
of the primeval wilderness on the preceding page is drawn from
fancy, and not from observation. It is, however, copied in every

Yet it would be false coloring to paint the half-savage *coureur de bois* as a romantic lover of Nature. He liked the woods because they emancipated him from restraint. He liked the lounging ease of the camp-fire, and the license of Indian villages. His life has a dark and ugly side, which is nowhere drawn more strongly than in a letter written by the Jesuit Carheil to the intendant Champigny. It was at a time when some of the outlying forest posts, originally either missions or transient stations of *coureurs de bois*, had received regular garrisons. Carheil writes from Michilimackinac, and describes the state of things around him like one whom long familiarity with them had stripped of every illusion.[1]

But here, for the present, we pause; for the father touches on other matters than the *coureurs de bois*, and we reserve him and his letter for the next chapter.

particular, without exception, from a virgin forest in a deep moist valley by the upper waters of the little river Pemigewasset in northern New Hampshire, where I spent a summer afternoon a few days before the passage was written.

[1] See the letter in Appendix I.

CHAPTER XXI.

1663–1702.

THE MISSIONS. — THE BRANDY QUESTION.

THE JESUITS AND THE IROQUOIS. — MISSION VILLAGES. — MICHILI-
MACKINAC. — FATHER CARHEIL. — TEMPERANCE. — BRANDY AND
THE INDIANS. — STRONG MEASURES. — DISPUTES. — LICENSE AND
PROHIBITION. — VIEWS OF THE KING. — TRADE AND THE JESUITS.

FOR a year or two after De Tracy had chastised
the Mohawks, and humbled the other Iroquois nations, all was rose-color on the side of that dreaded
confederacy. The Jesuits, defiant as usual of hardship and death, had begun their ruined missions
anew. Bruyas took the Mission of the Martyrs
among the Mohawks; Milet, that of Saint Francis
Xavier, among the Oneidas; Lamberville, that of
Saint John the Baptist among the Onondagas;
Carheil, that of Saint Joseph among the Cayugas;
and Raffeix and Julien Garnier shared between them
the three missions of the Senecas. The Iroquois,
after their punishment, were in a frame of mind so
hopeful that the fathers imagined for a moment that
they were all on the point of accepting the faith.
This was a consummation earnestly to be wished, not

only from a religious, but also from a political, point
of view. The complete conversion of the Iroquois
meant their estrangement from the heretic English
and Dutch, and their firm alliance with the French.
It meant safety for Canada, and it insured for her
the fur-trade of the interior freed from English
rivalry. Hence the importance of these missions,
and hence their double character. While the Jesuit
toiled to convert his savage hosts, he watched them
at the same time with the eye of a shrewd political
agent; reported at Quebec the result of his observations, and by every means in his power sought to
alienate them from England, and attach them to
France.

Their simple conversion, by placing them wholly
under his influence, would have outweighed in
political value all other agencies combined; but the
flattering hopes of the earlier years soon vanished.
Some petty successes against other tribes so elated
the Iroquois that they ceased to care for French
alliance or French priests. Then a few petty reverses
would dash their spirits, and dispose them again to
listen to Jesuit counsels. Every success of a war-
party was a loss to the faith, and every reverse was
a gain. Meanwhile a more repulsive or a more critical existence than that of a Jesuit father in an
Iroquois town is scarcely conceivable. The torture
of prisoners turned into a horrible festivity for the
whole tribe; foul and crazy orgies in which, as the
priest thought, the powers of darkness took a special

delight; drunken riots, the work of Dutch brandy, when he was forced to seek refuge from death in his chapel, — a sanctuary which superstitious fear withheld the Indians from violating, — these, and a thousand disgusts and miseries, filled the record of his days; and he bore them all in patience. Not only were the early Canadian Jesuits men of an intense religious zeal, but they were also men who lived not for themselves but for their Order. Their faults were many and great, but the grandeur of their self-devotion towers conspicuous over all.

At Caughnawaga, near Montreal, may still be seen the remnants of a mission of converted Iroquois, whom the Jesuits induced to leave the temptations of their native towns and settle here, under the wing of the Church. They served as a bulwark against the English, and sometimes did good service in time of war. At Sillery, near Quebec, a band of Abenakis, escaping from the neighborhood of the English towards the close of Philip's War, formed another mission of similar character. The Sulpitians had a third at the foot of the mountain of Montreal, where two massive stone-towers of the fortified Indian town are standing to this day. All these converted savages, as well as those of Lorette and other missions far and near, were used as allies in war, and launched in scalping-parties against the border settlements of New England.

Not only the Sulpitians, but also the seminary priests of Quebec, the Récollets, and even the

Capuchins, had missions more or less important, and more or less permanent. But the Jesuits stood always in the van of religious and political propagandism; and all the forest tribes felt their influence, from Acadia and Maine to the plains beyond the Mississippi. Next in importance to their Iroquois missions were those among the Algonquins of the northern lakes. Here was the grand domain of the beaver-trade; and the chief woes of the missionary sprang not from the Indians, but from his own countrymen. Beaver-skins had produced an effect akin to that of gold in our own day, and the deepest recesses of the wilderness were invaded by eager seekers after gain.

The focus of the evil was at Father Marquette's old mission of Michilimackinac. First, year after year came a riotous invasion of *coureurs de bois*, and then a garrison followed to crown the mischief. Discipline was very weak at these advanced posts, and, to eke out their pay, the soldiers were allowed to trade, — brandy, whether permitted or interdicted, being the chief article of barter. Father Étienne Carheil was driven almost to despair; and he wrote to the intendant, his fast friend and former pupil, the long letter already mentioned. "Our missions," he says, "are reduced to such extremity that we can no longer maintain them against the infinity of disorder, brutality, violence, injustice, impiety, impurity, insolence, scorn, and insult, which the deplorable and infamous traffic in brandy has spread universally among the

Indians of these parts. . . . In the despair in which
we are plunged, nothing remains for us but to abandon
them to the brandy-sellers as a domain of drunkenness and debauchery." He complains bitterly of the
officers in command of the fort, who, he says, far
from repressing disorders, encourage them by their
example, and are even worse than their subordinates,
"insomuch that all our Indian villages are so many
taverns for drunkenness and Sodoms for iniquity,
which we shall be forced to leave to the just wrath
and vengeance of God." He insists that the garrisons are entirely useless, as they have only four occupations, — first, to keep open liquor-shops for crowds
of drunken Indians; secondly, to roam from place to
place, carrying goods and brandy under the orders of
the commandant, who shares their profits; thirdly,
to gamble day and night; fourthly, to "turn the fort
into a place which I am ashamed to call by its right
name;" and he describes, with a curious amplitude
of detail, the swarms of Indian girls who are hired to
make it their resort. "Such, Monseigneur, are the
only employments of the soldiers maintained here so
many years. If this can be called doing the King
service, I admit that such service is done for him
here now, and has always been done for him here;
but I never saw any other done in my life." He
further declares that the commandants oppose and
malign the missionaries, while of the presents which
the King sends up the country for distribution to
the Indians, they, the Indians, get nothing but a

little tobacco, and the officer keeps the rest for himself.[1]

From the misconduct of officers and soldiers, the
father passes to that of the *coureurs de bois* and
licensed traders; and here he is equally severe.   He
dilates on the evils which result from permitting the
colonists to go to the Indians instead of requiring
the Indians to come to the settlements.   "It serves
only to rob the country of all its young men, weaken
families, deprive wives of their husbands, sisters of
their brothers, and parents of their children; expose
the voyagers to a hundred dangers of body and soul;
involve them in a multitude of expenses, some necessary, some useless, and some criminal; accustom
them to do no work, and at last disgust them with it
forever; make them live in constant idleness, unfit
them completely for any trade, and render them useless to themselves, their families, and the public.
But it is less as regards the body than as regards the
soul that this traffic of the French among the savages
is infinitely hurtful.   It carries them far away from
churches, separates them from priests and nuns, and
severs them from all instruction, all exercise of

[1] Of the officers in command at Michilimackinac while Carheil
was there, he partially excepts La Durantaye from his strictures,
but bears very hard on La Mothe-Cadillac, who hated the Jesuits
and was hated by them in turn.   La Mothe, on his part, writes that
" the missionaries wish to be masters wherever they are, and cannot
tolerate anybody above themselves."   (*N. Y. Colonial Docs.*, ix. 587.)
For much more emphatic expressions of his views concerning them,
see two letters from him, translated in Sheldon's *Early History of
Michigan.*

religion, and all spiritual aid. It sends them into places wild and almost inaccessible, through a thousand perils by land and water, to carry on by base, abject, and shameful means a trade which would much better be carried on at Montreal."

But in the complete transfer of the trade to Montreal, Father Carheil sees insuperable difficulties; and he proceeds to suggest, as the last and best resort, that garrisons and officers should be withdrawn, and licenses abolished, that discreet and virtuous persons should be chosen to take charge of all the trade of the upper country; that these persons should be in perfect sympathy and correspondence with the Jesuits; and that the trade should be carried on at the missions of the Jesuits and in their presence.[1]

This letter brings us again face to face with the brandy question, of which we have seen something already in the quarrel between Avaugour and the bishop. In the summer of 1648 there was held at the mission of Sillery a temperance meeting, — the first in all probability on this continent. The drum beat after mass, and the Indians gathered at the summons. Then an Algonquin chief, a zealous convert of the Jesuits, proclaimed to the crowd a late edict of the governor imposing penalties for drunkenness, and, in his own name and that of the other

---

[1] *Lettre du Père Étienne Carheil de la Compagnie de Jésus à l'Intendant Champigny, Michilimackinac, 30 Août, 1702 (Archives Nationales), Appendix I.*

chiefs, exhorted them to abstinence, declaring that all drunkards should be handed over to the French for punishment. Father Jerome Lalemant looked on delighted. "It was," he says, "the finest public act of jurisdiction exercised among the Indians since I have been in this country. From the beginning of the world they have all thought themselves as great lords, the one as the other, and never before submitted to their chiefs any further than they chose to do so."[1]

There was great need of reform; for a demon of drunkenness seemed to possess these unhappy tribes. Nevertheless, with all their rage for brandy, they sometimes showed in regard to it a self-control quite admirable in its way. When at a fair, a council, or a friendly visit, their entertainers regaled them with rations of the coveted liquor, so prudently measured out that they could not be the worse for it, they would unite their several portions in a common stock, which they would then divide among a few of their number, — thus enabling them to attain that complete intoxication which, in their view, was the true end of all drinking. The objects of this singular benevolence were expected to requite it in kind on some future occasion.

A drunken Indian, with weapons within reach, was very dangerous, and all prudent persons kept out of his way. This greatly pleased him; for, seeing everybody run before him, he fancied himself a great chief,

---

[1] Lalemant, *Relation*, 1648, p. 43.

and howled and swung his tomahawk with redoubled
fury.   If, as often happened, he maimed or murdered
some wretch not nimble enough to escape, his countrymen absolved him from all guilt, and blamed only
the brandy.   Hence, if an Indian wished to take a
safe revenge on some personal enemy, he would
pretend to be drunk; and not only murders but other
crimes were often committed by false claimants to
the bacchanalian privilege.

In the eyes of the missionaries, brandy was a fiend
with all crimes and miseries in his train; and, in
fact, nothing earthly could better deserve the epithet
infernal than an Indian town in the height of a
drunken debauch.   The orgies never ceased till the
bottom of the barrel was reached.   Then came
repentance, despair, wailing, and bitter invective
against the white men, the cause of all the woe.   In
the name of the public good, of humanity, and above
all of religion, the bishop and the Jesuits denounced
the fatal traffic.

Their case was a strong one; but so was the case
of their opponents.   There was real and imminent
danger that the thirsty savages, if refused brandy by
the French, would seek it from the Dutch and
English of New York.   It was the most potent lure
and the most killing bait.   Wherever it was found,
thither the Indians and their beaver-skins were sure
to go, and the interests of the fur-trade, vital to the
colony, were bound up with it.   Nor was this all,
for the merchants and the civil powers insisted that

religion and the saving of souls were bound up with
it no less; since, to repel the Indians from the
Catholic French, and attract them to the heretic
English, was to turn them from ways of grace to
ways of perdition.[1] The argument, no doubt, was
dashed largely with hypocrisy in those who used it;
but it was one which the priests were greatly perplexed to answer.

In former days, when Canada was not yet transformed from a mission to a colony, the Jesuits entered
with a high hand on the work of reform. It fared
hard with the culprit caught in the act of selling
brandy to Indians. They led him, after the sermon,
to the door of the church; where, kneeling on the
pavement, partially stript and bearing in his hand
the penitential torch, he underwent a vigorous flagel-
lation, laid on by Father Le Mercier himself, after
the fashion formerly practised in the case of refractory
school-boys.[2] Bishop Laval not only discharged
against the offenders volleys of wholesale excommunication, but he made of the offence a "reserved
case;" that is, a case in which the power of granting
absolution was reserved to himself alone. This produced great commotion, and a violent conflict between
religious scruples and a passion for gain. The
bishop and the Jesuits stood inflexible; while their

[1] " Ce commerce est absolument nécessaire pour attirer les
sauvages dans les colonies françoises, et par ce moyen leur donner
les premières teintures de la foy." — *Mémoire de Colbert, joint à sa
lettre à Duchesneau du* 24 *Mai,* 1678.

[2] *Mémoire de Dumesnil,* 1671.

opponents added bitterness to the quarrel by charging them with permitting certain favored persons to sell brandy, unpunished, and even covertly selling it themselves.[1]

Appeal was made to the King, who — with his Jesuit confessor, guardian of his conscience on. one side, and Colbert, guardian of his worldly interests on the other — stood in some perplexity. The case was referred to the fathers of the Sorbonne; and they, after solemn discussion, pronounced the selling of brandy to Indians a mortal sin.[2] It was next referred to an assembly of the chief merchants and inhabitants of Canada, held under the eye of the governor, intendant, and council, in the Château St.

[1] *Lettre de Charles Aubert de la Chesnaye*, 24 *Oct.*, 1693. After speaking of the excessive rigor of the bishop, he adds : " L'on dit, et il est vrai, que dans ces temps si fâcheux, sous pretexte de pauvreté dans les familles, certaines gens avoient permission d'en traiter, je crois toujours avec la réserve de ne pas enivrer." Dumesnil, *Mémoire de* 1671, says that Laval excommunicated all brandy-sellers, " à l'exception, néanmoins, de quelques particuliers qu'il voulait favoriser." He says further that the bishop and the Jesuit Ragueneau had a clerk whom they employed at 500 francs a year to trade with the Indians, paying them in liquors for their furs ; and that for a time the ecclesiastics had this trade to themselves, their severities having deterred most others from venturing into it. La Salle, *Mémoire de* 1678, declares that, " Ils [*les Jésuites*] refusent l'absolution à ceux qui ne veulent pas promettre de n'en plus vendre, et s'ils meurent en cet état, ils les privent de la sépulture ecclésiastique : au contraire, ils se permettent à eux mesmes sans aucune difficulté ce mesme trafic, quoyque toute sorte de trafic soit interdite à tous les ecclésiastiques par les ordonnances du Roy et par une bulle expresse du Pape." I give these assertions as I find them, and for what they are worth.

[2] *Délibération de la Sorbonne sur la Traite des Boissons*, 8 *Mars*, 1675.

Louis. Each was directed to state his views in writing. The great majority were for unrestricted trade in brandy; a few were for a limited and guarded trade; and two or three declared for prohibition.[1] Decrees of prohibition were passed from time to time, but they were unavailing. They were revoked, renewed, and revoked again. They were, in fact, worse than useless; for their chief effect was to turn traders and *coureurs de bois* into troops of audacious contrabandists. Attempts were made to limit the brandy-trade to the settlements, and exclude it from the forest country, where its regulation was impossible; but these attempts, like the others, were of little avail. It is worthy of notice that when brandy was forbidden everywhere else, it was permitted in the trade of Tadoussac, carried on for the profit of government.[2]

In spite of the Sorbonne, in spite of Père La Chaise, and of the Archbishop of Paris, whom he also consulted, the King was never at heart a prohibitionist.[3] His Canadian revenue was drawn from the fur-trade; and the singular argument of the partisans of brandy, that its attractions were needed

---

[1] *Procès-verbal de l'Assemblée tenue au Château de St. Louis de Québec, le 26 Oct., 1676, et jours suivants.*

[2] *Lettre de Charles Aubert de la Chesnaye*, 24 *Oct.*, 1693. In the course of the quarrel, a severe law passed by the General Court of Massachusetts against the sale of liquors to Indians was several times urged as an example to be imitated. A copy of it was sent to the minister, and is still preserved in the Archives of the Marine and Colonies.

[3] See, among other evidence, *Mémoire sur la Traite des Boissons*, 1678.

to keep the Indians from contact with heresy, served admirably to salve his conscience.   Bigot as he was, he distrusted the Bishop of Quebec, the great champion of the anti-liquor movement.   His own letters, as well as those of his minister, prove that he saw, or thought that he saw, motives for the crusade very different from those inscribed on its banners.   He wrote to Saint-Vallier, Laval's successor in the bishopric, that the brandy-trade was very useful to the kingdom of France; that it should be regulated, but not prevented; that the consciences of his subjects must not be disturbed by denunciations of it as a sin; and that "it is well that you [the bishop] should take care that the zeal of the ecclesiastics is not excited by personal interests and passions." [1]   Perhaps he alludes to the spirit of encroachment and domination which he and his minister in secret instructions to their officers often impute to the bishop and the clergy; or perhaps he may have in mind other accusations which had reached him from time to time during many years, and of which the following from the pen of the most noted of Canadian governors will serve as an example. Count Frontenac declares that the Jesuits greatly exaggerate the disorders caused by brandy, and that they easily convince persons "who do not know the interested motives which have led them to harp continually on this string for more than forty years. . . . They have long wished to have the fur-trade entirely

[1] *Le Roy à Saint-Vallier, 7 Avril*, 1691.

to themselves, and to keep out of sight the trade
which they have always carried on in the woods, and
which they are carrying on there now." [1]

TRADE OF THE JESUITS. — As I have observed in a former
volume, the charge against the Jesuits of trading in beaver-
skins dates from the beginning of the colony. In the private
journal of Father Jerome Lalemant, their superior, occurs the
following curious passage, under date of November, 1645:
Pour la traite des castors. Le 15 de Nov. le bruit estant qu'on
s'en alloit icy publier la defense qui auoit esté publiée aux
Trois Riuieres que pas vn n'eut à traiter auec les sauuages, le
P. Vimont demanda à Mons. des Chastelets commis general
si nous serions de pire condition soubs eux que soubs Messieurs
de la Compagnie. La conclusion fut que non et *que cela iroit
pour nous à l'ordinaire, mais que nous le fissions doucement.*"
(*Journal des Jésuites.*) Two years after, on the request of
Lalemant, the governor Montmagny, and his destined successor
Ailleboust, gave the Jesuits a certificate to the effect that "les
pères de la compagnie de Jésus sont innocents de la calomnie
qui leur a été imputée, et *ce qu'ils en ont fait a été pour le bien
de la communauté et pour un bon sujet.*" This leaves it to be
inferred that they actually traded, though with good intentions. In 1664, in reply to similar "calumnies," the Jesuits
made by proxy a declaration before the council, stating, "que
les dits Révérends Pères Jésuites n'ont fait jamais aucune
profession de vendre et n'ont jamais rien vendu, *mais seulement
que les marchandises qu'ils donnent aux particuliers ne sont que
pour avoir leurs nécessités.*" This is an admission in a thin
disguise. The word *nécessités* is of very elastic interpretation.
In a memoir of Talon, 1667, he mentions, "la traite de pelleteries qu'on assure qu'ils [*les Jésuites*] font aux Outaouacks et
au Cap de la Madeleine; ce que je ne sais pas de science
certaine."

That which Talon did not know with certainty is made
reasonably clear for us by a line in the private journal of

---

[1] *Frontenac au Ministre,* 29 *Oct.,* 1676.

Father Le Mercier, who writes under date of 17 August, 1665, "Le Père Frémin remonte supérieur au Cap de la Magdeleine, ou le temporel est en bon estat. *Comme il est delivré de tout soin d'aucune traite,* il doit s'appliquer à l'instruction tant des Montagnets que des Algonquins." Father Charles Albanel was charged, under Frémin, with the affairs of the mission, including doubtless the temporal interests, to the prosperity of which Father Le Mercier alludes, and the cares of trade from which Father Frémin was delivered. Cavelier de la Salle declared in 1678, "Le père Arbanelle [*Albanel*] jésuite a traité au Cap [*de la Madeleine*] pour 700 pistoles de peaux d'orignaux et de castors; luy mesme me l'a dit en 1667. Il vend le pain, le vin, le bled, le lard, et il tient magazin au Cap aussi bien que le frère Joseph à Québec. Ce frère gagne 500 pour 100 sur tous les peuples. Ils [*les Jésuites*] ont bâti leur collège en partie de leur traite et en partie de l'emprunt." La Salle further says that Frémin, being reported to have made enormous profits, "ce père répondit au gouverneur (*qui lui en avait fait des plaintes*) par un billet que luy a conservé, que c'estoit une calomnie que ce grand gain prétendu ; puisque tout ce qui se passoit par ses mains ne pouvoit produire par an que quatre mille de revenant bon, tous frais faits, sans comprendre les gages des domestiques." La Salle gives also many other particulars, especially relating to Michilimackinac, where, as he says, the Jesuits had a large stock of beaver-skins. According to Péronne Dumesnil, *Mémoire de* 1671, the Jesuits had at that time more than 20,000 francs a year, — partly from trade and partly from charitable contributions of their friends in France.

The King repeatedly forbade the Jesuits and other ecclesiastics in Canada to carry on trade. On one occasion he threatened strong measures should they continue to disobey him. (*Le Roi à Frontenac*, 28 *Avril*, 1677.) In the same year the minister wrote to the intendant Duchesneau : "Vous ne sauriez apporter trop de precautions pour abolir entièrement la coustume que les Ecclesiastiques seculiers et reguliers avaient pris de traitter ou de faire traitter leurs valets," 18 *Avril*, 1677.

The Jesuits entered also into other branches of trade and

industry with a vigor and address which the inhabitants of Canada might have emulated with advantage. They were successful fishers of eels. In 1646 their eel-pots at Sillery are said to have yielded no less than forty thousand eels, some of which they sold at the modest price of thirty sous a hundred. (Ferland, *Notes sur les Registres de N. D. de Québec*, 82.) The members of the Order were exempted from payment of duties, and in 1674 they were specially empowered to construct mills, including sugar-mills, and keep slaves, apprentices, and hired servants. *Droit Canadien*, 180.

CHAPTER XXII.

1663–1763.

PRIESTS AND PEOPLE.

CHURCH AND STATE. — THE BISHOP AND THE KING. — THE KING AND THE CURÉS. — THE NEW BISHOP. — THE CANADIAN CURÉ. — ECCLESIASTICAL RULE. — SAINT-VALLIER AND DENONVILLE. — CLERICAL RIGOR. — JESUIT AND SULPITIAN. — COURCELLE AND CHÂTELAIN. — THE RÉCOLLETS. — HERESY AND WITCHCRAFT. — CANADIAN NUNS. — JEANNE LE BER. — EDUCATION. — THE SEMINARY. — SAINT JOACHIM. — MIRACLES OF SAINT ANNE. — CANADIAN SCHOOLS.

WHEN Laval and the Jesuits procured the recall of Mézy, they achieved a seeming triumph; yet it was but a defeat in disguise. While ordering home the obnoxious governor, the King and Colbert made a practical assertion of their power too strong to be resisted. A vice-regal officer, a governor, an intendant, and a regiment of soldiers were silent but convincing proofs that the mission days of Canada were over, and the dream of a theocracy dispelled forever. The ecclesiastics read the signs of the times, and for a while seemed to accept the situation.

The King on his part, in vindicating the civil power, had shown a studious regard to the sensibilities of the bishop and his allies. The lieutenant-

general Tracy, a zealous devotee, and the intendant
Talon, who at least professed to be one, were not
men to offend the clerical party needlessly.   In the
choice of Courcelle, the governor, a little less caution
had been shown.   His chief business was to fight the
Iroquois, for which he was well fitted; but he
presently showed signs of a willingness to fight the
Jesuits also.   The colonists liked him for his lively
and impulsive speech; but the priests were of a
different mind, and so, too, was his colleague Talon,
— a prudent person, who studied the amenities of
life, and knew how to pursue his ends with temper
and moderation.   On the subject of the clergy he
and the governor substantially agreed, but the ebulli-
tions of the one and the smooth discretion of the
other were mutually repugnant to both.   Talon
complained of his colleague's impetuosity; and
Colbert directed him to use his best efforts to keep
Courcelle within bounds, and prevent him from
publicly finding fault with the bishop and the
Jesuits.[1] Next we find the minister writing to
Courcelle himself to soothe his ruffled temper, and
enjoining him to act discreetly, "because," said.
Colbert, "as the colony grows, the King's authority
will grow with it, and the authority of the priests
will be brought back in time within lawful bounds."[2]

Meanwhile, Talon had been ordered to observe
carefully the conduct of the bishop and the Jesuits,

[1] *Colbert à Talon,* 20 *Fév.,* 1668.
[2] *Colbert à Courcelle,* 19 *Mai,* 1669.

"who," says the minister, "have hitherto nominated governors for the King, and used every means to procure the recall of those chosen without their participation; [1] filled offices with their adherents, and tolerated no secular priests except those of one mind with them." [2] Talon, therefore, under the veil of a reverent courtesy, sharply watched them. They paid courtesy with courtesy, and the intendant wrote home to his master that he saw nothing amiss in them. He quickly changed his mind. "I should have had less trouble and more praise," he writes in the next year, "if I had been willing to leave the power of the Church where I found it." [3] "It is easy," he says again, "to incur the ill-will of the Jesuits if one does not accept all their opinions and abandon one's self to their direction even in temporal matters; for their encroachments extend to affairs of police, which concern only the civil magistrate," — and he recommends that one or two of them be sent home as disturbers of the peace. [4] They, on their part, changed attitude towards both him and the governor. One of them, Father Bardy, less discreet than the rest, is said to have preached a sermon against them at Quebec, in which he likened them to a pair of toadstools springing up in a night, — adding that a good remedy would soon be found, and

---

[1] *Instruction au Sieur Talon.*

[2] *Mémoire pour M. de Tracy.*

[3] *Talon au Ministre*, 13 *Nov.*, 1666.

[4] *Talon, Mémoire de* 1667.

that Courcelle would have to run home like other
governors before him.[1]

Tracy escaped clerical attacks. He was extremely
careful not to provoke them; and one of his first acts
was to restore to the council the bishop's adherents
whom Mézy had expelled.[2] And if, on the one hand,
he was too pious to quarrel with the bishop, so, on
the other, the bishop was too prudent to invite collision with a man of his rank and influence.

After all, the dispute between the civil and ecclesiastical powers was not fundamental. Each had
need of the other; both rested on authority, and
they differed only as to the boundary lines of their
respective shares in it. Yet the dispute of boundaries was a serious one, and it remained a source of
bitterness for many years. The King, though rigidly
Catholic, was not yet sunk in the slough of bigotry
into which Maintenon and the Jesuits succeeded at
last in plunging him. He had conceived a distrust
of Laval, and his jealousy of his royal authority
disposed him to listen to the anti-clerical counsels of
his minister. How needful they both thought it to
prune the exuberant growth of clerical power, and
how cautiously they set themselves to do so, their
letters attest again and again. "The bishop," writes
Colbert, "assumes a domination far beyond that of

---

[1] La Salle, *Mémoire de* 1678. This sermon was preached on the
12th of March, 1667.

[2] A curious account of his relations with Laval is given in a
letter of La Mothe-Cadillac, 28 September, 1694.

other bishops throughout the Christian world, and particularly in the kingdom of France."[1] "It is the will of his Majesty that you confine him and the Jesuits within just bounds, and let none of them overstep these bounds in any manner whatsoever. Consider this as a matter of the greatest importance, and one to which you cannot give too much attention."[2] "But," the prudent minister elsewhere writes, "it is of the greatest consequence that the bishop and the Jesuits do not perceive that the intendant blames their conduct."[3]

It was to the same intendant that Colbert wrote, "it is necessary to diminish as much as possible the excessive number of priests, monks, and nuns in Canada." Yet in the very next year, and on the advice of Talon, he himself sent four more to the colony. His motive was plain. He meant that they should serve as a counterpoise to the Jesuits.[4] They were mendicant friars, belonging to the branch of the Franciscans known as the Récollets; and they were supposed to be free from the ambition for the aggrandizement of their Order which was imputed, and with reason, to the Jesuits. Whether the Récollets were free from it or not, no danger was to be feared from them; for Laval and the Jesuits were sure to oppose them, and they would need the support of the

[1] *Colbert à Duchesneau, 1 Mai, 1677.*

[2] *Ibid., 28 Avril, 1677.*

[3] *Instruction pour M. Bouteroue, 1668.*

[4] *Mémoire succinct des principaux points des intentions du Roy sur le pays de Canada, 18 Mai, 1669.*

government too much to set themselves in opposition to it. "The more Récollets we have," says Talon, "the better will the too firmly rooted authority of the others be balanced."[1]

While Louis XIV. tried to confine the priests to their ecclesiastical functions, he was at the same time, whether from religion, policy, or both combined, very liberal to the Canadian Church, of which, indeed, he was the main-stay. In the yearly estimate of "ordinary charges" of the colony, the Church holds the most prominent place; and the appropriations for religious purposes often exceed all the rest together. Thus, in 1667, out of a total of 36,360 francs, 28,000 are assigned to Church uses.[2] The amount fluctuated, but was always relatively large. The Canadian curés were paid in great part by the King, who for many years gave eight thousand francs annually towards their support. Such was the poverty of the country that, though in 1685 there were only twenty-five curés,[3] each costing about five hundred francs a year, the tithes utterly failed to meet the expense. As late as 1700, the intendant declared that Canada without the King's help could

[1] *Talon au Ministre*, 10 *Oct.*, 1670.

[2] Of this, 6,000 francs were given to the Jesuits, 6,000 to the Ursulines, 9,000 to the cathedral, 4,000 to the seminary, and 3,000 to the Hôtel-Dieu. (*État de dépense, etc.*, 1677.) The rest went to pay civil officers and garrisons. In 1682 the amount for Church uses was only 12,000 francs. In 1687 it was 13,500. In 1689 it rose to 34,000, including Acadia.

[3] Increased soon after to thirty-six by Saint-Vallier, Laval's successor.

26

not maintain more than eight or nine curés. Louis XIV. winced under these steady demands, and reminded the bishop that more than four thousand curés in France lived on less than two hundred francs a year.[1] "You say," he wrote to the intendant, "that it is impossible for a Canadian curé to live on five hundred francs. Then you must do the impossible to accomplish my intentions, which are always that the curés should live on the tithes alone."[2] Yet the head of the Church still begged for money, and the King still paid it. "We are in the midst of a costly war," wrote the minister to the bishop, "yet in consequence of your urgency the gifts to ecclesiastics will be continued as before."[3] And they did continue. More than half a century later, the King was still making them, and during the last years of the colony he gave twenty thousand francs annually to support Canadian curés.[4]

The maintenance of curés was but a part of his bounty. He endowed the bishopric with the revenues of two French abbeys, to which he afterwards added a third. The vast tracts of land which Laval had acquired were freed from feudal burdens, and emigrants were sent to them by the government in such numbers that, in 1667, the bishop's seigniory of Beaupré and Orleans contained more than a fourth

---

[1] *Mémoire à Duchesneau*, 15 *Mai*, 1678 ; *Le Roy à Duchesneau*, 11 *Juin*, 1680.

[2] *Le Roy à Duchesneau*, 30 *Avril*, 1681.

[3] *Le Ministre à l'Évêque*, 8 *Mai*, 1694.

[4] Bougainville, *Mémoire*, 1757.

of the entire population of Canada.[1]   He had emerged
from his condition of apostolic poverty to find himself the richest land-owner in the colony.

If by favors like these the King expected to lead
the ecclesiastics into compliance with his wishes, he
was doomed to disappointment. The system of
movable curés, by which the bishop like a military
chief could compel each member of his clerical army
to come and go at his bidding, was from the first
repugnant to Louis XIV. On the other hand, the
bishop clung to it with his usual tenacity. Colbert
denounced it as contrary to the laws of the kingdom.[2]
"His Majesty has reason to believe," he writes, "that
the chief source of the difficulty which the bishop
makes on this point is his wish to preserve a greater
authority over the curés."[3] The inflexible prelate,
whose heart was bound up in the system he had
established, opposed evasion and delay to each
expression of the royal will; and even a royal edict
failed to produce the desired effect. In the height
of the dispute, Laval went to court, and, on the
ground of failing health, asked for a successor in the
bishopric. The King readily granted his prayer.
The successor was appointed; but when Laval pre-

[1] Entire population, 4,312 ; Beaupré and Orleans, 1185. (*Recense-
ment de* 1667.) Laval, it will be remembered, afterwards gave his
lands to the seminary of Quebec. He previously exchanged the
Island of Orleans with the Sieur Berthelot for the Island of Jesus.
Berthelot gave him a large sum of money in addition.

[2] *Le Ministre à Duchesneau,* 15 *Mai,* 1678.

[3] *Instruction à M. de Meules,* 1682.

pared to embark again for Canada, he was given to
understand that he was to remain in France. In vain
he promised to make no trouble; [1] and it was not till
after an absence of four years that he was permitted
to return, no longer as its chief, to his beloved
Canadian Church. [2]

Meanwhile Saint-Vallier, the new bishop, had
raised a new tempest. He attacked that organization
of the seminary of Quebec by which Laval had
endeavored to unite the secular priests of Canada
into an attached and obedient family, with the
bishop as its head and the seminary as its home, — a
plan of which the system of movable curés was an
essential part. The Canadian priests, devoted to
Laval, met the innovations of Saint-Vallier with an
opposition which seemed only to confirm his purpose.
Laval, old and worn with toil and asceticism, was
driven almost to despair. The seminary of Quebec
was the cherished work of his life, and, to his thinking, the citadel of the Canadian Church; and now he
beheld it battered and breached before his eyes. His
successor, in fact, was trying to place the Church of
Canada on the footing of the Church of France. The
conflict lasted for years, with the rancor that marks
the quarrels of non-combatants of both sexes. " He "

[1] *Laval au Père la Chaise*, 1687. This forms part of a curious
correspondence printed in the *Foyer Canadien* for 1866, from originals in the Archevêché of Quebec.

[2] From a *mémoire* of 18 Feb., 1685 (*Archives de Versailles*), it is
plain that the court, in giving a successor to Laval, thought that
it had ended the vexed question of movable curés.

[Saint-Vallier], says one of his opponents, "has made himself contemptible to almost everybody, and particularly odious to the priests born in Canada; for there is between them and him a mutual antipathy difficult to overcome."[1]   He is described by the same writer as a person "without reflection and judgment, extreme in all things, secret and artful, passionate when opposed, and a flatterer when he wishes to gain his point." This amiable critic adds that Saint-Vallier believes a bishop to be inspired, in virtue of his office, with a wisdom that needs no human aid; and that whatever thought comes to him in prayer is a divine inspiration to be carried into effect at all costs and in spite of all opposition.

The new bishop, notwithstanding the tempest he had raised, did not fully accomplish that establishment of the curés in their respective parishes which the King and the minister so much desired. The Canadian curé was more a missionary than a parish priest; and Nature as well as Bishop Laval threw difficulties in the way of settling him quietly over his charge.

On the Lower St. Lawrence, where it widens to an estuary, six leagues across, a ship from France, the last of the season, holds her way for Quebec, laden with stores and clothing, household utensils, goods for Indian trade, the newest court fashions, wine, brandy, tobacco, and the King's orders from Ver-

---

[1] The above is from an anonymous paper, written apparently in 1695, and entitled *Mémoire pour le Canada.*

sailles. Swelling her patched and dingy sails, she
glides through the wildness and the solitude where
there is nothing but her to remind you of the great
troubled world behind and the little troubled world
before. On the far verge of the ocean-like river,
clouds and mountains mingle in dim confusion; fresh
gusts from the north dash waves against the ledges,
sweep through the quivering spires of stiff and
stunted fir-trees, and ruffle the feathers of the crow,
perched on the dead bough after his feast of mussels
among the sea-weed. You are not so solitary as you
think. A small birch-canoe rounds the point of
rocks, and it bears two men, — one in an old black
cassock, and the other in a buckskin coat, — both
working hard at the paddle to keep their slender
craft off the shingle and the breakers. The man in
the cassock is Father Morel, aged forty-eight, — the
oldest country curé in Canada, most of his brethren
being in the vigor of youth, as they had need to be.
His parochial charge embraces a string of incipient
parishes extending along the south shore from Rivière
du Loup to Rivière du Sud, a distance reckoned at
twenty-seven leagues, and his parishioners number
in all three hundred and twenty-eight souls. He has
administered spiritual consolation to the one inhabitant of Kamouraska; visited the eight families of La
Bouteillerie and the five families of La Combe; and
now he is on his way to the seigniory of St. Denis
with its two houses and eleven souls.[1]

[1] These particulars are from the *Plan général de l'estat présent des
missions du Canada, fait en l'année* 1683. It is a list and description

The father lands where a shattered eel-pot high and dry on the pebbles betrays the neighborhood of man. His servant shoulders his portable chapel, and follows him through the belt of firs and the taller woods beyond, till the sunlight of a desolate clearing shines upon them. Charred trunks and limbs encumber the ground; dead trees, branchless, barkless, pierced by the woodpeckers, in part black with fire, in part bleached by sun and frost, tower ghastly and weird above the labyrinth of forest ruins, through which the priest and his follower wind their way, the cat-bird mewing, and the blue-jay screaming as they pass. Now the golden-rod and the aster, harbingers of autumn, fringe with yellow and purple the edge of the older clearing, where wheat and maize, the settler's meagre harvest, are growing among the stumps.

Wild-looking women, with sunburnt faces and neglected hair, run from their work to meet the curé; a man or two follow with soberer steps and less exuberant zeal; while half-savage children, the *coureurs de bois* of the future, bareheaded, barefooted, and half-clad, come to wonder and stare. To set up his altar in a room of the rugged log-cabin; say mass, hear confessions, impose penance, grant absolution; repeat the office of the dead over a grave made weeks before; baptize, perhaps, the last infant;

of the parishes with the names and ages of the curés, and other details. (See *Abeille*, i.) This paper was drawn up by order of Laval.

marry, possibly, some pair who may or may not have waited for his coming; catechise as well as time and circumstance would allow the shy but turbulent brood of some former wedlock, — such was the work of the parish priest in the remoter districts.   It was seldom that his charge was quite so scattered and so far extended as that of Father Morel; but there were fifteen or twenty others whose labors were like in kind, and in some cases no less arduous.   All summer they paddled their canoes from settlement to settlement; and in winter they toiled on snow-shoes over the drifts, while the servant carried the portable chapel on his back, or dragged it on a sledge.   Once, at least, in the year the curé paid his visit to Quebec, where, under the maternal roof of the seminary, he made his retreat of meditation and prayer, and then returned to his work.   He rarely had a house of his own, but boarded in that of the seignior or one of the *habitants*.   Many parishes or aggregations of parishes had no other church than a room fitted up for the purpose in the house of some pious settler. In the larger settlements there were churches and chapels of wood, thatched with straw, often ruinous, poor to the last degree, without ornaments, and sometimes without the sacred vessels necessary for the service.[1]   In 1683 there were but seven stone churches in all the colony.   The population was so thin and scattered that many of the settlers heard

---

[1] Saint-Vallier, *Estat présent de l'Église et de la Colonie Française,* 22 (ed. 1856).

mass only three or four times a year, and some of
them not so often. The sick frequently died without absolution, and infants without baptism.

The splendid self-devotion of the early Jesuit
missions has its record; so, too, have the unseemly
bickerings of bishops and governors. But the patient
toils of the missionary curé rest in the obscurity
where the best of human virtues are buried from age
to age. What we find set down concerning him is,
that Louis XIV. was unable to see why he should
not live on two hundred francs a year as well as a
village curé by the banks of the Garonne. The King
did not know that his cassock and all his clothing
cost him twice as much and lasted half as long; that
he must have a canoe and a man to paddle it; and
that when on his annual visit the seminary paid him
five or six hundred francs, partly in clothes, partly
in stores, and partly in money, the end of the year
found him as poor as before except only in his
conscience.

The Canadian priests held the manners of the
colony under a rule as rigid as that of the Puritan
churches of New England, — but with the difference
that in Canada a large part of the population was
restive under their control, while some of the civil
authorities, often with the governor at their head,
supported the opposition. This was due partly to
an excess of clerical severity, and partly to the continued friction between the secular and ecclesiastical
powers. It sometimes happened, however, that a

new governor arrived, who was so pious that the clerical party felt that they could rely on him. Of these rare instances the principal is that of Denonville, who, with a wife as pious as himself, and a young daughter, landed at Quebec in 1685. On this, Bishop Saint-Vallier, anxious to turn his good dispositions to the best account, addressed to him a series of suggestions or rather directions for the guidance of his conduct, with a view to the spiritual profit of those over whom he was appointed to rule. The document was put on file, and the following are some of the points in it. It is divided into five different heads, — "Touching feasts," "touching balls and dances," "touching comedies and other declamations," "touching dress," "touching irreverence in church." The governor and madame his wife are desired to accept no invitations to suppers, — that is to say, late dinners, — as tending to nocturnal hours and dangerous pastimes; and they are further enjoined to express dissatisfaction, and refuse to come again, should any entertainment offered them be too sumptuous. "Although," continues the bishop under the second head of his address, "balls and dances are not sinful in their nature, nevertheless they are so dangerous by reason of the circumstances that attend them and the evil results that almost inevitably follow, that, in the opinion of Saint Francis of Sales, it should be said of them as physicians say of mushrooms, that at best they are good for nothing;" and, after enlarging on their perils, he

declares it to be of great importance to the glory of
God and the sanctification of the colony, that the
governor and his wife neither give such entertain-
ments nor countenance them by their presence.
"Nevertheless," adds the mentor, "since the youth
and vivacity of mademoiselle their daughter requires
some diversion, it is permitted to relent somewhat,
and indulge her in a little moderate and proper dancing, provided that it be solely with persons of her
own sex, and in the presence of madame her mother;
but by no means in the presence of men or youths,
since it is this mingling of sexes which causes the
disorders that spring from balls and dances." Private
theatricals in any form are next interdicted to the
young lady. The bishop then passes to the subject
of her dress, and exposes the abuses against which
she is to be guarded. "The luxury of dress," he
says, "appears in the rich and dazzling fabrics
wherein the women and girls of Canada attire themselves, and which are far beyond their condition and
their means; in the excess of ornaments which they
put on; in the extraordinary head-dresses which they
affect, their heads being uncovered and full of
strange trinkets; and in the immodest curls so
expressly forbidden in the epistles of Saint Peter
and Saint Paul, as well as by all the fathers and
doctors of the Church, and which God has often
severely punished, — as may be seen by the example
of the unhappy Pretextata, a lady of high quality,
who, as we learn from Saint Jerome, who knew her,

had her hands withered, and died suddenly five months after, and was precipitated into hell, as God had threatened her by an angel; because, by order of her husband, she had curled the hair of her niece, and attired her after a worldly fashion." [1]

Whether the Marquis and Marchioness Denonville profited by so apt and terrible a warning, or whether their patience and good-nature survived the episcopal onslaught, does not appear on record. The subject of feminine apparel received great attention, both from Saint-Vallier and his predecessor, each of whom issued a number of pastoral mandates concerning it. Their severest denunciations were aimed at low-necked dresses, which they regarded as favorite devices of the enemy for the snaring of souls; and they also used strong language against certain knots of ribbons called *fontanges*, with which the belles of Quebec adorned their heads. Laval launches strenuous invectives against "the luxury and vanity of women and girls, who, forgetting the promises of their baptism, decorate themselves with the pomp of

---

[1] "Témoin entr'autres l'exemple de la malheureuse Prétextate, dame de grande condition, laquelle au rapport de S. Jérôme, dont elle étoit connue, eut les mains desséchées et cinq mois après mourut subitement et fut précipitée en enfer, ainsi que Dieu l'en avoit menacée par un Ange pour avoir par le commandement de son mari frisé et habillé mondainement sa nièce." (*Divers points à représenter à Mr. le Gouverneur et à Madame la Gouvernante, signé Jean, évesque de Quebec. Registre de l'Evêché de Québec.*) The bishop on another occasion holds up the sad fate of Pretextata as a warning to Canadian mothers; but in the present case he slightly changes the incidents to make the story more applicable to the governor and his wife.

Satan, whom they have so solemnly renounced; and, in their wish to please the eyes of men, make themselves the instruments and the captives of the fiend." [1]

In the journal of the superior of the Jesuits we find, under date of February 4, 1667, a record of the first ball in Canada, along with the pious wish, "God grant that nothing further come of it." Nevertheless more balls were not long in following; and, worse yet, sundry comedies were enacted under no less distinguished patronage than that of Frontenac, the governor. Laval denounced them vigorously, the Jesuit Dablon attacked them in a violent sermon; and such excitement followed that the affair was brought before the royal council, which declined to interfere. [2] This flurry, however, was nothing to the storm raised ten or twelve years later by other dramatic aggressions, an account of which will appear in the sequel of this volume.

The morals of families were watched with unrelenting vigilance. Frontenac writes in a mood unusually temperate, "They [the priests] are full of virtue and piety, and if their zeal were less vehement and more moderate, they would perhaps succeed better in their efforts for the conversion of souls; but

[1] *Mandement contre le luxe et la vanité des femmes et des filles*, 1682. (*Registres de l'Evéché de Québec.*) A still more vigorous denunciation is contained in *Ordonnance contre les vices de luxe et d'impureté*, 1690. This was followed in the next year by a stringent list of rules called *Réglement pour la conduite des fidèles de ce diocèse.*

[2] *Arrêts du 24 et 28 juin par lesquels cette affaire* (*des comédes*) *est renvoyée à Sa Majesté*, 1681. (?)   *Registre du Conseil Souverain.*

they often use means so extraordinary, and in France so unusual, that they repel most people instead of persuading them. I sometimes tell them my views frankly and as gently as I can, as I know the murmurs that their conduct excites, and often receive complaints of the constraint under which they place consciences. This is above all the case with the ecclesiastics at Montreal, where there is a curé from Franche Comté who wants to establish a sort of inquisition worse than that of Spain, and all out of an excess of zeal." [1]

It was this curé, no doubt, of whom La Hontan complains. That unsanctified young officer was quartered at Montreal, in the house of one of the inhabitants. "During a part of the winter I was hunting with the Algonquins; the rest of it I spent here very disagreeably. One can neither go on a pleasure party, nor play a game of cards, nor visit the ladies, without the curé knowing it and preaching about it publicly from his pulpit. The priests excommunicate masqueraders, and even go in search of them to pull off their masks and overwhelm them with abuse. They watch more closely over the women and girls than their husbands and fathers. They prohibit and burn all books but books of devotion. I cannot think of this tyranny without cursing the indiscreet zeal of the curé of this town. He came to the house where I lived, and, finding some books on my table, presently pounced on the romance

[1] *Frontenac au Ministre,* 20 *Oct.,* 1691.

of Petronius, which I valued more than my life because it was not mutilated. He tore out almost all the leaves, so that if my host had not restrained me when I came in and saw the miserable wreck, I should have run after this rampant shepherd and torn out every hair of his beard."[1]

La Mothe-Cadillac, the founder of Detroit, seems to have had equal difficulty in keeping his temper. "Neither men of honor nor men of parts are endured in Canada; nobody can live here but simpletons and slaves of the ecclesiastical domination. The count [Frontenac] would not have so many troublesome affairs on his hands if he had not abolished a Jericho in the shape of a house built by messieurs of the seminary of Montreal, to shut up, as they said, girls who caused scandal; if he had allowed them to take officers and soldiers to go into houses at midnight and carry off women from their husbands and whip them till the blood flowed because they had been at a ball or worn a mask; if he had said nothing against the curés who went the rounds with the soldiers, and compelled women and girls to shut themselves up in their houses at nine o'clock of summer evenings; if he had forbidden the wearing of lace, and made no objection to the refusal of the communion to women of quality because they wore a *fontange;* if he had not opposed excommunications flung about without sense or reason, — if I say, the count had been of this

---

[1] La Hontan, i. 60 (ed. 1709). Other editions contain the same story in different words.

way of thinking, he would have stood as a nonpareil, and have been put very soon on the list of saints, for saint-making is cheap in this country."[1]

While the Sulpitians were thus rigorous at Montreal, the bishop and his Jesuit allies were scarcely less so at Quebec. There was little good-will between them and the Sulpitians, and some of the sharpest charges against the followers of Loyola are brought by their brother priests at Montreal. The Sulpitian Allet writes: "The Jesuits hold such domination over the people of this country that they go into the houses and see everything that passes there. They then tell what they have learned to each other at their meetings, and on this information they govern their policy. The Jesuit, Father Ragueneau, used to go every day down to the Lower Town, where the merchants live, to find out all that was going on in their families; and he often made people get up from table to confess to him." Allet goes on to say that Father Châtelain also went continually to the Lower Town with the same object, and that some of the inhabitants complained of him to Courcelle, the governor. One day Courcelle saw the Jesuit, who was old and somewhat infirm, slowly walking by the château, cane in hand, on his usual errand, — on which he sent a sergeant after him to request that he would not go so often to the Lower Town, as the people were annoyed by the frequency of his visits. The father replied in wrath, "Go and tell Monsieur

[1] *La Mothe-Cadillac à ——, 28 Sept., 1694.*

de Courcelle that I have been there ever since he was governor, and that I shall go there after he has ceased to be governor;" and he kept on his way as before. Courcelle reported his answer to the superior, Le Mercier, and demanded to have him sent home as a punishment; but the superior effected a compromise. On the following Thursday, after mass in the cathedral, he invited Courcelle into the sacristy, where Father Châtelain was awaiting them; and here, at Le Mercier's order, the old priest begged pardon of the offended governor on his knees.[1]

The Jesuits derived great power from the confessional; and, if their accusers are to be believed, they employed unusual means to make it effective. Cavelier de la Salle says: "They will confess nobody till he tells his name, and no servant till he tells the name of his master. When a crime is confessed, they insist on knowing the name of the accomplice, as well as all the circumstances, with the greatest particularity. Father Châtelain especially never fails to do this. They enter as it were by force into the secrets of families, and thus make themselves formidable; for what cannot be done by a clever man devoted to his work, who knows all the secrets of every family; above all, when he permits himself to tell them when it is for his interest to do so?"[2]

[1] *Mémoire d'Allet.* The author was at one time secretary to Abbé Quélus. The paper is printed in the *Morale pratique des Jésuites.* The above is one of many curious statements which it contains.

[2] La Salle, *Mémoire*, 1678.

The association of women and girls known as the Congregation of the Holy Family, which was formed under Jesuit auspices, and which met every Thursday with closed doors in the cathedral, is said to have been very useful to the fathers in their social investigations.[1] The members are affirmed to have been under a vow to tell one another every good or evil deed they knew of every person of their acquaintance; so that this pious gossip became a copious source of information to those in a position to draw upon it. In Talon's time the Congregation of the Holy Family caused such commotion in Quebec that he asked the council to appoint a commission to inquire into its proceedings. He was touching dangerous ground. The affair was presently hushed, and the application cancelled on the register of the council.[2]

The Jesuits had long exercised solely the function of confessors in the colony, and a number of curious anecdotes are on record showing the reluctance with which they admitted the secular priests, and above all the Récollets, to share in it. The Récollets, of whom a considerable number had arrived from time to time, were on excellent terms with the civil powers, and were popular with the colonists; but with the bishop and the Jesuits they were not in

---

[1] See "La Salle, and the Discovery of the Great West," 111.

[2] *Représentation faite au conseil au sujet de certaines assemblées de femmes ou filles sous le nom de la Sainte Famille*, 1667. (*Registre du Conseil Souverain.*) The paper is cancelled by lines drawn over it; and the following minute, duly attested, is appended to it: "Rayé du consentement de M. Talon."

favor, and one or two sharp collisions took place. The bishop was naturally annoyed when, while he was trying to persuade the King that a curé needed at least six hundred francs a year, these mendicant friars came forward with an offer to serve the parishes for nothing; nor was he, it is likely, better pleased when, having asked the hospital nuns eight hundred francs annually for two masses a day in their chapel, the Récollets underbid him, and offered to say the masses for three hundred.[1] They, on their part, complain bitterly of the bishop, who, they say, would gladly have ordered them out of the colony, but, being unable to do this, tried to shut them up in their convent, and prevent them from officiating as priests among the people. "We have as little liberty," says the Récollet writer, "as if we were in a country of heretics." He adds that the inhabitants ask earnestly for the ministrations of the friars, but that the bishop replies with invectives and calumnies against the Order; and that when the Récollets absolve a penitent, he often annuls the absolution.[2]

In one respect this Canadian Church militant achieved a complete success. Heresy was scoured

---

[1] "Mon dit sieur l'evesque leur fait payer (aux hospitalières 800 l. par an pour deux messes qu'il leur fait dire par ses Séminaristes que les Récollets leurs voisins leur offrent pour 300 l." — La Barre au Ministre, 1682.

[2] Mémoire instructif contenant la conduite des PP. Récollets de Paris en leurs missions de Canada, 1684. This paper, of which only a fragment is preserved, was written in connection with a dispute of the Récollets with the bishop who opposed their attempt to establish a church in Quebec.

out of the colony. When Maintenon and her ghostly prompters overcame the better nature of the King, and wrought on his bigotry and his vanity to launch him into the dragonnades; when violence and lust bore the crucifix into thousands of Huguenot homes, and the land reeked with nameless infamies; when churches rang with *Te Deums*, and the heart of France withered in anguish, — when, in short, this hideous triumph of the faith was won, the royal tool of priestly ferocity sent orders that heresy should be treated in Canada as it had been treated in France.[1] The orders were needless. The pious Denonville replies, "Praised be God! there is not a heretic here." He adds that a few abjured last year, and that he should be very glad if the King would make them a present. The Jesuits, he further says, go every day on board the ships in the harbor to look after the new converts from France.[2] Now and then at a later day a real or suspected Jansenist found his way to Canada, and sometimes an *esprit fort*, like La Hontan, came over with the troops; but on the whole a community more free from positive heterodoxy perhaps never existed on earth. This exemption cost no bloodshed. What it did cost we may better judge hereafter.

If Canada escaped the dragonnades, so also she

[1] *Mémoire du Roy à Denonville*, 31 *Mai*, 1686. The King here orders the imprisonment of heretics who refuse to abjure, or the quartering of soldiers on them. What this meant, the history of the dragonnades will show.

[2] *Denonville au Ministre*, 10 *Nov.*, 1686.

escaped another infliction from which a neighboring colony suffered deplorably. Her peace was never much troubled by witches. They were held to exist, it is true; but they wrought no panic. Mother Mary of the Incarnation reports on one occasion the discovery of a magician in the person of a converted Huguenot miller, who, being refused in marriage by a girl of Quebec, bewitched her, and filled the house where she lived with demons, which the bishop tried in vain to exorcise. The miller was thrown into prison, and the girl sent to the Hôtel-Dieu, where not a demon dared enter. The infernal crew took their revenge by creating a severe influenza among the citizens.[1]

If there are no Canadian names on the calendar of saints, it is not because in byways and obscure places Canada had not virtues worthy of canonization. Not alone her male martyrs and female devotees, whose merits have found a chronicle and a recognition; not the fantastic devotion of Madame d'Ailleboust, who, lest she should not suffer enough, took to herself a vicious and refractory servant girl, as an exercise of patience; and not certainly the mediæval pietism of Jeanne Le Ber, the venerated recluse of Montreal, — there are others quite as worthy of honor, whose names have died from memory. It is difficult to conceive a self-abnegation more complete than that of the hospital nuns of Quebec and Montreal. In the almost total absence

[1] Marie de l'Incarnation, *Lettre de — Septembre*, 1661.

of trained and skilled physicians, the burden of the sick and wounded fell upon them. Of the two communities, that of Montreal was the more wretchedly destitute, while that of Quebec was exposed, perhaps, to greater dangers. Nearly every ship from France brought some form of infection, and all infection found its way to the Hôtel-Dieu of Quebec. The nuns died, but they never complained. Removed from the arena of ecclesiastical strife, too busy for the morbidness of the cloister, too much absorbed in practical benevolence to become the prey of illusions, they and their sister community were models of that benign and tender charity of which the Roman Catholic Church is so rich in examples. Nor should the Ursulines and the nuns of the Congregation be forgotten among those who, in another field of labor, have toiled patiently according to their light.

Mademoiselle Jeanne Le Ber belonged to none of these sisterhoods. She was the favorite daughter of the chief merchant of Montreal, — the same who, with the help of his money, got himself ennobled. She seems to have been a girl of a fine and sensitive nature; ardent, affectionate, and extremely susceptible to religious impressions. Religion at last gained absolute sway over her. Nothing could appease her longings or content the demands of her excited conscience but an entire consecration of herself to Heaven. Constituted as she was, the resolution must have cost her an agony of mental conflict. Her story is a strange, and, as many will think, a

very sad one. She renounced her suitors, and wished
to renounce her inheritance; but her spiritual directors,
too far-sighted to permit such a sacrifice, persuaded
her to hold fast to her claims, and content herself
with what they called "poverty of heart." Her
mother died, and her father, left with a family of
young children, greatly needed her help; but she
refused to leave her chamber where she had immured
herself. Here she remained ten years, seeing nobody
but her confessor and the girl who brought her food.
Once only she emerged, and this was when her
brother lay dead in the adjacent room, killed in a
fight with the English. She suddenly appeared
before her astonished sisters, stood for a moment in
silent prayer by the body, and then vanished without
uttering a word. "Such," says her modern biographer, "was the sublimity of her virtue and the
grandeur of her soul." Not content with this
domestic seclusion, she caused a cell to be made
behind the altar in the newly built church of the
Congregation, and here we will permit ourselves
to cast a stolen glance at her through the narrow
opening through which food was passed in to her.
Her bed, a pile of straw which she never moved, lest
it should become too soft, was so placed that her
head could touch the partition which alone separated
it from the Host on the altar. Here she lay wrapped
in a garment of coarse gray serge, worn, tattered,
and unwashed. An old blanket, a stool, a spinning-
wheel, a belt and shirt of haircloth, a scourge, and a

pair of shoes made by herself of the husks of Indian-corn, appear to have formed the sum of her furniture and her wardrobe. Her employments were spinning and working embroidery for churches. She remained in this voluntary prison about twenty years; and the nun who brought her food testifies that she never omitted a mortification or a prayer, though commonly in a state of profound depression, and what her biographer calls "complete spiritual aridity." When her mother died, she had refused to see her; and, long after, no prayer of her dying father could draw her from her cell. "In the person of this modest virgin," writes her reverend eulogist, "we see, with astonishment, the love of God triumphant over earthly affection for parents, and a complete victory of faith over reason and of grace over nature."

In 1711, Canada was threatened with an attack by the English; and Mademoiselle Le Ber gave the nuns of the Congregation an image of the Virgin on which she had written a prayer to protect their granary from the invaders. Other persons, anxious for a similar protection, sent her images to write upon; but she declined the request. One of the disappointed applicants then stole the inscribed image from the granary of the Congregation, intending to place it on his own when the danger drew near. The English, however, did not come, their fleet having suffered a ruinous shipwreck ascribed to the prayers of Jeanne Le Ber. "It was," writes the Sulpitian Belmont, "the greatest miracle that ever happened since the

days of Moses." Nor was this the only miracle of
which she was the occasion. She herself declared
that once when she had broken her spinning-wheel,
an angel came and mended it for her. Angels also
assisted in her embroidery, "no doubt," says Mother
Juchereau, "taking great pleasure in the society of
this angelic creature." In the church where she had
secluded herself, an image of the Virgin continued
after her death to heal the lame and cure the sick.[1]

Though Jeanne rarely permitted herself to speak,
yet some oracular utterance of the sainted recluse
would now and then escape to the outer world.
One of these was to the effect that teaching poor
girls to read, unless they wanted to be nuns, was
robbing them of their time. Nor was she far wrong,
for in Canada there was very little to read except
formulas of devotion and lives of saints. The
dangerous innovation of a printing-press had not
invaded the colony,[2] and the first Canadian news-
paper dates from the British conquest.

All education was controlled by priests or nuns.
The ablest teachers in Canada were the Jesuits.
Their college of Quebec was three years older than
Harvard. We hear at an early date of public dis-
putations by the pupils, after the pattern of those

---

[1] Faillon, *L'Héroine chrétienne du Canada, ou Vie de Mlle. Le Ber.*
This is a most elaborate and eulogistic life of the recluse. A
shorter account of her will be found in Juchereau, *Hôtel-Dieu.* She
died in 1714, at the age of fifty-two.

[2] A printing-press was afterwards brought to Canada, but was
soon sent back again.

tournaments of barren logic which preceded the reign of inductive reason in Europe, and of which the archetype is to be found in the scholastic duels of the Sorbonne. The boys were sometimes permitted to act certain approved dramatic pieces of a religious character, like the *Sage Visionnaire*. On one occasion they were allowed to play the *Cid* of Corneille, which, though remarkable as a literary work, contained nothing threatening to orthodoxy. They were taught a little Latin, a little rhetoric, and a little logic; but against all that might rouse the faculties to independent action, the Canadian schools prudently closed their doors. There was then no rival population, of a different origin and a different faith, to compel competition in the race of intelligence and knowledge. The Church stood sole mistress of the field. Under the old régime the real object of education in Canada was a religious and, in far less degree, a political one. The true purpose of the schools was: first, to make priests; and, secondly, to make obedient servants of the Church and the King. All the rest was extraneous and of slight account. In regard to this matter, the King and the bishop were of one mind. "As I have been informed," Louis XIV. writes to Laval, "of your continued care to hold the people in their duty towards God and towards me by the good education you give or cause to be given to the young, I write this letter to express my satisfaction with conduct so salutary, and to exhort you to persevere in it." [1]

[1] *Le Roy à Laval,* 9 *Avril,* 1667 (extract in Faillon).

The bishop did not fail to persevere. The school for boys attached to his seminary became the most important educational institution in Canada. It was regulated by thirty-four rules, "in honor of the thirty-four years which Jesus lived on earth." The qualities commended to the boys as those which they should labor diligently to acquire were "humility, obedience, purity, meekness, modesty, simplicity, chastity, charity, and an ardent love of Jesus and his Holy Mother."[1] Here is a goodly roll of Christian virtues. What is chiefly noticeable in it is, that truth is allowed no place. That manly but unaccommodating virtue was not, it seems, thought important in forming the mind of youth. Humility and obedience lead the list; for in unquestioning submission to the spiritual director lay the guaranty of all other merits.

We have seen already, that, besides this seminary for boys, Laval established another for educating the humbler colonists. It was a sort of farm-school; though besides farming, various mechanical trades were also taught in it. It was well adapted to the wants of a great majority of Canadians, whose tendencies were anything but bookish; but here, as elsewhere, the real object was religious. It enabled the Church to extend her influence over classes which the ordinary schools could not reach. Besides manual training, the pupils were taught to read and

[1] *Ancien réglement du Petit Séminaire de Québec*, see *Abeille*, viii. no. 32.

write; and for a time a certain number of them
received some instruction in Latin. When, in 1686,
Saint-Vallier visited the school, he found in all
thirty-one boys under the charge of two priests;
but the number was afterwards greatly reduced, and
the place served, as it still serves, chiefly as a retreat
during vacations for the priests and pupils of the
seminary of Quebec. A spot better suited for such a
purpose cannot be conceived.

From the vast meadows of the parish of St.
Joachim, which here border the St. Lawrence, there
rises like an island a low flat hill, hedged round with
forests like the tonsured head of a monk. It was
here that Laval planted his school. Across the
meadows, a mile or more distant, towers the mountain promontory of Cape Tourmente. You may climb
its woody steeps, and from the top, waist-deep
in blueberry-bushes, survey, from Kamouraska to
Quebec, the grand Canadian world outstretched
below; or mount the neighboring heights of St.
Anne, where, athwart the gaunt arms of ancient
pines, the river lies shimmering in summer haze, the
cottages of the *habitants* are strung like beads of a
rosary along the meadows of Beaupré, the shores of
Orleans bask in warm light, and far on the horizon
the rock of Quebec rests like a faint gray cloud; or
traverse the forest till the roar of the torrent guides
you to the rocky solitude where it holds its savage
revels. High on the cliffs above, young birch-trees
stand smiling in the morning sun; while in the abyss

beneath the snowy waters plunge from depth to depth, and, halfway down, the slender harebell hangs from its mossy nook, quivering in the steady thunder of the cataract. Game on the river; trout in lakes, brooks, and pools; wild fruits and flowers on meadows and mountains, — a thousand resources of honest and wholesome recreation here wait the student emancipated from books, but not parted for a moment from the pious influence which hangs about the old walls embosomed in the woods of St. Joachim. Around on plains and hills stand the dwellings of a peaceful peasantry, as different from the restless population of the neighboring States as the denizens of some Norman or Breton village.

Above all, do not fail to make your pilgrimage to the shrine of St. Anne. You may see her chapel four or five miles away, nestled under the heights of the Petit Cap. Here, when Ailleboust was governor, he began with his own hands the pious work, and a *habitant* of Beaupré, Louis Guimont, sorely afflicted with rheumatism, came grinning with pain to lay three stones in the foundation, in honor probably of Saint Anne, Saint Joachim, and their daughter the Virgin. Instantly he was cured. It was but the beginning of a long course of miracles continued more than two centuries, and continuing still. Their fame spread far and wide. The devotion to Saint Anne became a distinguishing feature of Canadian Catholicity, till at the present day at least thirteen parishes bear her name. But of all her shrines, none

can match the fame of St. Anne du Petit Cap.
Crowds flocked thither on the week of her festival,
and marvellous cures were wrought unceasingly, as
the sticks and crutches hanging on the walls and
columns still attest.   Sometimes the whole shore
was covered with the wigwams of Indian converts
who had paddled their birch canoes from the farthest
wilds of Canada.   The more fervent among them
would crawl on their knees from the shore to the
altar.   And, in our own day, every summer a far
greater concourse of pilgrims — not in paint and
feathers, but in cloth and millinery, and not in
canoes, but in steamboats — bring their offerings
and their vows to the "Bonne Sainte Anne." [1]

To return to Laval's industrial school.   Judging
from repeated complaints of governors and intendants
of the dearth of skilled workmen, the priests in
charge of it were more successful in making good
Catholics than in making good masons, carpenters,
blacksmiths, and weavers; and the number of pupils,
even if well trained, was at no time sufficient to meet
the wants of the colony,[2] for, though the Canadians

[1] For an interesting account of the shrine at the Petit Cap, see
Casgrain, *Le Pélérinage de la Bonne Sainte Anne,* a little manual of
devotion printed at Quebec.   I chanced to visit the old chapel in
1871, during a meeting of the parish to consider the question of reconstructing it, as it was in a ruinous state.   Passing that way again
two years later, I found the old chapel still standing, and a new one,
much larger, half finished.

[2] Most of them were moreover retained, after leaving the school,
by the seminary, as servants, farmers, or vassals.   (La Tour, *Vie de
Laval,* liv. vi.)

showed an aptitude for mechanical trades, they preferred above all things the savage liberty of the backwoods.

The education of girls was in the hands of the Ursulines and the nuns of the Congregation, of whom the former, besides careful instruction in religious duties, taught their pupils "all that a girl ought to know." [1] This meant exceedingly little besides the manual arts suited to their sex; and, in the case of the nuns of the Congregation, who taught girls of the poorer class, it meant still less. It was on nuns as well as on priests that the charge fell, not only of spiritual and mental, but also of industrial, training. Thus we find the King giving to a sisterhood of Montreal a thousand francs to buy wool, and a thousand more for teaching girls to knit. [2] The King also maintained a teacher of navigation and surveying at Quebec on the modest salary of four hundred francs.

During the eighteenth century, some improvement is perceptible in the mental state of the population. As it became more numerous and more stable, it also became less ignorant; and the Canadian *habitant*, towards the end of the French rule, was probably better taught, so far as concerned religion, than the mass of French peasants. Yet secular instruction was still extremely meagre, even in the *noblesse*.

---

[1] "À lire, à écrire, les prières, les mœurs chrétiennes, et tout ce qu'une fille doit savoir." — Marie de l'Incarnation, *Lettre du 9 Août,* 1668.

[2] *Denonville au Ministre,* 13 *Nov.,* 1685.

"In spite of this defective education," says the famous navigator, Bougainville, who knew the colony well in its last years, "the Canadians are naturally intelligent. They do not know how to write, but they speak with ease, and with an accent as good as the Parisian." [1] He means, of course, the better class. "Even the children of officers and gentlemen," says another writer, "scarcely know how to read and write; they are ignorant of the first elements of geography and history." [2] And evidence like this might be extended.

When France was heaving with the throes that prepared the Revolution; when new hopes, new dreams, new thoughts — good and evil, false and true — tossed the troubled waters of French society, — Canada caught something of its social corruption, but not the faintest impulsion of its roused mental life. The torrent surged on its way; while, in the deep nook beside it, the sticks and dry leaves floated their usual round, and the unruffled pool slept in the placidity of intellectual torpor. [3]

[1] Bougainville, *Mémoire de* 1757 (see Margry, *Relations inédites*).

[2] *Mémoire de* 1736; *Détail de toute la Colonie* (published by the Hist. Soc. of Quebec).

[3] Several Frenchmen of a certain intellectual eminence made their abode in Canada from time to time. The chief among them are the Jesuit Lafitau, author of *Mœurs des Sauvages Américains;* the Jesuit Charlevoix, traveller and historian; the physician Sarrazin; and the Marquis de la Galisonnière, the most enlightened of the French governors of Canada. Sarrazin, a naturalist as well as a physician, has left his name to the botanical genus *Sarracenia*, of which the curious American species, *S. purpurea*, the "pitcher-

plant," was described by him. His position in the colony was singular and characteristic. He got little or no pay from his patients; and though at one time the only genuine physician in Canada (*Callières et Beauharnois au Ministre*, 3 *Nov.*, 1702), he was dependent on the King for support. In 1699 we find him thanking his Majesty for 300 francs a year, and asking at the same time for more, as he has nothing else to live on. (*Callières et Champigny au Ministre*, 20 *Oct.*, 1699.) Two years later the governor writes, that, as he serves almost everybody without fees, he ought to have another 300 francs. (*Ibid.*, 5 *Oct.*, 1701.) The additional 300 francs was given him; but, finding it insufficient, he wanted to leave the colony. "He is too useful," writes the governor again; "we cannot let him go." His yearly pittance of 600 francs, French money, was at one time reinforced by his salary as member of the Superior Council. He died at Quebec in 1734.

CHAPTER XXIII.

1640–1763.

MORALS AND MANNERS.

THE mission period of Canada, or the period anterior to the year 1663, when the King took the colony in charge, has a character of its own. The whole population did not exceed that of a large French village. Its extreme poverty, the constant danger that surrounded it, and, above all, the contagious zeal of the missionaries, saved it from many vices, and inspired it with an extraordinary religious fervor. Without doubt an ideal picture has been drawn of this early epoch. Trade as well as propagandism was the business of the colony, and the colonists were far from being all in a state of grace; yet it is certain that zeal was higher, devotion more constant, and popular morals more pure, than at any later period of the French rule.

The intervention of the King wrought a change. The annual shipments of emigrants made by him were, in the most favorable view, of a very mixed character, and the portion which Mother Mary calls *canaille* was but too conspicuous. Along with them came a regiment of soldiers fresh from the license of camps and the excitements of Turkish wars, accustomed to obey their officers and to obey nothing else, and more ready to wear the scapulary of the Virgin in campaigns against the Mohawks than to square their lives by the rules of Christian ethics. "Our good King," writes Sister Morin, of Montreal, "has sent troops to defend us from the Iroquois, and the soldiers and officers have ruined the Lord's vineyard, and planted wickedness and sin and crime in our soil of Canada."[1] Few, indeed, among the officers followed the example of one of their number, — Paul Dupuy, who, in his settlement of Isle aux Oies, below Quebec, lived, it is said, like a saint, and on Sundays and fête days exhorted his servants and *habitants* with such unction that their eyes filled with tears.[2] Nor, let us hope, were there many imitators of Major La Fredière, who, with a company of the regiment, was sent to garrison Montreal, where he ruled with absolute sway over settlers and soldiers alike. His countenance naturally repulsive was made more so by the loss of an eye; yet he was irrepressible in gallantry, and women and girls fled in

<hr>

[1] *Annales de l'Hôtel-Dieu St. Joseph,* cited by Faillon.
[2] Juchereau, *Hôtel-Dieu de Québec,* 511.

terror from the military Polyphemus. The men, too,
feared and hated him, not without reason. One
morning a settler named Demers was hoeing his field,
when he saw a sportsman gun in hand striding
through his half-grown wheat. "Steady there,
steady!" he shouted in a tone of remonstrance; but
the sportsman gave no heed. "Why do you spoil a
poor man's wheat?" cried the outraged cultivator.
"If I knew who you were, I would go and complain of you." "Whom would you complain to?"
demanded the sportsman, who then proceeded to
walk back into the middle of the wheat, and called
out to Demers, "You are a rascal, and I'll thrash
you." "Look at home for rascals," retorted Demers,
"and keep your thrashing for your dogs." The sportsman came towards him in a rage to execute his threat.
Demers picked up his gun, which, after the custom
of the time, he had brought to the field with him,
and, advancing to meet his adversary, recognized La
Fredière, the commandant. On this he ran off. La
Fredière sent soldiers to arrest him, threw him into
prison, put him in irons, and the next day mounted
him on the wooden horse, with a weight of sixty
pounds tied to each foot. He repeated the torture
a day or two after, and then let his victim go, saying,
"If I could have caught you when I was in your
wheat, I would have beaten you well."

The commandant next turned his quarters into a
dram-shop for Indians, to whom he sold brandy in
large quantities, but so diluted that his customers,

finding themselves partially defrauded of their right
of intoxication, complained grievously. About this
time the intendant Talon made one of his domiciliary
visits to Montreal, and when, in his character of
father of the people, he inquired if they had any
complaints to make, every tongue was loud in accusation against La Fredière. Talon caused full depositions to be made out from the statements of Demers
and other witnesses. Copies were deposited in the
hands of the notary, and it is from these that the
above story is drawn. The tyrant was removed, and
ordered home to France.[1]

Many other officers embarked in the profitable
trade of selling brandy to Indians, and several garrison posts became centres of disorder. Others of
the regiment became notorious brawlers. A lieutenant of the garrison of Montreal named Carion,
and an ensign named Morel, had for some reason
conceived a violent grudge against another ensign
named Lormeau. On Pentecost day, just after
vespers, Lormeau was walking by the river with his
wife. They had passed the common and the seminary wall, and were in front of the house of the
younger Charles Le Moyne, when they saw Carion
coming towards them. He stopped before Lormeau,
looked him full in the face, and exclaimed, "Coward!"
"Coward yourself," returned Lormeau; "take your-

---

[1] *Information contre La Fredière.* (See Faillon, *Colonie Française*,
iii. 386.) The dialogue, as here given from the depositions, is
translated as closely as possible.

self off!" Carion drew his sword, and Lormeau
followed his example. They exchanged a few passes,
then closed, and fell to the ground grappled together.
Lormeau's wig fell off; and Carion, getting the
uppermost, hammered his bare head with the hilt of
his sword. Lormeau's wife, in a frenzy of terror,
screamed *murder*. One of the neighbors, Monsieur
Belêtre, was at table with Charles Le Moyne and a
Rochelle merchant named Baston. He ran out with
his two guests, and they tried to separate the com-
batants, who still lay on the ground foaming like a
pair of enraged bull-dogs. All their efforts were
useless. "Very well," said Le Moyne in disgust,
"if you won't let go, then kill each other if you
like." A former military servant of Carion now ran
up, and began to brandish his sword in behalf of his
late master. Carion's comrade, Morel, also arrived,
and, regardless of the angry protest of Le Moyne,
stabbed repeatedly at Lormeau as he lay. Lormeau
had received two or three wounds in the hand and
arm with which he parried the thrusts, and was
besides severely mauled by the sword-hilt of Carion,
when two Sulpitian priests, drawn by the noise,
appeared on the scene. One was Frémont, the curé;
the other was Dollier de Casson. That herculean
father, whose past soldier life had made him at home
in a fray, and who cared nothing for drawn swords,
set himself at once to restore peace, — upon which,
whether from the strength of his arm, or the mere
effect of his presence, the two champions released

their gripe on each other's throats, rose, sheathed their weapons, and left the field.[1]

Montreal, a frontier town at the head of the colony, was the natural resort of desperadoes, offering, as we have seen, a singular contrast between the rigor of its clerical seigniors and the riotous license of the lawless crew which infested it. Dollier de Casson tells the story of an outlaw who broke prison ten or twelve times, and whom no walls, locks, or fetters could hold. "A few months ago," he says, "he was caught again, and put into the keeping of six or seven men, each with a good gun. They stacked their arms to play a game of cards, which their prisoner saw fit to interrupt to play a game of his own. He made a jump at the guns, took them under his arm like so many feathers, aimed at these fellows with one of them, swearing that he would kill the first who came near him, and so, falling back step by step, at last bade them good-by, and carried off all their guns. Since then he has not been caught, and is roaming the woods. Very likely he will become chief of our banditti, and make great trouble in the country when it pleases him to come back from the Dutch settlements, whither they say he is gone along with another rascal, and a French woman so depraved that she is said to have given or sold two of her children to the Indians." [2]

---

[1] *Requête de Lormeau à M. d'Aillebout. Dépositions de MM. de Longueuil [Le Moyne] de Baston, de Belêtre, et autres.* Cited by Faillon, *Colonie Française,* iii. 393.

[2] Dollier de Casson, *Histoire de Montréal,* 1671–72.

When the governor, La Barre, visited Montreal, he found there some two hundred reprobates gambling, drinking, and stealing. If hard pressed by justice, they had only to cross the river and place themselves beyond the seigniorial jurisdiction. The military settlements of the Richelieu were in a condition somewhat similar, and La Barre complains of a prevailing spirit of disobedience and lawlessness.[1] The most orderly and thrifty part of Canada appears to have been at this time the *côte* of Beaupré, belonging to the seminary of Quebec. Here the settlers had religious instruction from their curés, and industrial instruction also if they wanted it. Domestic spinning and weaving were practised at Beaupré sooner than in any other part of the colony.

When it is remembered that a population which in La Barre's time did not exceed ten thousand, and which forty years later did not much exceed twice that number, was scattered along both sides of a great river for three hundred miles or more; that a large part of this population was in isolated groups of two, three, five, ten, or twenty houses at the edge of a savage wilderness; that between them there was little communication except by canoes; that the settlers were disbanded soldiers, or others whose lives had been equally adverse to habits of reflection or self-control; that they rarely saw a priest, and that a government omnipotent in name had not arms long enough to reach them, — we may listen without

[1] *La Barre au Ministre, 4 Nov.,* 1683.

surprise to the lamentations of order-loving officials over the unruly condition of a great part of the colony. One accuses the seigniors, who, he says, being often of low extraction, cannot keep their vassals in order.[1] Another dwells sorrowfully on the "terrible dispersion" of the settlements where the inhabitants "live in a savage independence." But it is better that each should speak for himself, and among the rest let us hear the pious Denonville.

"This, Monseigneur," he says, "seems to me the place for rendering you an account of the disorders which prevail not only in the woods, but also in the settlements. They arise from the idleness of young persons, and the great liberty which fathers, mothers, and guardians have for a long time given them, or allowed them to assume, of going into the forest under pretence of hunting or trading. This has come to such a pass, that, from the moment a boy can carry a gun, the father cannot restrain him and dares not offend him. You can judge the mischief that follows. These disorders are always greatest in the families of those who are *gentilshommes*, or who through laziness or vanity pass themselves off as such. Having no resource but hunting, they must spend their lives in the woods, where they have no curés to trouble them, and no fathers or guardians to constrain them. I think, Monseigneur, that martial law would suit their case better than any judicial sentence. Monsieur de la Barre suppressed a certain

[1] Catalogne, *Mémoire addressé au Ministre*, 1712.

order of knighthood which had sprung up here, but
he did not abolish the usages belonging to it. It was
thought a fine thing and a good joke to go about
naked and tricked out like Indians, not only on
carnival days, but on all other days of feasting and
debauchery. These practices tend to encourage the
disposition of our young men to live like savages,
frequent their company, and be forever unruly and
lawless like them. I cannot tell you, Monseigneur,
how attractive this Indian life is to all our youth. It
consists in doing nothing, caring for nothing, following every inclination, and getting out of the way of
all correction."

He goes on to say that the mission villages governed by the Jesuits and Sulpitians are models of
good order, and that drunkards are never seen there
except when they come from the neighboring French
settlements; but that the other Indians, who roam at
large about the colony, do prodigious mischief, because
the children of the seigniors not only copy their way
of life, but also run off with their women into the
woods.[1] "Nothing," he continues, "can be finer or
better conceived than the regulations framed for the
government of this country; but nothing, I assure
you, is so ill observed as regards both the fur-trade

---

[1] Raudot, who was intendant early in the eighteenth century, is
a little less gloomy in his coloring, but says that Canadian children
were without discipline or education, had no respect for parents or
curés, and owned no superiors. This, he thinks, is owing to "la
folle tendresse des parents qui les empêche de les corriger et de leur
former le caractère qu'ils ont dur et féroce."

and the general discipline of the colony. One great
evil is the infinite number of drinking-shops, which
makes it almost impossible to remedy the disorders
resulting from them. All the rascals and idlers of
the country are attracted into this business of tavern-
keeping. They never dream of tilling the soil; but,
on the contrary, they deter the other inhabitants
from it, and end with ruining them. I know seigniories where there are but twenty houses, and more
than half of them dram-shops. At Three Rivers
there are twenty-five houses, and liquor may be had
at eighteen or twenty of them. Villemarie [Montreal]
and Quebec are on the same footing."

The governor next dwells on the necessity of finding occupation for children and youths, — a matter
which he regards as of the last importance. "It is
sad to see the ignorance of the population at a distance from the abodes of the curés, who are put to
the greatest trouble to remedy the evil by travelling
from place to place through the parishes in their
charge." [1]

La Barre, Champigny, and Duchesneau write in a
similar strain. Bishop Saint-Vallier, in an epistolary
journal which he printed of a tour through the colony
made on his first arrival, gives a favorable account of
the disposition of the people, especially as regards
religion. He afterwards changed his views. An
abstract made from his letters for the use of the
King states that he "represents, like M. Denonville,

[1] *Denonville au Ministre* 13 *Nov.*, 1685.

that the Canadian youth are for the most part wholly demoralized." [1]

"The bishop was very sorry," says a correspondent of the minister at Quebec, "to have so much exaggerated in the letter he printed at Paris the morality of the people here." [2]   He preached a sermon on the sins of the inhabitants and issued a pastoral mandate, in which he says, "Before we knew our flock we thought that the English and the Iroquois were the only wolves we had to fear; but God having opened our eyes to the disorders of this diocese, and made us feel more than ever the weight of our charge, we are forced to confess that our most dangerous foes are drunkenness, luxury, impurity, and slander." [3]

Drunkenness was at this time the most destructive vice in the colony.   One writer declares that most of the Canadians drink so much brandy in the morning that they are unfit for work all day. [4]   Another says that a canoe-man when he is tired will lift a keg of brandy to his lips and drink the raw liquor from the bung-hole, after which, having spoiled his appetite, he goes to bed supperless; and that, what with drink and hardship, he is an old man at forty. Nevertheless the race did not deteriorate.   The prevalence of early marriages, and the birth of numerous offspring before the vigor of the father had been

[1] *N. Y. Colonial Documents*, ix. 278.   [2] *Ibid.*, ix. 388.

[3] *Ordonnance contre les vices de l'ivrognerie, luxe, et impureté*, 31 *Oct.,* 1690.

[4] *N. Y. Colonial Documents*, ix. 398.

wasted, insured the strength and hardihood which characterized the Canadians. As Denonville describes them, so they long remained. "The Canadians are tall, well-made, and well set on their legs [*bien plantés sur leurs jambes*], robust, vigorous, and accustomed in time of need to live on little. They have intelligence and vivacity, but are wayward, light-minded, and inclined to debauchery."

As the population increased, as the rage for bush-ranging began to abate, and, above all, as the curés multiplied, a change took place for the better. More churches were built, the charge of each priest was reduced within reasonable bounds, and a greater proportion of the inhabitants remained on their farms. They were better watched, controlled, and taught by the Church. The ecclesiastical power, wherever it had a hold, was exercised, as we have seen, with an undue rigor, yet it was the chief guardian of good morals; and the colony grew more orderly and more temperate as the Church gathered more and more of its wild and wandering flock fairly within its fold. In this, however, its success was but relative. It is true that in 1715 a well-informed writer says that the people were "perfectly instructed in religion;"[1] but at that time the statement was only partially true.

During the seventeenth century, and some time after its close, Canada swarmed with beggars, — a singular feature in a new country where a good farm could be had for the asking. In countries intensely

---

[1] *Mémoire addressé au Regent.*

Roman Catholic begging is not regarded as an unmixed evil, being supposed to promote two cardinal virtues, — charity in the giver, and humility in the receiver. The Canadian officials nevertheless tried to restrain it. Vagabonds of both sexes were ordered to leave Quebec, and nobody was allowed to beg without a certificate of poverty from the curé or the local judge.[1] These orders were not always observed. Bishop Saint-Vallier writes that he is overwhelmed by beggars,[2] and the intendant echoes his complaint. Almshouses were established at Montreal, Three Rivers, and Quebec;[3] and when Saint-Vallier founded the General Hospital, its chief purpose was to serve, not as a hospital in the ordinary sense of the word, but as a house of refuge, after the plan of the General Hospital of Paris.[4] Appeal, as usual, was made to the King. Denonville asks his aid for two destitute families, and says that many others need it. Louis XIV. did not fail to respond, and from time to time he sent considerable sums for the relief of the Canadian poor.[5]

Denonville says, "The principal reason of the

[1] *Réglement de Police*, 1676.

[2] *N. Y. Colonial Documents*, ix. 279.

[3] *Édits et Ordonnances*, ii. 119.

[4] On the General Hospital of Quebec, see Juchereau, 355. In 1692, the minister writes to Frontenac and Champigny that they should consider well whether this house of refuge will not "augmenter la fainéantise parmi les habitans," by giving them a sure support in poverty.

[5] As late as 1701 six thousand livres were granted. *Callières au Ministre*, 4 *Nov.*, 1701.

poverty of this country is the idleness and bad conduct of most of the people. The greater part of the
women, including all the *demoiselles*, are very lazy."[1]
Meules proposes as a remedy that the King should
establish a general workshop in the colony, and pay
the workmen himself during the first five or six
years.[2] "The persons here," he says, "who have
wished to make a figure are nearly all so overwhelmed
with debt that they may be considered as in the last
necessity."[3] He adds that many of the people go
half-naked even in winter. "The merchants of this
country," says the intendant Duchesneau, "are all
plunged in poverty, except five or six at the most; it
is the same with the artisans, except a small number,
because the vanity of the women and the debauchery
of the men consume all their gains. As for such of
the laboring class as apply themselves steadily to
cultivating the soil, they not only live very well, but
are incomparably better off than the better sort of
peasants in France."[4]

All the writers lament the extravagant habits of
the people; and even La Hontan joins hands with
the priests in wishing that the supply of ribbons, laces,
brocades, jewelry, and the like might be cut off by
act of law. Mother Juchereau tells us, that, when
the English invasion was impending, the belles of

[1] *Denonville et Champigny au Ministre,* 6 *Nov.,* 1687.
[2] *Meules au Ministre,* 12 *Nov.,* 1682.
[3] Meules, *Mémoire touchant le Canada et l'Acadie,* 1684.
[4] *Duchesneau au Ministre,* 10 *Nov.,* 1679.

Canada were scared for a while into modesty in order
to gain the favor of Heaven; but, as may be imagined,
the effect was short, and Father La Tour declares
that in his time all the fashions except *rouge* came
over regularly in the annual ships.

The manners of the mission period, on the other
hand, were extremely simple. The old governor,
Lauzon, lived on pease and bacon like a laborer, and
kept no man-servant. He was regarded, it is true,
as a miser, and held in slight account.[1] Magdeleine
Bochart, sister of the governor of Three Rivers,
brought her husband two hundred francs in money,
four sheets, two table-cloths, six napkins of linen
and hemp, a mattress, a blanket, two dishes, six
spoons and six tin plates, a pot and a kettle, a table
and two benches, a kneading-trough, a chest with
lock and key, a cow, and a pair of hogs.[2] But the
Bocharts were a family of distinction, and the bride's
dowry answered to her station. By another marriage
contract, at about the same time, the parents of the
bride, being of humble degree, bind themselves to
present the bridegroom with a barrel of bacon, deliver-
able on the arrival of the ships from France.[3]

Some curious traits of this early day appear in the
license of Jean Boisdon as innkeeper. He is required
to establish himself on the great square of Quebec,
close to the church, so that the parishioners may con-

1 *Mémoire d'Aubert de la Chesnaye*, 1676.

2 *Contrat de mariage*, cited by Ferland, *Notes*, 73.

3 *Contrat de mariage*, cited by Benjamin Sulte in *Revue Canadi-
enne*, ix. 111.

veniently warm and refresh themselves between the
services; but he is forbidden to entertain anybody
during high mass, sermon, catechism, or vespers.[1]
Matters soon changed; Jean Boisdon lost his
monopoly, and inns sprang up on all hands. They
did not want for patrons, and we find some of their
proprietors mentioned as among the few thriving men
in Canada. Talon tried to regulate them, and, among
other rules, ordained that no innkeeper should furnish
food or drink to any hired laborer whatever, or to
any person residing in the place where his inn was
situated. An innkeeper of Montreal was fined for
allowing the syndic of the town to dine under his
roof.[2]

One gets glimpses of the pristine state of Quebec
through the early police regulations. Each inhabitant was required to make a gutter along the middle
of the street before his house, and also to remove
refuse and throw it into the river. All dogs, without
exception, were ordered home at nine o'clock. On
Tuesdays and Fridays there was a market in the
public square, whither the neighboring *habitants*,
male and female, brought their produce for sale, as
they still continue to do. Smoking in the street was
forbidden, as a precaution against fire; householders
were required to provide themselves with ladders,
and when the fire alarm was rung all able-bodied

[1] *Acte officielle*, 1648, cited by Ferland, *Cours d'Histoire du Canada*,
i. 365.

[2] Faillon, *Colonie Française*, iii. 405.

persons were obliged to run to the scene of danger
with buckets or kettles full of water.[1] This did not
prevent the Lower Town from burning to the ground
in 1682.   It was soon rebuilt, but a repetition of the
catastrophe seemed very likely.   "This place," says
Denonville, "is in a fearful state as regards fire; for
the houses are crowded together out of all reason,
and so surrounded with piles of cord-wood that it is
pitiful to see."[2]   Add to this the stores of hay for
the cows kept by many of the inhabitants for the
benefit of their swarming progeny.   The houses were
at this time low, compact buildings, with gables of
masonry, as required by law; but many had wooden
fronts, and all had roofs covered with cedar shingles.
The anxious governor begs, that, as the town has not
a *sou* of revenue, his Majesty will be pleased to make
it the gift of two hundred crowns' worth of leather
fire-buckets.[3]   Six or seven years after, certain citizens were authorized by the council to import from
France, at their own cost, "a pump after the Dutch
fashion, for throwing water on houses in case of
fire."[4]

How a fire was managed at Quebec appears from a
letter of the engineer, Vasseur, describing the burning of Laval's seminary in 1701. Vasseur was then
at Quebec, directing the new fortifications. On a
Monday in November, all the pupils of the seminary

---

[1] *Réglement de Police*, 1672. *Ibid.*, 1676.
[2] *Denonville au Ministre*, 20 *Août*, 1685.
[3] *Ibid.*
[4] *Réglement de* 1691, extract in Ferland.

and most of the priests went, according to their
weekly custom, to recreate themselves at a house and
garden at St. Michel, a short distance from town.
The few priests who remained went after dinner to
say vespers at the church.   Only one, Father Petit,
was left in the seminary, and he presently repaired to
the great hall to rekindle the fire in the stove and
warm the place against the return of his brethren.
His success surpassed his wishes.   A firebrand snapped
out in his absence and set the pine floor in a blaze.
Father Boucher, curé of Point Levi, chanced to come
in, and was half choked by the smoke.   He cried
fire ! the servants ran for water; but the flames soon
mastered them; they screamed the alarm, and the
bells began to ring.   Vasseur was dining with the
intendant at his palace by the St. Charles, when he
heard a frightened voice crying out, " Monsieur, you
are wanted! you are wanted!"   He sprang from
table, saw the smoke rolling in volumes from the top
of the rock, ran up the steep ascent, reached the
seminary, and found an excited crowd making a
prodigious outcry.   He shouted for carpenters.   Four
men came to him, and he set them at work with such
tools as they had to tear away planks and beams, and
prevent the fire from spreading to the adjacent parts
of the building; but when he went to find others to
help them, they ran off.   He sent new men in their
place, and these too ran off the moment his back was
turned.   A cry was raised that the building was to
be blown up, on which the crowd scattered for their

lives. Vasseur now gave up the seminary for lost, and thought only of cutting off the fire from the rear of the church, which was not far distant. In this he succeeded, by tearing down an intervening wing or gallery. The walls of the burning building were of massive stone, and by seven o'clock the fire had spent itself. We hear nothing of the Dutch pump, nor does it appear that the soldiers of the garrison made any effort to keep order. Under cover of the confusion, property was stolen from the seminary to the amount of about two thousand livres, — which is remarkable, considering the religious character of the building, and the supposed piety of the people. "There were more than three hundred persons at the fire," says Vasseur; "but thirty picked men would have been worth more than the whole of them." [1]

August, September, and October were the busy months at Quebec. Then the ships from France discharged their lading, the shops and warehouses of the Lower Town were filled with goods, and the *habitants* came to town to make their purchases. When the frosts began, the vessels sailed away, the harbor was deserted, the streets were silent again, and like ants or squirrels the people set at work to lay in their winter stores. Fathers of families packed their cellars with beets, carrots, potatoes, and cabbages; and, at the end of autumn, with meat, fowls, game, fish, and eels, all frozen to stony hardness.

---

[1] *Vasseur au Ministre*, 24 *Nov.*, 1701. Like Denonville before him, he urges the need of fire-buckets.

Most of the shops closed, and the long season of leisure and amusement began.   New Year's day brought visits and mutual gifts.   Thence till Lent dinner-parties were frequent, sometimes familiar and sometimes ceremonious.   The governor's little court at the château was a standing example to all the aspiring spirits of Quebec, and forms and orders of precedence were in some houses punctiliously observed. There were dinners to the military and civic dignitaries and their wives, and others, quite distinct, to prominent citizens.   The wives and daughters of the burghers of Quebec are said to have been superior in manners to women of the corresponding class in France.   "They have wit," says La Potherie, "delicacy, good voices, and a great fondness for dancing. They are discreet, and not much given to flirting; but when they undertake to catch a lover, it is not easy for him to escape the bands of Hymen."[1]

So much for the town.   In the country parishes, there was the same autumnal stowing away of frozen vegetables, meat, fish, and eels, and unfortunately the same surfeit of leisure through five months of the year.   During the seventeenth century, many of the people were so poor that women were forced to keep at home from sheer want of winter clothing.   Nothing, however, could prevent their running from house to house to exchange gossip with the neighbors, who all knew one another, and, having nothing else to do, discussed each other's affairs with an industry

[1] La Potherie, i. 279.

which often bred bitter quarrels. At a later period, a more general introduction of family weaving and spinning served at once to furnish clothing and to promote domestic peace.

The most important persons in a parish were the curé, the seignior, and the militia captain. The seignior had his bench of honor in the church. Immediately behind it was the bench of the militia captain, whose duty it was to drill the able-bodied men of the neighborhood, direct roadmaking and other public works, and serve as deputy to the intendant, whose ordinances he was required to enforce. Next in honor came the local judge, if any there was, and the church-wardens.

The existence of slavery in Canada dates from the end of the seventeenth century. In 1688 the attorney-general made a visit to Paris, and urged upon the King the expediency of importing negroes from the West Indies as a remedy for the scarcity and dearness of labor. The King consented, but advised caution, on the ground that the rigor of the climate would make the venture a critical one.[1] A number of slaves were brought into the colony; but the system never flourished, the climate and other circumstances being hostile to it. Many of the colonists, especially at Detroit and other outlying posts, owned slaves of a remote Indian tribe, the Pawnees. The fact is

[1] *Instruction au Sr. de Frontenac*, 1689. On Canadian slavery, see a long paper, *L'Esclavage en Canada*, published by the Historical Society of Montreal.

remarkable, since it would be difficult to find another of the wild tribes of the continent capable of subjection to domestic servitude.   The Pawnee slaves were captives taken in war and sold at low prices to the Canadians.   Their market value was much impaired by their propensity to run off.

It is curious to observe the views of the Canadians taken at different times by different writers.   La Hontan says: "They are vigorous, enterprising, and indefatigable, and need nothing but education.   They are presumptuous and full of self-conceit, regard themselves as above all the nations of the earth, and, unfortunately, have not the veneration for their parents that they ought to have.   The women are generally pretty; few of them are brunettes; many of them are discreet, and a good number are lazy.   They are fond to the last degree of dress and show, and each tries to outdo the rest in the art of catching a· husband." [1]

Fifty years later, the intendant Hocquart writes: "The Canadians are fond of distinctions and attentions, plume themselves on their courage, and are extremely sensitive to slights or the smallest corrections.   They are self-interested, vindictive, prone to drunkenness, use a great deal of brandy, and pass for not being at all truthful.   This portrait is true of many of them, particularly the country people: those of the towns are less vicious.   They are all attached to religion, and criminals are rare.   They are vola-

[1] La Hontan, ii. 81 (ed. 1709).

tile, and think too well of themselves, which prevents their succeeding as they might in farming and trade. They have not the rude and rustic air of our French peasants. If they are put on their honor and governed with justice, they are tractable enough; but their natural disposition is indocile."[1]

The navigator Bougainville, in the last years of the French rule, describes the Canadian *habitant* as essentially superior to the French peasant, and adds, " He is loud, boastful, mendacious, obliging, civil, and honest; indefatigable in hunting, travelling, and bush-ranging, but lazy in tilling the soil."[2]

The Swedish botanist, Kalm, an excellent observer, was in Canada a few years before Bougainville, and sketches from life the following traits of Canadian manners. The language is that of the old English translation: " The men here [at Montreal] are extremely civil, and take their hats off to every person indifferently whom they meet in the streets. The women in general are handsome; they are well bred and virtuous, with an innocent and becoming freedom. They dress out very fine on Sundays, and though on the other days they do not take much pains with the other parts of their dress, yet they are very fond of adorning their heads, the hair of which is always curled and powdered and ornamented with glittering bodkins and aigrettes. They are not averse to taking part in all the business of housekeeping;

---

[1] *Mémoire de* 1736.
[2] *Mémoire de* 1757, printed in Margry, *Relations Inédites.*

and I have with pleasure seen the daughters of the better sort of people, and of the governor [of Montreal] himself, not too finely dressed, and going into kitchens and cellars to look that everything be done as it ought. What I have mentioned above of their dressing their heads too assiduously is the case with all the ladies throughout Canada. Their hair is always curled, even when they are at home in a dirty jacket and short coarse petticoat that does not reach to the middle of their legs. On those days when they pay or receive visits, they dress so gayly that one is almost induced to think their parents possess the greatest honors in the state. They are no less attentive to have the newest fashions, and they laugh at one another when they are not dressed to one another's fancy. One of the first questions they propose to a stranger is, whether he is married; the next, how he likes the ladies of the country, and whether he thinks them handsomer than those of his own country; and the third, whether he will take one home with him. The behavior of the ladies seemed to me somewhat too free at Quebec, and of a more becoming modesty at Montreal. Those of Quebec are not very industrious. The young ladies, especially those of a higher rank, get up at seven and dress till nine, drinking their coffee at the same time. When they are dressed, they place themselves near a window that opens into the street, take up some needlework and sew a stitch now and then, but turn their eyes into the street most of the time. When a

young fellow comes in, whether they are acquainted
with him or not, they immediately lay aside their
work, sit down by him, and begin to chat, laugh,
joke, and invent *double-entendres ;* and this is reckoned
being very witty. In this manner they frequently
pass the whole day, leaving their mothers to do the
business of the house. They are likewise cheerful
and content, and nobody can say that they want
either wit or charms. Their fault is that they think
too well of themselves. However, the daughters of
people of all ranks without exception go to market
and carry home what they have bought. The girls
at Montreal are very much displeased that those at
Quebec get husbands sooner than they. The reason
of this is that many young gentlemen who come over
from France with the ships are captivated by the
ladies at Quebec and marry them; but as these
gentlemen seldom go up to Montreal, the girls there
are not often so happy as those of the former place." [1]

Long before Kalm's visit, the Jesuit Charlevoix, a
traveller and a man of the world, wrote thus of
Quebec in a letter to the Duchesse de Lesdiguières:
"There is a select little society here which wants
nothing to make it agreeable. In the *salons* of the
wives of the governor and of the intendant, one finds
circles as brilliant as in other countries." These
circles were formed partly of the principal inhabitants, but chiefly of military officers and government

---

[1] Kalm, *Travels into North America*, translated into English by
John Reinold Forster (London, 1771), 56, 282, etc.

officials, with their families. Charlevoix continues:
"Everybody does his part to make the time pass
pleasantly, with games and parties of pleasure, —
drives and canoe excursions in summer, sleighing
and skating in winter. There is a great deal of
hunting and shooting, for many Canadian gentlemen
are almost destitute of any other means of living at
their ease. The news of the day amounts to very
little indeed, as the country furnishes scarcely any,
while that from Europe comes all at once. Science
and the fine arts have their turn, and conversation
does not fail. The Canadians breathe from their
birth an air of liberty, which makes them very pleasant in the intercourse of life, and our language is
nowhere more purely spoken. One finds here no rich
persons whatever, and this is a great pity; for the
Canadians like to get the credit of their money, and
scarcely anybody amuses himself with hoarding it.
They say it is very different with our neighbors the
English; and one who knew the two colonies only
by the way of living, acting, and speaking of the
colonists would not hesitate to judge ours the more
flourishing. In New England and the other British
colonies there reigns an opulence by which the people
seem not to know how to profit; while in New
France poverty is hidden under an air of ease which
appears entirely natural. The English colonist keeps
as much and spends as little as possible; the French
colonist enjoys what he has got, and often makes a
display of what he has not got. The one labors for

his heirs; the other leaves them to get on as they can, like himself. I could push the comparison further, but I must close here; the King's ship is about to sail, and the merchant vessels are getting ready to follow. In three days, perhaps, not one will be left in the harbor."[1]

And now we, too, will leave Canada. Winter draws near, and the first patch of snow lies gleaming on the distant mountain of Cape Tourmente. The sun has set in chill autumnal beauty, and the sharp spires of fir-trees on the heights of Sillery stand stiff and black against the pure cold amber of the fading west. The ship sails in the morning; and before the old towers of Rochelle rise in sight there will be time to smoke many a pipe, and ponder what we have seen on the banks of the St. Lawrence.

---

[1] Charlevoix, *Journal Historique*, 80 (ed. 1744).

CHAPTER XXIV.

1663–1763.

CANADIAN ABSOLUTISM.

FORMATION OF CANADIAN CHARACTER. — THE RIVAL COLONIES. — ENGLAND AND FRANCE. — NEW ENGLAND. — CHARACTERISTICS OF RACE. — MILITARY QUALITIES. — THE CHURCH. — THE ENGLISH CONQUEST.

NOT institutions alone, but geographical position, climate, and many other conditions unite to form the educational influences that, acting through successive generations, shape the character of nations and communities.

It is easy to see the nature of the education, past and present, which wrought on the Canadians and made them what they were. An ignorant population, sprung from a brave and active race, but trained to subjection and dependence through centuries of feudal and monarchical despotism, was planted in the wilderness by the hand of authority, and told to grow and flourish. Artificial stimulants were applied, but freedom was withheld. Perpetual intervention of government, — regulations, restrictions, encouragements sometimes more mischievous than restrictions, a constant uncertainty what the authorities would do next, the fate of each man resting less with himself than with another, volition enfeebled, self-reliance paralyzed, — the condition, in short, of a child held always under the rule of a father, in the main well-meaning and kind, sometimes generous, sometimes neglectful, often capricious, and rarely very wise, — such were the influences under which Canada grew up. If she had prospered, it would have been sheer miracle. A man, to be a man, must feel that he holds his fate, in some good measure, in his own hands.

But this was not all. Against absolute authority there was a counter influence, rudely and wildly antagonistic. Canada was at the very portal of the great interior wilderness. The St. Lawrence and the Lakes were the highway to that domain of savage freedom; and thither the disfranchised, half-starved seignior, and the discouraged *habitant* who could find no market for his produce naturally enough betook themselves. Their lesson of savagery was well learned, and for many a year a boundless license and a stiff-handed authority battled for the control of Canada. Nor, to the last, were Church and State fairly masters of the field. The French rule was drawing towards its close when the intendant complained that though twenty-eight companies of regular troops were quartered in the colony, there were not soldiers enough to keep the people in order.[1] One cannot but remember that in a neighboring colony,

[1] *Mémoire de* 1736 (printed by the Historical Society of Quebec).

far more populous, perfect order prevailed, with no other guardians than a few constables chosen by the people themselves.

Whence arose this difference, and other differences equally striking, between the rival colonies? It is easy to ascribe them to a difference of political and religious institutions; but the explanation does not cover the ground. The institutions of New England were utterly inapplicable to the population of New France, and the attempt to apply them would have wrought nothing but mischief. There are no political panaceas, except in the imagination of political quacks. To each degree and each variety of public development there are corresponding institutions, best answering the public needs; and what is meat to one is poison to another. Freedom is for those who are fit for it; the rest will lose it, or turn it to corruption. Church and State were right in exercising authority over a people which had not learned the first rudiments of self-government. Their fault was not that they exercised authority, but that they exercised too much of it, and, instead of weaning the child to go alone, kept him in perpetual leading-strings, making him, if possible, more and more dependent, and less and less fit for freedom.

In the building up of colonies, England succeeded and France failed. The cause lies chiefly in the vast advantage drawn by England from the historical training of her people in habits of reflection, forecast, industry, and self-reliance, — a training which enabled them to adopt and maintain an invigorating system of self-rule, totally inapplicable to their rivals.

The New England colonists were far less fugitives from oppression than voluntary exiles seeking the realization of an idea. They were neither peasants nor soldiers, but a substantial Puritan yeomanry, led by Puritan gentlemen and divines in thorough sympathy with them. They were neither sent out by the King, governed by him, nor helped by him. They grew up in utter neglect, and continued neglect was the only boon they asked. Till their increasing strength roused the jealousy of the Crown, they were virtually independent, — a republic, but by no means a democracy. They chose their governor and all their rulers from among themselves, made their own government and paid for it, supported their own clergy, defended themselves, and educated themselves. Under the hard and repellent surface of New England society lay the true foundations of a stable freedom, — conscience, reflection, faith, patience, and public spirit. The cement of common interests, hopes, and duties compacted the whole people like a rock of conglomerate; while the people of New France remained in a state of political segregation, like a basket of pebbles held together by the enclosure that surrounds them.

It may be that the difference of historical antecedents would alone explain the difference of character between the rival colonies; but there are deeper causes, the influence of which went far to determine the antecedents themselves. The Germanic race, and especially the Anglo-Saxon branch of it, is peculiarly masculine, and, therefore, peculiarly fitted for self-government. It submits its action habitually to the guidance of reason, and has the judicial faculty of seeing both sides of a question. The French Celt is cast in a different mould. He sees the end distinctly, and reasons about it with an admirable clearness; but his own impulses and passions continually turn him away from it. Opposition excites him; he is impatient of delay, is impelled always to extremes, and does not readily sacrifice a present inclination to an ultimate good. He delights in abstractions and generalizations, cuts loose from unpleasing facts, and roams through an ocean of desires and theories.

While New England prospered and Canada did not prosper, the French system had at least one great advantage. It favored military efficiency. The Canadian population sprang in great part from soldiers, and was to the last systematically reinforced by disbanded soldiers. Its chief occupation was a continual training for forest war; it had little or nothing to lose, and little to do but fight and range the woods. This was not all. The Canadian government was essentially military. At its head was a soldier nobleman, often an old and able commander; and those beneath him caught his spirit and emulated his example. In spite of its political nothingness, in spite of poverty and hardship, and in spite even of trade, the upper stratum of Canadian society was

30

animated by the pride and fire of that gallant *noblesse* which held war as its only worthy calling, and prized honor more than life.   As for the *habitant*, the forest, lake, and river were his true school; and here, at least, he was an apt scholar.   A skilful woodsman, a bold and adroit canoe-man, a willing fighter in time of need, often serving without pay, and receiving from government only his provisions and his canoe, he was more than ready at any time for any hardy enterprise; and in the forest warfare of skirmish and surprise there were few to match him.   An absolute government used him at will, and experienced leaders guided his rugged valor to the best account.

The New England man was precisely the same material with that of which Cromwell formed his invincible "Ironsides;" but he had very little forest experience.   His geographical position cut him off completely from the great wilderness of the interior. The sea was his field of action.   Without the aid of government, and in spite of its restrictions, he built up a prosperous commerce, and enriched himself by distant fisheries, neglected by the rivals before whose doors they lay.   He knew every ocean from Greenland to Cape Horn, and the whales of the north and of the south had no more dangerous foe.   But he was too busy to fight without good cause; and when he turned his hand to soldiering, it was only to meet some pressing need of the hour.   The New England troops in the early wars were bands of raw fishermen and farmers, led by civilians, decorated with military titles, and subject to the slow and uncertain action of legislative bodies. The officers had not learned to command, nor the men to obey. The remarkable exploit of the capture of Louisburg, the strongest fortress in America, was the result of mere audacity and hardihood, backed by the rarest good luck.

One great fact stands out conspicuous in Canadian history, — the Church of Rome. More even than the royal power, she shaped the character and the destinies of the colony. She was its nurse and almost its mother; and, wayward and headstrong as it was, it never broke the ties of faith that held it to her. It was these ties which, in the absence of political franchises, formed under the old régime the only vital coherence in the population. The royal government was transient; the Church was permanent. The English conquest shattered the whole apparatus of civil administration at a blow, but it left her untouched. Governors, intendants, councils, and commandants, all were gone; the principal seigniors fled the colony; and a people who had never learned to control themselves or help themselves were suddenly left to their own devices. Confusion, if not anarchy, would have followed but for the parish priests, who, in a character of double paternity, half spiritual and half temporal, became more than ever the guardians of order throughout Canada.

This English conquest was the grand crisis of Canadian history. It was the beginning of a new life. With England came Protestantism, and the

Canadian Church grew purer and better in the
presence of an adverse faith. Material growth; an
increased mental activity; an education, real though
fenced and guarded; a warm and genuine patriotism,
— all date from the peace of 1763. England imposed
by the sword on reluctant Canada the boon of rational
and ordered liberty. Through centuries of striving
she had advanced from stage to stage of progress,
deliberate and calm, — never breaking with her past,
but making each fresh gain the base of a new success,
— enlarging popular liberties while bating nothing of
that height and force of individual development
which is the brain and heart of civilization; and now,
through a hard-earned victory, she taught the conquered colony to share the blessings she had won.
A happier calamity never befell a people than the
conquest of Canada by the British arms.

APPENDIX.

———•———

SECTION FIRST.

———

A.

LA TOUR AND D'AUNAY.

Procès verbal d'André Certain.

[Literatim.]

Collection de M. Margry.

L'an mil six cent quarante quatre le vint cinq jour d'octobre deux mois après la signification faits de l'arrest du conseil en date du 5 mai de la mesme année au Sieur de la Tour et à tous ceux qui estoient avec luy dans le fort de la Rivière St. Jean par la Montjoie le 15 8bre 1644 Mr Charles de Menou chevalier Seigneur d'Aunay Charnisay, gouverneur et Lieutenant général pour le Roy dans toute l'Etendue descostes d'Acadie pais de la Nouvelle France, veu le refus du d. de la Tour et l'obstination dans laquelle estoient ses gens, equipa de rechef deux de ses chaloupes pour tenter par les voies de douceur de ramener ces esprits rebelles à l'obeissance qu'ils doivent à sa Majeste pour lequel effet mon dit Sieur deputa un lieutenant de son vaisseau pour commander une d'icelles et son sergent pour l'autre auec commandement de sa part d'aller à la riviere

St. Jean faire tout effort pour adroitement remonter quelqu'uns de ces esprits rebelles, les emboucher et leur donner
lettres pour leur camarades signés de mon dit Sieur avec
assurance d'abolition de leurs crimes et payements de leurs
gages s'ils se rangeoient à leur devoir de veritables sujets,
leur devant montrer comme les arrets du conseil obligeoient
mon dit Sieur à pareils traitemens. Ce qu'ayant fidellement
executé ils ne receurent pour toute reponse qu'injures et
imprecations de ces malheureux et huit jours après la
femme du dit Sieur de la Tour arrivant à la riviere de
St. Jean conduite par un vaisseau anglois obligea son
mary d'aller à Boston vers les Anglois se declarer de leur
religion, comme elle venoit de faire et leur demander
un ministre pour son habitation et par là obliger tout le
corps des Anglois à les maintenir dans leurs biens avec offre
qu'ils partageroient toute la coste d'Acadie après qu'ils s'en
seroient rendus maistres: Et le 28 de Janvier 1645 la dite
dame parla si insolemment aux réverends peres Recollects
qui pour lors estoient dans son habitation que faisant la
Démoniaque et mepris scandaleux de la religion Catholique,
apostolique et Romaine son mary présent, qui adhéroit à
toutes ses actions, ils furent contraints de sortir et chercher
moyen de se retirer quoyque dans ces contrées l'Hiver soit
très rigoureux, ce que le dit Sieur de la Tour et sa femme
leur octroierent avec dérision et injures leur donnant pour
cet effet une vieille pinasse qui couloid quasy bas d'eau avec
deux bariques de bled d'Inde pour toutes vitailles, ce qui
sera justifié par une attestation de ceux mesmes qui estoient
dans le service du Sr de la Tour et sa femme et une lettre
d'un des susdits pères Recollects superieur dans le d. lieu
et huit ou neuf des gens du d. Sr de la Tour counoissant le
deplorable estat de cette habitation ed la formelle rebellion
du Sr de la Tour sa femme et du reste de leurs camarades
contre le devoir qu'ils doivent à dieu et au Roy se retirérent

semblablement et accompagnerent les dits reverends pères
Recollects, lesquels avec beaucoup de perils se vinrent rendre
dans le Port Royal demeure ordinaire du Sr. d'Aunay,
lequel après avoir esté imbu de tout ce que dessus les receut
tous humainement envoiant les deux religieux Recollects
dans la maison des Reverends peres Capucins missionaires
qui les receurent avec tant d'affection et les firent tant de
charité et saints offices qu'ils en demeurent tous confus aussy
bien que les huid personnes qui les accompagnoient voyant
le favorable accueil que leur fit mon dit Sieur qui ne se con-
tenta pas de les loger et nourrir comme les siens propres mais
les paya leurs gages que le dit La Tour de tant d'années qu'ils
l'avoient servy leur avoid refusé. Ce qui est prouvé par une
reconnoissance de ces mesmes personnes pour les sommes qui
leur ont esté mises entre les mains, signée de leurs mains.
Ce régalement ayant esté donné comme dessus est dit, Mon
dit sieur s'informant plus particulierement de l'estat au quel
estoient ces miserables esprits, l'obstination du reste de ceux
qui estoient demeurez avec le dit la Tour, et qu'il estoit
party pour aller vers les Anglois dans Boston pour tascher
de renvoyer comme jà cy dessus est dit le traitté de paix fait
avec les dits Anglois et le sieur Marie confident de Mon
d. Sieur D'Aunay et engager par mesme moyen quelque
marchand pour amener quelques vitailles dans la riviere de
Saint Jean dans la quelle il n'avoit laissé que quarante cinq
personnes, ce que mon dit sieur considerant fit assemblées de
tous les officiers qui pour lors estoient auprès de sa personne,
où il fut conclud de prendre cette occasion aux cheveux. Et
quoyque ne le peut quasy permettre et qu'il falloit risquer
pour une affaire de telle consequence, ce qui obligea mon dit
sieur de monter le plus grand de ces navires du port de trois
cents tonneaux, equipé en guerre, pour se mettre en garde à
l'entrée de la Rivière St. Jean afin de surprendre le dit La
Tour avec une partie de son monde, qui pensoit à la faveur

de la rigueur de l'Hiver faire son voyage sans qu'il en fust aucune nouvelle, ce que mon dit sieur ayant executé et pris rade à une lieue du fort de la Rivière St. Jean assisté d'un religieux Capucin missionnaire et des deux susdits Recollects, envoya de rechef vers la dite femme La Tour et tous ceux qui pour lors estoient avec elle le Révérend Père André Recollect par une de ses chaloupes, le quel se promettoit d'attirer peutestre quelquuns à resipiscence, leur faisant connoitre le bon accueil que luy et leurs camarades avoient receu de mon dit Sieur, ce qui ne reussit non plus que les autres fois du passé. Deux mois s'ecoulèrent dans semblable attente, après quoy mon dit Sieur prid resolution de battre le fer pendant qu'il estoit chaud, voyant un de ses navires aussy equipé en guerre qui l'estoit venu trouver du Port Royal selon qu'il l'avoit ainsy ordonné accompagné d'une pinasse aussi chargée de monde et après avoir reallié de toutes ses Habitations les personnes capables de porter mousquets, il fit descendre une bonne partie de ses hommes à terre ed mettre deux pièces de canon avec ordre de les mettre promptement en batterie le plus proche du fort de la Rivière de St. Jean qu'ils pourroient avec assurance qu'aussytost qu'ils avoient effectué son commandement ils approcheroient ce navire à la portée du pistolet, afin que sans donner jour aux assiegés de se reconnoistre on pust faire un tonnerre et par mer et par terre, donner à mesme temps qu'il y auroit breche faite, pendant l'exécution de ces ordres un petit navire Anglois se présenta pour entrer dans la dite rivière chargé de vitailles et munitions de guerre, dans lequel il y avoit un des domestiques du d. La Tour qui estoit chargé de Lettres de son maistre pour la ditte dame sa femme qui l'assuroit dans un mois ou deux venir la trouver en meilleur estat et posture qu'il pourroit. Le dit domestique avoit outre plus une lettre du gouverneur de la grande baye des anglois addressante à la dite dame par

laquelle il l'exhortoit à faire son profit des instructions
qu'elle avoit recues pendant sa residence.   Le dit navire
fut pris et arresté par mon dit Sieur et l'equipage renvoyé
au lieu d'où il estoit party, avec une chaloupe que mon dit
sieur leur donna pour cet effet, lequel estant une fois de
retour fit rapport à Messieurs les magistrats du gouvernement
des Anglois que leur navire avoid esté pris en negotiant avec
les francois et que le traité de paix quils avoient fait avec le
Sieur Marie nestoit gardé avec mil autres plaintes dont ils
vouloient couvrir le sujet de leur voyage, ce qui obligea ces
Messieurs de deputer un exprès vers mon dit Sieur pour luy
demander raison du bien pris par luy sur un de leurs marchands contre les articles de paix que le Sieur Marie, confident, leur avoit laissé signer de sa part — À quoy mon dit
Sieur leur fit response et déclara à leur député la fourbe de
leur dit marchand, le quel par un désir de lucre abusoit de
leur commission et au lieu d'aller négotiant dans les Habitations des véritables François, Il alloit rompant par luy
mesmes ce traité de paix passé entre ses magistrats et le
Sieur Marie, confident, portant ainsi frauduleusement des
munitions de vivres et de guerre pour maintenir des rebelles dans leur desobeissance et contre le devoir qu'ils
doivent à leur prince naturel.   Toutes les quelles raisons
payerent entièrement et le député et Messieurs les Magistrats de la Grande Baie le susdit député estant party et mon
dit Sieur D'Aunay ayant recue nouvelle que la batterie
estoit en estat et ses gens qui estoient à terre disposés
à faire ce quil leur ordonneroit, se resolut de haster le
pas et avant que le d. Sieur De la Tour en eust le
vent faire tout son effort, ce qui luy arriva si Heureuse-
ment qu'après avoir encore une fois sommé ces malheureux,
lesquels lui envoierent pour response une vollée de canon à
balle, aborant le pavillon rouge sur leurs bastions avec mil
injures et blasphemes et avoir fait battre le dit fort de la

Rivière de St Jean tant par terre que par son **grand navire,**
qu'il avoit emmené à portée de pistolet d'iceluy ce qui rasa
une partie de leur parapets il s'en rendit maistre par un
assaut général qu'il fit donner sur le soir de la mesme
Journée le Lendemain Pasques ce qui fut accompagné d'une
si grande benediction de Dieu, que quoyque la perte des
Hommes que mon dit sieur a fait soit grande elle eut esté
encore plus sanglante. Une partie des assiegéz furent tuez
dans la chaleur du combat et l'autre fait prisonniers entre
autres la femme du dit La Tour, son fils et sa fille de
Chambre et une autre femme qui est tout cequ'il y avoit
dans le dit fort de sexe feminin toutes lesquelles ne recurent
aucun tort ny à leur Honneur ny à leurs personnes. Une
partie des prisonniers recut grace de mon dit Sieur et le reste
des plus seditieux fut pendu et etranglé pour servir de
memoire et d'exemple, à la postérité d'une si obstinée ré-
bellion ce qui est prouvé par l'attestation qu'en ont rendue
et signée une bonne partie de ceux qui ont recue la vie et
pareille gratification. Le Lendemain 18 Avril 1645 mon
dit sieur fit inhumer tous les morts tant de part que d'autre
avec la distinction pour tant requise en telle rencontre du
party faisant prier Dieu et faire un service solemnel à tous
ceux que deux révérends pères Capucins missionnaires qui
avoient esté presens à tout jugement estre deu, ce qui est
prouvé aussi bien que tout ce que dessus par une attestation
authentique des mesmes susd. révérends pères Capucins
missionnaires après quoy mon dit Sieur fit travailler pour
combler les travaux de dehors faits par les assiegeans et re-
parer ceux de la place mettre ordre aux deffauts d'icelle par
luy reconnus et faire inventaire de tout ce qui se trouva de
reste dans icelle après le pillage fait par les compagnons que
mon dit sieur leur avoit donné et faire ensuite renvituailler
le dit lieu de toutes choses necessaires pour la conservation
d'iceluy et enfin poser une personne capable et fidele pour

le service du Roi ce que dura l'espace de trois semaines ou un mois pendant le quel la femme du dit La Tour qui estoit dans le Commencement en Liberté fut resserrée par une Lettre qu'on trouva qu'elle ecrivoit à son mary et pratique qu'elle faisoit de lui faire tenir par le moyen des Sauvages afin de la pouvoir par la première occasion envoyer en France à nos Seigneurs du Conseil en bonne sauve garde, ce qui l'alarma de telle sorte que de depit et de rage elle tomba malade et nonobstant tous les bons traitemens et Charités que L'on exerça en son endroit mourut le 15 Juin après avoir abjuré publiquement dans le chapelle du mesme fort L'Heresie qu'elle avoit professée parmy les Anglois àla grande Baye. Ce qui est justifié par l'attestation désjà cy dessus alleguée des deux réverends pères Capucins Missionaires.

Le présent procés verbal a esté fait par nous, André Certain prevost et garde du Scel Royal de La Coste d'Acadie pays de la Nouvelle france à la requeste de Monsieur d'Aunay Charnisay Gouverneur et Lieutenant general pour le Roy en toute l'Etendue de la Coste d'Acadie pays de la Nouvelle France le 10ᵉ jour de may 1645 et rendu et dès le mesme jour et an que dessus pour lui servir et valoir aussi que de raison. Le tout en présence de tesmoins et principaux chefs des Francois qui sont dans la dite coste signé Longvilliers Poincy, Bernard Marot, Dubreuil Vismes, Javille, Jean Laurent, Henry Dansmartin, Barthelemy Aubert, Leclerc et Certain prevost et Garde du Sceau Royal.

[The following extracts are printed, letter for letter, from copies of
the original documents.]

SECTION SECOND.

B.

THE HERMITAGE OF CAEN.

MÉMOIRE POUR FAIRE CONNOISTRE L'ESPRIT ET LA
CONDUITE DE LA COMPAGNIE ESTABLIE EN LA VILLE
DE CAEN, APPELÉE L'HERMITAGE.

(Extrait.) [1] *Bibliothèque Nationale.*

C'EST en ce fameux Hermitage que le dit feu Sieur de
Bernières a eslevé plusieurs jeunes gens auxquels il en-
seignoit une espèce d'oraison sublime et transcendante que
l'on appelle l'oraison purement passive, parceque l'esprit
n'y agit point, mais reçoit seulement la divine opération;
c'est cette espèce d'oraison qui est la source de tant de
visions et de révélations, dont l'Hermitage est si fécond; et
après qu'il leur avoit subtilizé et presque fait évaporer
l'esprit par cette oraison rafinée, il les rendoit capables de
reconnoistre les Jansenistes les plus cachéz; en sorte que
quelques uns de ces disciples ont dit qu'ils le connoissoient
au flairer, comme les chiens font leur gibier, pour ensuite
leur faire la chasse, néantmoins le dit Sieur de Bernières
disoit qu'il n'avoit pas l'odorat si subtil, mais que la
marque à laquelle il connoissoit les Jansénistes estoit quand

[1] This *mémoire* forms 116 pages in the copy in my possession.

on improuvoit sa conduite ou que l'on estoit opposé aux
Jésuites. . . . Au commencement les personnes de cette
compagnie ne se mesloient que de l'assistance des pauvres,
mais depuis que le feu Sieur de Bernières qui estoit un
simple laïque, qui n'avoit point d'estude, s'en estant rendu
le maistre, il persuada a ceux qui en sont qu'elle n'estoit
pas seulement establie pour prendre soin des pauvres, mais
de toutes les autres bonnes œuvres, publiques ou particulières, qui regardent la Piété et la Religion et que Dieu
les avoit suscitez, principalement pour suppléér aux défauts
et négligences des Prélats, des Pasteurs, des Magistrats, des
Juges et autres Supérieurs Ecclésiastiques et Politiques qui
faute de s'appliquer assez aux devoirs de leurs charges, ob-
mettent dans les occasions beaucoup de bien qu'ils pourroient procurer, et négligent de résister à beaucoup de maux,
d'abus et d'erreurs qu'ils pourroient empêcher; et que pour
remédier à ces manquements, il estoit expédient que Dieu
suscitat plusieurs gens de bien de toutes sortes de conditions
qui s'unissent ensemble pour travailler à l'avancement du
bien qui se peut faire en chaque profession, et pour extirper
les erreurs, les abus et les vices qui s'y glissent souvent, par
la négligence ou connivence mesme de ceux qui sont le plus
obligez par leur ministère d'y donner ordre.

Et c'est dans cette pensée que ces messieurs croyent avoir
droit à se mesler de toutes choses, de s'ingérer de toutes les
actions un peu éclantes qui regardent la Religion, de
s'ingérer en censeurs publics, pour corriger et controller
tout ce qui leur deplaist, d'entrer et de pénétrer dans les
secrets des maisons et des familles particulières, comme
aussi dans la conduite des communautez Religieuses pour y
gouverner toutes choses à leur gré; et bien que ces messieurs
soient fort ignorans, bien qu'ils n'ayent aucune experience
des affaires et qu'ils passent dans le jugement de tous ceux
qui les connoissent pour personnes qui n'ont qu'un Zèle

impetueux et violent, sans lumières et sans discrétion, neantmoins ils présument avoir assez de capacité pour réformer la vie, les mœurs, les sentimens et la doctrine de tous les autres. Et ce qu'il y a de plus fascheux et de plus dangereux en cela, c'est que si on ne défère aveuglément à tous leurs sentimens, si on improuve leur conduite et si l'on oppose la moindre résistance à leurs entreprises, quoyqu'injustes et violentes, ils unissent toutes leur forces pour les faire réussir et pour cet effet ils réclament les secours de tous ceux qui leur sont unis, à Paris, à Rouen et ailleurs, pour décrier, pour diffamer et pour perdre ceux qui leur résistent et qui veulent s'opposer au cours de leurs violences et de leurs injustice, de sorte qu'on peut assurer avec vérité que cette compagnie a dégénéré en une cabale et en une faction dangereuse et pernicieuse, tant à l'Eglise qu'à la Patrie, estant certant que depuis peu d'années ils ont excité beaucoup de troubles et de divisions dans toute la ville de Caen, et notamment dans le clergé et mesme en plusieurs autres lieux de la Basse-Normandie ainsi qu'il paroistra par les articles suivants de ce mémoire.

Il est arrivé quelques fois qu'ayant eu de faux avis que des maris maltroitoient leurs femmes ou que des femmes n'estoient pas fidèles à leurs maris ou que des filles ne se gouvernoient pas bien, ils se sont ingérez sur le rapport qui en estoit fait en leur assemblée de chercher les moyens de remédier à ces maux, et ils en ont choisi de si impertinents et de si indiscrets que cela a esté capable de causer bien du désordre et de la division dans les familles et dans toute la ville; car souvent voulant empescher une légère faute, on en fait naistre de grands scandales, lorsque l'on agit par emportement plustost que par prudence.

Ce n'est pas seulement dans les familles particulières qu'ils s'introduisent pour en fureter les secrets, pour en connoitre les défauts et pour en usurper la direction et le gouverne-

ment, mais encore dans les maisons Religieuses, dont les
unes se sont soumises à leur domination, comme les Ursulines de Caen, les moynes de l'Abbaye d'Ardenne de l'ordre
de Premontré, proche de cette ville et depuis peu les filles de
Sainte-Marie ; et les autres leur ayant tesmoigné quelque
résistance, ils ont employé toute leur industrie pour en
venir à bout ; et où l'artifice a manqué, ils y ont adjouté les
violences et les menaces. . . .

Mais il ne faut point chercher de marques plus visibles de
la persévérance, pour mieux dire du progrès de ces faux
ermites dans leurs emportemens que ce qu'ont fait cet hiver
passé cinq jeunes hommes nourris en l'Hermitage et élevés
sous la direction et discipline du feu Sieur de Bernières.
On leur avoit si bien imprimé dans l'esprit que tout estoit
rempli de Jansénistes dans la ville de Caen, et que les curez
en estoient les fauteurs et protecteurs, qu'un d'entre eux
s'imagina que Dieu l'inspiroit fortement advertir le peuple
de Caen que les curez estoient des fauteurs d'Hérétiques et
par conséquent des excomuniez ; et ayant persuadé à ses
compagnons d'annoncer publiquement à toute la ville ce
crime prétendu des Curez d'une manière qui touchast le
peuple et qui fut capable de l'exciter contre ces Pasteurs,
ils résolurent de faire cette publication le mercredi quatrième du mois de Febvrier dernier, et jugèrent que pour
se disposer à exécuter dignement ce que Dieu leur avoit in-
spiré, il falloit faire ensemble une communion extraordinaire,
immédiatement avant que de l'entreprendre. Ils assistèrent
donc pour cet effet et dans la paroisse de Saint-Ouen à la
messe d'un prestre qu'on dit estre de leur cabale, et conmu-
nièrent tous cinq de sa main ; et après leur communion, le
plus zélé mit bas son pourpoint et le laissa avec son chapeau
dans l'Eglise ; et accompagné des quatre autres qui le sui-
voient sans chapeaux, sans colets et le pourpoint deboutonné,
non-obstant la rigueur extrème du froid ; ils marchèrent en

cet équipage par toute la ville, annonçant à haute voix que
les curez de Caen à l'exception de deux qu'ils nommoient
étoient fauteurs de Jansénistes et excommuniez, parce qu'ils
avoient signé un acte devant l'official de Caen, où ils attestent
qu'ils ne connoissent point de Jansenistes dans la dite ville
et répétoient cet advertissement de dix pas en dix pas, ce
qui emeut toute la ville et attira à leur suite une grande
multitude de populace qui se persuadant que ces gens estoient envoyés de Dieu pour leur donner cet advertissement,
témoignoient desja de l'emotion contre les curez. Mais les
magistrats qui estoient alors au siège en ayant esté advertis,
ils envoyèrent leurs huissiers pour les arrester et les emme-
ner, et ayant esté interrogez par le juge sur le sujet d'une
action si extraordinaire, ils respondirent hardiment qu'ils
l'avoient entreprise pour le service de Dieu et qu'ils estoient
prests de souffrir la mort pour soustenir la vérité de ce qu'ils
annonçoient, qu'ils avoient connoissance certaine qu'il y avoit
grand nombre de Jansénistes en la ville de Caen, et que les
curez s'en estoient declarez les fauteurs, par la déclaration
qu'ils avoient donnée qu'ils n'en connoissoient point ; ensuitte
de quoy quatre d'entre eux furent renvoyez en prison et le
cinquième fut mis entre les mains de ses parents sur une
attestation que donnèrent les médecins qu'il estoit hypo-
condriaque et peu de jours après le lieutenant criminel ayant
instruit le procez, les quatre prisonniers furent condamnez à
cent livres d'amende ; il leur fut deffendu et à tous autres de
s'assembler ni d'exciter aucun scandale, il fut ordonné qu'ils
seroient mis entre les mains de leur parents pour s'en
charger et en faire bonne et seure garde, avec deffense de
les laisser entrer dans la ville et aux fauxbourgs, sur peines
au cas appartenantes. . . .

Car de quelles entreprises ne sont pas capables des personnes d'esprit faible et d'humeur atrabilaire que d'ailleurs
on a desséchées par des jeûnes, des veilles et d'autres

austéritez continuelles et par des méditations de trois ou quatre heures par jour, lorsque l'on ne les entretient presque d'autre chose, si non que leur Religion et l'Eglise sont en un très grand danger de se perdre, par la faction et la conspiration des Jansénistes lesquels on leur représente dans les livres, dans les sermons et dans les conférences, comme des gens qui veulent renverser les fondements de la Religion et de la Piété Chrestienne, qui veulent détruire le mystère de l'Incarnation, qui ne croyent point à la Transubstantation ni l'Invocation des Saints, ni les Indulgences, qui veulent abolir le sacrifice de la messe et le sacrement de la Pénitence, qui combattent la dévotion et la culte de la Sainte-Vierge, qui nient le franc arbitre et qui substituent en sa place le destin et la fatalité des Turcs, et enfin qui machinent la ruine de l'authorité des Souverains Pontifes. Qu'y a-t-il de plus aisé que d'animer les esprits imbéciles d'eux mesmes et prévenus de ces fausses imaginations contre des Evesques, des Docteurs, des Curez, et contre d'autres personnes très vertueuses et très catholiques, lorsqu'on leur fait croire que toutes ces personnes conspirent à establir une hérésie abominable !

C.

LAVAL AND ARGENSON.

LETTRE DE L'EVESQUE DE PETRÉE A M. D'ARGENSON, FRÈRE DU GOUVERNEUR.

(*Extrait.*)   *Papiers d'Argenson.*

J'AI reçeu dans mon entrée dans le pays de Monsieur votre frère toutes les marques d'une bienveillance extraordinaire; iay fait mon possible pour la recongnoistre et luy ay rendu

31

tous les respects que je dois à une personne de sa vertu et
de son mérite joint à la qualité qu'il porte ; comme son plus
véritable amy et fidelle serviteur iay cru estre obligé de luy
donner un advis important pour le bien de l'Eglise et qui
luy devoit estre utile s'il l'eust pris dans la mesme disposition que ie suis asseuré que vous l'auries receu ; cestoit seul
à seul à cœur ouvert avec marques assez évidentes que ce
que ie luy disois estoit vray veu qu'il estoit fondé sur des
sentimens que i'avois veu moy mesme paroistre en diverses
assemblées publiques ; cependant il ne fist que trop cong-
noistre qu'il ne trouvoit auqunnement bon que ie luy don-
naisses cet advertissement et me voullut faire embrasser le
party de ceux qui avaient tout subject de se plaindre de son
procédé envers eux, mais que je ne pretendois auqunnement justifier n'en ayant auqunne plainte de leur part pour
luy faire et d'ailleurs estans asses desintéressés ; vous pouvez
bien iuger quels sont ceux dont ie veux parler sans vous les
nommer puisque vous mesme qui avez une affection sincère
et bien réglée pour ces dignes ouvriers évangéliques m'avez
avoué que vous aviez doulleur de le voir partir dans les
sentiments où il estoit à leur esgard sans beaucoup de fonde-
ment du moins suffisamment recongneu pour lors ; ce que ie
luy dis avoir sceu de vous pour ne rien omettre de ce que je
me persuadois qui estoit capable de lui faire avouer une vérité
qui nestoit que trop apparente, ce qui devoit un peu le
calmer son esprit sembla l'aigrir et se fascha de ce que vous
m'aviez faict cette ouverture, ie ne scais depuis ce qu'il a
pensé de moy, mais il semble que je luy sois suspect et qu'il
aye crû que i'embrasse la cause de ces bons serviteurs de
Dieu à son preiudice, mais ie puis bien asseurer qu'ils n'ont
pour luy que des sentimens de respect et que la plus forte
passion que iaye est de le voir dans une parfaite union et
intelligence avec eux.

QUEBEC, ce 20 Octobre 1659.

Lettre de M. d'Argenson, 1660.

(*Extrait.*) *Papiers d'Argenson.*

Monsieur de Petrée a une telle adherence à ses sentiments et un zèle qui le porte souvent hors du droict de sa charge qu'il ne faict aucune difficulté d'empieter sur le pouvoir des aultres et avec tant de chaleur qu'il n'écoute personne. Il enleva ces jours derniers une fille servente d'un habitant d'icy, et la mit de son autorité dans les Hursulines sur le seul prétexte qu'il vouloit la faire instruire, et par là il priva cet habitant du service qu'il prétendoit de sa servente qui luy avoit faict beaucoup de dépense a amener de France. Cet habitant est M.* Denis lequel ne cognoissant pas qui l'avoit soubstret me présenta requeste pour l'avoir. Je gardé [*sic*] la requeste sans la répondre trois jours pour empescher l'éclat de cette affaire. Le R. P. Lalement avec lequel j'en communiqué et lequel blasma fort le procedé de M.* de Petrée s'employa de tout son pouvoir pour la faire rendre sans bruit et n'y gaigna rien, si bien que je fus obligé de repondre la requeste et de permettre à cet habitant de reprendre sa servente où il la trouveroit, et si je n'eusse insinué soubs main d'accommoder cette affaire et que l'habitant a qui on refusa de la rendre l'eut poursuivi en justice j'eusse esté obligé de la luy rendre et de pousser tout avec beaucoup de scandal et cela (*à cause de*) la volonté de M.* de Petrée qui dict *qu'un evesque peult se qu'il veult, et ne menace que dexcommunication.*

Lettre de M. d'Argenson.

(*Extraits.*) *Papiers d'Argenson.*

Kebec le 7 Juillet, 1660.

M.* de Petrée a faist naistre cette contestation et ie puis dire auec verité que son zêle en plusieurs rencontres approche

fort d'une grande atache à son sentiment et d'empietement
sur la charge des aultres comme vous le verrez par un
billet icy joint. . . . De toutes ces contestations que i'ay
eu auec M.ʳ de Petrée i'ay tousjours faist le R. P. Lalemand
médiateur; c'est une personne d'un si grand merite et d'un
sens si achevé que ie pense qu'on ne peult rien y adjouter;
il seroit bien à souhaiter que touts ceux de sa maison
suivissent ses sentiments; ils ne se mesleroient pas de
censurer plusieurs choses comme ils font et laisseroient le
gouvernement des affaires a ceux que Dieu a ordonné pour
cela.

D.

PÉRONNE DUMESNIL.

Le Sieur Gaudais du Pont à Monseigneur de Colbert. 1664.

(*Extrait.*) *Archives de la Marine.*

Quelque 7 ou 8 jours après l'etablissement du Conseil
Souverain, en consequence des lettres patentes de Sa
majesté, le Procureur Général du dit Conseil jugeant qu'il
était de sa charge de reprendre les (*papiers*) de cette plainte
pour ne pas laisser un tel attentat impuni, fit sa requête
verbale au dit Conseil tendante à ce qu'il lui fut donné
commission pour informer contre le dit Sieur Du Mesnil; et
que si le dit Sieur Du Mesnil, avait avis de la dite commission qu'il ne manquerait pas de détourner ces dits papiers
demandant qu'il lui fut permis de saisir et de sequestrer ici
et apposer le sceau au coffre ou armoire en laquelle se
trouveraient les dits papiers, et pour ce faire qu'il plut au
dit Conseil nommer tel Commissaire qu'il jugerait à propos.

Le dit Conseil entérinant la requête du dit Procureur Général, nomma le Sieur de Villeray, pour, en la presence du dit Procureur Général et assistance de son Greffier vaquer à la dite information, &c.

Et d'autant que le dit Sieur Du Mesnil était estimé homme violent et qu'il pourrait faire quelque boutade, pour donner main forte à la justice, Mr. le Gouverneur fut prié par les dits Conseillers de faire escorter le dit Sieur Commissaire par quelque nombre de soldats.

Le dit Sieur de Villeray assisté, comme dit est pour l'execution de sa commission, se transporta au logis du dit Sieur Du Mesnil, laissant à quartier l'escorte de soldats pour s'en servir en cas de besoin.

Le dit Sieur Du Mesnil ne trompa pas l'opinion que l'on avait eue de sa violence, fit grand bruit, cria aux voleurs, voulant emouvoir son voisinage, outrageant d'injures les dits Sieurs de Villeray et Procureur Général au grand mépris de l'autorité du Conseil, refusant même de le reconnaître. Ce qui n'empêcha pas le dit Sieur de Villeray d'exécuter sa commission de saisir les papiers du dit Sieur Du Mesnil, qui en donna la clef, y fit apposer le sceau et icelui sequestrer es mains d'un voisin du dit Sieur Du Mesnil et de son consentement.

Le lendemain le dit Sieur de Villeray rapporta son procès verbal au dit conseil, attesté du dit Procureur Général, et signé du Greffier du dit Conseil et sur les injures, violences et irrévérences y contenues tant contre le dit Sieur Commissaire que l'autorité du Conseil, fit decerner un décret de prise de corps contre le dit Sieur Du Mesnil, dont j'empêchai l'exécution.

MEMOIRE DE DUMESNIL CONCERNANT LES AFFAIRES DU CANADA.

(*Extrait.*)   *Archives de la Marine.*

10 SEPTEMBRE, 1671.

Les dits Sieurs de Mésy, Gouverneur, de Pétrée, Evêque, et Dupont Gaudais, arrivés au dit Quebec le 16ᵉ jour de Septembre 1663, furent le lendemain salués et visités par le dit Du Mesnil précédent juge, lequel par devoir et civilité leur dit par forme d'avis que par des arrêts du conseil du Roi, qu'il leur représenta en date du 27 Mars 1647 et 13 Mai 1659 tous les commis et receveurs des dits deniers publics étaient exclus de toutes charges publiques, jusqu'à ce qu'ils eussent rendu et assuré leurs comptes, et le nommé Villeray chassé du conseil de la traite pour y avoir entré par voies et moyens illicites; et ordonné qu'il viendrait en France pour le purger de ses crimes; ce qu'il n'a pas fait, et pour nommer les autres commis, receveurs, auxquels il aurait commencé à faire le procès pendant qu'il était juge.

Nonobstant lesquels dires, actes et arrêts représentés, les dits Sieurs de Mésy, Evêque de Pétrée, et Dupont Gaudais, n'ont délaissé de prendre et admettre avec eux au dit Conseil Souverain les dits comptables; lesquels par ce moyen se prétendent à couvert et exempts de rendre les dits comptes. Le dit établissement de conseil fait et arrêté par les dits Commissaires le 18 du mois de Septembre, deux jours après leur arrivée; et pour Procureur Général prennent un nommé Jean Bourdon, boulanger et cannonier au fort et aussi comptable de 8 à 900,000 livres, comme il sera montré et qu'il a prêté son nom.

Le 20 du mois de Septembre, deux jours après l'établissement du dit conseil, les dits Villeray soi-disant conseiller et commissaire et Bourdon, Procureur Général accompagnés de deux sergents, d'un serrurier et de dix soldats du fort, bien

armés vont en la maison du dit Du Mesnil, Intendant et
Contrôleur Général, et peu auparavant leur juge souverain,
sur les 7 a 8 heures du soir pour piller sa maison ; ce qu'ils
firent ; ayant fait rompre la porte de son cabinet, ses
armoires et un coffret ; pris et emporté ce qu'ils ont trouvé
dedans et notamment tous ses papiers dans lesquels étaient
leurs procès presque faits, et les preuves de leurs péculats,
concussions et malversations, sans aucun inventaire ni forme
de justice, étant le dit Du Mesnil, lors des dites violences,
tenu et arrêté sur un siége et rudement traité par les soldats
jusques à l'empêcher d'appeler du secours et des témoins
pour voir ce qui se passait en sa maison et comme il était
lié et arrêté.

Cette action violente ainsi faite et le dit Du Mesnil se
voyant délivré du massacre de sa personne dont il était
menacé, et d'être assassiné comme son fils s'en va trouver le
dit Sieur Dupont Gaudais prenant qualité d'Intendant pour
lui en faire plainte, qu'il ne voulut entendre, disant que
c'était de son ordonnance et du dit Conseil que la dite action
et prise de papiers avait été faite ; à quoi le dit Du Mesnil
repartit qu'il s'en plaindrait au Roi, et lui en demanderait
justice, ce qui obligea le dit Dupont Gaudais de dire au dit
Du Mesnil qu'il donnât sa requête ; ce qui fut fait, et sur
laquelle fut par le dit Conseil ordonné le 22 du dit mois de
Septembre, deux jours après cette violence que le dit
Dupont Gaudais serait commissaire pour vérifier les faits
d'icelle requête ; ce que poursuivant le dit Du Mesnil, il
eut ordre verbal du dit Sr. Gaudais de mettre au Greffe ses
causes et moyens de récusation, de nullité de prise à partie
et de demandes ; ce que le dit Du Mesnil fit comme appert
par l'acte signé du Greffier du dit Conseil du 28 du dit mois
de Septembre sur lesquelles récusations, prises à partie et
demandes, le dit Conseil n'a rien voulu ordonner, comme
appert par autre acte du dit Greffier du 21 Octobre ensuivant,

jour ordonné pour l'embarquement et départ des vaisseaux du dit Quebec pour retourner en France.

Mais au lieu de statuer et ordonner sur les faits, moyens et conclusions du dit Du Mesnil, le dit Conseil sans plainte, sans partie et sans information a dressé emprisonnement du dit Du Mesnil et caché le décret sans le mettre au Greffe dans l'intention de le faire paraître et executer du même temps que le dit Du Mesnil se voudrait embarquer pour revenir en France, afin qu'il n'eût pas le temps de donner avis des violences qu'on lui faisait: de quoi averti il s'embarqua quelques jours auparavant les autres et fut reçu par le Capitaine Gardeur dans son navire, nonobstant les défenses qui lui en avaient été faites par le dit nouveau Conseil et que six pièces de canon de la plate forme d'en bas fussent pointées contre son navire pour le faire obéir à leurs ordonnances.

Tous ces massacres, assassins et pillages n'ont été faits au dit Du Mesnil, Intendant, par les dits comptables, ordonnateurs et preneurs de bien public et leurs parents et alliés que pour tâcher à couvrir et s'exempter de compter, payer et rendre ce qu'ils ont pillé, savoir. . . .

E.

LAVAL AND MÉSY.

Ordre de Mr de Mésy de faire sommation a l'Evêque de Pétrée.

(*Extrait.*)　*Registre du Conseil Supérieur.*

13 Fevrier, 1664.

Le Sieur d'Angoville, Major de la Garnison entretenue par le Roi dans le Fort de St Louis à Québec pays de la Nouvelle France, est commandé par nous Sieur de Mésy,

Lieutenant Général et Gouverneur pour Sa Majesté dans toute l'étendue du dit pays, aller dire et avertir Monsieur l'Evêque de Pétrée étant présentement dans la chambre qui servait ci-devant aux Assemblées du Conseil au dit pays, que les Sieurs nommés pour Conseillers et le Sieur Bourdon pour Procureur du Roi au dit conseil à la persuasion du dit Sieur de Pétrée qui les connaissait entièrement ses créatures s'étant voulu rendre les maîtres declarés et portés en diverses manières dans le dit Conseil contre les Intérêts du Roi et du public pour appuyer et autoriser les intérêts d'autrui en particulier, il leur a été commandé par notre ordre pour la conservation des intérêts du Roi en ce pays, de s'absenter du dit Conseil jusqu'à ce que à notre diligence par le retour des premiers vaisseaux qui viendront. Sa Majesté ait été informée de leur conduite, et qu'ils se soient justifiés des cabales qu'ils ont formées, fomentées et entretenues contre leur devoir et le serment de fidélité qu'ils étaient obligés de garder à Sa dite Majesté.

Priant le dit Sieur Evêque acquiescer à la dite interdiction pour le bien du service du Roi, et vouloir procéder par l'avis d'une Assemblée publique à nouvelle nomination des Conseillers en la place des dits Sieurs Interdits pour pouvoir rendre la justice aux peuples et habitants de ce pays, Déclarant que nous Sieur de Mésy ne pouvons en nommer aucun de notre part en la façon en laquelle nous avons été surpris par notre facilité lors de la première nomination manque d'une parfaite connaissance, et que s'il est fait quelque chose au préjudice de cet avertissement par aucun des dits Conseillers interdits, ils seront traités comme désobeissants, fomenteurs de rebellions et contraires au repos public.

 (Signé)   MÉSY.

Réponse de l'Eveque de Pétrée.

Registre du Conseil Supérieur.

16 Fev. 1664.

Laissant à part les paroles offensives et accusations injuri-
euses qui me regardent dans l'affiche mise au son du tambour
le treizième de ce mois de Fevrier, au poteau public, dont
je prétends me justifier devant Sa Majesté je réponds à la
prière que Monsieur le Gouverneur m'y fait d'agréer l'interdiction des personnes qui y sont comprises, et de vouloir
procéder à la nomination d'autres Conseillers ou Officiers
et ce par l'avis d'une assemblée publique, que ni ma conscience ni mon honneur, ni le respect et obéissance que je
dois aux volontés et commandements du Roi, ni la fidélité
et l'affection que je dois à son service ne me le permettent
aucunement jusques à ce que dans un jugement légitime
les desnommés dans la susdite affiche soient convaincus des
crimes dont on les y accuse.

A Quebec ce seizième Février mil-six-cent-soixante-
quatre.

(Signé)   FRANCOIS, EVÊQUE DE QUEBEC.

Enrégistré à la requête de Mgr. l'Evêque de Pétrée ce
16 Fevrier 1664 par moi Secrétaire au Conseil Souverain
soussigné.

(Signé)   .   PEUVRET, Secret^{re}
avec paraphe.

Lettre de Mésy aux Jésuites.

(Extrait.)   Collection de l'Abbé Ferland.

Comme ainsi soit que la gloire de Dieu, le service du
Roi et le service du public nous aient engagés de venir en
ce pays pour y rencontrer notre salut par la sollicitation de

M. l'Evêque de Pétrée qui nous a fait agréer au Roi pour avoir l'honneur d'être son Lieutenant Général et Gouverneur de toute la Nouvelle France, représenter sa personne dans le Conseil Souverain qu'il a établi dans ce dit pays pour exercer la justice, police et finance, ce qui nous tient lieu d'obligation vers mon dit Sieur l'Evêque pour lui donner des marques de reconnaissance en toutes rencontres. A quoi nous sommes aussi obligés par son mérite particulier et par le respect qui est dû à son caractère, mais qui ne doit entrer en nulle consideration pour le regard du service et de la fidélité que nous sommes obligé de rendre à S. M.; n'étant pas ni de notre conscience ni de notre honneur d'avoir accepté la commission dont il nous a honoré, pour n'en pas faire le deub de notre charge et de trahir les intérêts de Sa dite Majesté; lui en ayant fait le serment de fidélité entre ses mains et d'en avoir reçu le commandement par sa bouche. Pourquoi ayant rencontré plusieurs pratiques que nous avons cru en conscience par devoir être obligé d'en empêcher la suite, nous aurions fait publier notre déclaration du 13e jour de Février dernier, et ne l'ayant pu faire faire sans y intéresser le Sr Evêque, notre dite déclaration nous fait passer dans son esprit et de tous Messieurs les Ecclésiastiques qui considèrent ce point d'une prétendue offense sans avoir égard aucunement aux intérêts du Roy pour un calomniateur, mauvais juge, un ingrat et conscience erronnée et plusieurs autres termes injurieux qui se publient journellement contre l'autorité du Roy, en faisant un point de réprobation de la dite prétendue offense, un des principaux nous étant venu avertir que l'on nous pourrait faire fermer la porte des Eglises et nous empêcher de recevoir les Sts Sacrements, si nous ne réparions la dite prétendue offense, ce qui nous donne un scrupule en l'âme; et de plus ne pouvant nous adresser pour nous en éclaircir qu'à des personnes qui se déclarent nos parties et qui jugent

du fait sans en savoir la cause; mais n'y ayant rien de si important au monde que le salut et la fidélité que nous devons garder pour les intérêts du Roi que nous tenons inséparables l'un de l'autre, et reconnaissant qu'il n'y a rien de si certain que la mort et rien de si inconnu que l'heure, et que le temps est long pour informer Sa Majesté de ce qui se passe, pour en recevoir ses ordres, et qu'en attendant, une âme est toujours dans la crainte quoiqu'elle se connaisse dans l'innocence, nous sommes obligé avoir néanmoins recours aux Révérends Pères Casuistes de la maison de Jesus pour nous dire en leur conscience ce que nous pouvons pour la décharge de la nôtre et pour garder la fidélité que nous devons avoir pour le service du Roi, les priant qu'ils aient agréable signer ce qu'ils jugeront au bas de cet écrit, afin de nous servir de garantie vers sa Majesté.

Fait au Château de Quebec, ce dernier jour de Fevrier, 1664.

MÉSY.

SECTION THIRD.

F.

MARRIAGE AND POPULATION.

LETTRE DE COLBERT A TALON.

(*Extrait.*) *Archives de la Marine.*

PARIS, 20 FEVRIER, 1668.

SA Majesté a fait une gratification de 1500 livres à Mr de Lamotte, 1er Capitaine au Régiment de Carignan-Salières, tant en considération du service qu'il rend en Canada, de la construction des forts et de ses expéditions qui ont été faites contre les Iroquois, que du mariage qu'il a contracté dans le pays, et de la résolution qu'il a prise de s'y habituer. Elle a ordonné de plus la somme de 6000 livres pour être distribuées aux officiers des mêmes troupes, ou qui s'y sont dejà mariés ou qui s'y marieront afin de leur donner des moyens de s'établir et de mieux s'affermir dans la pensée ou ils sont de ne pas revenir en France. Elle fait un autre fond de 12,000 livres pour être distribué aux soldats qui resteront aux pays et qui s'y marieront, autres que ceux des quatre compagnies qu'elle y laisse, ces derniers étant entretenus par le paiement de leur solde. . . . 1200 livres pour celui des meilleurs habitants qui a 15 enfants, et 800 livres pour l'autre qui en a dix. Elle a aussi gratifié M. l'Evêque de Pétrée d'une somme de 6000 livres pour continuer à l'assister pour soutenir sa dignité, fournir aux besoins de son Eglise et de son séminaire, et enfin 40,000 livres pour être employées à la levée de 150 hommes et de 50 filles depuis 16 jusqu'a 30 ans et non au dela ; outre 235 que la Compagnie y fait passer cette année, et qui devaient y être passées l'année dernière ; 12 Cavales, 2 étalons, 2 gros ânes de Mirbelais et 50 brebis ; à quoi l'on travaille dans les provinces du royaume, et l'on n'oublie rien pour l'embarquement partant de la Rochelle vers la fin du mois prochain.

. . . Je vous prie de bien faire considérér à tout le pays que leur bien, leur subsistance, et tout ce qui peut les regarder de plus près dépend d'une résolution publique à laquelle il ne soit jamais contrevenu de marier les garçons à 18 ou 19 ans, et les filles à 14 ou 15 ans ; que les oppositions de n'avoir pas suffisamment pour vivre doivent être rejetées, parceque dans ces pays et le Canada premièrement où tout le monde travaille, il se produit pour tous la subsistance et que l'abondance ne peut jamais leur venir que par l'abondance des hommes. . . . Il serait bon de rendre les charges et servitudes doubles à l'égard des garçons qui ne se marieraient point à cet age . . . et à l'egard de ceux qui sembleraient avoir absolument renoncé au mariage, il serait à propos de leur augmenter les charges, de les priver de tous honneurs, même d'y ajouter quelque marque d'infamie.

. . . Bien que le Royaume de France soit autant peuplé qu'aucun pays du monde, il est certain qu'il serait difficile d'entretenir de grandes armées et de faire passer en même temps de grandes Colonies dans les pays éloignés. . . . Il faut donc se réduire à tirer seulement chaque année avec précaution un nombre d'habitants de l'un et de l'autre sexe, pour les envoyer au Canada, et fonder principalement l'augmentation de la colonie sur l'augmentation des mariages, à mesure que le nombre des colons augmentera.

Lettre de Talon a Colbert.

(Extrait.) *Archives de la Marine.*

10 Novembre, 1670.

. . . De toutes les filles venues cette année au nombre de 165, il n'en reste pas 30 à marier. Après que les soldats venus cette année auront travaillé à faire une habitation, il se porteront au mariage ; pour quoi il serait bon qu'il plût à Sa Majesté d'envoyer encore 150 à 200 filles.

. . . Il serait bon de recommander que les filles destinées à ce pays ne soient nullement disgrâciées de la nature, qu'elles n'aient rien de rebuttant à l'extérieur ; qu'elles soient saines et fortes pour le travail de campagne, ou du-moins qu'elles aient quelqu'industrie pour les ouvrages de main.

. . . Trois ou quatre filles de naissance et distinguées par la qualité serviraient peut-être utilement à lier par le mariage des officiers qui ne tiennent au pays que par les appointements et l'emolument de leurs terres, et qui par la disproportion des conditions ne s'engagent pas davantage. Si le Roi fait passer d'autres filles ou femmes veuves de l'Ancienne à la Nouvelle-France, il est bon de les faire accompagner d'un certificat de leur Curé ou du juge du lieu qui fasse connaître qu'elles sont libres et en état d'être mariées, sans quoi les Ecclésiastiques d'ici font difficulté de leur conférer ce sacrement ; à la vérité ce n'est pas sans raison, 2 ou 3 doubles mariages s'étant reconnus ici ; on pourrait prendre la même précaution pour les hommes veufs.

LETTRE DE TALON A COLBERT.

(*Extrait*.)   *Archives de la Marine.*

2 Novembre, 1671.

. . . Le nombre des enfants nés cette année est de 6 à 700. . . . J'estime qu'il n'est plus nécessaire de faire passer des demoiselles, en ayant reçu cette année quinze ainsi qualifiées au lieu de quatre que je demandais pour faire des alliances avec les officiers ou les principaux habitants d'ici. . . .

G.

CHÂTEAU ST. LOUIS.

THIS structure, destined to be famous in Canadian history, was originally built by Samuel de Champlain. The cellar still remains, under the wooden platform of the present Durham Terrace. Behind the château was the area of the fort, now an open square. In the most famous epoch of its history, the time of Frontenac, the château was old and dilapidated, and the fort was in a sad condition. "The walls are all down," writes Frontenac in 1681; "there are neither gates nor guard-house; the whole place is open." On this the new intendant, Meules, was ordered to report what repairs were needed. Meanwhile La Barre had come to replace Frontenac, whose complaints he repeats. He says that the wall is in ruin for a distance of a hundred and eighty *toises*. "The workmen ask 6,000 francs to repair it. I could get it done in France for 2,000. The cost frightens me. I have done nothing." (*La Barre au Ministre*, 1682.) Meules, however, received orders to do what was necessary; and, two years later, he reports that he has re-built the wall, repaired the fort, and erected a building, intended at first for the council, within the area. This building stood near the entrance of the present St. Louis Street, and was enclosed by an extension of the fort wall.

Denonville next appears on the scene, with his usual dis-position to fault-finding. The so-called château, he says (1685), is built of wood, "and is dry as a match. There is a place where with a bundle of straw it could be set on fire at any time; . . . some of the gates will not close; there is no watch-tower, and no place to shoot from." (*Denonville au Ministre*, 20 *Août*, 1685.)

When Frontenac resumed the government, he was much disturbed at the condition of the château, and begged for slate to cover the roof, as the rain was coming in everywhere. At the same time the intendant, Champigny, reports it to be rotten and ruinous. This was in the year made famous by the English attack and the dramatic scene in the hall of the old building, when Frontenac defied the envoy of Admiral Phipps, whose fleet lay in the river below. In the next summer, 1691, Frontenac again asks for slate to cover the roof, and for 15,000 or 20,000 francs to repair his mansion. In the next year the King promises to send him 12,000 francs, in instalments. Frontenac acknowledges the favor; and says that he will erect a new building, and try in the mean time not to be buried under the old one, as he expects to be every time the wind blows hard. (*Frontenac au Ministre*, 15 *Sept.*, 1692.) A misunderstanding with the intendant, who had control of the money, interrupted the work. Frontenac writes the next year that he had been obliged to send for carpenters, during the night, to prop up the château, lest he should be crushed under the ruins. The wall of the fort was however strengthened, and partly

32

rebuilt to the height of sixteen feet, at a cost of 13,629 francs. It was a time of war, and a fresh attack was expected from the English. (*Frontenac et Champigny au Ministre*, 4 *Nov.*, 1693.) In the year 1854, the workmen employed in demolishing a part of this wall, adjoining the garden of the château, found a copper plate bearing an inscription in Latin as follows: "In the year of Redemption 1693, under the reign of the most august, most invincible, and most Christian King of France, Louis the Great, fourteenth of that name, the most excellent Louis de Buade, Count of Frontenac, governor for the second time of all New France, seeing that the rebellious inhabitants of New England, who three years ago were repulsed, routed, and completely vanquished by him when they besieged this town of Quebec, are threatening to renew the siege this very year, has caused to be built, at the expense of the king, this citadel, with the fortifications adjoining thereto, for the defence of the country, for the security of the people, and for confounding yet again that nation perfidious alike towards its God and its lawful king. And he [Frontenac] has placed here this first stone."

A year later, the rebuilding of the château was begun in earnest. Frontenac says that nothing but a miracle has saved him from being buried under its ruins; that he has pulled everything down, and begun again from the foundation, but that the money has given out. (*Frontenac au Ministre*, 4 *Nov.*, 1694.) Accordingly, he and the intendant sold six licenses for the fur trade; but at a rate unusually low, for they brought only 4,400 francs. The King, hearing of this, sent 6,000 more. Frontenac is profuse in thanks; and at the same time begs for another 6,000 francs, "to complete a work which is the ornament and beauty of the city" (1696). The minister sent 8,000 more, which was soon gone; and Frontenac drew on the royal treasurer for 5,047 in addition. The intendant complains of his extravagance, and says that he will have nothing but perfection; and that, besides the château, he has insisted on building two guard-houses, with Mansard roofs, at the two sides of the gate. " I must do as he says," adds the intendant, " or there will be a quarrel." (*Champigny au Ministre*, 13 *Oct.*, 1697.) In a letter written two days after, Frontenac speaks with great complacency of his château, and asks for another 6,000 francs to finish it. As the case was urgent, he sold six more licenses, at 1,000 francs each; but he died too soon to see the completion of his favorite work (1698). The new château was not finished before 1700, and even then it had no cistern. In a pen-sketch of Quebec on a manuscript map of 1699, preserved in the Dépôt des Cartes de la Marine, the new château is distinctly represented. In front is a gallery or balcony, resting on a wall and buttresses at the edge of the cliff. Above the gallery is a range of high windows along the face of the building, and over these a range of small windows and a Mansard roof. In the middle is a porch opening on the gallery; and on the left extends a battery, on the ground now occupied by a garden along the brink of the cliff. A water-color sketch of the château taken in 1804, from the land-side, by William Morrison, Jr., is in my possession. The building appears to have been completely remodelled in the interval. It is two stories in height; the Mansard roof is gone, and a row of attic windows surmounts the second story. In 1809 it was again remodelled, at a cost of ten thousand pounds sterling. A third story was added; and the building, resting on the buttresses which still remain under the balustrade of Durham Terrace, had an imposing effect when seen from the river. It was destroyed by fire in 1834.

H.

TRADE AND INDUSTRY.

(Extrait.) *Archives de la Marine.*

LETTRE DE DENONVILLE AU MINISTRE.

A QUEBEC LE 13 NOVEMBRE, 1685.

. . . J'AI remarqué, Monseigneur que les femmes et filles, y sont assez paresseuses par le manque de menus ouvrages à se donner, il y a un peu trop de luxe dans la pauvreté génerale des demoiselles ou soi disantes; les menus ouvrages de capots et de chemises de traite les occupent un peu, pendant l'hiver, et leur font gagner quelque chose, mais cela ne dure pas, l'endroit de pauvreté de ce pays, est le manque de toilles et de serges ou draps, cependant c'est ici le pays du monde le plus propre à faire des chanvres, et du fil, et par consequent de la toille, si on s'en voulait donner la peine. Mr. Talon s'y est donné du soin pour cela, aussi y a-t-il une côte qui est celle de Beaupré, ou on en fait, mais ce n'est que chez quelques habitans. J'ai fort exorté la dessus tous les peuples d'y travailler, pour y réussir, il faut y apporter de la sévérité et de l'utilité si il y a moyen, ce dernier avec le temps et l'industrie arrivera, et le premier de ma part ne manquera pas, je n'ai pu avoir d'autre raison, pourquoi on ne faisait point de chanvres, si ce n'est que l'on n'avait pas assez de temps, à cause que les saisons de labourer, semer et recueillir sont trop courtes, car en ce pays le bled ne se sème qu'en Avril et May. Si le Roy voulait acheter les chanvres un peu plus cher jusques à ce que l'on fut en train, cela pourait les animer, avec un ordre à chacun d'en fournir une certaine quantité on pourra les faire agir, si outre cela on avait quelques ouvriers tisserands à distribuer par paroisses, et qui ne fussent à la charge du peuple

que pour leurs nouritures, ce serait un moyen pour faire apprendre aux enfants. Les Curés nous rendraient compte du nombre de ceux qui apprendraient à préparer la chanvre et fillasse, et à faire de la toille; avant que d'en venir là il faudrait montrer à filer aux filles et aux femmes, car il y en a très peu, qui sachent tenir le fuseau, c'est en cela que les filles de la congrégation de Montréal feront merveilles. Il nous est venu de la part de Mr. Arnoul deux bariques de graine de chanvre que je ferai distribuer et dont je me ferai rendre compte.

Je croyais, Monseigneur, une ordonnance necessaire encore à faire pour engager chaque habitant à avoir deux ou trois brebis, n'y en ayant pas suffisament dans le pays.

. . . Il n'est pas possible qu'on ne puisse faire une verrerie en ce pays, la plus grande affaire sont les ouvriers qui enchérissent tout car l'on donne ordinairement et communément à chaque ouvrier par jour quarente sols nouris, cinquante sols et un écu, et tous ces maraux n'en sont pas plus riches car ils mettent tout à boire.

(Signé)   LE M^{quis} DE DENONVILLE.

MÉMOIRE A MONSEIGNEUR LE MARQUIS DE SEIGNELAY,
SUR L'ÉTABLISSEMENT DU COMMERCE EN CANADA,
PRÉSENTÉ PAR LES SIEURS CHALONS ET RIVERIN.

(*Extrait.*)   *Archives de la Marine.*

(JOINT A LA LETTRE DU SIEUR DE RIVERIN, DU 7 FEVRIER, 1686.)

. . . En effet si cette colonie n'a pas avancé depuis le temps de son établissement, c'est que les habitants qui la composent ou par leur négligence ou par leur peu d'expérience dans les affaires, ou enfin par leur impuissance ne se sont pas mis en estat de se servir des avantages qu'elle renferme

en elle-mesme, et des moyens qu'elle leur fournit pour **un**
commerce solide et considerable.

Car il ne faut pas regarder la traitte des pelleteries à
laquelle seule on s'est attaché jusqu'à présent et qui finira
avec le temps par la destruction des bestes, comme un
moyen propre à son avancement, au contraire l'expérience a
fait connoistre qu'elle rend les habitans fainéans et vagabonds, qu'elle les détourne de la culture des terres, de la
pesche, de la navigation et des autres entreprises.

MÉMOIRE DU SIEUR DE CATALOGNE, INGÉNIEUR, SUR LES
PLANS DES HABITATIONS ET SEIGNEURIES DES GOU-
VERNEMENS DE QUEBEC, DE MONTRÉAL ET DES TROIS-
RIVIÈRES.

(*Extrait.*[1])   *Archives de la Marine.*

7 NOVEMBRE, 1712.

. . . .

Observations sur l'établissement. — Que par rapport à
la grande étendue qu'on a donnée à l'établissement, il n'y a
pas le quart des ouvriers qu'il faudroit pour bien étendre et
cultiver les terres.

Que les laboureurs ne se donnent pas assez de soin pour
cultiver les terres, étant certain que la semence d'un minot
de blé, semé sur de la terre cultivée comme en France,
produira plus que deux autres comme on sème en Canada.

Que comme les saisons sont trop courtes et souvent très
mauvaises, il serait à souhaiter que l'Eglise permit les
travaux indispensables, que les fêtes d'été obligent de
chômer, étant très vrai que depuis le mois de Mai que les
semences commencent jusques à la fin de Septembre, il n'y

---

[1] This *mémoire* is 70 pages in length.

a pas 90 journées de travail, par rapport aux fêtes et au mauvais temps. C'est pourtant dans cette espace que roule la solidité de cet établissement. Il faudrait assujetir les habitans négligens à travailler à la culture des terres, en les privant des voyages qui les dispensent de travailler, et cela parce qu'un voyage de deux ou trois mois leur produit 30 ou 40 escus en perdant la saison du travail à la terre, qui les fait demeurer en friche.

Les obliger de semer quantité de chanvre et lin qui vient en ce pays plus gros qu'en Europe. Ils s'en relâchent parceque, disent-ils, il y a trop de peine et de soins à le mettre en œuvre. Il est vrai qu'il y a peu de gens qui s'entendent et qui le font payer bien cher.

Assujetir les habitans à nourrir et à élever des bêtes à cornes, au lieu du grand nombre de chevaux qui ruinent le Pacage et qui entrainent les habitans à des grosses dépenses, tant que pour leurs équipages qui sont fort chers que par la grande quantité de fourages et de grains qu'il faut pendant 7 ou 8 mois de l'année, étant très vrai que l'entretien d'un cheval coûte autant que deux bœufs.

Obliger les Seigneurs pour faciliter l'établissement de leurs Seigneuries de donner suffisamment des terres pour commencer à un prix modique et à construire des moulins et les commodités publiques; plusieurs consomment le tiers de leur temps à aller faires leur farines à 15 ou 20 lieues, et que les Seigneurs, dès que les Seigneuries sont établies, concèdent des terres sans que les tenanciers soient obligés de payer des rentes qu'après 6 ans que les terres soient en valeur.

Ordonner au grand voyer de donner son application à faire établir les chemins et ponts nécessaires au public, qui est une nécessité fort essentielle.

Obliger les habitans ou ceux qui sont en état, de faire des greniers pourque chacun fût en état de conserver du

grain pour deux années; cela fait une fois, l'abondance se trouvera toujours au Canada au lieu que la plupart, faute de cette commodité, en manquent très souvent, étant obligé de le vendre à vil prix.

Châtier sévérement tous ceux qui sont convaincus de fraude, mauvaise foi et imposture, qui est un mal qui commence à être bien en racine et qui indubitablement le privera de tout commerce, les marchands des îles et de Plaisance s'en étant déjà plaints.

Que comme il n'y a pas de notaires dans tous les lieux, que les conventions et les marchés faits en présence de deux témoins vaudront pendant un temps fixé.

Il serait à souhaiter que S. M. voulût établir dans chaque ville des conseils à juger sans frais sur le fait du commerce et des affaires qui n'entrent pas dans la coutume. Ces sortes de procédures aussi bien que les autres, ne prennent aucune fin que lorsque les parties n'ont plus d'argent pour plaider, qui est la ruine des familles.

Engager un certain nombre de gens du pays à étudier le pilotage, même les officiers des troupes, particulièrement du fleuve St. Laurent qui est très dangereux, la plupart du temps ne se trouvant pas un seul pilote en Canada, et cependant on commence à donner dans la construction; le capitaine du Port et M. Duplessis ayant mis un vaisseau de 3 à 400 tonneaux sur les chantiers.

Congédier de temps en temps des soldats en leur permettant de se marier, après qu'ils auront un établissement.

Il s'est établi une coutume dans ce pays autorisée par le magistrat, qui même ne me parait pas naturelle, de laisser des bestiaux à l'abandon qui la plupart gâtent les grains et les prairies, n'y ayant presque point de terres closes qui causent des contestes et de la mesintelligence entre les voisins; pour obvier à cela il faudrait qu'il y eut des gardiens pour chaque nature d'animaux pour les mener

dans les communes, car tel qui n'a pas un pouce de terre, envoie ses animaux paître sur les terres de ses voisins, en disant que l'abandon est donné; si S. M. voulait couper la racine à une pépinière de procès et de mésintelligence entre les Seigneurs et habitans, il serait à souhaiter qu'elle voulut donner une ordonnance tendante à ce que les Seigneuries et autres concessions demeureraient dans les limites qu'elles se trouvent à présent, sans avoir égard aux titres portés dans les contrats, pour la quantité et les rumbs de vent qui y sont annoncés, étant à remarquer que les anciens Seigneurs et habitans se sont établis de bonne foi, que les terres ont été limitées par des arpenteurs peu intelligens, et aujourd'hui que la chicane est en vogue, chacun veut suivre les termes de son contrat qui tendent la plupart à l'impossible. Mr. Raudot a donné une ordonnance à ce sujet pour l'île de Montréal seulement.

Comme la plupart des rues de Quebec et de Montréal sont souvent impraticables, tant par les rochers que par les bourbiers, s'il plaisait à S. M. d'ordonner que les deniers qui proviennent des amendes et certaines confiscations seraient employés à les mettre en état.

Que la subordination du vassal à son Seigneur n'est point objet à   . Cette erreur vient qu'il a été accordé des Seigneuries à des roturiers qui non pas su maintenir le droit que la raison leur donne à l'égard de leur co-sujets, même les officiers de milice qui leur sont dépendants, n'ont la plupart aucun égard pour leur superiorité et veulent dans les occasions passer pour indépendants.

Il serait à souhaiter que S. M. voulût envoyer dans ce pays toute sorte d'artisans, particulièrement des ouvriers en cordages et filages, des potiers et un verrier, et ils trouveraient à s'occuper. Si S. M. voulait faire envoyer en marchandises une partie des appointemens de Messrs. les officiers, cela leur adoucirait la dureté qu'eux seuls trouvent

dans le pays, par la grande cherté des marchandises causée
par le mauvais retour de la monnaie de cartes qui fait
acheter 3 et 4 pour 100.

     Veu: Vaudreuil.

     Veu: Bégon.   Catalogne.

I.

LETTER OF FATHER CARHEIL.

Lettre du Père Etienne de Carheil, de la Compagnie de Jésus, a l'Intendant de Champigny.

(*Extrait.*)[1] *Archives Nationales.*

A Michilimakina, le 30 d'Aoust, 1702.

. . . Nos Missions sont réduites à une telle extrémité,
que nous ne pouvons plus les soutenir contre une multitude
infinie de désordres, de brutalitez, de violences, d'injustices,
d'impietez, d'impudicitez, d'insolences, de mépris, d'insultes
que l'infâme et funeste traitte d'eau-de-vie y cause univer-
sellement dans toutes les nations d'icy haut, où l'on vient
la faire, allant de villages en villages et courant les lacs
avec une quantité prodigieuse de barils, sans garder aucune
mesure. Si Sa Majesté avoit veu une seule fois ce qui se
passe et icy et à Montréal, dans tous les temps qu'on y fait
cette malheureuse traitte, je suis sur qu'elle ne balanceroit
pas un moment, dès la première vue, à la déffendre pour
jamais sous les plus rigoureuses peines.

Dans le désespoir où nous sommes, il ne nous reste point
d'autre party à prendre que celui de quitter nos Missions et
de les abandonner aux traittants d'eau-de-vie, pour y établir

---

[1] This letter is 45 pages long.

le domaine de leur traitte, de l'ivrognerie et de l'impureté.
C'est ce que nous allons proposer à nos supérieurs en
Canada et en France, y étant contraints par l'état d'inutilité
et d'impuissance de faire aucun fruit où l'on nous a réduits
par la permission de cette déplorable traitte, permission que
l'on n'a obtenue de Sa Majesté que sous un pretexte aparent
de raisons que l'on scait être fausses, permission qu'elle
n'accorderoit point, si ceux auxquels elle se raporte de la
vérité la lui fesoient connoistre comme ils la connoissent
eux-mêmes et tout le Canada avec eux, permission enfin
qui est le plus grand mal et le principe de tous les maux qui
arrivent présentement au pays, et surtout des naufrages
dont on n'entendoit point encore parler ici et que nous
apprenons arriver maintenant presque touttes les années ou
dans la venue ou dans le retour de nos vaisseaux en France,
par une juste punition de Dieu qui fait périr par l'eau ce
que l'on avoit mal acquis par l'eau-de-vie, ou qui entend
empêcher le transport pour prévenir le mauvais usage qu'on
en feroit. Si cette permission n'est révoquée par une déf-
fense contraire, nous n'aurons plus que faire de demeurer
dans aucune de nos Missions d'icy haut, pour y perdre le
reste de notre vie, et touttes nos peines dans une pure
inutilité sous l'empire d'une continuelle ivrognerie et d'une
impureté universelle qu'on ne permet pas moins aux traitteurs d'eau-de-vie que la traitte même dont elle est l'accom-
pagnement et la suite. Si Sa Majesté veut sauver nos
missions et soutenir l'établissement de la Religion, comme
nous ne doutons point qu'elle le veuille, nous la suplions
très-humblement de croire, ce qui est très véritable, qu'il
n'y a point d'autre moyen de le pouvoir faire que d'abolir
les deux infâmes commerces qui les ont réduites à la nécessité prochaine de périr et qui ne tarderont pas à achever de
les perdre, s'ils ne sont au plus tost abolis par ses ordres et
mis hors d'état d'être rétablis. Le premier est le commerce

de l'eau-de-vie; le second est le commerce des femmes sauvages avec les François, qui sont tous deux aussy publics l'un que l'autre, sans que nous puissions y remédier, pour n'estre pas appuyez des commandans qui, bien loin de les vouloir empêcher par les remontrances que nous leur faisons, les exercent eux-mêmes avec plus de liberté que leurs inférieurs, et les autorisent tellement par leur exemple qu'en le regardant on s'en fait une permission générale et une assurance d'impunité qui les rend communs à tout ce qui vient icy de François en traitte, de sorte que tous les villages de nos Sauvages ne sont plus que des cabarets pour l'ivrognerie et des Sodomes pour l'impureté, d'où il faut que nous nous retirions, les abandonnant à la juste colère de Dieu et à ses vengeances.

Vous voyez par là que, de quelque manière qu'on établisse le commerce François avec les Sauvages, si l'on veut nous retenir parmi eux, nous y conserver et nous y soutenir en qualité de missionnaires dans le libre exercice de nos fonctions avec espérance d'y faire du fruit, il faut nous délivrer des commandans et de leur garnisons qui, bien loin d'estre nécessaires, sont au contraire si pernicieuses que nous pouvons dire avec vérité qu'elles sont le plus grand mal de nos missions, ne servant qu'à nuire à la traitte ordinaire des voyageurs et à l'avancement de la Foy. Depuis qu'elles sont venues icy haut, nous n'y avons plus veu que corruption universelle qu'elles ont répandues par leur vie scandaleuse dans tous les esprits de ces nations qui en sont présentement infectées. Tout le service prétendu qu'on veut faire croire au Roy qu'elles rendent se réduit à quatre principales occupations dont nous vous prions instamment de vouloir bien informer le Roy.

La première est de tenir un cabaret public d'eau-de-vie où ils la traittent continuellement aux Sauvages qui ne cessent point de s'enyvrer, quelques opositions que nous y puissions faire. C'est en vain que nous leur parlons pour les arrêter; nous n'y gagnons rien que d'être accusez de nous oposer nous-mêmes au Service du Roy en voulant empêcher une traitte qui leur est permise.

La seconde occupation des soldats est d'estre envoyez d'un poste à l'autre par les Commandans, pour y porter leurs marchandises et leur eau-de-vie, après s'être accommodés ensemble, sans que les uns et les autres ayent d'autre soin que celuy de s'entr'ayder mutuellement dans leur commerce, et afin que cela s'exécute plus facilement des deux costez comme ils le souhaitent, ils faut que les commandans se ferment les yeux pour user de connivence et ne voir aucun des désordres de leur soldats, quelques visibles, publics et scandaleux qu'ils soient, et il faut réciproquement que les soldats, outre qu'ils traittent leurs propres marchandises, se fassent encore les traitteurs de celles de leurs Commandans qui souvent même les obligent d'en acheter d'eux pour leur permettre d'aller où ils veulent.

Leur troisième occupation est de faire de leur fort un lieu que j'ay honte d'apeler par son nom, où les femmes ont apris que leurs corps pouvoient tenir lieu de marchandises et qu'elles seroient mieux reçues que le castor, de sorte que c'est présentement le commerce le plus ordinaire, le plus continuel et le plus en vogue. Quelques efforts que puissent faire tous les missionnaires pour décrier et pour l'abolir, au lieu de diminuer, il augmente et se multiplie tous les jours de plus en plus; tous les soldats tiennent table ouverte à toutes les femmes de leur connaissance dans leur maison; depuis le matin jusqu'au soir, elles y passent les journées entières, les unes après les autres, assises à leur feu et souvent sur leur lit dans des entretiens et des actions propre de leur commerce qui ne s'achève ordinairement que la nuit, la foule étant trop grande pendant la journée pour qu'ils puissent l'achever, quoyque souvent aussy ils s'entrelaissent

une maison vide de monde pour n'en pas différer l'achêve-
ment jusqu'à la nuit.

La quatrième occupation des soldats est celle du jeu qui a
lieu dans les tems où les traitteurs se rassemblent; il y va
quelquefois à un tel point que n'étans pas contens d'y passer
le jour, ils y passent encore la nuit entière, et il n'arrive
même que trop souvent dans l'ardeur de l'aplication qu'ils
ne se souviennent pas, ou s'ils s'en souviennent, qu'ils
méprisent de garder les postes. Mais ce qui augmente en
cela leur désordre, c'est qu'un attachement si opiniâtre au
jeu n'est presque jamais sans une ivrognerie commune à
tous les joueurs, et que l'ivrognerie est presque toujours
suivie de querelles qui s'excitent entre eux lesquelles venant
à paroître publiquement aux yeux des Sauvages, causent
parmi eux trois grands scandales: le premier de les voir
ivres, le second de les voir s'entrebatre avec fureur les uns
contre les autres jusqu'à prendre des fusils en main pour
s'entretuer, le troisième de voir que les Missionnaires n'y
peuvent apporter aucun remède.

Voila, Monseigneur, les quatre seules ocupations des garnisons que l'on a tenues ici pendant tant d'années. Si ces
sortes d'ocupations peuvent s'apeler le service du Roy,
j'avoue qu'elles luy ont actuellement et toujours rendu
quelqu'un de ces quatre services, mais je n'en ai point veu
d'autres que ces quatre-là; et par conséquent, si on ne juge
pas que ce soit là des services nécessaires au Roy, il n'y a
point eu jusqu'à présent de nécessité de les tenir icy, et
après leur rapel, il n'y en aura point de les y rétablir.

Cependant comme cette nécessité prétendue des Garnisons
est l'unique pretexte que l'on prend pour y envoyer des
Commandans, nous vous prions, Monseigneur, d'être bien
persuadé de la fausseté de ce prétexte, afin que, sous ces
spécieuses aparences du service du Roy, on ne se fasse pas
une obligation d'en envoyer, puisque les Commandans ne

viennent icy que pour y faire la traitte de concert avec leurs
soldats sans se mettre en peine de tout le reste.   Ils n'ont
de liaison avec les Missionnaires que par les endroits où ils
les croient utiles pour leur temporel, et hors de là ils leur
sont contraires dès qu'ils veulent s'opposer au désordre qui,
ne s'accordant ny avec le service de Dieu ny avec le service
du Roy, ne laisse pas d'être avantageux à leur commerce,
au quel il n'est rien qu'ils ne sacrifient.   C'est là l'unique
cause qui a mis le déréglement dans nos Missions, et qui les
a tellement désolées par l'ascendant que les Commandans
ont pris sur les Missionnaires en s'attirant toute l'autorité
soit à l'égard des François, soit à l'égard des Sauvages, que
nous n'avons pas d'autre pouvoir que celui d'y travailler
inutilement sous leur domination qui s'est élevée jusqu'à
nous pour nous faire des crimes civils et des accusations
prétendues juridiques des propres fonctions de notre état et
de notre devoir, comme l'a toujours fait Monsieur de la
Motte qui ne voulait pas même que nous nous servissions
du mot de désordre et qui intente en effet procez au père
Pinet pour s'en être servi.

. . . Vous voyez, Monseigneur, que je me suis beaucoup étendu sur les articles des Commandans et des garnisons pour vous faire comprendre que c'est là qu'est venu
tout le malheur de nos Missions.   Ce sont les Commandans,
ce sont les garnisons, qui, se joignant avec les traitteurs
d'eau-de-vie les ont entièrement désolées par l'ivrognerie et
par une impudicité presque universelle que l'on y a établie
par une continuelle impunité de l'une et de l'autre, que les
puissances civiles ne tolèrent pas seulement, mais qu'elles
permettent, puisque les pouvant empêcher, elles ne les
empêchent pas.   Je ne crains donc point de vous déclarer
que si l'on remet icy haut dans nos missions des Commandans traitteurs et des garnisons de soldats traitteurs, nous
ne doutons point que nous ne soyons contraints de les

quitter, n'y pouvant rien faire pour le salut des âmes. C'est à vous d'informer Sa Majesté de l'extrémité où l'on nous réduit et de luy demander pour nous notre délivrance, afin que nous puissions travailler à l'établissement de la Religion sans ces empêchemens qui l'ont arrêté jusqu'à présent.

J.

THE GOVERNMENT AND THE CLERGY.

Mémoire de Talon sur l'Etat présent du Canada, 1667.

(*Extrait.*)   *Archives de la Marine.*

. . . L'Ecclésiastique est composé d'un Evesque, ayant le tiltre de Pétrée, In partibus infidelium, et se servant du caractère et de l'autorité de Vicaire Apostolique.

Il a soubs [*sous*] luy neuf Prestres, et plusieurs clercs qui vivent en communauté quand ils sont près de lui dans son Séminaire, et séparément à la campagne quand ils y sont envoyez par voye de mission pour desservir les cures qui ne sont pas encore fondées. Il y a pareillement les Pères de la Compagnie de Jésus, au nombre de trente-cinq, la pluspart desquels sont employez aux Missions étrangères: ouvrage digne de leur zèle et de leur piété s'il est exempt du meslange de l'intérest dont on les dit susceptibles, par la traitte des pelleteries qu'on assure qu'ils font aux 8ta8aks [*Outaouaks*], et au Cap de la Magdelaine; ce que je ne sçay pas de science certaine.

La vie de ces Ecclésiastiques, par tout ce qui paroist au dehors, est fort réglée, et peut servir de bon exemple et d'un bon modèle aux séculiers qui la peuvent imiter; mais comme ceux qui composent cette Colonie ne sont pas tous d'esgale force, ny de vertu pareille, ou n'ont pas tous les mesmes dispositions au bien, quelques-uns tombent aysément dans leur disgrâce pour ne pas se conformer à leur manière de vivre, ne pas suivre tous leurs sentimens, et ne s'abandonner pas à leur conduite qu'ils estendent jusques sur le temporel, empiétant mesme sur la police extérieure qui regarde le seul magistrat.

On a lieu de soupconner que la pratique dans laquelle ils sont, qui n'est pas bien conforme à celle des Ecclésiastiques de l'Ancienne France, a pour but de partager l'autorité temporelle qui, jusques au temps de l'arrivée des troupes du Roy en Canada, résidoit principalement en leur personnes.

À ce mal qui va jusques à géhenner [*gêner*] et contraindre les consciences, et par là desgoûter les colons les plus attachez au pays, on peut donner pour remède l'ordre de balancer avec adresse et modération cette autorité par celle qui réside ez [*dans les*] personnes envoyées par Sa Majesté pour le Gouvernement: ce qui a desjà été pratiqué; de permettre de renvoyer un ou deux Ecclésiastiques de ceux qui reconnoissent moins cette autorité temporelle, et qui troublent le plus par leur conduite le repos de la Colonie, et introduire quatre Ecclésiastiques entre les séculiers ou les réguliers, les faisant bien autoriser pour l'administration des Sacremens, sans qu'ils puissent estre inquiétez: autrement ils deviendroient inutiles au pays, parce que s'ils ne se conformoient pas à la pratique de ceux qui y sont aujourd'huy M. l'Evesque leur deffendroit d'administrer les Sacremens.

Pour estre mieux informé de cette conduite des consciences, on peut entendre Monsieur Dubois, Aumosnier au régiment de Carignan, qui a ouy plusieurs Confessions en secret, et a la desrobée, et Monsieur de Bretonvilliers sur ce qu'il a appris par les Ecclésiastiques de son Séminaire establi à Mont-Réal.   33

Lettre du Ministre a Mr. Talon, 20 Fevrier, 1668.

(Extrait.)   *Archives de la Marine.*

. . . Il faut que l'application d'un Gouverneur et d'un Intendant aide a adoucir le mal, et non à l'effet que le Gouverneur ne se porte à aucune extrémité, contre les Sieurs Evêque et les P. P. Jésuites, quand bien même ils auraient abusé du pouvoir que leur habit et le respect qu'on a naturellement pour la religion leur donne.   En se contentant par des conférences particulières de resserrer ce pouvoir, autant que se pourra, dans les bornes d'une légitime autorité et espérant que, quand le pays sera plus peuplé, qui est la seule et unique chose que doit convier le dit Sr. Gouverneur et Intendant à y donner leurs soins quand à présent, l'autorité Royale qui sera la plus reconnue des peuples prévaudra sur l'autre et la contiendra dans de justes limites.

. . . Je ne m'explique point avec vous sur ce sujet, parceque je sais qu'à part ses bonnes qualités il [*M. de Courcelle*] a usé d'emportement dont il est bon qu'il se corrige.   Insinuez lui aussi honnêtement les sentiments qu'il doit avoir et ce que je viens de vous dire au sujet du Sieur de Ressan, et qu'il ne doit jamais blâmer la conduite de l'Evêque de Pétrée ni des Jésuites en public, étant assez d'en user avec eux avec grande circonspection, se contentant seulement lorsqu'ils entreprendront trop de leur faire connaître et d'en envoyer des mémoires, afin que je confère avec leurs Supérieurs de ces entreprises et en cas qu'ils en fassent qu'on puisse les interdire.

Instruction pour M. de Bouteroue, 1668.

(*Extrait.*)   *Archives de la Marine.*

Il faut empescher autant qu'il se pourra la trop grande quantité des prestres, religieux, et religieuses . . . s'entremettre quelquefois et dans les occasions pour les porter à adoucir cette trop grande séverité, estant très-important que lesdits evesque et Jésuites ne s'aperçoivent jamais qu'il veuille blasmer leur conduite.

(Signé)   Colbert.

For the instructions on this subject, more precise and emphatic than the above, given by the King to Talon in 1665, see N. Y. Colonial Docs., ix. 24.

Lettre de Colbert a Duchesneau, 15 Avril, 1676.

(*Extrait.*)   *Archives de la Marine.*

Eviter les contestations . . . sans toutefois préjudicier aux précautions qui sont à prendre et aux mesures à garder pour empescher que la puissance ecclésiastique n'entreprenne rien sur la temporelle, à quoy les ecclésiastiques sont assez portés.

Lettre du Ministre a Duchesneau, le 28 Avril, 1677.

(*Extrait.*)   *Archives de la Marine.*

. . . Je vous dirai premièrement que Sa Majesté est bien persuadée de la piété de tous les Ecclésiastiques et de leurs bonnes intentions pour le succez du sujet de leurs missions,

mais Sa Majesté veut que vous preniez garde qu'ils n'entre-
prennent rien tant sur son authorité Royalle que sur la
justice et police du pays et que vous les resserriez précise-
ment dans les bornes de l'authorité que les Ecclésiastiques
ont dans le Royaume, sans souffrir qu'ils les passent en
quelque sorte et manière que ce soit, et cette maxime géné-
ralle vous doit servir pour toutes les difficultez de cette
nature qui pourront survenir; mais pour parvenir à ce point
il seroit nécessaire que vous-mesme vous travailliassiez à
vous rendre habil sur ces matières en lisant les autheurs qui
en ont traitté, observer tout ce qui se passe et à envoyer
tous les ans des mémoires sur les difficultez que vous aurez
et auxquelles vous n'aurez pas pu remédier; considerez cette
matière comme très importante et à laquelle vous ne sçauriez
donner trop d'application.

Lettre du Ministre a Duchesneau, le premier May, 1677.

(*Extrait.*) *Archives de la Marine.*

. . . Je suis encore obligé de vous dire que l'on voit claire‧
ment qu'encore que le dit Sieur Evesque soit un homme
de bien et qu'il fasse fort bien son devoir, il ne laisse pas
d'affecter une domination qui passe de beaucoup au delà
des bornes que les Evesques ont dans tout le monde
chrestien et particulièrement dans le Royaume et ainsy
vous devez vous appliquer à bien connoistre et à sçavoir
le plus parfaitement que vous pourrez l'estendue du pouvoir
des Evesques et les remèdes que l'authorité Royalle a
apporté pour en empescher l'abus et leur trop grande
domination, afin que vous puissiez de concert avec Monsieur
le Comte de Frontenac dans les occasions importantes y
apporter les mesmes remèdes, en quoy vous devez toujours

les jours pour renverser le plan et les projets d'un Gouverneur. Il faut une tête aussi ferme et aussi plombée que
celle de Monsieur le Comte pour se soutenir contres les
ambusches que partout on lui dresse; s'il veut la paix cela
suffit pour qu'on s'y oppose et qu'on crie que tout est perdu;
s'il veut faire la guerre, on lui expose la ruine de la collonie.
Il n'auroit pas tant d'affaires sur les bras, s'il n'avoit pas
aboli un Hiericho qui etait une maison que Messieurs du
Séminaire de Montreal avoient fait bâtir pour renfermer,
disoient-ils, les filles de mauvaise vie. S'il avoit voulu leur
permettre de prendre des soldats et leur donner des officiers
pour aller dans les maisons arracher des femmes à minuit et
couchées avec leurs maris, pour avoir été au bal ou en
masque et les faire fesser jusques au sang dans ce Hiericho;
s'il n'avait rien dit encore contre des Curés qui faisoient la
ronde avec des soldats et qui obligeoient en esté les filles et
les femmes à se renfermer à neuf heures chez elles, s'il avoit
voulu déffendre de porter de la dentelle, s'il n'avoit rien dit
sur ce qu'on refusoit la communion à des femmes de qualité
pour avoir une fontange, s'il ne s'opposoit point encore aux
excommunications qu'on jette à tort et à travers, aux scandales qui s'en suivent, s'il ne faisoit les officiers que par la
voye des communautés, s'il vouloit déffendre le vin et l'eau
de vie aux sauvages, s'il ne disoit mot sur le sujet des cures
fixes et droits de patronage, si Monsieur le Comte estoit de
ces avis-là, ce seroit assurément un homme sans pareil et il
seroit bientôt sur la liste des plus grands saints, car on les
canonise dans ce pais à bon marché.

K.

CANADIAN CURÉS. EDUCATION. DISCIPLINE.

LETTRE DU MARQUIS DE DENONVILLE AU MINISTRE.

(*Extrait.*) *Archives de la Marine.*

A QUEBEC 15 NOVEMBRE, 1685.

. . . Vous me permettrez, Monseigneur, de vous demander la grâce de faire quelques réflections sur les moyens d'occuper la jeunesse du pays, dans son bas âge, et dans l'âge le plus avancé, que je vous rende compte de mes pensées la dessus, puisque c'est une des choses la plus essentielle de la colonie.

Pour y parvenir, Monseigneur, le premier moyen à mon gré, est de multiplier le nombre des Curés, et de les rendre plus fixes et résidentaires, Mr. notre Evêque en est si convaincu par la connaissance qu'il a prise de son diocèse dans ses visites, et dans le voyage que nous avons fait ensemble, qu'il n'a point de plus grand empressement que de pouvoir contribuer à cet établissement qui serait un moyen sur, pour faire des écoles, auxquelles les curés s'occuperaient et ainsi accoutumeraient les enfans de bonne heure à s'assugétir et à s'occuper: Mais, Monseigneur, pour faire cet établissement utilement, il faudrait multiplier le nombre des curés jusques au nombre de cinquante et un. Le mémoire que je vous en envoye, vous fera assez bien voir, que si on les étend davantage et qu'il faille que les curés passent et repassent la rivière, comme ils font à présent pour faire leurs fonctions, ils employent avec bien du travail tout le temps qu'ils pourraient donner à instruire la jeunesse, si leurs cures étaient moins étendues. Outre cela, Monseigneur, à l'entrée

et à la sortie de l'hiver, il y a près de deux mois que l'on ne saurait passer la rivière, qui en bien des endroits a une lieue de largeur, et beaucoup plus en d'autres. Si bien que dans ces temps il faut que les malades demeurent sans aucun secours spirituel.

C'est une pitié, Monseigneur, que de voir l'ignorance dans laquelle les peuples éloignés du séjour des Curés vivent en ce pays, et les peines que les missionnaires et Curés se donnent pour y remédier en parcourant leurs cures, sur le pied qu'elles sont selon le mémoire que je vous en envoye. Vous y verrez, Monseigneur, le chemin qu'il leur faut faire pour visiter leurs paroisses dans les rigueurs de l'hiver.

Puisque j'ai entamé l'affaire des Curés vous me permettrez d'achever de vous dire que pour la subsistance d'un curé selon les connaissances que j'ai pu prendre du pays, depuis que j'y suis, selon le prix des denrées, on ne saurait donner moins à un curé pour sa subsistance que quatre cents livres, monoye de France, attendu qu'il ne faut pas compter sur aucun revenant bon du dedans de l'Eglise. Il est bien vrai qu'il y a quelques cures qui sont mieux peuplées dont les dismes sont assez raisonables pour pouvoir suffir à leur entretien, mais il y en a très peu sur ce pied là.

J'ai trouvé ici dans le Séminaire de l'Evêché, le commencement de deux établissements qui seraient admirables pour la Colonie, si on les pouvait augmenter, ce sont, Monseigneur, deux maisons où l'on retire des enfans pour les instruire, dans l'une on y met ceux auxquels on trouve de la disposition pour les lettres, auxquelles on s'attache de les former pour l'Eglise, qui dans la suite peuvent rendre plus de service que les prêtres Français étants plus faits que les autres aux fatigues et aux manieres du pays.

Dans l'autre maison on y met ceux qui ne sont propres que pour être artisans, et à ceux là on apprends des métiers.

Je croirais que ce serait là un moyen admirable pour commencer un établissement de manufactures, qui sont absolument nécessaires pour le secours de ce pays.

Mr. notre Evêque est charmé de ces établissements, et voudrait bien être en etat de les soutenir et augmenter. Mais comme tout cela ne se peut faire sans dépense tant pour l'augmentation du nombre des Curés que pour cette espèce de manufacture, et qu'il conviendrait d'en faire de grandes, pour y réussir, je ne vois qu'un moyen assuré pour cela, qui serait que le Roy voulut bien donner une grosse abbaye à Mr. notre Evêque sans l'attacher à l'Evêché, comme il n'a l'esprit et le cœur occupés que des soins de faire du bien aux pauvres et augmenter la foi et le salut des âmes, il est certain que Sa Majesté, aurait le plaisir de voir employer le revenu de ce bénéfice en bonnes et saintes œuvres, qui feraient merveille pour le bien de la colonie son soutien et son augmentation.

J'ai trouvé à Villemarie en l'isle de Montreal, un établissement de sœurs de la congrégation, sous la conduite de la sœur Bourgeois, qui fait de grands biens à toute la colonie, elles furent brulées l'an passé où elles perdirent tout; il seroit fort nécessaire qu'elles se rétablissent, elles n'ont pas le premier sol, j'y ai trouvé un autre établissement de filles de la providence qui travaillent ensemble, elles pourront commencer quelque manfacture de ce côté là, si vous avez la bonté de continuer la gratification de mil livres pour les laines, et mil livres pour apprendre à tricoter. Il y a encore un troisième établissement pour faire des maîtres d'écoles.

Il faut revenir s'il vous plait, Monseigneur, à voir ce qui se peut faire pour dissipliner les grands garçons, et pour donner de l'occupation aux enfans des gentilshommes et autres soi-disans et vivans comme tels.

Avant tout, Monseigneur, vous me permettrez de vous

dire que la noblesse de ce pays nouveau, est tout ce qu'il y a de plus gueux et que d'en augmenter le nombre est augmenter le nombre des fainéants. Un pays neuf demande des gens laborieux et industrieux, et qui mettent la main à la hache et à la pioche. Les enfans de nos conseillers ne sont pas plus laborieux, et n'ont de ressource que les bois, où ils font quelque traite, et la plupart font tous les désordres dont j'ai eu l'honneur de vous entretenir, je ne m'oublierai en rien de ce qu'il y aurait à faire pour les engager à entrer dans le commerce, mais comme nos nobles et conseillers sont tous fort pauvres et accablés de debtes, ils ne sauraient trouver de crédit pour un écu.

Le seul moyen qui me parait le plus assuré pour discipliner cette jeunesse serait que le Roy voulut bien entretenir en ce pays, quelques compagnies, dont on donnerait le commandement à gens d'authorité et de bonnes mœurs et appliqués, comme à Mr. le Chevalier de Caillière, a Mr. de Varénes, Gouverneur des trois Rivières, ou au Sr. Prévot, Major de Quebec, avec des Lieutenants du pays que l'on choisirait, lesquels ne devraient point avoir peine d'obeir, a ceux auxquels naturellement ils doivent obéir.

INDEX.

INDEX.

Upper Lakes, the, Saint-Lusson takes possession of the country of, 274.

Ursuline Convent at Quebec, the, 171, 300; engraving of, 300; burned, 300.

Ursulines, the, of Caen, 479.

Ursulines, the, of Quebec, 125, 145, 243, 272, 300, 347, 401, 422, 431.

Utrecht, the Peace of, 362.

Valois, 229.

Varennes, town of, 294, 302.

Varennes, René Gaultier de, 289, 523.

Vasseur, describes the burning of Laval's seminary, 450.

Vaudreuil, 506.

Vendôme, Duc de, Madame d'Aunay applies for help to, 51.

Verchères, town of, 294, 302.

Verd, Cape, 234.

Verrazzano, voyage of, 3.

Versailles, 325, 348, 405.

Viger, J., 144, 255.

Vignal, Guillaume de, the priest, 96; killed by the Iroquois, 112, 113.

Villemarie, see Montreal.

Villeray, Rouer de, appointed councillor at Quebec, 195; Argenson's opinion of, 196; becomes the richest man in Canada, 197; 203; removed from the council by Mézy, 208; 213; banished to France, 214; 485, 486.

Vimont, Father, 393.

Virginia, English heretics in, 15; 46, 234.

Vismes, Dubreuil, 475.

Vitry, Sieur, 357.

Walckenaer, 230.

Ward, Nathaniel, signs the "Ips-

wich Letter," 30; Governor Winthrop's reply to, 31.

Washington, site of, 4.

West, the Company of the, 234.

West India Company, the, 329, its charter revoked, 353; extinguished, 366; revived, 373; given a monopoly of exporting beaver-skins, 373.

West Indies, the, 44, 237, 241; Talon's efforts to establish trade between Canada and, 272, 355, 360; 370; slaves imported into Canada from, 454.

William Henry, Fort, 253.

Williamson, 7.

Winthrop, Fort, 21.

Winthrop, Governor, 19; La Tour asks aid against D'Aunay from, 22; entertains La Tour, 23–27; allows La Tour to hire allies, 28, 29; sharply criticised for giving assistance to La Tour, 29; his action approved by the majority, 30; the "Ipswich Letter," 30; his reply to, 31; letter from Bradstreet to, 31; entertains D'Aunay's envoys, 42; arranges a treaty with D'Aunay, 43, 44; deceived in La Tour, 46.

Witches, Canada never troubled by, 421.

Wolf Indians, the, 124.

Wolfe, 308.

Women, political influence among the Iroquois of, 84.

Wood, 22, 23.

Wooster River, 123.

Xavier, Saint Francis, fête of, 166; 225.

York, the Duke of, 249.

Zrin, the fortress of, 188.

Francis Parkman's Works

NEW LIBRARY EDITION

Printed from entirely new plates, in clear and beautiful type, upon a choice laid paper. With portraits of Parkman, and illustrated with twenty-four photogravure plates executed by Goupil from historical portraits, and from original drawings and paintings by Howard Pyle, De Cost Smith, Thule de Thulestrup, Frederic Remington, Orson Lowell, Adrien Moreau, and other artists.

Thirteen volumes, medium octavo, cloth, gilt top, price, $26.00; half calf, extra, gilt top, $58.50; half crushed Levant morocco, extra, gilt top, $78.00; half morocco, gilt top, $58.50. Any work supplied separately in cloth, $2.00 per volume.

LIST OF VOLUMES.

Parkman in perfect form. . . . That the books are light in the hand and present a clean page to the eye is particularly gratifying, because an historian is not merely an authority for purposes of reference alone; he is an imaginative word painter, to be read for the sheer pleasure of reading him. — *New York Tribune.*

Of all American historians he is the most peculiarly American, and yet he is the broadest and most cosmopolitan. — *Prof. John Fiske.*

LITTLE, BROWN, & COMPANY, Publishers
254 WASHINGTON STREET, BOSTON, MASS.

THE LIFE OF
FRANCIS PARKMAN
By CHARLES HAIGHT FARNHAM

NEW LIBRARY EDITION, WITH PHOTOGRAVURE PORTRAIT. 8VO.
CLOTH, GILT TOP $2.00
ALSO BOUND TO MATCH THE ORIGINAL LIBRARY EDITION OF
PARKMAN'S WORKS. SMALL 8VO. CLOTH $2.00

THE author of this work knew Mr. Parkman, and his work has been done with the sanction of the historian's nearest relatives, and with their assistance as far as information of a personal character is concerned. He has devoted much study and labor to the preparation of his work, and has had access to all the available material in the hands of Mr. Parkman's family and friends, including such letters as have been preserved, the diary of his vacation journals, and the extremely interesting autobiographic letters written by the historian to his friends, Dr. George H. Ellis and Martin Brimmer.

On every page of Mr. Farnham's volume one's admiration is roused for this man of indomitable will, courage, and cheerfulness that failed but few times in a half-century of suffering and disability, chivalrous spirit, and tremendous energy and perseverance. — *Boston Herald.*

Should come to be recognized as a masterpiece of literary portraiture. . . . As you read it, you feel a growing sense that you are once more in the presence of the man, in his habit, as he lived. The hours which you pass with this book are like renewed ones with the friend whose memory it will help to preserve. You lay it down with a feeling of grave, tender content. The future, if it will, may know more than Parkman's work; it may know Parkman, too. — BARRETT WENDELL, in the *American Historical Review.*

LITTLE, BROWN, & COMPANY, Publishers
254 WASHINGTON STREET, BOSTON, MASS.